Management Accounting: A Contemporary Approach

Consultant Editor: Robert W Scapens

Management Accounting: A Contemporary Approach

Bob Ryan

Principal Lecturer in Accounting and Head of the Division of Business
Hatfield Polytechnic

John Hobson

Senior Lecturer in Statistics and Operations Research
Hatfield Polytechnic

Pitman

PITMAN PUBLISHING LIMITED
128 Long Acre, London WC2E 9AN

PITMAN PUBLISHING INC
1020 Plain Street, Marshfield, Massachusetts 02050

Associated Companies
Pitman Publishing Pty Ltd, Melbourne
Pitman Publishing New Zealand Ltd, Wellington
Copp Clark Pitman, Toronto

© Robert J Ryan and John B Hobson

First published in Great Britain 1985

British Library Cataloguing in Publication Data
Ryan, Bob
    Management accounting: a contemporary approach.
    1. Managerial accounting
    I. Title   II. Hobson, John
    658.1'511   HF5635

ISBN 0-273-01958-9

Printed in Great Britain at The Bath Press, Avon

Contents

Part 4: Conclusions

Preface

This book is our view of what a first course in management accounting should be like. First, such a course should place management accounting in its wider context as an interdisciplinary subject with close and clear connections with the other social sciences, mathematics and statistics. Second, such a course should place the subject in its industrial and commercial context and, third, it should also provide an adequate basis for further study in management accounting and the closely related subject area of financial management.

This book should appeal to the following:

- Teachers and students of degree courses teaching or studying management accounting for the first time. In our experience, the material in this book can be easily covered in one year of a single-module (one lecture per week) course. Management accounting is only given a full treatment in the second year of the Business Studies Degree at the Hatfield Polytechnic. This book is ideal for a course such as that. Other institutions offering degrees in accounting and business studies offer a full course in management accounting in the first year. Teachers and students on such courses should find that this book gives a comprehensive treatment of the necessary material and will help the students in the very important task of interrelating their study of management accounting with other subjects taught on their course.

- Teachers and students of polytechnic and other courses leading to exemption from the foundation examinations of the various professional accounting bodies. Again, the material can be easily covered in a one-year single-module (one lecture per week) course.

- Teachers and students on BTEC courses in Business Studies. Such courses are often characterized by a high degree of interdisciplinary work. This book should provide excellent support for BTEC courses in management accounting and interdisciplinary studies.

- Teachers and students on post-experience and postgraduate management courses. We have found much of this book's material invaluable in teaching Management Studies Diploma courses and it should also provide a very thorough 'first appreciation' of the subject for MBA and other postgraduate management students.

No single text in management accounting can provide a complete and exhaustive treatment of the subject. There are just too many different treatments of the subject and different perspectives which can be offered.

However, if this book is used as a principal course text with supplementary reading taken from the references cited at the end of each chapter, the student should be in a very strong position to pursue further academic or professional study in management accounting at a later date.

The book is partnered by a suite of computer software which covers many of the problem areas discussed in this book. The programs in the software suite are designed to match the methods taught in this text and are sufficiently flexible to permit the solution of substantial-sized problems. Further details of this suite can be found in the Appendix to this book.

Teachers may apply to the publisher for a free copy of the solutions manual for this text. The solutions manual is so designed that teachers can take direct photo-transparencies of the material for class use. We would welcome suggestions from teachers for improvements in the solutions manual as well as for the book and program suite.

We would like to acknowledge the efforts of the many people who have helped us in the preparation of this book and the accompanying software. We enter the usual caveat under which such acknowledgements are made—we alone are responsible for any defects which this book, the software or the teaching manual may have. We would like to thank the following for their very helpful advice and encouragement during the development of this book: Simon Archer, Michael Bourn, Michael Bromwich, Dr J. B. Coates, Geoff Clinton, Alan Lovell, T. J. Thompson, and two other anonymous referees. A special word of thanks must go to Bob Scapens who has given us invaluable advice in his role as consultant editor on the project. Thanks also to Eric Dalton of Pitmans who bullied and cajoled us as appropriate and provided us with considerable help and advice throughout. Finally, love and thanks to Char and Jan for putting up with us.

Hatfield,   BOB RYAN
April 1985   JOHN HOBSON

Part 1 Basic concepts

1 An introduction to management accounting ───────

The purpose of this introductory chapter is to introduce you to the nature of management accounting and the context in which it operates within the firm. First of all, we will give you some guidance on how to study this book and how to cope with the type of questions which you will meet in the subject. We then commence our discussion of management accounting with some preliminary observations about the purpose of the firm and the role that management plays within it. Following that we will offer a general definition of management accounting and summary of the work of the management accountant. Once we have established the purpose of management accounting we will then move on to examine both its technical role as a provider of information for managerial decision-making and its general organizational role within the firm. Finally, we will outline the overall plan of this book.

By the end of this chapter we will have covered the following points:

- How to study this book
- A statement of its perspective
- The function of the firm and its management
- The objectives of the firm
- The decision-orientated approach to management accounting
- The behavioural and organizational context of management accounting
- The contribution other disciplines can make to the study of management accounting
- The overall plan of the book

How to study this book

This book is intended to be a foundation text in that it will provide you with the conceptual and technical background for further academic or professional study in management accounting. Because it is the first, this will probably be the most important management accounting book which you will ever read, so it will repay careful study.

Chapters 1–3, inclusive, cover the basic conceptual tools of the management accountant's trade. They are an important prerequisite for the material covered in later chapters. Given this foundation you can then choose to study either the section on short-term decision-making first (Chapters 4–10 inclusive) or the section on long-term decision-making (Chapters 11–13 inclusive) first. Chapter 14 can be read at any stage although it will be more meaningful if left until the end. Most of the terms used in this text are explained in context or in the form of a note. However, a glossary is provided at the end of the book in order to save you the problem of searching back through the text for meanings you have forgotten.

Each chapter of this book (except Chapters 4 and 11 which are introductions to new areas of study) represents approximately four to six hours' study time depending upon the support which you can get from lectures, tutorials and seminars. We have found that most students of the subject benefit when they follow a systematic plan of study:

- Read a chapter quickly once, marking off in the margin of the book those sections which supplement any lectures notes you may have obtained.

- Read that chapter through carefully a second time, making notes where appropriate. If you have lecture or seminar notes covering the topic areas discussed in the particular chapter you are studying you may simply need to supplement them with notes from the book.

- During this second reading of the chapter material try the self-test questions in the text. You will note that an answer clue is given at the end of those questions which require a numerical solution. If, after having attempted the question, the answer clue means nothing to you, you should read the relevant section again.

- Once you have read the chapter thoroughly and mastered the self-test questions, try the end of chapter questions. Where more than one numerical question is given they are ranked in what we believe to be an ascending order of difficulty. These questions represent the standard you might reasonably expect in any examination testing an initial year of study in this subject.

- When you have completed a chapter you will gain considerable benefit from reading as many of the supplementary references as you can manage. We have been extremely selective in the material we suggest for further study, so you should find the references of considerable use in expanding your knowledge of the subject.

- At the end of each part of the book quickly reread through the material studied in that part before proceeding to the next.

Nearly all of this book can be studied with only a rudimentary knowledge of mathematics. Where greater knowledge is required we will either explain in full the mathematical principles involved or, where this disrupts the flow of the text, we will relegate the exposition of the mathematics to a chapter appendix. Finally, before embarking on our study of management accounting we offer some suggestions for tackling the types of questions set in this subject area:

- Read each question thoroughly and assess the relative importance of numbered parts to questions. In an examination the marks given to each question and, in some cases, to the parts of questions define the maximum time which you should allocate to the question

- If a part of a question is what can be described as a 'general rider', i.e. a part which requires some comment on a general point of principle, make sure you do that part. These 'riders' are often neglected through lack of time. Marshal your thoughts carefully; if comments are called for—comment; if a discussion is required—state and then evaluate the alternative points of view. Never give notes unless you are specifically required to do so

- If a numerical type question contains a lot of detail always work from the beginning to the end, transferring factual points to your working sheet as you go. It is dangerous to backtrack in lengthy questions. Note down on a working sheet any crucial assumptions you are required to make (these are often given just before the 'requirements' part of the question)

- Do not avoid general essay-type questions. They are becoming more popular in all types of accounting examinations. It is important to realize that these questions often appear to be marked on a narrower band than numerical/analytical-type questions. To attract the best marks with essay-type questions: read the question, plan your answer carefully, develop your answer from a concise introduction, summarize clearly and write legibly

- Be precise in answering questions, cultivate a neat 'spacious' style of presentation. Your handwriting should be such that it can be easily read and typed by a competent typist

- Explain any points of principle you have followed in answering a question

- Always but always answer the question set. Make the simplest assumptions commensurate with the question. If more than one assumption can be made, adopt the one which takes you to an answer through the quickest route. Do not impute deviousness to the examiners.

This book's perspective

Whenever individuals come together to produce goods or services a firm is created. Some of those individuals will perform a managerial function and as a result the need for management accounting will arise. In this book we view management accounting as an activity which arises because of the needs of managers for relevant and timely information not only for their decision-making purposes but also to help them control the activities of the firm.

This book adopts a 'decision-orientated' approach in determining the subject-matter of management accounting. However, as we will show in the chapters which follow, there is also a wider dimension to management accounting. Because the managerial-accounting activity imposes rules and procedures upon the organization it will profoundly influence (and be influenced by) the structure of relationships which exist within the firm. It will influence not only the way individuals behave personally, but also the way they interrelate and communicate with one another. This 'behavioural' dimension to management accounting is extremely important and too often neglected in many books which profess to be about management accounting.

Note, however, that this book is about 'management accounting' and, therefore, contains only a small element of traditional 'cost accounting'. Cost accounting is concerned with a range of techniques specifically devoted to the control of costs within the firm. As such, cost accounting is one part of the study of management accounting. Out of context, cost accounting makes little sense, but within its proper context as part of the firm's overall management-accounting activity, it has a vital role to play in the control of the firm (see Chapters 8 and 9).

This book, in summary, takes a 'contextual approach' to management accounting; that is, we place management accounting in its context as part of the information production and decision support systems of the organization. If you follow through the story we tell in the following pages of this book you will gain:

- A clear idea of the role of management accounting in its context within the modern industrial or commercial firm

- A thorough grounding in the methods management accountants apply in collecting and analysing information for use by managers

- A foundation of knowledge which will serve you well both in the practical environment and in any future studies you may wish to pursue in this subject.

As we examine management accounting from both an information and an organizational perspective we will soon see that management accounting is intrinsically concerned with the management information system of the firm. This means that management accountants have to be thoroughly familiar with the use of computers—not only in their traditional role as high-speed number crunchers, but also as important parts of a firm's information and communication system.

In this book we will discuss the usefulness of computers to the management accountant and, if you obtain the suite of software which goes with this book, you will (provided you can get access to an appropriate computer) be able to see how a computer can be used to solve a number of the problems discussed in the following chapters. The Appendix gives you some important notes on the software suite and the types of computer on which it will operate.

The function of the firm and its management

When we talk about a 'firm' we mean a group of individuals who have come together in order to produce goods and services, cash and the satisfaction which comes through cooperative effort. The firm may be established by an informal agreement between the parties concerned although it is much more usual for there to be some legal relationship between the 'owners' of the firm (as is found in a legal partnership agreement or in the Articles and Memorandum of Association of a limited company). In addition, it is very likely that a legal relationship will exist between owners and employees in the form of a contract of employment.

> *Note:* 'Company law' is that part of the law which is concerned with the way companies are established and administer themselves. The law lays down the duties and responsibilities of the directors of a company and the rights and powers of company shareholders. The principal Acts of Parliament concerned with company law are the Companies Acts 1948, 1967 and 1981.

Firms come in many different shapes and sizes and we, in writing this book, have in mind a 'typical firm'. Of course, most of what we say in the following pages also applies to the sole trader or, indeed, to the very largest multinational corporation as much as to our typical firm. Our typical firm has the following characteristics:

- It is a public limited company

- It produces a range of physical products and services

- It has 'in-house' expertise in research and development, market research and personnel

- It has, approximately, 500 employees.

We define our typical firm as a single company although the size of organization we have outlined above would not be untypical for a division or subsidiary of a much larger company.

Some of the problems we consider in this book are not applicable to a firm of this type. Where that is the case we will define the type of organization to which the problem does relate.

If we consider our archetypical firm not just as a legal entity, but in its full social and economic context, we have the phenomenon of different individuals coming together each with some particular purpose in mind. The purpose of the individuals concerned may be ill-defined but its pursuit with others within the firm must produce some net benefit which is the reward for cooperation.

Firms exist to produce either goods or services for sale either:

- in the open market, which is typified by a range of potential customers from private individual to other companies (open-market selling),

- or to the government or some other single purchaser (contract selling).

In Chapters 5 and 6 we will discuss these different types of market and the problems they pose for management in determining prices and output.

One role of management is to collect the resources of the firm, decide upon their allocation between competing uses, and channel the output of the firm into the appropriate market. It is this ability to make decisions which separates the manager from the other employees of the organization and, generally speaking, the greater the decision-making power possessed by a particular manager the more 'senior' that manager is said to be.

In the large majority of firms in the UK, senior managers also enjoy the privileges of ownership, because they not only have a say in the control and distribution of the firm's surplus (which we will loosely term 'profit'), but also often have a considerable personal financial stake in the business as well. Indeed, many large firms operate share bonus schemes for their senior executives as part of their overall remuneration package. As a result, senior managers may well see their own interests and that of the shareholders as being one and the same thing and as a consequence are unlikely to be entirely neutral when conflict arises between the interests of shareholders and other groups within the firm.

The management function within industry and commerce is character-ized by its discretionary and decision-making nature. Of course, in a large firm, the range of discretion which a particular manager possesses will be constrained by his or her role within the organization. Indeed, the boundaries of any particular management group are often impossible to define. However, we can generalize about the tiers of management on the basis of the level and time-scale of decisions taken:

- Senior management: long-term decisions on corporate policy, major capital investment and financing

- Upper middle management: technical support and advice for the long-term decision-making of senior management. Significant short- and medium-term decisions on pricing, purchasing, employment, etc.

- Lower middle management: short-term decisions, especially in the areas of production, quality control, purchasing, etc.

- Operations management: control of processes, short-term labour management, etc.

As we will explain in the next section, management accounting has a role to play in all of these areas of decision-making and is, therefore, a major component of the firm's management information system.

Objectives of the firm

We know from history that the rigid economic and social order of the Middle Ages, and later the capitalism of the merchant adventurers, gave way to the production-based capitalism of the Industrial Revolution in the nineteenth century. The new industrial organizations which arose were highly 'owner orientated' and, as a consequence, had very authoritarian management structures. The owner of the Victorian firm would have been its principal manager and the idea that the firm's employees should have any say in the strategic policy making of the firm would have been quite unthinkable. This very authoritarian and paternalistic approach to the management of business evolved into the conception of the 'bureaucratic' organization in this century.

Given the authoritarian nature of Victorian firms and the rigid organizational structures of the bureaucratic firms which followed, it is not surprising that the notion that firms exist to 'maximize the profits of their owners' became so important. With the Victorian firm, the employees were expected to serve a single principal goal: the maximization of the interest of the owner who may well have been the firm's senior manager as well. This principal goal was translated over time into the belief that a firm should exist to maximize the profit it could distribute to its shareholder owners who may not, necessarily, have been engaged in the day-to-day management of the firm. Indeed, in much of the early development of economic thought it was assumed that individuals would seek to maximize their utility (or personal satisfaction) and firms their profit. Even today, this view of the motives of individuals and firms forms the central presumption of the traditional or 'neo-classical' school of economic theory.

In Chapter 2 we will consider bureaucracy in more detail and explain some of the reasons why bureaucratic organizations are not always very effective in what they set out to do. For the moment, what we can say is that in recent years there has been a gradual weakening of belief in the legitimacy of authority wielded by owners of capital as such. Most people now expect that the exercise of authority should be supported by a reasonable moral right to that authority. As a result, it is very difficult to support the view that the ultimate reason for a firm's existence is to maximize the wealth of shareholders who often have little say (and often very little interest) in the management of their firms.

Given this alteration in social attitudes, we now see less emphasis placed, even by senior managers, upon the single-minded pursuit of the interests of the shareholders above all others.

Self test: There have been a number of different attempts to formulate overall objectives which both describe and prescribe the ways in which firms should behave. Some suggestions are as follows:

- Firms should work to maximize the profit which is distributable to their owners.

- Firms should act to maximize the market value of the firm's shares.
- The principal aim of a firm is to ensure its long-term survival.

To what extent do you think these objectives presume that shareholders are the most important group within a firm and what reasons can you give to support that view?

Two important writers, Cyert and March, in their *A Behavioural Theory of the Firm*, contributed a radically new perspective to our understanding of corporate behaviour. They argued that:

- Only individuals have objectives.
- Company objectives, in as far as they exist, represent a negotiated settlement of the conflict of interest of the various participant groups within the firm.

In Cyert and March's view, the firm is viewed as a collectivity of individuals who form themselves into a number of different interest groups. These interest groups include a number who exist outside the formal structure of the firm.

In most firms we would expect the following groups to have a significant interest in its activities:

- Suppliers of capital (the shareholders).
- Suppliers of loans and other fixed-interest capital.
- Employees and their union representatives (the latter may well form a separate interest group).
- Suppliers of goods and services.
- Customers for the firm's products.
- Tax authorities.
- Government including its various representatives.
- Various social pressure groups and other interest lobbies.
- Different management functions such as purchasing, marketing, research and development and even accounting.

These different groups will conflict in their basic aims: the suppliers of finance will seek a situation of high return with minimum risk and, other things being equal, argue against increased salaries for the firm's employees which, of course, would reduce their return. Employees, in trying to satisfy their interest, would be opposed to this position.

At a different level, the production and sales managers (especially if they are rewarded according to performance) may well disagree over the range of products to be offered to the market. The production manager sees many products in terms of short production runs with difficult scheduling problems; the sales manager, on the other hand, would like to offer to his potential markets as wide a range of products as possible.

Management occupies a unique position within the firm. As well as forming an interest group in its own right, management acts as the principal mediator in achieving a negotiated settlement between the interests of other groups. This negotiated settlement takes shape as management's plan or 'budget' which lays down the targets for expenditure and for sales during the coming period. These expenditure targets will also include the management's projection of cash distributions which can be made to the various interest groups within the firm in the form of increased wages and salaries, bonuses and dividends, which can be paid to investors.

> *Self test:* **What limits the power of management to:**
>
> **1 Hire and fire employees?**
> **2 Influence the quality of supplies?**
> **3 Introduce new technology or products?**
>
> **With which groups must management negotiate in each case and to what extent are their interests likely to conflict?**

Figure 1.1 depicts the mediatory role taken by management. This mediatory role of management gives us a clue as to what could be a reasonable, operational objective for the management group itself. We assume that management will attempt to increase its power and the range of options open to it in negotiation (which we call 'negotiating discretion') by:

- Neutralizing conflict between other groups when and wherever such conflict arises.

- Maximizing the cash surplus from operations and hence its ability to reward other individuals and groups who perform well.

We also assume that management will also attempt to:

- Maximize its own financial and non-financial rewards.

As we shall see in later chapters, managerial negotiation is a continuous and often covert activity which is principally conducted through the budget-setting process. In this view of the firm, the budget becomes an important device for monitoring performance, an important vehicle for settling conflict and also, in the short run, a means for formalizing the expectations of the various interest groups within the firm.

Given this contemporary view of the firm, we can now be specific about the function of management accounting as part of the firms's management information system:

First: management accounting is concerned with the collection of data within and outside the firm and its translation into information suitable for managerial decision-makers at all levels in the firm and for setting their 'bids' in the negotiating process.

Second: management accounting is concerned with the translation of the outcome of the negotiating process into formal representations of the expectations of the interest groups within the firm (the budgeting process).

Fig 1.1 The mediatory role of management

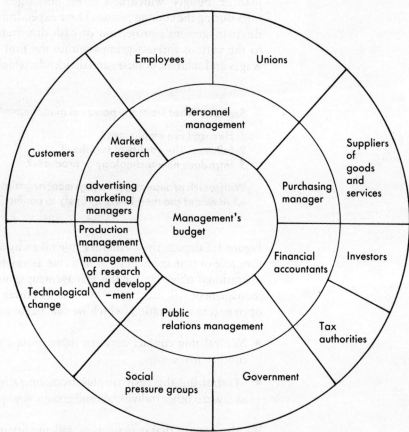

The decision-orientated approach

Traditionally, management-accounting texts classify managerial decision-making into either the long or the short run. This is a useful, but not completely unproblematic, classification which closely follows the economist's distinction between the long and the short run.

Note: We sometimes use the words 'tactical' and 'strategic' when we refer to short- and long-run decisions, respectively.

Long-run decisions entail the procurement of the fixed resources of the firm and their commitment to a particular process or activity. For example, raising new long-term finance, investing in plant and machinery, undertaking a merger, opening a new product market, all entail long-term commitments of effort and resources. And, in most cases, the making (and reversal) of such decisions will bring major upheaval and disturbance to the firm over a number of years.

Short-run decisions do not normally involve altering the fixed resources of the firm and would not, in most practical situations, influence the firm over longer than a single planning period (usually a year). Of course, short-run decisions entirely presuppose some prior long-term decision. For example, the decision to produce a fixed tonnage of a particular chemical presupposes that some long-run decision has been made to build the plant in which the chemical will be made. However, long-run decision-making always assumes a feasible set of consequent short-run decisions. In Chapter 4 we will discuss more fully the distinction between short- and long-run decisions.

Fig 1.2 The interrelationship of decisions

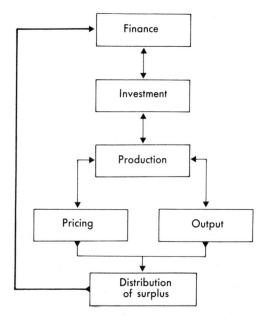

In Fig. 1.2 we show how the short- and long-run decisions of the firm can be viewed as a series of interacting activities. One major problem in writing a text such as this is that there is a tendency to present the decision-making process as a sequence of independent activities where, in practice, they are closely interrelated. For example, the price at which a firm can sell its product depends upon the price which the market will pay, given the degree of competition which exists, the output level the firm operates at, and its particular advertising and other marketing efforts. Pricing is also influenced by the skill with which managers can exploit the seasonality of demand for the firm's product by building stocks of goods during 'off-season' and selling them when demand (and hence prices) are likely to be at their highest. Thus, the pricing decision is also connected to the decisions management make concerning inventory policy (see Chapter 8).

Note: In the following chapters particular types of decisions are identified and their important characteristics isolated from one another. However, managerial decision-making is very much an interrelated activity. All we can really do in a book like this is to show you the salient, distinguishing features of each class of decision and indicate the problems which arise through the interdependencies of one type of decision with another.

For the purpose of this book, we have classified the broad areas of decision-making to which management accounting can contribute, in our typical firm, as follows:

Short-run decisions:

- Output decisions (Chapter 5): how much of a particular product or service should be produced?

- Pricing decisions (Chapter 6): given the market context, at what price should a particular product or service be sold?

- Allocation decisions (Chapter 7): how can the available resources of the firm be allocated between their various uses?

- Control decisions (Chapter 8 and 9): how can the short-term resources of the firm such as stock and cash be controlled? How can the usage of resources on processes be monitored and controlled?

- Distribution decisions (Chapter 10): how can the firm's surplus be distributed between the various competing interest groups? In this chapter we specifically consider the problem of wage negotiation and the sorts of management accounting information required in those negotiations.

Long-run decisions:

- The financing decision (Chapter 12): how can new capital resources be raised from the capital markets and in what proportions should that capital be raised from the owners of the firm in the form of equity or from lenders in the form of debt?

- The investment decision (Chapter 13): how can the firm's captial resources and managerial and labour skills be invested in new processes?

In the long run all of the above decisions, both short- and long-run, interrelate and in the chapters devoted to them we will discuss such issues as:

- The sequencing of decisions.

- The behavioural factors which influence management decision-making.

- Avoiding the situation where different decisions produce conflicting results.

We have depicted management accounting as an advisory function serving the needs of the management group. Of course, the realities of decision-making are not so straightforward; many management accountants are involved directly in the decision-making process as well as in the preparation and interpretation of accounting information.

But one important issue does arise in the way we view the discipline of management accounting which is: how far can we take the 'decision-orientated' approach to the subject? To what extent should the management accountant be a passive supplier of management's information needs rather than an active participant in the decision-making process? There is no easy answer to this question and in practice it often reduces down to the attitude management has concerning the provision of information. If management believes that its way of making decisions is correct, even though those decisions are not made in any apparently rational way, then it is still the duty of the management-accounting function to produce information relevant for those decisions. In this case, as in many others, he who pays the piper calls the tune. However, in some situations management may be quite unclear as to the type of information needed for a particular decision. In such circumstances the management accountant may have an educative role in providing information in a form which clearly suits the decision model the management acountant believes to be most appropriate.

In this book we will describe some of the different ways of being 'rational' in decision-making and outline some of the consequences of these 'models' of rationality for actual decision-making behaviour. Therefore, even within the decision-orientated approach, management accounting must call upon the intellectual insights of the psychologist and the social psychologist.

The main thrust of our analytical discussion of the techniques of management accounting will presume that the decision-maker is adhering to what economists understand as 'rationality'. We will outline in Chapter 2 the notion of economic rationality, so suffice it to say at the moment that this notion of rationality is highly formalized and sets a framework from which prescriptions for actual decision-making can be deduced.

Note: **Many other sciences also follow this procedure of defining certain axioms or self-evident truths from which certain logical consequences can** be deduced. In physics, classical mechanics is based upon Newton's three laws of motion. Three laws also form the basis of thermodynamics where they are used to define the behaviour of gases under 'ideal' conditions. In economics, certain axioms of human behaviour (which we will discuss in the next chapter) are used to prescribe how individuals will behave in decision-making situations. Note that we use the word 'prescribe' to indicate that these axioms of rational human behaviour are not used to describe what actually happens but to propose what should happen in an ideal state.

Because a number of other models of rationality can be put forward (and are observed in practice) economic rationality cannot be looked upon as a particularly good description of the way decision-makers, in general, behave. The great advantage of adopting the economic model of rationality in decision-making is that it is, analytically, very convenient. The economic analysis of consumer behaviour and of the firm provides much of the ground upon which management-accounting techniques can be based. Our approach toward management accounting (like the approach adopted by many of the professional examining bodies) is that management accounting techniques should be developed in a formal, lytical environment and should prescribe methods which are available to the practising management accountant. Where we differ from most other management accounting texts (at this level) is in explaining the context in which management accounting operates and the behavioural complexities which distort the 'purity' of the formal, analytical approach to the subject.

The behavioural and organizational context

There is, however, a completely different dimension of management accounting to the decision-orientated approach outlined in the last section. Because firms, as they grow, become more complex in their social structure, they also become increasingly dependent upon effective means of communication and on an effective framework of rules and procedures to maintain their internal coherence and efficiency of operation. Management accounting and the related study of 'management information systems' (MIS) are both concerned with communication within organizations. Management accounting is primarily concerned with the communication of the financial consequences of decision-making while the study of MIS covers the communication of all types of information. These lines of communication influence and are influenced by the organizational structure of the firm (a topic which we will examine in more detail in the next chapter). In Chapter 14 we will consider, in more detail, the influence management accounting has upon the management information systems of the firm.

Management-accounting information is not received and acted upon neutrally by those who receive it. Indeed, the very method of presentation of information can have different significance for different groups. For example, the presentation of methods of performance in terms of 'profitability' assumes that profit represents an appropriate measurement base. However, the very notion of profit makes a presumption of shareholder supremacy in the company—a view which might not be whole-heartedly endorsed by the representatives of the labour force. Information can also have a motivational effect on individuals. A good performance in comparison with budget may bring advancement or some other benefit for a particular departmental manager, a bad performance may bring undesirable consequences. In this book we will examine these other dimensions to the management-accounting function.

Fig 1.3 Other disciplines and management accounting

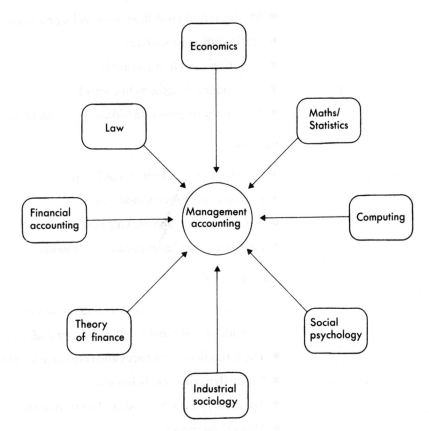

Other disciplines and management accounting

In Fig. 1.3 we show the various disciplines which bear upon the work of the modern management accountant and which we will draw upon in this book. The main contributions of these disciplines can be outlined as follows:

Economic theory:

- The theory of consumer behaviour
- The theory of supply and demand
- Microeconomic theory of the firm
- Some aspects of macroeconomic theory (such as the effect of inflation, interest rates and exchange rates)
- The economics of information

Mathematical and statistical method:

- Mathematical modelling of financial processes
- Optimization procedures
- Statistical sampling and analysis
- Mathematical methods in control
- The theory of games (in bidding for contracts)

Computing:

- Data handling and control techniques
- Financial and process modelling
- Monitoring decision-making performance
- Information and communication systems

Social psychology:

- Models of human personality and rationality
- Decision-making and problem solving under stress
- The formation of attitudes and resistance to attitude change
- Group dynamics and behaviour
- The theory of conflict and conflict resolution
- Motivation theory

Industrial sociology and industrial relations:

- The role of the firm in its social context
- The social analysis of groups
- Employee relations
- Wage bargaining and union negotiations

The theory of finance:

- The operation of the capital market
- The costing of capital funds
- Sources of finance and distribution policy
- The analysis of investment opportunities

Financial accounting:

- The relationships between financial and management reporting
- The interpretation of company accounts

Law:

- Contract law and the law of agency
- The law of industrial relations
- Consumer protection and civil liability

These topic areas are not intended to be exhaustive nor, indeed, would we wish to give the impression that they are all covered in detail in this book. However, the list above should give some indication of the range of subject areas which may be appropriate for understanding management accounting problems and processes.

Plan of the book

Part 1: In the first three chapters of this book we introduce the basic concepts and the context of management accounting. In Chapter 2 we outline the organizational context of management accounting and some of the basic models of rationality which can be invoked in order to understand the process of managerial decision-making. In Chapter 3 we will introduce the very fundamental concepts of wealth and cost and show how they form the basis of our analysis of long- and short-term decision-making.

Part 2: This part of the book is devoted to short-term decision-making. In Chapter 4 we briefly introduce the general problems of short-term decision-making before entering into a more formal analysis of the problems of output, pricing, production and control decision-making in Chapters 5–9, inclusively. Finally, in Chapter 10, we look at an area which lies very much on the borderline between short- and long-term decision-making, namely an investigation of the problems of distributing the surplus earned by the firm and the sort of information which the management accountant should produce for this sort of decision-making.

Part 3: This part of the book is concerned with the problems of long-term decision-making. In Chapter 11 we introduce the general problems of long-term decisions followed by a detailed discussion of the types of finance available to companies (Chapter 12) and how those funds should be allocated to different production projects (Chapter 13).

Part 4: This book finishes with a chapter devoted to an examination of the role of management accounting in the management information systems of the firm and the impact which modern information technology has had upon the management accountant's task (Chapter 14).

Supplementary reading

PARKER, R. H., History of accounting for decisions, in Arnold, J., Carsberg, B., and Scapens, R. (eds) *Topics in Management Accounting,* Philip Allan, 1980

RYAN, R. J., Scientific method, in Arnold, J., Carsberg, B., and Scapens, R. (eds), *Topics in Management Accounting,* Philip Allan, 1980

SCAPENS, R., Closing the gap between theory and practice, *Management Accounting,* January 1983

Questions

1   Outline your objectives in purchasing this book. What criteria will you use for determining the success of this purchase?

2   List the principal financial decisions which you make during the course of every month. What information do you require in order to make those decisions?

3   Outline the 'decision-orientated approach' to management accounting and try to construct a brief definition of management accounting.

4   Distinguish between the long and short run in decision-making. What personal financial decisions have you made which could be regarded as long run?

5   Distinguish between different levels of management and identify, in your own place of work or study, those individuals who occupy the levels of management you have specified. Outline the types of acounting information which you think those managers might require in the normal course of their work.

2 The organizational and behavioural context of management accounting

In this chapter we consider, in some detail, the different markets in which the firm operates and how the conditions of those markets introduce uncertainty into management's decision-making. We will also examine how uncertainty interacts with the structure of relationships within the firm and how different market conditions and different organizational structures influence the role and purpose of the management-accounting activity within a firm. Finally, we will consider the problem of decision-making, what it means to be 'rational' and the way that different ways of being rational can influence the perception of what is, and what is not, relevant information.

Our outline for this chapter is as follows:

- A brief examination of the different markets in which the firm operates
- The general characteristics of those markets
- The ways in which the firm must adapt, both structurally and behaviourally, to cope with those markets
- The 'contingency' view of the organization
- The organizational dimension to management acounting
- The concept of 'rationality' and its implications for managerial decision-making

The firm's markets

There are two important aspects to any commercial or industrial firm which combine together to give uniqueness to its character:

- Its productive or technological aspect and,
- Its social or human aspect.

A firm is an organization of individuals who, as a consequence of their joint activity, produce products and services for sale. A firm of architects or accountants offers the services of its members to anyone who has need of them and the ability to pay its fees. An industrial firm produces physical goods such as chemicals, industrial equipment, cars, etc., for sale, again to anyone who has the means and the willingness to pay.

But, over and above this productive aspect, firms are social organizations and they do, in their way, exhibit the same phenomena as other social institutions. They exhibit a culture, have rules and norms and even possess what appear to be myths and rituals. Indeed, some writers have suggested that accountants form the equivalent of a 'priesthood' for business and have tried to give an anthropological description of the periodic 'rituals', such as budgeting and financial reporting, which are performed at regular intervals by accountants.

In this book we assume that a firm is an embodiment of reason and order. We make this assumption in order to structure the methods and techniques which are the tools of the management accountant's trade. Toward the end of this chapter we will discuss what we mean by being rational and, in particular, we will look at the concept of 'economic rationality' which forms the basis of much of our analytical work in later chapters.

However, it is important to recognize that there are other ways of viewing the behaviour of firms and the role that management accounting plays within those firms. Where appropriate, in this book, we will point out the alternative interpretations which can be made of the management-accounting process.

At an overall level we can think of the firm as a simple input/output system, as shown in Fig. 2.1, where goods or services are produced from a variety of inputs. In addition to the products and services made by the firm a cash surplus or deficit will be produced. Any cash surplus is then available for distribution, to government through taxes and duties

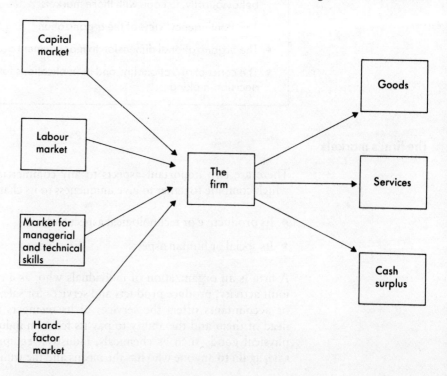

Fig 2.1 The imputs and outputs of the firm

and to any other interest groups who have a claim upon the firm. The creation of cash surplus through the activites of the firm can be termed 'value added'—a concept we will return to later.

> *Note:* The terms 'surplus', 'income' and 'profit' are used throughout this book. The terms 'income' and 'profit' can be considered synonymous at this stage (see Chapter 10). Income is normally defined as the amount which can be withdrawn from a business during an accounting period (in either goods, services or cash) leaving the business in the same economic position as it was at the beginning of the period. Normally, income is measured relative to an individual (we can talk about an individual's income) or, less precisely, relative to an identifiable group (the income of the firm's owners, for example).

Management's (and especially senior management's) control over the firm's cash surpluses gives them their principal means of control through the variety of 'side payments' that they can make to the various interest groups engaged in the bargaining process. These side payments are the inducements which management can offer to other interest groups within the firm to gain their compliance in pursuing the goals specified by management.

Everything else being equal, the search for the highest level of cash surplus possible and the resultant increase in the power of the management group, will lead management to seek the highest output revenues with the minimum input costs. The overall effect of this behaviour by management in the various firms participating in a particular market leads to what economists call 'competitive pressure'. Generally, the greater the competitive pressure in a particular market, the less discretion managers possess over the prices they can charge (in output markets) or the prices they have to pay (in input markets).

> *Note:* A 'decision' involves a choice between a range of alternative actions which will have different future consequences for the decision-maker. By their very nature decisions always involve future possibilities. Past events have no relevance except in so far as they influence the decision-maker's judgement about what will happen in the future. Uncertainty is said to attach to a decision when the outcomes of the choices open to the decision-maker cannot be predicted with a reasonable degree of statistical confidence. In practice, such uncertainty can arise because of the degree of complexity and change exhibited in the firm's technological, economic and social environment.

The competitive nature of the firm's input and output markets is, however, only one dimension of managerial concern. In addition managers must also anticipate and deal with the rate of change in particular markets. Apart from price, some markets may remain relatively stable while others exhibit rapid change. Technologically, many products change little through time. For example, primary products such as basic chemicals, fossil fuels, metals, minerals, textiles, etc., change little over the years. Of course, refinements in production techniques may occur and some developments in technical specifications or packaging may come about, but the basic product remains very much the same. Other products change very rapidly; for example, the modern microelectronics industry is producing 'jumps' in technology at ever increasing speed.

The 'life cycle' of a particular product can give us some idea of the technological and marketing uncertainty which managers must face. We can characterize the development of a product through its 'life cycle' from invention to redundancy as in Fig. 2.2.

Fig 2.2 The product life cycle

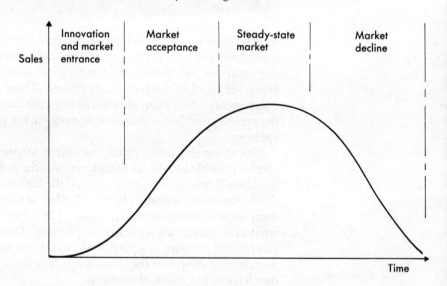

In Fig. 2.2 we show the passage of a product through four important stages in its life:

- The stage of innovation and market entrance
- The stage of market acceptance
- A stage where the market for the product is in a steady state
- A final stage of market decline for the product.

The first stage of innovation represents the stage of product discovery and the development of a technique for its production. A number of attempts have been made to explain why some firms are more successful at innovation than others. In one study it was discovered that on average, in the UK, only one product in sixty survived from discovery to full market production. In addition, there is often a considerable gap (the so-called 'technology gap') between the discovery of a new process or product and its commercial development. In some cases this gap can be as long as 30–40 years.

The second stage of market acceptance represents the period during which the market 'learns' about a new product or process. With some products this stage may take a long time, perhaps because some other competing product already holds the market place and extra costs would be incurred by consumers in making the switch. For example, the introduction of colour televisions into the UK came at a time when a substantial proportion of the population had black-and-white sets. Unless one has seen a colour television, a black-and-white set may appear perfectly adequate and this, combined with the high cost of making the switch, had to be overcome before television manufacturers could make substantial inroads into what was largely a replacement market.

The third stage of steady-state demand can cover any length of time depending upon the product. The stable products referred to earlier all enjoy very long periods of full market exploitation perhaps with some gradual expansion in demand through time. Other products, for example in the fashion industry and pharmaceuticals, have very short periods where the market is fully exploited. Indeed, the fashion-clothing industry, almost by definition, cannot enjoy periods of stable market sales.

The fourth and final stage of product decline can come about through a variety of reasons. In the case of some stable products, market decline may brought about by a failure on the supply side. It is not hard to predict that the various fossil fuels will enter decline simply through the depletion of the world's reserves. Other stable products may enter into sudden decline because they are no longer regarded as socially desirable or safe. But, the most common causes of market decline are either the availability of a new, superior product or because the product's principal use disappears.

> **Self test:** At what stage of their life cycle would you place the following products and why?
>
> 1 Video recorders
> 2 Asbestos
> 3 Electronic calculators
> 4 Jumbo jets
> 5 This book

To summarize, managers must contend with market uncertainty in, at least, two dimensions: first, the degree of competitiveness characteristic of a particular market and, second, the susceptibility of that market to technological change.

The life-cycle diagram gives us some clues as to the types of uncertainty which management must face as a product proceeds through its life. In the first two stages, uncertainty will arise from the problems of penetrating new and possibly unknown technologies and market-places. In the third stage of the product's life uncertainty will attach to the of time over which stable sales can be expected before decline sets in. Finally, in the last stage the question arises: when should the firm stop producing?

Characteristics of the firm's markets

The principal input markets in which the firm must operate can be classified in the following way:

- The hard-factor market
- The labour market
- The market for managerial and technical skills
- The capital market.

The hard-factor markets

The hard-factor markets are those for raw materials, plant, equipment, land and buildings and so forth. Indeed, any physical asset can be regarded as a 'hard factor'. The discipline of microeconomics is devoted to understanding (amongst other things) the operation of these markets. Economists seek to explain the mechanisms by which these markets attain equilibrium, that is, where the supply of a particular product is equal to its demand. Problems arise, however, because the concept of economic equilibrium does not lend itself readily to situations where markets are in a state of rapid change. The manager is in the front line trying to foresee changes in these markets such as changes in the patterns of supply and demand through changes in tastes, product characteristics and so forth. He or she may also be faced with problems of procurement in markets where only one or two suppliers exist or where special difficulties arise in transportation or handling.

The economic characteristics of particular markets will determine the way in which managers can respond to those markets. In a perfectly competitive market (see note below), management's range of action in the area of pricing is severely limited. Management must either work within the market, as it exists, or attempt to alter the market type in which they are either buying or selling the product concerned. This can often be achieved by introducing some degree of imperfection into the market by giving their product special attributes to separate it from the competition.

Note: In Chapter 6 we examine the differences between the principal market types. However, perfect competition is an 'ideal' market type so we will, at this point, briefly outline the assumptions necessary for such a market to exist. With a perfect market for any commodity there are:

- A large number of buyers and sellers of the commodity in question

- A single ruling price which both buyers and sellers must take as given

- No transaction costs or taxes which either buyers or sellers must pay in order to trade

- No barriers of entry into the market. That is, anyone who has a mind to set up as a producer of the commodity in question may do so without restriction.

A market is said to be 'imperfect' if one or more of these conditions do not hold. Monopoly, for example, is a situation where the first assumption is violated and only one supplier exists in the market.

The concept of a perfect market is important for a number of reasons:

- It defines an 'ideal case' against which reality can be compared

- The movement toward perfection in particular markets is regarded, in certain political senses, as desirable.

Perfect markets do lead to an efficient allocation of resources within an economy with the minimum of political control. However, the individuals involved in those markets have no control over the supply–demand relationship which exists. In one sense, perfectly competitive markets are pure, self-regulating anarchies.

However, perfect competition is an ideal market type and is rarely, if ever, met in practice. Most markets possess some degree of imperfection and managers will attempt to exploit these imperfections in order to increase the surplus they make from operations. Indeed, the famous economist J. K. Galbraith argues that the managers of modern corporations try to accumulate power over markets in a number of ways.

- Through gaining control of prices by the acquisition of monopoly powers both as a seller and as a buyer in their markets

- By gaining access to the power of government (which often comes through increased size):

  '... the bigger it is (the organization), the better it can minimize risk and plan operations and investment with assurance as to the outcome' (See the reference to Galbraith and Salinger at the end of this chapter)

- By gaining access to foreign markets and creating and influencing the foreign policy of others.

Uncertainty is a characteristic feature of management's dealings with external markets. Often, this uncertainty cannot be quantified, perhaps because of a lack of prior experience in a particular market situation or because the market is in a state of rapid change. In as far as uncertainty can be quantified (a problem we discuss in more detail in Chapter 11) it can be managed, otherwise it just has to be avoided! Uncertainty is an all pervasive problem in all sorts of decision-making, and much of management accounting is concerned with its measurement and the analysis of its effects.

The labour market

A firm's total labour force includes the various levels of management within the firm as well as those actively engaged in operational tasks such as production, sales, research and development, etc. The total labour force lies along a spectrum; at one end is the firm's senior management, at the other the person who does the most menial (but often very necessary) tasks in the organization. However, we do, in this text, make the somewhat artificial distinction between managerial and non-managerial labour. As we have indicated before, management is characterized by its decision-making powers. The remainder of the labour force is formally directed although, in practice, non-managerial labour may have considerable informal decision-making power.

New labour is hired by the firm through the medium of the labour market. However, labour is not a commodity which can be purchased like raw materials or, indeed, capital. Society now imposes severe restrictions on managerial discretion over the conditions of service and the firing of employees. These restrictions reflect the social view (often very imperfectly) that an employee donates to the firm not just part of his or her surplus wealth, as is the case with capital holders, but what may be a substantial proportion of the individual's lifetime and intellectual resources.

As well as a variety of legal constraints concerning labour relations the interests of many employees are protected by representative groups such as the unions and professional societies and organizations. In Chapter 10 we consider the information needs of management in its negotiations with these various representative bodies over wage rates and other conditions of service. At this point we can note the problem areas in dealing with the labour market which will influence management's perception of the uncertainty it faces:

- The changing state of labour law, particularly in the areas of industrial relations, employment protection and conditions of service

- The effect of various union agreements on representation and closed shops

- Changes in technology which alter the degree of mechanization in particular processes

- Altering patterns of employment within the economy such as the availability of employees with particular skills in the firm's catchment area.

In any firm, substantial management resources are devoted to the management of its industrial relations and its dealings with the labour market.

The market for technical and managerial skills

A firm's dealings with the market for technical and managerial skills present the same sort of problems as those encountered with the general labour market except that the influence of unionization is less pronounced. However, technical, scientific and professional staff often regard themselves as members of, and hold allegiance to, certain outside bodies or peer groups. The various professional bodies lay down ethical as well as technical guidelines governing the behaviour of their members including those members employed in industry. Scientific and technical staff also regard themselves as members of their peer group of fellow scientists which provides a degree of external validation of their activities. As a consequence of this external allegiance, firms have to recognize and account for the changing influence of the various professional and technical associations, not only in the terms of conditions of service they offer to new staff but also in terms of their own practices.

The capital market

The capital market is the medium through which the firm must obtain its supplies of long-term investment funds. That is, money for investment in land and buildings, capital equipment and so forth. The capital market is an economic market and not a physical market as it is fixed neither in time nor place. It represents the aggregate activity of all those individuals and organizations which have surplus funds which they wish to invest and all those who have a use for those funds and the ability to pay the necessary rate of return to those investors.

Money can therefore be regarded as a commodity; at any given time the balance of supply and demand for investment funds will lead to a market price which is measured in terms of its interest rate. However, money is not a homogenous commodity. The ruling price or interest rate will be determined both by the requirements of the suppliers and by the potential uses to which the funds will be put by their users.

On the supply side, the capital market can be split into two sectors:

- The equity market
- The debt market.

Suppliers of equity finance take a share in the ownership of the firm when they subscribe their money. Typically, in large, public companies the rights of the equity investors are somewhat restricted. Normally, equity shareholders have:

- No right to repayment of their capital

- No right to any interest or dividends
- No right to manage the business
- A right to vote at the company's general meetings and appoint the senior management of the firm (the directors)
- A right to the assets of the business upon winding up once all of its other debts have been paid
- A right to certain statutory information concerning the affairs of the business as defined by the Companies Acts 1948, 1967 and 1981.

In practice most large companies do pay regular dividends to their equity investors (or 'ordinary share holders' as they are referred to in the UK or 'common stock holders' in the USA). The equity investors receive, in exchange for the funds they subscribe, a title of part ownership in the company in the form of a share certificate. These share certificates can be subsequently traded on the Stock Exchange in the case of public limited companies or by private arrangement in the case of private companies. The price at which they are bought and sold in this 'secondary' market reflects the investors' expectations of the future dividends they will receive from the company concerned. As we see in Chapter 12, the price of shares in this second-hand market has an important effect in determining the cost of equity finance for the firm. Uncertainty in the future level of share prices has, therefore, an important effect upon the cost management will impute to the equity funds it uses in capital investment.

The principal suppliers of debt finance are financial insititutions such as the banks (although they see themselves primarily as suppliers of short- and medium-term finance), the merchant banks, pension funds, insurance companies and trust funds of various sorts. With debt capital:

- The borrower promises to pay a specified rate of interest
- There may be a contractual repayment date (redeemable stock)
- The debt may be 'secured' on the assets of the business. In the event of default, the debt holder has the right to sell the assets which act as security in order to redeem the debt
- The debt holder has no say in the management of the business except in the event of default in either interest payments or capital repayment. In that situation, the debt holder will usually have the power (depending upon the terms of the loan agreement) to appoint a 'receiver' to run the business until the capital and interest are repaid.

In some cases, where the debt has been offered to the general public, a secondary market may come into existence where the debt stock is traded like ordinary shares on the Stock Exchange.

In Chapter 12 we will consider, in much more detail, the advantages and disadvantages of different sources of finance. We will also consider, in that chapter, some of the important economic characteristics which the capital market must possess in order to operate efficiently in providing funds for investing firms. At this stage, we can say that the uncertainty managers face, in their capital market operations, arise from:

- Sudden and unpredictable changes in the cost of financing their capital requirements
- New opportunities for raising new finance or refurbishing existing capital
- Government interference in the money markets (raising and lowering interest rates and altering credit conditions).

Structure and behaviour of organizations

In the last section we described, in outline, some of the problems which managers face in their relationship with their firm's markets. With each market category we indicated some of the sources of uncertainty which arise from those markets and which management must face in their decision-making. We also pointed out that market conditions can rapidly change. To cope with these problems, management accounting must be able effectively to translate data from the firm's environment into information suitable for management decisions.

However, the structure of the organization itself has a crucial role in determining the ability of the firm to respond to environmental change. Because the communication of management information is also greatly influenced by the structure of relationships which exist between managers themselves we will spend some time examining the problem of organizational structure and the way it is influenced by forces inside and outside the firm.

There has been considerable effort over the years by theorists to discover what constitutes the ideal organizational structure. In the next section we will describe three different types of structure and the problems which arise with each. In practice, few organizations exactly conform to any prescribed structural model; all are modified, to a certain extent, by the peculiarities of their environment.

Bureaucratic organizations

In the last chapter we outlined the ways in which firms developed through and after the Industrial Revolution. As we have already noted, Victorian firms were highly owner-dominated and controlled. The concept of the bureaucratic organization arose in this century because of this 'Victorian' preoccupation with the need for strict control and predictability in behaviour.

Max Weber, one of the fathers of modern sociology, described the features of what he believed to be the ideal organization. Weber's conception of a bureaucracy was an organization ruled by a hierarchy of 'officials', i.e. individuals who, for the time being, held an office within the organization. Each office had its own specific tasks and privileges and the incumbent would be responsible to a single superior officer. In its ideal form, according to Weber, a bureaucracy should have the following characteristics:

- The incumbents of particular offices should be personally free, apart from the duties and responsibilities of their office

- Individuals should hold their office and earn advancement by merit only

- Discipline and control should be exercised through the formal lines of authority using the 'one man, one boss' rule.

Within the ideal bureaucracy, all individuals have the freedom to develop their technical competence within a closely defined job description (the office) and to use the expertise so gained to solve the problems of the organization. Weber's perception was that individuals work best and can use their skills most effectively in a closely controlled and disciplined situation.

In Fig. 2.3 we show a typical 'line management chart' for an organization such as would be found in many firm's manual of procedures or as pinned on a director's wall. Note the arrangement of offices into levels to create a hierarchy of responsibility and the degree (or 'span') of control which each office holds over those under it. Normally, the more important offices within bureaucratic organizations have a greater span of control than those lower down the hierarchy, although there is a limit to the degree of control which can be effectively exercised by one individual.

Note, also, that an organization which relies upon strict control and discipline within a highly formalized set of relationships must have, at the very top of the hierarchy, a source of authority which is accepted unquestioningly by those underneath it. In other words, the authority must be accepted by all within the organization as legitimate otherwise the authority of the various officials down through the organization will be weakened and control made less effective. It is for this reason that modern bureaucracies try to 'distance' and impersonalize their ultimate authority figure—the sovereign in many of our social organizations in the UK, the 'shareholders' in the case of many of our large firms.

The interesting feature of a bureaucratic organization is that all the formal lines of communication pass up and down through the hierarchy. Therefore, information within the organization is constrained into vertical rather than horizontal movements. For example, if, in Fig. 2.3, a subordinate official in the laboratories had a suggestion for a modification to a plant process, that suggestion would have to be considered at the directorate level before it could be passed down to the head of plant. Clearly, this could lead to considerable delays in the implementation of any decision. This slowness to respond to changes, either externally or internally, can in certain circumstances be a great strength of bureaucracies, hasty

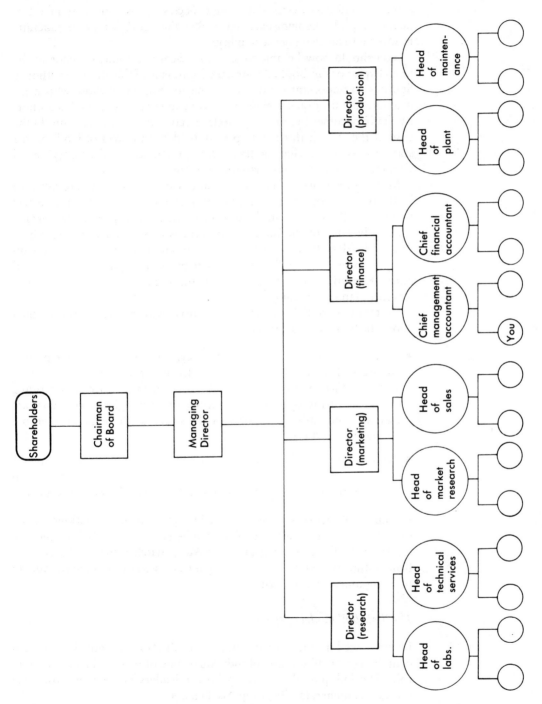

Fig 2.3 Typical line management chart

decisions can be avoided and crises managed by inactivity. But, where rapid and effective decision-making is necessary, as is the case in a firm facing a rapidly changing external market, the rigidity of the bureaucratic model could be an immense liability.

You should now be able to see more clearly a point we made in the first chapter of this book. Because the legitimacy of the ultimate authority figure is so important for obtaining the compliance of those who work in a bureaucratic organization, the satisfaction of the needs of that authority figure becomes the primary, declared goal of the organization. In the case of the church this is interpreted as 'doing the will of God', in the state it may be 'serving the flag', 'doing for Queen and country' or, in Communist countries, just 'serving the state'.

In the framework of the bureaucratic firm, shareholders are taken to be the primary source of authority although they have very little effective power (which is vested in the directors). As a consequence, the formal, stated objective of the bureaucratic firm is to maximize the wealth of its shareholders. Because the primary reason for the existence of a bureaucracy is to serve the will of its ultimate authority figure(s) the personal aims of specific office holders within the organization should be subservient to this overriding aim.

Certain undesirable side effects can arise within organizations which adopt the bureaucratic model:

- Office holders within the bureaucracy, perceiving that their performance will be measured and controlled in terms of the performance of their office, will tend to view the goals of their office as overriding the goals of the overall organization. In sociological terms they are said to 'internalize' the goals of the office at the expense of those of the organization

- Because, in principle, only one valid claim on the surplus of the organization exists, i.e. that made by the owners, any other claim is seen as a subversion of their rights and therefore an issue of overt conflict.

A number of theorists have attempted to prescribe organizational structures which overcome the problems inherent in Weber's bureaucratic model of the firm. One attempt, by Likert, switched the emphasis away from authority and control to an organization based upon good human relations and group performance.

The 'link-pin' model of the organization

Likert viewed the ideal organization as a collection of family groups each containing a small number of individuals one of whom filled a 'link-pin' role. The link-pins themselves, who are leaders of their groups, form a separate, higher, family group. See Fig. 2.4.

The principal advantages claimed for the Likert model are that it:

- Reduces conflict between various levels of the organization as heads of family groups (the 'link-pins') are responsible not to a single superior but to members of a higher family group

- Reduces barriers to communication between peers, as lateral communications are enhanced through the operation of groupings of superiors

- Brings about a greater level of agreement and commitment among participants within each family group.

Fig 2.4 Likert's link-pin model of organizational structure

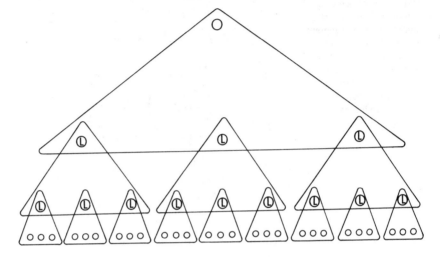

Ⓛ   'Link-pin' member of family group

Likert's model of the organization has a number of difficulties. First, it does nothing to help resolve the conflicts between individuals and groups over the distribution of the firm's surplus and, second, it relies upon individual members of the organization being prepared to sublimate their identities within the family group. The second point raises a problem about personality types and organizational structure which we will deal with in the next section.

Self test: Take any organization with which you are familiar and draw up its management structure in terms of a bureaucratic hierarchy of offices then redesign it in terms of Likert's 'link-pin' model. Outline the advantages and disadvantages of the structure based upon the link-pin as opposed to the bureaucratic model.

Matrix organizations

The trend, in practice, toward less formal control within organizations as a way of attaining higher adaptability has led to the concept of the 'matrix' organization. In Fig. 2.5 we depict this type of organization as a 'cell' structure with the most highly specialized areas of activity lying around the periphery of the organization. Within this outer layer of the organization lie progressively less specialized, integrative areas of operation and, indeed, at the centre, like the nucleus of a living cell, lies the central management function. In this concept of the organization, again taking its analogy from biology, the outer layers form a 'protective shell' for the more senior, strategic management functions.

Fig 2.5 Matrix model of the organization. F = Functional management groups (management accounting, marketing, etc); S = Specialized groups (sales teams, production staff, etc.); I = Intergroup teams.

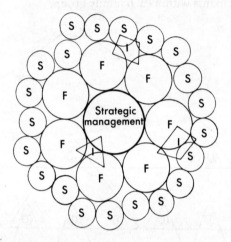

The matrix organization permits:

- A high level of differentiation into different units responsible for different organizational functions

- A high degree of freedom in communication through the use of intergroup teams

- Minimal formal control through the use of liaison committees between groups.

The problems with the Likert model are, however, much magnified in the matrix organization which relies very heavily upon interpersonal co-operation for its success.

Another, more formal version of the matrix organization is specifically designed to cope with two basic needs of organizations:

- The need to separate (or differentiate) the organization into functional groups where employees can perform their duties and gather expertise in their particular specialist areas

- The need to integrate these functional activities into overall organizational activities such as specific production projects.

This variant of the matrix organization presupposes that many employees will have to report to two authority figures: the first being that employee's group manager, the second being the activity or project manager. In Fig.

2.6 we show the matrix organization which exists in many universities and polytechnics where staff are separated into different academic discipline groups (the functional units) along one dimension and into different scheme groupings along the other.

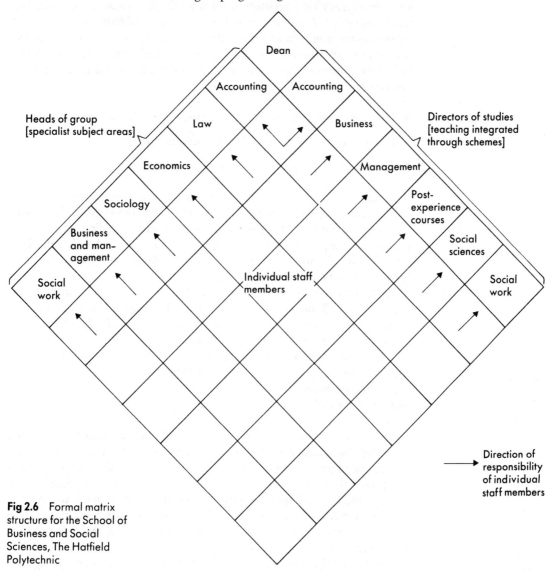

Fig 2.6 Formal matrix structure for the School of Business and Social Sciences, The Hatfield Polytechnic

This formal model of a matrix organization presupposes a 'contingency view' of the organization which we will discuss in the next section. It is also important to note that this matrix model emphasizes structure and the importance of a hierarchy in managerial relations. As well as having many of the defects of the bureaucratic model discussed above, this matrix model can also engender conflict between the functional and the integrating hierarchies as members of the organization must report to two supervisors who may have quite different objectives.

The contingency view of the organization

In recent years, the search for an ideal organization structure has been replaced by what is called the 'contingency view' of the organization. The contingency view presupposes that no single organizational structure will be suitable for each and every firm irrespective of its market, economic and social environment and that a firm's structure will change in response to changing environmental conditions. Organization theorists have identified three important 'contingent' variables which play a crucial role in determining organizational structure:

- The complexity and changability of the technological environment
- The uncertainty in the social and economic environment
- The personality style of the organization concerned.

We have already outlined the nature of the first two variables and we will develop our discussion of their importance throughout this book. The third variable is of great importance in understanding what makes particular companies 'tick' and why their managers behave in the way that they do. In addition, the personality style of a particular firm will have a subtle but none the less decisive influence upon the development of its formal organizational structure. Managers with an authoritarian personality will favour strict control of their subordinates through a clearly defined system of hierarchical relationships. On the other hand, more gregarious individuals are likely to prefer the more cooperative environment of the Likert or matrix model. The personality style of the organization as a whole is usually determined by the personalities of the senior management group although many other factors (such as the organization's personnel and marketing policy, for example) will also have an effect.

However, a firm will only survive if the organizational structure favoured by management is in sympathy with the contingent forces impacting upon it from its external environment. This tension between the personality (and resultant managerial) style of the organization and the demands placed upon it by its external environment leads to a phenomenon we call 'organizational stress'. The degree to which an organization can resolve this stress determines its managerial health and consequently its ability to survive.

Unfortunately, it is extremely difficult to measure the personality style of an organization although many writers have tried to do so. Part of the problem is that there is no single, well-developed theory of individual personality which would enable us to either explain or predict how individuals relate to one another in an organizational setting. It is easy to classify firms as 'paternalistic' or 'entrepreneurial' and to see how, for example, a paternalistic, authoritarian, bureaucratic organization would have trouble coping with a rapidly changing external environment. However, this sort of crude distinction between personality styles does not give us the detail we require to predict how a firm will cope with its organizational stress.

The contingency view of organizational structure does produce two interesting implications concerning organization structure. First, as the external environment becomes more complex and 'threatening' to the firm so it will become more differentiated in its activities in order to cope. What this means is that a firm facing changing markets, for example, will set up specialist functional units such as special marketing teams in order to deal with the problem. The Law of 'Requisite Variety' states that organizations become sufficiently differentiated in their activities in order to cope with the contingencies of their external environment. The second implication arises directly from this in that it becomes more difficult to control an organization as it becomes more differentiated. In other words, the need grows within the organization to reintegrate or harmonize its overall activities in order to achieve its overall goals. These two forces of differentiation and the need for integration work against one another and represent an important source of conflict in the management of an organization.

Organizational implications

The management-accounting function within the firm will impact upon its organizational structure in two important ways:

- By providing information for the specialist information needs of the firm and thus helping it toward the optimal degree of differentiation required to meet the uncertainty of its external environment

- By providing an integrative mechanism through its formal rules and procedures.

Management accounting cannot create differentiation where the need for it does not exist. But, where particular specialist functions have been created through necessity, management accounting can focus the activities of performance measurement into those areas. For example, a company undergoing long-term reinvestment in plant and machinery may create a specialist group to appraise new projects and coordinate their development within the firm. Management accounting will enter into this group's activities in two ways:

- At the functional level of providing data on the financial implications of the projects considered by the group

- Monitoring the performance of the group as new projects come into existence and the group's forecasts can be compared with actual results.

In the first case, the management accounting function has provided information relevant to the task of the group itself, and thus, by responding in this specific way it has supported the required degree of differentiation within the organization. In the second case, it has aided in the process of integrating the group's activities within the firm as a whole.

When we examine the purpose of budgeting in Chapter 4 we will note that the periodic budgeting and resultant control procedures are an important integrating mechanism within the organization. Not only do budgets provide a means whereby the various conflicting interests within the organization can be reconciled through negotiation, they also present management with the opportunity to control and harmonize the firm's activities.

Rationality and its implications for managerial decision-making

We assume in this book that a decision-maker, when faced with a choice between a set of different outcomes, will make a choice in a 'rational' way. By this we mean that the decision-maker will select a course of action (make a decision) which will achieve some goal or preference which he or she has. The difficulty is that there is much debate about what the concept of rationality entails. As it is a task of the management accountant to provide information for managerial decision-makers it is important to have some idea of what is meant by 'rationality' in decision-making and how the different models of rationality can affect the choices which are made.

The concept of 'rationality', and its implications for our understanding of how individual decision-makers behave, has been a fundamental problem in the social sciences for a number of years. Some social-science disciplines, economics being the prime example, have developed a very rigorous definition of the concept of rationality and have had to live with the problem that very few individuals appear to be rational in the way their definition implies. However, the advantage of this very formal definition (encapsulated within a set of rationality 'axioms') is that it provides the basis for a (relatively) easy formal analysis of many decision-making situations. Other disciplines, more concerned with the explanatory power of their theories rather than with their amenability to formal analysis, have settled for less rigorous but more descriptive concepts of rationality.

The economist's concept of rationality

Economists argue that when an individual is faced with a set of possible choices he or she will select that alternative which they regard, at that point in time, to be most desirable. Or, in slightly more technical terms, each individual will attempt to maximize his or her 'utility' by selecting from the range of alternatives available that alternative which is most 'preferred'. All this is saying is that if a particular individual happens to prefer a blue to a red car and, everything else being equal, goes ahead and buys the red car then he or she is behaving irrationally.

In order to formalize this self-evident truth two choice 'axioms' are proposed:

- An individual can compare alternatives and decide which is preferred or come to the conclusion that they are equally satisfactory (the axiom of comparison)

- An individual is 'intransitive' in his or her ordering of alternatives. For example, if an individual prefers a red car to a blue car and a blue car to a white car then, everything else being equal, he/she would be irrational in expressing a preference for the white car as opposed to the red car (the axiom of 'transitivity').

The combination of these two axioms produces the 'proposition of the rank ordering of preferences' which states that:

- A rational decision-maker can rank all available alternatives in a consistent order of preference.

In this book, as is usual elsewhere, we will term this type of rationality 'economic rationality'. Individuals who make choices in accordance with these axioms and the proposition of rank ordering of preferences are said to be maximizing their 'utility'. Utility being, simply, a variable which measures the strength of an individual's preferences.

It is difficult to fault the contention that individuals will always choose the most highly preferred course of action open to them. However, the difficulties with this concept of 'rational economic man' lie in the validity of the axioms outlined above. In any choice situation the rational economic man or woman will:

- Know and examine all possible courses of action open to them

- Rank the various courses of action according to their attributes even though many of the objects of choice may well have a range of different attributes

- Keep their tastes and preferences constant during their search of all possible alternatives.

In some cases, the attributes attaching to a particular option may only be potentially rather than actually realizable. For example, consider the following four alternatives available for your lunchtime refreshment and the various attributes which attach to them (you may be able to think of some others):

Objects of choice

Pint of Grotney's Real Ale
Pint of Grottenburg Lager
Pint of milk
Pint of Espana-Lax orange juice

Attributes

Ability to quench thirst
Calorific value
Taste
Health-giving properties
Hangover potential
Vitamin C content

Some of the attributes (such as cost and, perhaps, calorific value and vitamin C content) are readily and objectively identifiable although only cost will be known for certain. All the other attributes rely on a degree of subjective judgement and estimates of likelihood (maybe using probabilities) of an outcome occurring. In fact, much of the evidence collected by researchers over the years indicates that it is in just these areas of subjective judgement—especially where probabilities are involved—that people exhibit less than rational behaviour.

Much research has been conducted into individual decision-making and the results are not encouraging for those who would argue that economic rationality is found in actual decision-making behaviour. Apart from very simple choices where there is a clearly identifiable payoff in terms of money or some other tangible reward, economic rationality, as we have described it above, does not appear to represent real decision-making behaviour.

In order to sidestep the problem that individuals do not appear to exhibit consistent economic rationality, Milton Friedman argued that all we need assume is that individuals act 'as if' they were rational. This would appear, at first sight, to be a satisfactory solution for economists, as their investigations often look at market-wide or aggregate effects. Therefore, even if individuals do not act rationally, in the economic sense of the term, all the time, we could argue that markets behave 'as if' the individual participants within those markets were acting rationally. There are a number of problems with this reinterpretation of the concept of economic rationality although it is true to say that many of the economic models based upon it provide powerful explanations of real market processes.

Multiattribute elimination models of rationality

One of the most realistic attempts to surmount the growing evidence of less than optimal behaviour on the part of individual decision-makers was proposed by Tversky. Tversky's model assumes that individuals enter the decision-making situation with a list of attributes which they have ranked in descending order of importance. These attributes form a 'filter' through which alternatives, as soon as they are recognized, can be passed. For example, the individual who contemplates purchasing a car will identify a set of attributes such as price, make, age, mileage, colour, state of the tyres, etc., which he or she regards as important, and will test each alternative with each of these attributes. This search and selection procedure is only completed once all of the attributes are satisfied, although in practice some of the lower attributes may be dispensed with if the set of alternatives discovered is found to be too small and the costs of continuing the search are too high. The experimental evidence gathered so far seems to suggest that this model represents the most satisfactory description of the mode of rationality actually used by individuals in their actual decision-making behaviour.

Satisficing models

Herbert A Simon, who won a Nobel prize for his work in behavioural economics, has argued that individuals, for a number of reasons, are unable to optimize in anything other than simple decision-making situations. Simon termed this inability 'bounded rationality' and observed that bounded rationality is the norm when individuals are required to make intuitive statistical judgements. Simon proposed that instead of seeking optimal solutions to their decision problems, decision-makers invariably settle for the first 'satisfactory' alternative which appears (hence the term 'satisficing'). Thus, there is no attempt, as is prescribed by the economic-man model, to appraise the attributes of all possible alternatives and to seek an optimal solution, given the decision-maker's particular preference ranking.

Some writers have suggested that if we take into account all of the hidden costs of searching and appraising all possible alternatives then the optimizing and satisficing models reduce to the same thing. Unfortunately, as there is no way of ascertaining these hidden costs there is no way of proving this suggestion right or wrong!

Quasi-satisficing models

The three attempts at describing rationality discussed above, assume that:

- The decision-maker has in mind the satisfaction of some goal or goals

- Decisions will be made in order to achieve either a satisfactory or an optimal solution

- Choices will be based upon either a complete (in the case of economic rationality) or a less than complete search of the available alternatives.

With quasi-satisficing however, alternatives are not accepted if they are just satisfactory but rather if they fulfil a moral or normative criterion which the decision-maker regards as sacrosanct and, indeed, the only morally acceptable criterion in the given situation. Politicians offer the most obvious examples of this approach when simple criteria such as 'reducing the money supply', 'achieving a broad consensus', etc., are used as the one and only acceptable justification for action. In understanding managerial behaviour, this description of rationality accounts for the rigidity of behaviour and inflexibility of attitudes often observed in actual decisions (most noticeably in the area of industrial relations but in other areas as well).

Incrementalist models

Lindblom in his paper 'The Science of Muddling Through' proposed what has become a very influential view of the way policy decisions are made. He argued that the preferred strategy of decision-makers is to search the set of alternatives starting with the one closest to the currently held policy option. Only very minor variations on current practice are acceptable and the search for a solution is halted as soon as a satisfactory outcome is achieved. The selection rule may resemble either the simple satisficing approach or may take on the complexion of a moral rule as in the quasi-satisficing model. Incrementalism presents a particularly seductive view of the way in which policy decisions are made especially in government and law. Indeed, the concept of judicial precedence—the epitome of the incrementalist approach—is firmly embodied in the English legal system. By their nature, wherever bureaucratic organizations exist there will be a tendency toward the caution exemplified by the incrementalist approach.

Dramaturgical models of man

Some of the oldest theories of human decision-making behaviour view individuals not as careful balancers of utilitarian gains and losses, but rather as actors who play out given decision situations in accordance with their own perception of how they should act. In fact we often notice that individuals rehearse decision-making situations, working out what to do and so forth. The perception of self-role and the rules by which such roles must be acted out is a crucial characteristic of human rationality. The captain who goes down with his sinking ship is hardly acting according to the rules of rational economic man.

In some respects this dramaturgical model is an extension of the quasi-satisficing model discussed above. Individuals under stress slip easily into moral judgements and decision-making based upon rules whose validity they see no need to inspect. Often, under stress, decision-making will be dominated by the individuals 's perception of his or her self-role—especially in those situations where the maintenance of particular roles and the style with which they are carried out have heavy moral or ethical overtones.

To summarize this section: we have considered a range of different models of rationality which have been proposed at one time or other to explain how people actually make decisions. At one extreme we have the formal model of economic rationality with its high analytical, but poor explanatory power. At the other extreme we have the dramaturgical model which presupposes that individual action is determined by a preset role which is often rehearsed and then acted out. However, it does seem likely that under relatively calm, unpressurized decision-making conditions, choices will be made along the lines prescribed by either the economist's, the multi-attribute or the satisficing models of rationality. On the other hand, under pressure, we would expect decision-makers to slip into pre-rational rules and roles in their decision-making.

In terms of the economist's model of rationality, the problem faced by the management accountant is quite straightforward. If we assume that the principal role of the management accountant is to provide information for decision-making then, given an environment where decisions are made in line with the prescriptions of economic analysis, the management accountant need only establish the information inputs to those economic models and be prepared to supply as much of that information as he or she can.

However, once we move away from the formal definition of rationality supplied by the economist, the problems of the management accountant become much more complex. It is much more difficult to impose a structure on the decision-making situation and to predict (*ex-ante*) the sort of information management will require. In this situation, management accountants often find themselves in the position of imposing structures in which the way they present information limits the range of choice which managers perceive to be open to them.

Supplementary reading

COOPER, D., Models of personal choice, in Arnold, J., Carsberg, B. V., and Scapens, R. (eds), *Topics in Management Accounting*, Philip Allan, 1980

COOPER, D., A social and organizational view of management accounting, in Bromwich, M., and Hopwood, A. (eds), *Essays in British Accounting Research*, Pitman, 1981

GALBRAITH, J. K., and SALINGER, N., *Almost Everyone's Guide to Economics*, Pelican, 1981

JANIS, I. L., and MANN, L., *Decision Making*, Free Press, 1977. Especially parts 1 and 2

LAWRENCE, P. R., and LORSCH, J. W., *Organization and Environment*, Harvard School of Business Adminstration, Boston, 1967

LIKERT, R., The principle of supportive relationships, in Pugh, D., (ed.), *Organization Theory*, Penguin, 1971

LOWE, E. A. and TINKER, A. M., New directions for management accounting, in Chenhall, R. H., *et al.* (eds), *The Organizational Context of Management Accounting*, Pitman, 1981. This is an excellent book of readings containing numerous articles for those interested in the wider aspects of the subject

MARCH, J. B., and SIMON, H. A., The dysfunctions of bureaucracy, in Pugh, D. (ed.), *Organization Theory*, Penguin , 1971

WEBER, M., Legitimate authority and bureaucracy, in Pugh, E. (ed.), *Organization Theory*, Penguin, 1971

Questions

1   Discuss the meaning of the following terms:

   (a) Organization

   (b) Market

   (c) Organizational structure

   (d) Requisite variety

   (e) Perfect competition.

2   We have split input factors used by firms into four groups: capital, labour, managerial and technical skills and 'hard factors'. Suggest how these four inputs could be further subdivided for a motor-car manufacturer.

3   Discuss the different sorts of uncertainty which a manager might have to face in the sale of a new product. How does that uncertainty differ from the situation where a company is selling an established product?

4   Outline the differences between debt and equity capital. What does it mean to say that a loan is secured and what sorts of security would an individual be able to offer to a bank in order to obtain a loan?

5   Outline the influence which the structure of an organization could have on the management accounting carried on within it.

6   For each model of rationality outlined in this chapter describe:

   (a) The search strategy involved

   (b) The behavioural objectives assumed for the decision-maker.

3 Concepts and costs for decision-making —————

In this chapter we take a look at the concepts of wealth and opportunity cost. These two concepts form the foundation of accounting for decision-making because they form a basis for the measurement of the financial consequences of managerial decision-making. In order to operationalize these concepts and make them analytically useful we define them purely in cash terms.

Time and again in this book we return to the cash implications of decision-making. However, in order to place our subsequent discussions in a wider context we present some general arguments against this cash approach in general and the opportunity cost concept in particular at the end of this chapter.

The following topics are discussed in this chapter:

- The financial consequences of decision-making

- The concept of wealth

- The concept of cost

- The irrelevance of certain types of cost for decision-making purposes

- The importance of 'cash flow' in decision-making

- Opportunity cost and the measurement of the 'true cost' of past actions

- The criticisms of the opportunity cost concept.

Financial consequences of decision-making

In a decision-making situation, each of the possible courses of action open to the decision-maker can set in motion a wide range of different consequences. At the point in time that a decision is made the expected outcomes from that decision will have varying degrees of uncertainty attached to them. We assume, however, that there is one component, or one attribute, of the consequence of a given decision which will always be of interest to the decision-maker. This attribute is the wealth change (in cash terms) brought about by the decision concerned. If a manager is trying to pursue the objective of maximizing the cash surplus over which he or she has control, we assume:

- The manager will only consider the net alteration in wealth brought about by each alternative.

- The manager will choose that alternative which offers the highest positive net wealth change.

The management accountant is therefore narrowing down the range of attributes attaching to each alternative course of action to the single one of net wealth change. It may be that in the process of actual decision-making management will not regard the financial outcome as conclusive in deciding which course of action to pursue. Other more important, but financially unquantifiable, factors may be conclusive in making a particular decision.

For example:

- Certain outcomes may be seen as conflicting with the firm's ethical or commercial policies and would be rejected on that basis.

- Certain courses of action may be seen as affecting the firm's goodwill with others.

The concept of wealth

In order to examine the implications of the assumptions made above we must derive an operational definition for the concept of wealth. An operational definition of wealth must be one which permits its objective measurement so that it can be used in practical decision-making situations. 'Objectivity' means, in this sense, that given the definition of wealth arrived at, a number of accountants in possession of the same raw data concerning past events or with common expectations of future events would produce the same estimate of wealth.

At an abstract level wealth measures the power which a particular individual or firm has over consumption, that is, the ability to purchase goods or services. In a money-based economy, this reduces down to the total financial resources of the individual or firm.

Of course, in common parlance we normally mean more than this when we use the term 'wealth'. Such things as quality of lifestyle and even the social class of the individual concerned may influence our judgement of how wealthy that individual is. However, our definition ignores these intangibles unless they are measurable. Therefore, for an individual or firm we define wealth as:

- The total net cash balances held (C) plus

- the 'present value' (PV) of all future cash flows which are recognizable at the point of measurement (we explain this concept in detail below) plus

- the net realizable (sale) value (NRV) of all assets which are not held with the view to earning cash until the eventual date of sale (non-productive assets).

Therefore, at the point in time (t) at which a decision is made the decision-maker's wealth W_t is given by:

$$W_t = C_t + PV_t + NRV_t$$

Long-term decisions usually entail alterations in the holding of cash-generating assets as well as cash in hand, while short-term decisions usually involve only changes in the cash balances currently held.

Some assets are owned in order to produce cash in the future. A job, for example, is an asset in that a person who has a job will earn a 'stream' of future cash payments in the form of salary, wages, pension payments and so forth. Other benefits accrue with a job as well—self-esteem, job satisfaction, etc.—but in one important sense it can be regarded as a cash-producing asset. Similarly, firms hold plant and equipment, not for their intrinsic merit, but to generate future cash flows through use.

Other assets are held not for their ability to generate cash but rather to increase their owners' quality of life. Property, old masters, antiques, cellars of wine and other chattels are assets which can be used to enhance their owners' quality of life rather than as a cash-yielding investment. As far as we are concerned, the amount of wealth tied up in such assets is the amount they would realize if they were sold immediately. The reason for this is that at any point in time, holding such assets implies that the owner is forgoing the opportunity of selling and putting the cash proceeds to another use. The wealth tied up in such assets is, therefore, the cash proceeds from sales forgone. But, to avoid double counting, we do not include the realizable value of productive, cash-generating assets in our measure of wealth. The full value of these assets is reflected in the present value of their future cash flows.

Note: The 'net realizable value' of an asset is the amount which would be realized upon its sale less the charges and expenses of the actual sale. We sometimes refer to the net realizable value of an asset at the end of its life as its 'scrap value'. The net realizable value of a cash-generating asset should always be lower than the present value of the cash flows generated by that asset. If not, the most rational course would be for the firm to sell the asset and realize its cash value.

The one term in our definition of wealth which has, up to this point, been unexplained is the concept of 'present value'. Because the concept of present value is so important to our understanding of wealth we will spend some time examining it now.

The concept of present value

Because cash is the means by which we purchase goods and services and, because most people prefer to enjoy goods and services sooner rather than later, we can infer that cash will be preferred sooner rather than later. This is what we mean when we say that money has 'time value'. But, note, this phenomenon is not simply a function of inflation, because even in a world of zero inflation a sum of money available now is preferable to the same sum available at a future date. Inflation simply exaggerates the effect of time as people take into account the declining purchasing power of money as well as the fact that their ability to purchase has been delayed.

For every individual there is an interest rate which will just induce them to invest, that is, give up a current sum of money in the hope of receiving a cash return some time in the future. In an ideal world, where everything in the future is known for certain, where there is no inflation, taxes or transactions costs and where the amount of cash invested is relatively small, most individuals require only a small rate of interest to induce them to invest. The actual rate will depend upon the other potential uses the individual has for the sum involved.

For example, let us assume that in a given situation Mr Paco (a musician of slender means) is prepared to invest at a minimum rate of 5 per cent per annum. Any rate in excess of this figure of 5 per cent he would regard as very satisfactory, anything less and he would not invest. We will assume that Mr Paco lives in a very stable economy with zero inflation and, also, that there are no expected price changes in his own pattern of consumption. We will also assume that the amount Mr Paco is planning to invest is very small compared with his overall level of wealth (i.e. the investment is 'marginal' with respect to his current wealth level). Therefore, over one year Mr Paco would expect to receive £1 plus the interest payment (his reward for investment) of £0.05.

Using this rate of 5 per cent which is just enough to 'trigger' Mr Paco into investment we can infer that he is 'indifferent' between £1 now and £1.05 in one year's time. In other words he regards the two sums of money as equivalent. The £1 is the 'present value' of £1.05 receivable in one year's time. Similarly, assuming that Mr Paco's indifference rate of 5 per cent per annum does not alter he would regard £1 held now as equivalent to £1.1025 receivable in two years' time as:

$$1.05^2 = 1.1025$$

This rate of 5 per cent is very important to Mr Paco because it allows him to determine the equivalent present value of any future cash sum which he expects to receive. In theory, individuals possess their own unique rate of interest which allows them to calculate the present value of cash which they expect to receive at some time in the future. This personal rate of interest which allows an individual to translate future sums of money into their present cash equivalents is often referred to as that individual's 'marginal rate of time preference for money'. To see how this rate can be used in personal investment decisions consider the following example:

Mr Paco expects to receive £60 in one year following an investment of £50. Determine whether this investment is worth while for Mr Paco.

The present value of £60 receivable in one year's time is:

$$\frac{60}{1.05} = £57.14$$

Using the same reasoning as before, Mr Paco is indifferent between a present sum of £57.14 and a future sum, receivable in one year's time, of £60. Indeed, Mr Paco's wealth appears to have risen by £7.14, the difference between what he has to pay out (£50) and the present value which he places upon the £60 receivable in one year's time.

Now, if the £60 had been receivable in two years' time we would have to divide by 1.05^2, i.e.

$$\frac{60}{1.05^2} = £54.42$$

Again, the investment of £50 is worth while although in this case Mr Paco's wealth has risen by the smaller amount of £4.42.

Note: Formally, we calculate the future value (*FV*) of a present sum of money by the process of 'compounding':

$$FV = PV(1 + i)^n$$

where *PV* is the present sum of money, *i* is the rate of interest and *n* is the number of periods in the future when the sum will be received.

In the example above we assume annual rates of interest and annual periods. The present value is calculated by the inverse of the compounding process. We refer to this process as 'discounting':

$$PV = \frac{FV}{(1 + i)^n}$$

Using this concept we can estimate the present value of any future cash flows which an individual might receive. In principle we can do the same for the firm, although the rate of interest which we use in the discounting process should represent the return required by all the different donors of capital. In Chapter 13 we consider some ways of 'costing' the capital resources of the firm.

Example: Mr Paco expects to receive three annual payments of £2000 on a recording contract. Assume that the rate at which money can be borrowed or lent by Mr Paco is 5 per cent per annum (free of bank charges) and that Mr Paco's indifference rate is also 5 per cent. The wealth which these three payments represent can be calculated as follows:

	Now t_0	1 year's time, t_1	2 years' time, t_2	3 years' time, t_3
Receipt		£2000	£2000	£2000
Divide by:		1.05	1.05^2	1.05^3
Present value:				
t_1	£1904.76 ←			
t_2	1814.06 ←			
t_3	1727.68 ←			
	£5446.50			

Given that Mr Paco can borrow at 5 per cent interest he can enjoy the full benefit of the wealth tied up in the recording contract immediately. If he borrows £5446.50 from a bank his loan can be cleared by the annual receipts of £2000 from the recording contract:

t_0	Initial borrowing from bank	£5446.50
t_1	*add:* 1 year's interest at 5 per cent	272.32
		5718.82
	less: First cash receipt from the recording contract paid to bank	2000.00
	Balance carried forward	3718.82
t_2	*add:* Interest on balance brought forward	185.94
		3904.76
	less: Second cash receipt from the recording contract paid to bank	2000.00
	Balance carried forward	1904.76
t_3	*add:* Interest on balance brought forward	95.24
		2000.00
	less: Third cash receipt from the recording contract paid to bank	2000.00
	Final nil balance	—

This simple example illustrates an important financial concept. When an individual or firm has the opportunity of unlimited borrowing or lending at a fixed rate of interest, free of transactions charges, the full benefit of wealth held in the form of future cash flows can be enjoyed immediately or, by borrowing and lending, at any time in the future.

We can summarize the technique for calculating the present value of a series of future cash flows in mathematical form:

Present value (PV)

$$= \frac{A_1}{1+i} + 0\frac{A_2}{(1+i)^2} + \frac{A_3}{1(+i)^3} + \ldots + \frac{A_n}{(1+i)_n}$$

$$= A_1 \times \frac{1}{1+i} + A_2 \times \frac{1}{(1+i)^2} + A_3 \times \frac{1}{(1+i)^3} + \ldots + A_n \times \frac{1}{(1+i)_n}$$

Where $A_1, A_2, A_3, \ldots, A_n$ are the cash values receivable (or if negative, payable) in the future and i is the investor's indifference rate or marginal rate of time preference for money.

The expression: $1/(1+i)_n$ is called the 'discount factor' and is given the symbol $V_{\overline{i}|n}$. For example, the discount factor for 5 per cent over two years is given by:

$$V_{0.05|2} = 1/1.05^2 = 0.907$$

Using this notation Mr Paco's problem becomes:

$$PV = \frac{2000}{1.05} + \frac{2000}{1.05^2} + \frac{2000}{1.05^3}$$

$$= 2000 \times V_{0.05|1} + 2000 \times V_{0.05|2} + 2000 \times V_{0.05|3}$$

$$= 2000 \times 0.952 + 2000 \times 0.907 + 2000 \times 0.864$$

$$= £5446$$

With this type of problem, a labour-saving device is available to us. Where we have a constant series of cash flows we can withdraw them as a factor from the present-value equation:

$$PV = 2000(V_{0.05|1} + V_{0.05|2} + V_{0.05|3})$$

The term in brackets is referred to as an 'annuity' which is, in this case, the present value of £1 receivable over three years discounted at 5 per cent per annum. We use the general symbol:

$$A_{\overline{i}|n} = (V_{\overline{i}|1} + V_{\overline{i}|2} + V_{\overline{i}|3} + \ldots + V_{\overline{i}|n})$$

In this example:

$$A_{0.05|3} = 0.952 + 0.907 + 0.864$$

$$= 2.723$$

Therefore:

$$PV = 2000 \times 2.723$$

$$= £5446$$

At the end of this chapter we show how a simple formula can be derived to calculate the present value of an annuity.

Self test: Lucia, Pena and Algericas have assets as follows:

	Lucia (£)	Pena (£)	Algericas (£)
Cash in hand	200	100	10
House and chattels (resale value)	18 000	25 000	27 000

Algericas has a bank deposit account in which he has invested £1000 per annum over the last five years. He has earned 10 per cent per annum throughout the period. Pena expects to earn £6000 this year although, at the moment, he has no further employment prospects beyond that time. Lucia, on the other hand, has just won a recording contract for five years which is worth £4000 per annum. Lucia feels that 10 per cent per annum is the best rate he could get on either borrowing or lending. The value of £1 per annum invested for five years at 10 per cent is £6.716. The present value of an annuity of £1 discounted over 5 years at 10 per cent is £3.790. Which of the three has the greatest wealth?

Solution clue: One has £31 100, the other has £2626 more and the final one £2260 more.

In Chapter 13 we return to the concept of present value when we discuss the problems of long-term decision-making. In the short term we can usually ignore the problems of discounting when considering wealth changes. Wealth change, in the short term, reduces to change in the net cash resources of the individual or firm concerned (i.e. change in C_t in the definition of wealth given above).

To summarize: when we talk about the 'financial implications' of a given course of action we mean the net wealth change to the decision-maker (whether it be an individual or a firm) brought about if that course of action is adopted. The concept of cost flows naturally from this idea.

The concept of cost

When we consider any given course of action we can usually identify the cause of the change in the decision-maker's cash balances which will result. Cash inflows will arise from revenues earned through the sale of goods and services, repayments of taxes, dividends and interest received, etc. Cash outflows arise through expenditure on the resources required to pursue the course of action decided upon.

However, when we look for a change in cash balance we must consider the difference between adopting the option in question and the next best alternative open to the decision-maker. We assume that a 'rational' decision-maker would adopt his or her most preferred alternative if the particular option being considered happened to be unavailable.

A cost is any decrease in wealth brought about by a decision to use up a particular resource or set of resources. In the short term this will be the same as the change in the decision-maker's net cash balances brought about by the decision to use up the resource concerned.

By asking the question: what would the total cash resources of the individual or firm have been had the particular course of action not been adopted?, we can easily identify the financial consequences of the given decision.

The concept of cost we have just outlined forces us to consider the cash consequences of a decision in the light of the next-best alternative. Our concept of cost is an operationalization, in cash terms, of the economist's definition of 'opportunity cost'. In economics cost is defined as the benefits forgone through not adopting the next-best alternative—although 'benefits' in this case can relate to any economic benefits, not just those which are measurable in cash terms.

Before we consider the application of this cost concept to an actual case we can draw out certain implications or guidelines for identifying cost items which will be relevant for a given decision.

Relevant costs for decisions

We can make the following general points concerning costs for decision-making purposes:

- Only cash costs are relevant. Any cost which does not bring about a cash change to the decision-maker, now or in the future, is irrelevant. Depreciation charges are a common example of this type of irrelevant cost. A charge for depreciation is an arbitrary allocation of part of the original cost of a particular fixed asset to a production period. The charge may be based on the part of the asset's anticipated life used up or on some other estimate of the asset's service potential which has been reduced by production. As depreciation charges do not represent actual cash changes they do not measure the wealth lost through using the asset. For this reason they are ignored in the analysis of the opportunity cost of a given decision.

- Cash costs to the business as a whole, which will be paid whatever the outcome of a particular decision, should be ignored when costing the alternatives available.

- Costs incurred or committed prior to the decision being made are irrelevant for decision-making purposes. Decisions are only concerned with future outcomes. Costs incurred or committed prior to a decision are irrecoverable—they are what are often called 'sunk costs'. Only future costs are relevant for decision-making purposes.

In any given decision situation it is important to distinguish those cost elements that are true opportunity costs (i.e. ones which represent actual consequential cash changes) from those which may appear as costs in accounting statements but are not directly attributable to the decision itself.

In order to clarify the issues and concepts introduced in the last two sections consider the following problem.

An example of the opportunity cost concept

Diego plc is considering the terms of a small construction project. The building could be completed in four weeks and the client is prepared to pay a cash price, upon completion, of £30 000.

The project will involve the use of the following:

Labour: 1500 unskilled labour hours will be required. Men and women capable of doing this work can be hired on subcontract at a rate of £8 per labour hour. In addition, three supervisors will be required: one supervisor is due to be served with an immediate redundancy notice which could be delayed until the end of the project; a second supervisor could be redeployed from other supervision duties which would have to be subcontracted at a cost of £450. The third supervisor would have been on 'standby' duties for the month, on full pay, as no other work is available. Each supervisor is paid £12 000 per annum (gross) inclusive of employer's pension contribution and National Health Insurance (NHI).

Materials: The following materials will be required:

- 200 tons of concrete mix which Diego currently holds in stock. The mix was purchased two months ago at a cost of £18 per ton, but the contract on which it was to be used has fallen through. Due to the short self life of the mix, Diego had planned to sell it to another company at £9 per ton net.

- 100 cubic yards of timber had been ordered, on contract, at a purchase price of £6 per cubic yard although it is only now due for delivery. This type of timber is used on a number of different jobs within the firm. Since ordering, the purchase has risen to £7.50 per cubic yard.

- Other materials will have to be purchased at a net cost of £3700. Stock is valued by the firm's accountants at the lower of its cost or net realizable value.

Plant and equipment: One excavator, which was due to be sold for £18 000 can be held for the life of the project. However, the renegotiated price for delivery one month late will be £17 000. The original purchase price of the excavator was £30 000. The other necessary equipment can be hired at a cost of £5500 for the duration of the project. Diego normally charges 10 per cent of original cost of equipment as a depreciation charge in its accounts.

Other information: To date, design costs of £4800 have been spent in preparing for the new project. Diego normally allocates part of its fixed overheads to projects. In this case, Diego's accountants have decided to allocate £6000 to this project. The managing director has estimated that he will incur an extra £800 of entertainment expenses if the project proceeds. If we assume that the facts as given above fully reflect the problem facing Diego's management we can proceed to identify the consequential change in cash which will occur if they decide to go ahead.

Cash outflows (cost items)

Unskilled labour will cost the firm £12 000, i.e. 1500 hours at £8 per hour. During the course of the project (or very shortly afterwards) Diego's bank account should show a payment of £12 000. This figure represents the direct wealth change attributable to the use of unskilled labour following acceptance of the project.

Unskilled labour (cash outflow)   £12 000

The first supervisor was due to be made redundant. Because his redundancy payments will be made at the end of the project rather than at the beginning, no additional cash change on that account will be incurred. This supervisor will simply cost Diego £1000, being one month's salary £12 000/12) which would not be paid if the project does not proceed. The second supervisor will be paid his salary irrespective of whether the project goes ahead or not. The only cash change which will result if this supervisor is employed upon the project is the subcontract charge of £450. The third supervisor would have been idle for the month in any event so no cash change follows his use on the project.

First supervisor (cash outflow)   £1000
Second supervisor (cash outflow on redeployment)   £450
Third supervisor   nil

The materials costs raise slightly more complicated issues: in the case of the concrete mix, the decision to proceed with the project entails the loss of the opportunity to sell. In other words, proceeding means that £1800 (£9 per ton × 200) will be forgone. The purchase price of £18 per ton is irrelevant as the company will not be replacing the concrete mix once it is used.

 With the timber, the decision to proceed with the project implies that it will have to be replaced as we are told that it has a variety of other uses within the firm. As a result of its use, the replacement will cost £750, i.e. there will be a cash flow out of the firm of £750 which will have arisen as a direct result of accepting the project. Note, however, that the original contract price of £6 per cubic yard is irrelevant as the contract has already been entered into and the commitment to pay the £6 per cubic yard already made. The figure of £6 per cubic yard will be paid irrespective of whether or not the contract proceeds. The remaining materials must be purchased at their full cost (which will represent an actual cash outflow) of £3700.

Cement mix (sale proceeds forgone)   £1800
Timber (replacement cost)   £750
Other materials (cash outflow)   £3700

The use of the excavator means that its sale must be delayed by one month, as a result of which the immediate sale price of £18 000 will be forgone and £17 000 received instead. The cash change resulting from the decision is, therefore, £1000. The remaining plant represents an actual cash flow of £5500. Note, however, that the depreciation charge (which is shown in Diego's accounts as a deduction from the original cost of the asset and as a charge against income in the profit and loss account) does not represent a cash flow during the period. Indeed, the amount which is written off each period may bear little relationship to either the physical deterioration or economic value of the asset. Depreciation charges are usually set using the accounting conventions adopted by the firm. In this case the monthly depreciation charge of:

$$10\% \times 30\,000 \times \tfrac{1}{12} = £250$$

is irrelevant for this decision.

Excavator (cash forgone through delay of sale)   £1000
Hire charges for other equipment   £5500

Note: In Fig. 3.1 we show the decision rules for determining the opportunity cost of materials or, indeed, any other resource, in the three situations most often encountered in practice.

Fig 3.1   Decision rule for determining opportunity cost

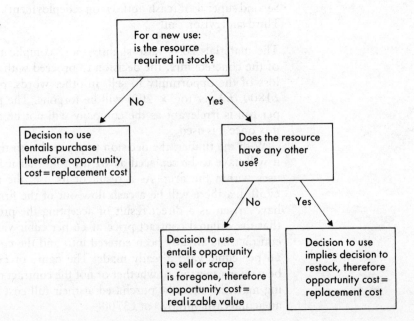

The design costs have already been incurred prior to the time at which the decision is being made. The design costs are, therefore, a 'sunk cost'. The sum of £4800 has already been paid out and is irrecoverable. Similarly, the allocation of £6000 for fixed overheads is an arbitrary allocation of expenses which will be incurred irrespective of whether or not the project proceeds. On the other hand, the sum of £800 for additional entertainment will only be incurred if the decision to proceed is made.

Entertainment expenses (cash outflow)   £800

We can now summarize the effect on Diego's cash flows if the option to proceed is adopted:

Statement of cash changes
(cash revenues less opportunity costs)

Cash inflow from revenues		£30 000
Cash outflows:		
Unskilled labour	£12 000	
First supervisor	1 000	
Second supervisor	450	
Third supervisor	—	
Materials:		
Cement mix	1 800	
Timber	750	
Other materials	3 700	
Plant and equipment:		
Excavator	1 000	
Other	5 500	
Entertainment expenses	800	
		27 000
Net cash receipts to Diego		£3 000

In an overall sense we can say that accepting the project leaves Diego £3000 better off. Turning the argument around the other way, failing to accept the project would have meant that the firm's cash balances would have been £3000 lower than they would have been if the project were accepted. Thus, the figure of £3000 is the opportunity cost of not accepting the project.

We have assumed in our analysis that proceeding with the project does not entail forgoing any other productive opportunity. In only one instance, in the case we have examined, is a redeployment cost incurred. With the second supervisor a redeployment cost is incurred (the cost of subcontracting his supervision duties). Although redeployment charges such as this are cash costs incurred as a direct result of the decision to proceed with the project, they arise indirectly through the redeployment of a resources internally. In Chapter 7 we consider in more detail the problems associated with these internal transfers of resources.

On the basis of our analysis a 'rational' manager would undertake the project concerned. By accepting the project, Diego is £3000 better off than it would have been, i.e. £3000 has been earned.

Self test: Below is a statement of profit and loss for Diego's project:

Revenue			£30 000
Direct costs:			
Labour costs:			
Unskilled	£12 000		
Supervisors	3 000		
		£15 000	
Materials costs:			
Concrete mix	2 800		
Timber	600		
Other	3 700		
		6 100	
Total direct costs			21 100
Gross profit			8 900
Less: Other charges			
Plant and equipment:			
Depreciation	250		
Hire charges	5 500		
		5 750	
Entertainment expenses		800	
Fixed costs		6 000	
Total indirect costs			12 550
Net loss on project			£(3 650)

Check the calculation of each figure using the information in the Diego plc example. Make sure that you understand the reasons why this statement differs from the calculation of the cash contribution from the project. Also, note the layout. We have followed the usual accounting practice of classifying together and insetting cost items.

Opportunity cost and 'true cost'

Because of the way we have defined the concept, opportunity cost gives the cash change of one decision alternative against the next best available. We refer to opportunity cost as an *ex-ante* cost measure, i.e. one which is measured prior to the event which is expected to give rise to the cost in question. Opportunity costs differ from accounting costs which are determined after rather than before an event has occurred. Accounting costs are, therefore, *ex-post* costs based upon realized economic events.

It is possible to use the opportunity-cost concept on past events in much the same way as we have used it on the anticipated future consequences of current decisions. Using the opportunity-cost measurement concept on past events we are measuring the cash change to the individual or firm which has come about because one actual course of action materialized rather than another. We will refer to the opportunity-cost concept when used in this way as the 'true economic cost' of a particular event.

For example, a fire broke out in the finishing department of Martin's pine furniture factory. As a result production of finished tables and cupboards was halted for four weeks while repairs were carried out. Martin was due to deliver 50 refectory-style tables to a public school at the end of the month. This delivery could not be made and so the school went to an alternative supplier. The profit per table, on the contract, was calculated as follows:

		£/unit
Sales revenue		£225
Costs:		
Materials	£85	
Labour	60	
Overheads	30	
	—	175
Profit per table		£50

The materials cost shown above was based upon the original cost of the pine and other materials required to make the tables.

There had been a 5 per cent rise in materials prices between the time of their purchase and the date of the fire. None of the materials was damaged in the fire and was used in subsequent production.

None of the company's workforce was laid off during the month of lost production. Some of the firm's labour was used in relaying a wooden floor in the firm's canteen. This saved the company employing an outside contractor who had quoted a cost of £2500. The materials required for laying the new floor cost £900.

The company received £12 500 from its insurers for the fire damage and paid £14 000 for the full restoration of the finishing room plus some additional improvements which would have cost £2000 if done separately.

The company managed to fulfil its other customers' requirements by overtime working in the subsequent month. Additional overtime payments of £300 were made in that month and additional overheads for heating and lighting the workshops during the overtime period were estimated to be £150. There was no apparent reduction in overheads during the month of lost production.

Even though this is an event which has already occurred it is still possible to use the opportunity-cost concept to determine the true economic cost of the fire to Martin. In order to do this we need to calculate the change in the firm's cash balances which arose because the fire occurred.

If the fire had not occurred the company would have fulfilled its contract and earned sales revenue of (50 × £225) £11 250. Therefore the sales revenue lost was £(11 250.00)

Because the contract was not carried out, materials worth £4462.50 (50 × £85 × 1.05) were not used up. As these materials were not used on the contract the firm avoided having to replace them, therefore their replacement value at the time of the fire (original cost plus 5 per cent) represents the cost saved 4 462.50

There was no cash saving on labour costs because the labour force was retained during the period in question. However, labour was used to carry out work on the canteen floor. As a result the company saved a quoted cost of £2500 but had to pay for the necessary materials. The cash saving to the company was, therefore, £2500 less £900 1 600.00

The insurers paid £12 500 to Martin which was a cash gain. This was used to cover the cost of restoration (£14 000) of which £2000 was improvement work. The net cost of restoration due to the fire only was £12 000. As a result the fire itself brought a net cash benefit to Martin of £12 500 less £12 000, i.e. 500.00

Finally, extra overtime costs were incurred as a direct result of the production required to catch up after the fire. The amount involved was £300 plus £150 which were both cash losses incurred directly by the firm (450.00)

There were no other cash changes which can be directly attributed to the fire. Therefore the true economic cost of the fire was £(5 137.50)

This means that, following the fire, Martin's total cash balances and hence the firm's wealth were reduced by £5137.50. As you can see, the principle of calculation is exactly the same as that followed in the previous example except that we are now working with the realized consequences of some previous event rather than with the future expected outcomes from present decisions.

Objections to the opportunity-cost approach

To conclude this chapter, we identify some of the difficulties and objections to the rational decision-making approach outlined in this chapter. In particular we will examine some of the arguments levied against the concept of opportunity cost.

1   We assume that managers can correctly identify the next-best course of action in any given situation. But, as we indicated earlier when we talked about the problems of rationality, we must also account for the different modes of rationality which will be present in any given individual. At the more pragmatic level, the hidden search costs may appear

too high to the decision-maker to justify seeking out and evaluating all courses of action. For example, the sale price of concrete mix in Diego's production problem could well be improved beyond the £9.00 per ton specified especially if vigorous marketing of the product were to be undertaken. Any increase in the realizable value of concrete mix would bring about an increased cash loss associated with proceeding with the project.

2   Decisions can rarely be isolated from their economic and social context. For any project, the process of negotiation and the setting up of exploratory studies (which are reflected in the sunk costs) may well commit the firm to a particular course of action, abandonment of which may well not be reflected fully in the analysis of cash change.

3   In the case of an individual the decision-maker is clearly defined. However, the determination of opportunity cost is not so straightforward when a firm or some other entity is the decision-maker concerned. Indeed, in some situations it may be very difficult to identify who the decision-making entity is and for whom the cash change should be measured. For example a division within a highly diversified firm may wish to regard cash transfers between itself and other parts of the firm as either revenues or opportunity costs, whereas, for the firm as a whole, these transactions may be regarded as pure, internal cash transfers with a zero net cash effect overall. Similarly, if we examine the effect of cash changes at the firm level individuals who hold shares in different companies will see cash movements as purely internal transfers of wealth whereas the firms themselves will see them as genuine opportunity costs. Nationalized firms face exactly the same problem: is the individual firm the decision-making unit or should the State be the entity for which opportunity costs are measured?

4   Opportunity costs are 'forward looking', or *ex-ante* estimates of future, decision-related cash movements. However, estimates of future cash movements must be made largely on the basis of past experience of costs and revenues associated with similar projects. As we shall see in Chapter 5 the translation of 'historic' data into future estimates can be a tricky business.

5   Traditional accountants are often suspicious of costs which have not been actually incurred and authenticated by an invoice or some other contractual obligation and a cash payment. An opportunity cost is always measured with respect to a sale or purchase price on a hypothetical transaction which the firm may never carry out. This objection reduces to the old argument as to whether it is better to be accurately wrong or approximately right.

6   Finally, many decisions are made under considerable pressure. Indeed, social psychologists tell us that the calm, evaluative behaviour implied by the decision-orientated approach may well be the exception rather than the rule in actual human problem-solving and decision-making. We have already suggested that under stress decision-makers may well switch from one model of rationality to another. In many situations decisions are not made through rational choices but as a result of the roles which the individual decision-maker wishes to play out.

The point which we want you to draw from this section is that while opportunity-costing techniques are vital for analysing the financial effects of particular decisions they are not without criticism.

Supplementary reading

AMEY, L. R., On opportunity costs and decision making, *Accountancy*, July 1968. An easy and interesting discussion of the topic

ARNOLD, J., Budgets for decisions, in Arnold J, Carsberg, B., and Scapens, R. (eds), *Topics in Management Accounting*, Philip Allan, 1980

ARNOLD, J. and SCAPENS, R., The British contribution to opportunity-cost theory, in Bromwich, M., and Hopwood, A. G. (eds), *Essays in British Accounting Research*, Pitman, 1981

LUTZ, M. A. and LUX, K., *The Challenge of Humanistic Economics*, Benjamin/Cummings, 1979. Chapters 1–4 offer a thought-provoking critique of the basic tenets of economic rationality and the concept of opportunity cost

Questions

1 Define the concepts of wealth and cost and discuss their relevance for management accounting.

2 To what extent do you think that the economist's concept of opportunity cost represents an absolute definition of the concept of cost.

3 The following materials are necessary for the production of a new chemical:

1 Boro-grot: held in stock but otherwise obsolete for other production.

2 Boro-primo: on order from a supplier. The contract for delivery has been made at the price stated as the 'historic cost' below although the materials have not, as yet, been paid for. The original order was made in the belief that the company would be making another chemical altogether. However, for technical reasons the use of Boro-primo on that process was not feasible and the company had planned to sell its stock of Boro-primo as soon as it was received from the supplier.

3 Boro-secundo: none in stock but currently available from suppliers.

The costs per kilogram of each of these raw materials are as follows:

	Historic cost (£)	Replacement cost (£)	Realizable value (£)
Boro-grot	15	12	5
Boro-primo	32	35	26
Boro-secundo	—	17	13

Required:
(a) State the relevant cost of each of the three raw materials in the production decision.
(b) Define opportunity cost and classify (giving reasons) the main types of cost which are irrelevant for decision-making purposes.

4 Seville Ltd manufactures scientific instruments. It is considering whether to manufacture a batch of oscilloscopes. The contract would last 12 weeks. The following statement has been prepared on the basis that the contract should not be accepted:

Materials:		
A—already in stock (original cost)	£750	
B—ordered (original contract price)	900	
	——	£1 650
Labour		3 500
Machinery:		
Leased at £50 per week	2 600	
Depreciation	2 000	
	——	4 600
General overheads		3 500
		———
		13 250
Contract price offered		10 000
		———
		£(3 250)
		═══

The following additional information is also available:

1 Materials: material A was purchased two years previously at a cost of £750. If sold now it would realize £500. Alternatively, it could be adapted and used on another job as a substitute for material currently costing £800. It would cost £150 to make the necessary adaptation.

Material B was ordered 6 months ago when the price was £900. Since that time the original use for the material had disappeared but Seville had planned to use the materials on the production of some laser-beam scanners. It would cost £100 to modify the materials for that use. The current buying price for material B is £1000 and its selling price with modification would be £1200 and without modification £850. The supplier of material B has offered a 5 per cent discount because of the delayed delivery although, under the terms of the original purchase agreement, delay would not be an excuse for Seville to rescind the contract.

2 The labour charge of £3500 includes £1000 in respect of a foreman's wages. Unlike the rest of the labour to be used on the contract the foreman will be employed whether or not the contract is accepted. However, if he does work on the contract the company will have to pay an extra £15 per week to take over his duties on other production. The remainder of the workforce earn half of their income by piecework payments, the other half is a basic payment.

3 Two machines will have to be used on the contract. The first machine is already leased at £50 per week. This machine is currently being used in another department and if it is used on the contract a replacement machine will have to be leased at a revised rate of £60 per week. The second machine is due to be sold. If it is kept in use for the life of the contract its sale value will fall by £1200.

4 General overheads cover such items as rent and rates and other administrative overheads. These overheads are charged to contracts on the basis of £1 for every pound of direct labour cost. All of the general overheads will be paid even if the contract is forgone.

5 Some preliminary design costs have already been incurred which amount to £2400.

Required:
(a) Fill in the following revised statement to obtain the surplus or loss on the contract:

	£	£
Materials:		
A		
B		
	_____	
Total materials		
Labour:		
Foreman		
Other		
	_____	
Total labour		
Machinery:		
Leased		
Owned		
	_____	
General overheads		
Design costs		
	_____	
Total opportunity cost		
Contract price offered		£10 000
		_____
Surplus/loss on the contract		
		=====

(b) Write a note explaining fully the reasons why you have entered the numbers you have done in the above statement.

5 Phrygian and Co. produces metal containers. They have been approached by an instrument manufacturer who requires 10 000 boxes of set dimensions with fancy clasps and letterings. Phrygian realize that in order to win the contract they must price very competitively. There are a number of other potential suppliers in the market.

Phrygian's management accountant has identified the following facts:

0.001 gauge mild steel (this gauge is no longer used on any other of the firm's production processes):

Requirement	8000 square feet
Stock held	5000 square feet
Original cost	£0.25/square foot
Replacement cost	£0.75/square foot
Sale price	£0.45 square foot

Labour requirements:

Machinists and cutters—1000 labour hours. The firm has sufficient labour to meet the production requirements of this contract as well as its existing work although 500 hours overtime would have to be worked. The current wage rate is £4 per hour with overtime paid at time and a half. New staff could be employed for this contract and this would ensure that the work was completed in normal time although 1100 labour hours would then be required as 100 hours would have to be devoted to training.

Finishers—1500 labour hours. Finishers belong to a highly skilled trade. They are paid £8 per hour (normal time) with double time paid for any overtime worked. Their current deployment means that half of the hours required on the new job would have to be worked as overtime. In addition a number of other jobs would have to be left undone. This will result in a loss of cash to the firm of £1800 in total excluding the additional overtime which will have to be paid to this class of labour.

Incidental expenses:

Clasps, letter punches and special tools	£600
Design costs (already incurred)	£550
Supervision of machinists during overtime	£1000
Variable overheads (with production)	£650
Fixed overheads charged per labour hour worked	£1.50

Cutting and welding equipment will also be used on this job. Its use on this job is unlikely to affect its useful life.

Required:
(a) Evaluate the minimum price Phrygian would require to cover the cost of production.
(b) Discuss the criticisms which can be levied at the use of opportunity cost in managerial decision-making

6   Following a strike of production workers at their Knaughtitory factory, Scottish Weyland lost 1000 units of production of their new car, the Ratcher. The Ratcher is a downmarket version of the Weyland Sovereign. Each car would have been sold at a final retail

price of £5700. The *Daily Gotcha* announced that the strike had cost the company £6.0 million. You discover the following:

1 Each Ratcher nets from retailers £4600 on average.
2 The net factory cost of each car is made up as follows:

Materials and components purchased	£1600
Labour costs averaging 130 man hours per car	£1200
Paint division costs	£200
Energy costs	£155
General fixed overheads	£1105

3 The annual production of Ratchers is budgeted at 80 000 units.
4 Two-thirds of the workforce devoted to Ratcher production was laid off during the strike.
5 After the strike which resulted in an 8 per cent increase for all non-supervisory employees engaged in car production, 400 cars were produced by extra time working. Overtime was paid at time and a quarter. Additional management time was paid at a total cost of £15 000.
6 A 10 per cent rise in the retail price of all Weyland cars was made following the strike.

Required:
(a) Estimate the cost of the strike to the company. Comment upon any figures which you produce.
(b) Outline the problems which you might expect in estimating the entry and exit values of components in a company such as Scottish Weyland.

Mathematical note

It is fairly straightforward to derive a simple formula for the present value of a series of receipts of £1 receivable over a number of years.

Case 1 (where the number of years (n) is infinitely long, i.e. $n = \infty$)

If £1 is receivable each year (or other period of time) into the indefinite future and i is the discount rate then the present value of the infinite series of pounds (the 'perpetuity') is given by the formula:

$$A_{\overline{i}|\infty} = \frac{1}{1+i} + \frac{1}{(1+i)^2} + \frac{1}{(1+i)^3} + \ldots \infty \tag{3.1}$$

Multiply the entire equation on both the left- and the right-hand side of the equation by $1 + i$:

$$A_{\overline{i}|\infty} = \frac{1+i}{1+i} + \frac{1+i}{(1+i)^2} + \frac{1+i}{(1+i)^3} + \ldots \infty$$

$$= 1 + \frac{1}{1+i} + \frac{1}{(1+i)^2} + \ldots \infty \tag{3.2}$$

Take Eq. (3.2) from Eq. (3.1):

$$A_{\overline{\infty}|i} - A_{\overline{\infty}|i} \times (1+i) = \frac{1}{1+i} + \frac{1}{(1+i)^2} + \frac{1}{(1+i)^3} + \ldots \infty$$

$$- 1 + \frac{1}{1+i} + \frac{1}{(1+i)^2} + \ldots \infty$$

$$= -1$$

Notice that apart from the 1 in the second equation and a final, implied term at infinity, in Eq. (3.1), each term in Eq. (3.1) has a corresponding term in Eq. (3.2). Both equations represent infinite, ie. never-ending, progressions. Furthermore, as the value of $(1+i)^n$ increases with each successive term, the value of its inverse approaches zero. Thus, the apparent loss of the final, infinitely small term in the progression has no effect on its solution.

By rearrangement and reversing signs:

$$A_{\overline{\infty}|i} = \frac{1}{i}$$

Therefore, to obtain the present value of a perpetuity, multiply the constant cash sum receivable by the inverse of the interest rate. For example, the present value of £1000 receivable each year into the indefinite future with an assumed rate of interest of 10 per cent is given by:

$$\text{present value} = £1000 \times A_{\overline{\infty}|i} = £1000 \times \frac{1}{0.1}$$

$$= £10\,000$$

Case 2 (where n is of a finite number of years)

$$A_{\overline{n}|i} = \frac{1}{1+i} + \frac{1}{(1+i)^2} + \frac{1}{(1+i)^3} + \ldots + \frac{1}{(1+i)^n} \tag{3.3}$$

multiply throughout by $1+i$ as we did in case 1:

$$A_{\overline{n}|i} \times (1+i) = \frac{1+i}{1+i} + \frac{1+i}{(1+i)^2} + \frac{1+i}{(1+i)^3} + \ldots + \frac{1+i}{(1+i)^n}$$

$$= 1 + \frac{1}{1+i} + \frac{1}{(1+i)^2} + \ldots + \frac{1}{(1+i)^{n-1}} \tag{3.4}$$

Taking (3.4) from Eq. (3.3) as before:

$$A_{\overline{n}|i} - A_{\overline{n}|i}(1+i) = -1 + \frac{1}{(1+i)^n}$$

By rearrangement and reversing signs:

$$A_{\overline{n}|i} = \frac{1 - 1/(1+i)^n}{i}$$

For example, the present value of £1 receivable over five years at 10 per cent per annum is:

$$A_{0.1\rceil 5} = \frac{1 - 1/1.1^5}{0.1}$$

$$= £3.791$$

If cash has been invested over a number of years then we may wish to know the accumulated value of the investment. This terminal value of £1 invested in each of n years at i per cent is given by the formula:

$$S_{\rceil n} = 1 \times (1 + i)^n + 1 \times (1 + i)^{(n-1)} + 1 \times (1 + i)^{(n-2)} + \ldots + 1 \times (1 + i)$$

$$= \frac{(1 + i)^{(n+1)} - (1 + i)}{i}$$

For example, at the beginning of each of the last 5 years £1000 has been placed on deposit at 10 per cent:

$$\text{terminal value} = 1000 \times S_{0.1\rceil 5}$$

$$= 1000 \times \frac{(1.1)^6 - 1.1}{0.1}$$

$$= 1000 \times 6.716$$

$$= £6716$$

Equations such as these can be calculated under all sorts of assumptions concerning the timing of the cash flows.

Self test: **Derive the formula for the terminal value of £1 invested annually at the end of each year assuming a rate of *i* per cent per annum over *n* years.**

Part 2 Accounting for short-term decisions ─────────

4 An introduction to short-term decision-making ——

In this chapter we will distinguish between short- and long-term decision-making and outline the characteristic features of those decisions which we normally regard as 'short term'. We will then discuss some of the practical problems of short-term decision-making before rounding off our discussion with some preliminary observations on budgeting which we will develop in later chapters.

> By the end of this chapter you should be aware of:
>
> - The differences between long- and short-term decisions.
>
> - The different classes of short-term decision.
>
> - The importance of short-term decisions to managers.
>
> - The role of budgeting within the firm especially as a tool for short-term decision-making.

Long- and short-term decision-making

Our discussion, in Chapter 1, of the decision-making approach adopted in this book led us to make a distinction between the long and the short term. However, this distinction is rarely absolute and will depend upon the attributes of the decision in question.

In the long run the firm will make certain commitments in markets for its product, in research and in production. These commitments entail the expenditure of capital funds and the acceptance of costs (which will be unavoidable in the short term) which are required to maintain the firm's ability to operate. In the very long run all costs are avoidable (i.e. none are fixed); production can be discontinued, employees laid off, buildings and factories closed and so forth.

In the very short run few costs are truly avoidable except, perhaps, the cost of raw materials and labour if it is paid on a piece-rate basis. So, in the short run managers only have discretion over the level of activity within the range specified by the resources available; the long-run decision to produce has already been made.

Note: We use the word 'activity' in a very general way. When we talk about a plant's activity level, for example, we mean the amount of product being made in a particular process. When we talk about 'marketing activity' we mean the level of effort being made to sell the firm's products, i.e. the numbers of salesmen's visits made and so on.

The classification of decisions into short and long run is somewhat arbitrary. Short-run decisions always presume some prior, long-run decision and a whole set of fixed costs, although these fixed costs will have been opportunity (avoidable) costs of the long-run decision concerned. Long-run decision-making must also assume a feasible set of consequent short-run decisions. We give some examples in Fig. 4.1.

Fig 4.1 Long-run versus short-run decisions

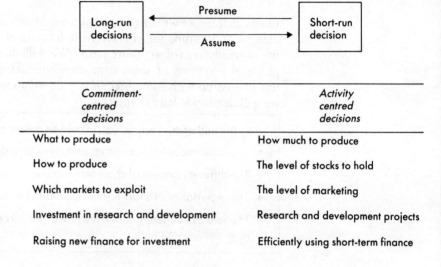

Commitment-centred decisions	Activity centred decisions
What to produce	How much to produce
How to produce	The level of stocks to hold
Which markets to exploit	The level of marketing
Investment in research and development	Research and development projects
Raising new finance for investment	Efficiently using short-term finance

Once a long-run decision is made, a constraint is placed upon the range and type of short-run activity in which a firm can engage. For example, if an airline invests exclusively in short-haul jets it effectively precludes itself, in the short term, from entering the long-distance travel markets even assuming it could get the necessary licences. Likewise, a company which opts for oil-fired heating will not be able to change to coal-fired heating in the short term. Long- and short-run decisions are, therefore, highly interrelated.

The following are some of the characteristics indicative of short-run decisions:

• The consequences of a short-run decision should be realized in a very short period of time which will, in the majority of cases, be no longer than the firm's normal trading cycle. Many companies find that their normal trading pattern follows an annual cycle because of seasonal influences upon the demand for their products.

• A short-run decision will normally include some activity variable such as: the amount of stock held, the number of miles covered by a lorry, the output level of a plant, the level of advertising.

• In some cases a short-run decision may involve a straightforward 'yes–no' choice. An example would be a short-term production contract where a particular level of output is specified by the terms of the contract between the buyer and seller. The decision would be whether to accept or reject such a contract.

- All short-run decisions presume that some prior, long-run decision has already been made. As a result of that long-run decision, the firm will have already incurred expenditures and will be committed to the payment of certain fixed costs which are independent of the activity variable under consideration.

From a technical point of view, the obvious distinction between long- and short-run decisions is that the former involve changes in all three components of the wealth measure, as defined in the last chapter, while with short-term decisions only changes in the net cash balances of the decision-making entity need be considered. In other words, the effects of short-term decisions can be measured in terms of net cash changes and the timing problem can be ignored while with long-term decisions the effect of time on future cash flows is crucial and the decision-maker must make explicit recognition of the fact.

Note: Economists define the short run as a period of time so brief that none of the firm's fixed commitments come to an end and the long run as that where all of the firm's fixed commitments can come to an end.

Classes of short-run decision

The short-run decisions faced by most industrial or commercial enterprises can be classified into five broad types:

- Output decisions.
- Pricing decisions.
- Resources allocation (or production) decisions.
- Control decisions
- Distribution decisions.

We will now make some introductory remarks concerning each of these five classes of decision. Each of these classes of decision-making will be discussed in much more detail over the next six chapters of this book.

The output decision

All organizations which produce goods or services for sale must select an appropriate level at which to produce. However, the decision concerning output level is tightly linked to the pricing decision. At any point in time, the quantity of a particular product which can be sold at a given price will be determined by the market's demand for that product at that price.

The only situations where this linkage between price and demand is of less importance is in the rather artificial situations of either perfect competition or pure monopoly. In the case of perfect competition, the managers of the producing firm have no discretion over the price charged. Perfect competition implies that all producers in the market are price takers, that is they must take the price as given and select the output quantity which maximizes their profit. The optimal output quantity will be determined, therefore, by the firm's cost structure. In the case of a monopoly producer, management has the opportunity to earn abnormal profits and has a much higher discretion over the price and output for the product concerned.

Note: (i) Strictly, when we discuss market behaviour of firms we should talk about 'economic profit' which is total revenue less the full opportunity cost of production where opportunity cost in this case includes the cost of the managerial and capital resources employed. In a perfect market no firm will earn positive economic profits because, as we shall see later, the mere existence of surplus profits will induce additional competitors to enter the market.

(ii) In reality, markets are not perfect and firms employ many tactics to break the linkage between output and price. The commonest way of doing this is by the creation of stocks. If a firm attempts to sell all it produces immediately it must take the market price dictated by its demand curve for that output level. However, with many products, the creation of stocks allows the firm to release its production onto the market when demand conditions are most favourable.

The short-run output decision will be constrained by a prior, long-run decision to invest in the capacity to produce. Obviously, a chemical company deciding upon the appropriate output level for a given plant must have made some prior, long-run decision to invest in building the factory, the plant and all of the support systems which it needs to operate. In addition it must also have decided to hire the necessary labour and managerial skills to build the plant in the first instance and subsequently to operate it. In Chapter 7 we consider the problem where these long-run decisions impose an effective constraint upon the levels of activity at which the firm can produce.

The pricing decision

As indicated above, pricing and output decisions are linked through a market relationship. In the majority of markets, firms face situations where decreases in price increase the demand for their product and vice versa. This idea can be represented by a downward sloping curve of price against quantity. Such a 'demand curve' expresses the well-known fact that the lower the price at which a commodity is offered to the market the greater will be the demand for that product. In Fig. 4.2 we show the demand curve faced by (for example) a producer of video recorders.

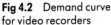

Fig 4.2 Demand curve for video recorders

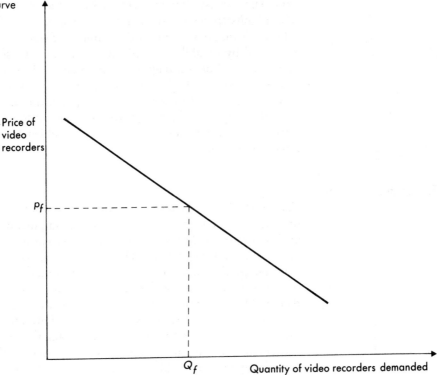

The important point to be made at this stage is that the video manufacturer cannot expect to expand output indefinitely and still command the same price per unit sold. Likewise, if the firm operates at a given output level (say Q_f in Fig. 4.2) it cannot impose an arbitrary price for its product upon the market place. The ruling market conditions specify a price p_f and the firm is stuck with that price unless it can alter the shape of the product's demand curve through its advertising or other marketing activities.

In Chapter 6 we consider, in more detail, the implications of different market conditions for corporate pricing policy. We will also examine the nature and limitations of cost-based pricing rules and some of the reasons why they are used in practice.

The resources allocation (or production) decision

In Chapter 2 we characterized the firm as an 'input–output' system where labour, 'hard factors', managerial and capital resources are transformed into cash, products and/or services. For many reasons, however, the firm may not have free access to all the input factors which it needs to use in production. Therefore, choices must be made by management in the allocation of those resources, which are available, between their competing uses. In addition, prior long-run decisions may have set operational capacity constraints which limit the firm's freedom of action in the short term. These constraints may set physical (e.g. plant capacity) limits or labour limits upon the firm's ability to produce.

In such situations the firm's opportunities to adopt new processes may be limited by its ability to redeploy, internally, those resources which cannot be freely obtained upon the open market. This means that a hidden cost will be incurred when the uses to which the scarce resources were previously put are depleted by their redeployment. In Chapter 7 we consider the ways in which resources can be most effectively allocated between their competing uses and how the hidden costs of redeployment can be measured.

The control decision

The marshalling of the resources required for production: cash, stocks of materials, plant, other equipment and labour, involves a careful analysis of need and the maintenance of sufficient stocks of consumables to smooth out delivery delays. However, holding large stocks of raw materials or, indeed, cash balances, while smoothing the production process will incur interest charges on the capital resources invested therein. One aspect of the short-term control decision is concerned with maintaining adequate supplies of the means of production so that productive capacity is not left idle. But, in total, the control decision also entails choosing stocking policies which minimize the cost of the capital employed in holding stock and the cost of reordering when stocks become depleted.

Another aspect of short-term control is concerned with maintaining adequate supplies of finished products to satisfy the needs of the firm's customers while keeping the cost of holding such stocks at a minimum. We will discuss, in Chapter 8, the problems of choosing appropriate credit polices so as to minimize the delay in receiving payment from customers while achieving the most favourable terms of trade with the firm's suppliers. In Chapter 9 we consider the problems of collecting costs for the various short-term decisions discussed in Chapters 5–8 inclusive.

The distribution decision

In the introduction to this book we depicted the firm as a set of different groups whose interests are reconciled over time by management. All of these different interest groups have claims upon the cash surpluses generated by the firm's activities. Investors require a reward for risking their financial capital, employees require a reward for risking their 'human capital' and, likewise, management will, at its various levels, seek rewards in the form of increased salaries and bonus payments.

An important concern of management is to decide how the firm's surplus should be allocated between the various interest groups. It follows that, in order to make these decisions, management must be aware of the firm's ability to pay in any given situation. For example, wage-rate negotiations can involve the firm in lengthy and costly industrial disputes. The reconciliation of such disputes can often be achieved more quickly if agreement is reached on the ability of the firm to pay in the short term. We examine these and related issues in Chapter 10.

Importance of short-term decisions

Because the rewards earned by various levels of management are often related to short-term performance there will be an inbuilt, systematic tendency for managers to attend to the short run rather than the long run in their decision-making. In addition, within the various functional areas of the firm, individual managers are likely to be rewarded according to their performance within that area. A sales manager, who is rewarded according to the number of new sales made, will attempt to maximize the variables which influence the level of new sales. For example, a sales manager would argue for wide stock ranges and high finished stock levels. A production manager, on the other hand, might wish to operate his plant on long production runs so as to maximize its efficiency and hence his or her productivity. A production manager would rather work toward the production of large quantities rather than the wide range of items required by the sales manager.

Given that managers will, if the reward structure is so designed, look for short-run rather than long-run payoffs from the decisions with which they are concerned, we would expect bias toward those decisions which maximized their short-run decision-making discretion. As we shall see later, this bias often shows up in the ways in which companies formulate their budgets. This leads us naturally into the final area to be discussed in this chapter—the role of budgeting within organizations. Budgeting is an activity which has a profound influence on management's decision-making behaviour. For this reason, a number of issues in budgeting are left until the areas of decision-making to which they relate are discussed in the text.

The role of budgeting

Budgeting is an activity we all engage in some time or other—often because we have discovered that our cash outgoings have exceeded our cash income for some reason. Cash, having many of the attributes of water, flows away with amazing rapidity and, as one sage put it, life is a cash-flow problem.

Companies find themselves in exactly the same situation as the individual who is trying to manage his or her own personal affairs, except that the sums of money involved are usually much larger. We can identify six important purposes for budgeting in firms:

- As a method of planning the use of the firm's resources in the light of potential market opportunities.

- As a regular and systematic vehicle for the firm's forecasting activities (although these forecasts, allied with the planning aspect of budgeting, are likely to be self-fulfilling).

- As a means of controlling the activities of various groups within the firm.

- As a means of motivating individuals within the firm to achieve the performance levels agreed and set for them.

- As a means of communicating the wishes and aspirations of senior management to other interest groups within the firm.

- As a means of resolving conflicts of interest between the various groups within the firm.

As we pointed out in Chapter 2, any increase in the technological and economic uncertainty facing the firm will lead to an increase in the specialization of its various functional activities. We called this process 'differentiation'. However, increased differentiation leads to an opposing force or need within the firm to integrate the disparate interests of these different functional areas. This process of 'integration' is a primary task of management and is strongly supported by the budgeting procedures of the firm.

Firms differ in the requisite degree of differentiation required to cope with the uncertainties of their particular economic and technical environment. Likewise, the effort necessary to achieve integration of each firm's activities will differ according to the degree of differentiation which has been achieved. Therefore, the role of budgeting within different firms will differ, depending upon the organizational needs of each. Each company will have different practices and procedures depending upon its own organizational characteristics. Therefore, very few general rules can be laid down concerning the practice of budgeting. Budgeting is not a simple technical skill which can be divorced from the context in which it is carried out.

In this section we will briefly discuss the six reasons for budgeting outlined above.

Self test: Construct a personal (or family) budget for yourself over the next month. Plan on the basis of cash inflows (wages or salary, grants, etc.) and cash outflows under different expenditure headings (food, clothing, drink, entertainment, etc.). Regard any permanent savings as an 'expenditure' to a deposit or other long-term savings account. Keep a record of all the cash receipts and expenditure you make during the month and then, at the end of the month, answer the following questions:

> (i) **What aim did you set yourself when drawing up your budget (making a cash surplus, breaking even, reducing your overdraft, etc.)?**
> (ii) **What information did you use to make your plans?**
> (iii) **How carefully did you have to time your cash payments in order to avoid running into deficit?**
> (iv) **Can you allocate causes to the differences between your planned and actual figures?**
> (v) **Can you reconcile the figure on your bank statement and credit-card bills with your summary of actual receipts and payments?**
> (vi) **How did you motivate yourself to keep within your budget?**

Budgeting and planning

At each of the different levels within the firm, management faces the need to plan the resources under its control. Senior management, with its primary concern with strategic decision-making will wish to ensure that the firm achieves its long-term targets. This will entail:

- Planning the long-term aggregate cash resources of the firm.

- Planning the deployment of physical resources to meet new market opportunities.

- Planning to increase the welfare of the various groups who have an interest within the firm.

Of course, senior managers will also attempt to maximize their own interests as far as they can. In Chapter 1 we suggested that all of these different objectives can be distilled into the simple principle that managers, and senior managers especially, will work so as to maximize their decision-making discretion.

The planning acivity at the lower levels of management will be determined by the degree of discretion which particular managers have over the types of decision they can make. However, the success of the budgeting exercise is largely dependent upon the degree of involvement of all levels of management in the planning process. A desirable feature of any budgeting system is the degree of consensus which it promotes throughout all levels of the firm. Unless levels of management are involved in the planning process the formal budgets will be seen, by those who are not involved in their preparation, as a simple extension of senior management's authority. In the long run, imposed budgets are less effective than budgets agreed through negotiation and consensus.

Budgeting and forecasting

The planning aspect of the budgeting process is concerned with extending the control of management over as many variables in its decision-making process as possible. However, a number of decision variables will be outside the control of management at the point in time when the budgets are drawn up. We give two possible reasons why this may be so:

- The variables may be exogenous to the firm (i.e. determined by some group or agency outside the firm's control). Examples of such variables are: government interest rate policy, the future demand for the company's product (although this can be controlled to a limited extent through the firm's marketing activity), the level of inflation, nationally agreed wage claims which affect the company's labour force, exchange rate movements, the impact of new technology and so on.

- The variables concerned are not expected to arise for a considerable period of time (the eventual sales level of a novel product still in the early stages of development).

In the first case, management will have to make forecasts or rely upon the forecasts of others when drawing up its budgets. The Treasury, for example, makes periodic forecasts of inflation and interest rates which are included in the national budgeting process. Similarly, many of the large stockbroking firms also prepare and publish forecasts of the macro-economic variables which may be useful to an individual firm.

For very long-range forecasting, management may have to resort to technological forecasting methods which can only give the order of magnitude for the second type of variable mentioned above. At the end of this chapter you will find a reference to technological forecasting which discusses those instances where such methods can be useful.

Where management has some control over the variables in question the process of forecasting merges into that of planning. In other words, the forecasts which management make become self-fulfilling and this is most pronounced where there is only a short time difference between the budgeting process and the incidence of the variables in question.

Budgeting as a method of organization control

Firm budgets are a very important instrument of managerial control. Once plans have been agreed and implemented, the need will arise to compare them with actual results as they occur. Differences (or variances) between actual and budgeted figures will guide management in:

- Identifying areas where performance has been better or worse than anticipated and deciding what (if any) corrective action is appropriate.

- Rewarding those individuals who have performed better than expected and punishing those who have failed to come up to expectations.

- Deciding the necessary revisions to future plans and targets in the light of current actual results.

An important technique of short-term control is called 'management by exception'. This technique entails identifying differences between actual and budgeted figures (variance analysis) and where these differences exceed certain preset bounds management will attempt to assign causes and take corrective action if appropriate. A crucial feature of any control system is the speed and reliability with which actual results can be collected, evaluated and corrective action applied. We will discuss more general problems of control in Chapter 8.

Note: A 'reward' can be either:

- A financial reward for performance to a particular preset standard.

- A non-financial reward such as advancement, the granting of external symbols of status (such as a new office carpet or better company car), etc.

Within a budgeting system, rewards and punishments must be closely allied to an understanding of those things which will motivate given individuals or groups to better performance.

Budgets and motivation

The idea of controlling performance through a firm's reward system is closely related to an understanding of how financial and non-financial rewards and punishments can motivate individuals. Indeed, one of the most important spin-offs from the budgeting procedure is its use for relating performance to motivation. A number of theories have been put forward to explain what motivates individuals to perform tasks to a specific standard.

Most of these theories revolve around the idea that men and women act so as to fulfil their 'needs'. One of the earliest theorists in the area of motivation through the satisfaction of personal needs was A. H. Maslow. Maslow argued that:

- Needs are the basis of the human drive to act.

- Human needs can be arranged in a hierarchy of relative prepotency (Fig. 4.3). At the bottom of this hierarchy are the most basic needs for warmth, food and security. At higher levels we have the need to be loved (this even applies to accountants) rising at the highest level to the need for 'self-actualization' (the need to realize one's fullest potential). The lowest needs in this hierarchy will be satisfied first and if one of these lower needs is thwarted the individual concerned will switch attention to the satisfaction of that need at the expense of those above it.

- Once a need has been satisfied, the individual will then shift attention toward satisfying needs at the next level in the hierarchy.

- Those individuals in whom a need has always been satisfied are best able to tolerate deprivation in the future.

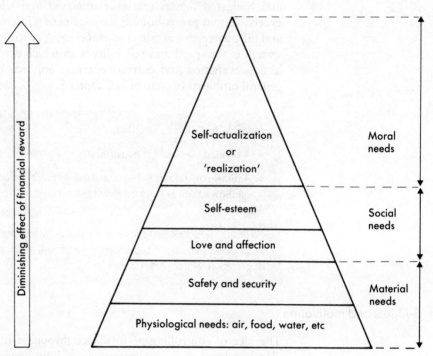

Fig 4.3 Maslow's hierarchy of needs

Maslow's model has been criticized and developed since it was first formulated in 1943. However, what is interesting about the model, from the budgeting point of view, is that it suggests that financial rewards are unlikely to be successful motivators beyond a certain point. Money is most effective at satisfying lower needs. Higher needs, such as those concerned with self-esteem and self-actualization, are often more effectively rewarded through rewards which enhance job satisfaction. There is much more to be learnt about the role of motivation and the effectiveness of rewards and punishments in achieving budget targets. What is certain is that a budgeting system cannot operate in isolation from its human context. It is the behavioural rather than the technical aspects of a budget which will govern its success as an integrative mechanism within the firm.

Budgets and senior management

As the dominant power group within the organization, senior management will see the budgeting process as one mechanism for establishing and maintaining its authority throughout the firm. Because senior managers, of all the groups within the firm, have the most discretion over the distribution of the firm's surplus they will form the dominant group in any negotiation procedure. In highly bureaucratic organizations with formal 'line' management systems the budgeting system will reflect the hierarchy of management within the firm. For example, compare the diagram of a typical budgeting system (Fig. 4.4) with the management line diagram in Chapter 2 (Fig. 2.3). The responsibility for different levels of budgeting can be clearly related to the different levels of managerial responsibility in the line diagram.

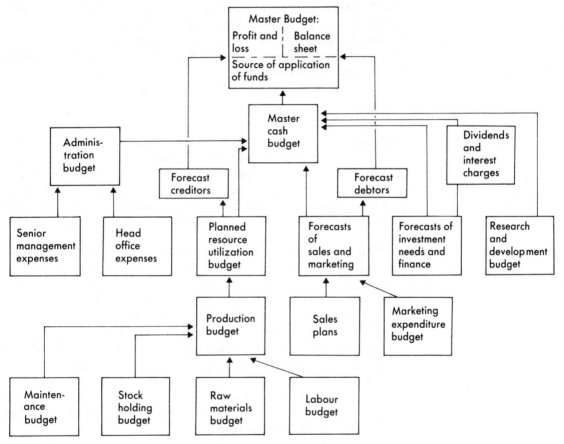

Fig 4.4 Formal budgeting system

At each stage going up through the organization, the various budgets, reflecting the operating and tactical planning decisions made within the firm (sales, purchases, production, cash, labour, marketing, etc.), are consolidated into a 'master budget'. The master budget is usually expressed in terms of the company's financial statements: budgeted profit and loss account, balance sheet and source and application of funds. These budgeted financial statements take the same form as the statements which, at the end of the accounting period, will be published and which form the principal vehicle for senior management accountability to the firm's shareholders and other external user groups. In a system such as we have outlined in Fig. 4.4. the budgeting procedure is designed to reflect the aspirations of senior management and also reflect their performance.

In less formal organizations, the budgeting system should support the informal lines of communication within the firm and the shared nature of authority common in such organizations. The highly centralized authority associated with the formal, bureaucratic firm has high 'compliance' costs associated with enforcing senior management's will throughout the firm. In such organizations senior management will have to spend considerable time ensuring that its wishes are properly complied with and that the firm's control systems are working effectively. In the less formal organization these compliance costs will be much lower, but management must work much harder to integrate the overall activities of the various differentiated aspects of the firm.

Budgeting and conflict resolution

In Chapter 1 we painted a picture of the firm as a coalition of different groups with different interests and aspirations. The budgeting system can provide an important means for resolving the conflicts of interest which arise and producing the consensus necessary for the continued operation of the firm. A number of ways in which budgeting can help to resolve conflicts between various groups are indicated below:

- By providing a mechanism for negotiation (both overt and covert) between different groups within the firm. Overt negotiation is normally conducted in the formal committees and other meetings set up to settle the budgets for the coming period. On the other hand, covert negotiation can occur in many different ways. For example, if a particular group within the firm (say a research and development department) realized that it was likely to underspend in a particular financial year then we would expect a large amount of 'catch-up' spending as the financial year came to a close. Often this spending is done not so much because the group concerned needs the items purchased at that particular time but rather to inform senior management that its budget should not be cut in future years.

- By the 'planned' creation of slack within the system so that incompatible aims can be satisfied without destructive internal competition between the various interest groups. Indeed, at any point in time a large proportion of a firm's planned surplus will be devoted to allowing groups with incompatible aims to exist side by side.

- By directing the attention of the organization at different times to different aims. For example, within a production group one month's budget may be aimed toward enhancing the quality of materials produced. Another month's budget, on the other hand, could well be orientated toward cutting costs. Thus the budgeting system can, sequentially, focus attention upon two different aspects of production performance which are in conflict.

Summary

To summarize, the firm's budgeting system represents an important part of management's control function. In addition the budgeting procedures provide an all-important means whereby the various power groups within the firm can reconcile their different interests.

Supplementary reading

HOPWOOD, A., *Accounting and Human Behaviour*, Accountancy Age, 1974. Chapters 1–3 of this excellent book provide a good introduction to behaviour in organizations and the problems of budgeting.

HOPWOOD, A., Organizational and behavioural aspects of budgeting and control, in Arnold, J., Carsberg, B. V., and Scapens, R. (eds), *Topics in Management Accounting*, Philip Allan, 1980.

MULLINS, L., Behavioural implications of management accounting, *Management Accounting*, January 1981.

THEOBALD, M., Forecasting models, in Arnold, J., Carsberg, B. V., and Scapens, R. (eds), *Topics in Management Accounting*, Philip Allan, 1980.

WOOD, D., and FILDES, R., *Forecasting for Business*, Longman, 1976. This is an excellent book which covers all of the basic forecasting methods which are likely to be needed in management-accounting applications. Chapter 1 makes good reading at this stage, the rest of the book should be used for reference purposes.)

Questions

1   Discuss the extent to which the distinction between the long and the short run is a distinction of convenience rather than a distinction of fact.

2   In the following situations indicate whether the decisions to be taken should be considered long or short run and specify any further information you would require in order to confirm your choice.
(a) A company is deciding the price at which to sell the maximum output of a particular plant. The plant is in continuous operation.
(b) A pharmaceutical company is considering opening a new research centre into anti-viral agents. Few such agents are available commercially.
(c) A cosmetics manufacturer is considering the level of advertising which should be commissioned for its new range of male cosmetics. Male cosmetics usually have a product life of less than three years.

(d) A football club is wondering whether to strengthen its defence by buying a South American international star of many years' experience.

(e) A motor-car manufacturer is drawing up its production budget for three versions of the same basic model line. Each version differs from the others in terms of engine size, quality of trim and extras. All three models are produced on the same production facility.

(f) A firm of chartered accountants is deciding upon the maximum level of taxation work which the firm should undertake and the number of partners who should specialize in that aspect of the firm's work.

3   Outline the principal features of a personal budget for a single person with only one major source of income. The individual concerned holds both a current and deposit account at a bank, two credit cards and a building society share account which requires seven days' notice of withdrawal. The individual's monthly salary cheque is paid into the current account by monthly direct credit and certain important monthly payments are made by standing orders and direct debits. (Use your personal experience and imagination.)

4   Outline the role which budgets play in industrial organizations.

5 The output decision

In this chapter we show how costs and revenues vary with output. We then explain how, in practice, the relationship between cost and output can be found and the role that statistical methods can play in determining the behaviour of costs as output changes. We then proceed to an examination of the different ways in which output decisions can be made and the assumptions which underlie the various methods of analysis discussed.

By the end of the chapter you should have an understanding of:

- The basics of the output decision.
- The way revenues vary with output and the concept of demand elasticity.
- The way that costs vary with output.
- How to estimate cost–output relationships in practice.
- The role of stocks in output decisions.
- The technique of break-even analysis and its practical application.
- The methods of marginal analysis.
- The concept of flexible budgeting.

Basics of the output decision

In the last chapter we noted some preliminary points about the output decision. We catagorized the output decision as a short-run decision because, first, it presumes that some prior long-run decision (in this case the decision to produce) has already been made and, second, because we can normally disregard the timing problem when measuring the impact of wealth changes upon the decision-maker's wealth. We also noted that pricing and output decisions are interrelated and that a decision-maker who attempts to make one without recognizing the impact of the other may be in for some unpleasant surprises.

In order to make output decisions we need to understand four things:

- The aims and objectives behind the decision.
- The time period over which the output is to be planned.

- The way in which revenues vary with output (which is linked to the pricing decision).
- The way in which costs vary with output.

The aims and objectives of the output decision

As we noted in Chapter 3, the single-minded pursuit of optimizing goals may not be really representative of typical decision-making behaviour. It may well be that under stress, or, indeed, in situations of imperfect knowledge, decision-makers will opt for satisfactory rather than optimal solutions. In this chapter we will examine an important technique in output decision-making called 'break-even' analysis. This technique can be regarded, for reasons we will discuss later, as a satisficing procedure.

Following our discussion of break-even analysis we will consider how output decisions can be made in an optimizing framework using a very simple form of mathematical analysis. The optimizing model we use assumes that management wishes to maximize its firm's economic profit (see Chapter 4) given that output can be set at any level within the capacity of the production system.

The time period of the output decision

In continuous-production systems such as an oil refinery, a chemical plant or a continuous car-production line, the output decision must be made over an arbitrary time period. In batch processes, however, the period defined by the beginning and the end of the batch may form a more natural decision-making period. The time period chosen is important on two counts: first, the length of time determines the maximum physical output possible on a particular production process and, therefore, the basis upon which output is measured; second, the function of stocks as an intermediary between production and the firm's product market becomes more important as we move from continuous-time to discrete-time (batch) processes.

Variation of revenues with output level

The revenue gained from selling a particular quantity of product is directly related to the number of units sold:

total revenue = price per unit sold × total number of units sold

Consider the demand curve for video recorders facing the electronics company discussed in the last chapter. We show this demand curve again (Fig. 5.1). However, we can now note that the straight line relating price per unit (p) to the quantity sold (Q) can be defined by the formula:

$$p = a - bQ$$

where a is the point where the line relating price to quantity cuts the price axis of the graph and b is the slope of the line. The negative sign indicates that there is a negative relationship between price and quantity, i.e. as the price of the product rises the quantity demanded in the market, and therefore sold, falls. Similarly, as the price falls so the quantity sold will rise.

Fig 5.1 A linear demand curve

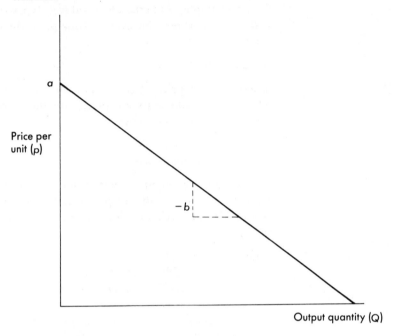

You will note that the formula above is similar to the general formula for any straight line.

$$y = a + bx$$

where y and x are the two variables which are linearly related to one another and a and b are the point of intercept with the y axis and the slope of the line, respectively. The sign (plus or minus) which attaches to the slope coefficient b tells us whether the line expresses an upward-sloping (positive) or a downward-sloping (negative) relationship between the two variables.

Given the definition of total revenue as price per unit times the quantity sold we can restate total revenue using the demand relationship above:

$$\text{total revenue} = \text{price} \times \text{quantity}$$
$$= pQ$$

but, using the demand relationship, $p = a - bQ$, it follows that:

$$\text{total revenue} = (a - bQ)Q$$
$$= aQ - bQ^2$$

This formula represents an inverted quadratic relationship between total revenue and quantity as shown in Fig. 5.2. The conclusion to be drawn from this curve is that the simplest type of downward-sloping demand curve will produce a total revenue function which is upward sloping over the first part of its range and then, after reaching a point of maximum total revenue, turns down giving decreasing total revenue with increasing output.

For example, Almeria plc produces typewriters. Almeria's market research department believes that the price–quantity relationship for its typewriters is as follows:

$$p = 290 - 0.1Q$$

where p is the price of each typewriter sold at the output quantity Q. Therefore, if 500 units are placed on the market, the price at which they can be sold is given by:

$$p(500) = 290 - 0.1 \times 500$$
$$= \text{£}240 \text{ per unit}$$

Given the price–quantity relationship expressed by this demand curve, we can draw up a table of prices and total revenues which will result from different levels of sales. Almeria's total revenue function is given by:

$$\text{total revenue} = pQ$$
$$= (290 - 0.1Q)Q$$
$$= 290Q - 0.1Q^2$$

Sales of typewriters	Price at specified level of sales (£)	Total revenue from sales (£)
0	290	0
250	265	66 250
500	240	120 000
750	215	161 250
1 000	190	190 000
1 250	165	206 250
1 500	140	210 000
1 750	115	201 250

The graph of total revenue from sales is shown in Fig. 5.2

The shape of any total revenue function is determined by the shape of the underlying relationship between price and output which a firm faces in the relevant product market. The quadratic function shown in Fig. 5.2 is derived from the simplest type of demand curve. More complicated functions generate more complex relationships between total revenue and output.

The concept of elasticity

The sensitivity of the amount demanded of a particular product to changes in its price is measured by its 'price-elasticity of demand'. The price-elasticity of demand measures the proportionate change in the quantity

Fig 5.2 Total revenue from typewriter sales

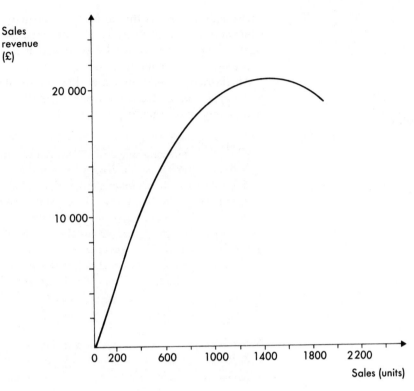

of a product demanded by the market following a small change in the product's price.

It is also possible to measure the elasticity of demand with respect to other variables: advertising expenditure is one example, changes in the income of consumers are another.

If Almeria's typewriters currently retail at £240 and their price is reduced to £215 then the proportionate change in price is given by:

$$\frac{\text{new price} - \text{current price}}{\text{current price}} = \frac{\Delta p}{p} = \frac{215 - 240}{240} = -0.104\,17$$

As a consequence of this fall in price the demand for Almeria's typewriters will rise. The corresponding proportionate change in demand is, therefore:

$$\frac{\text{demand at new price} - \text{demand at current price}}{\text{demand at current price}} = \frac{\Delta Q}{Q} = \frac{750 - 500}{500} = 0.5$$

The demand levels at a price of £215 and £240 can be read from the sales/price/total revenue table above.

The price-elasticity of demand at the point on Almeria's demand curve where price = £240 and quantity = 500 units is given by the ratio of the two proportionate changes:

$$\text{elasticity at point } (p, Q) = \frac{\Delta Q/Q}{\Delta p/p} = \frac{\Delta Q}{\Delta p} \times \frac{p}{Q}$$

therefore $e(240, 500) = 0.5/0.104\,17 = 4.80$

where $e(240, 500)$ is the point price-elasticity of demand at a price of £240 and an output quantity of 500 units. Note: by convention, price-elasticity of demand is usually expressed as a positive value, irrespective of the sign of its component ratios.

An elasticity of 4.80 indicates that, for small price changes only, every percentage change from the price of £240 will bring about a 4.80 per cent change in the quantity demanded.

Note: With a linear demand curve the ratio of price to quantity (p/Q) will change, and hence the elasticity will also change as we move up and down the curve. In addition to this, with non-linear demand curves the ratio of change in quantity to change in price (the slope of the demand curve) will also depend upon the point at which we wish to measure elasticity. Therefore, when we talk about elasticity about a point we must talk about very tiny changes in price and output. These tiny or 'marginal' changes are given by the first differential of quantity with respect to price, i.e. the price-elasticity of demand about a point is given by:

$$e(p, Q) = \frac{dQ}{dp} \times \frac{p}{Q}$$

In this chapter we will assume linearity in all those demand curves we deal with. In business it is safest to assume, initially, that a given product's demand curve is linear unless there is some overwhelming reason for believing otherwise. The simple reason for this is that it is much easier to disprove the existence of linearity than to disprove some more esoteric price–quantity relationship. Indeed, a good working rule in business, as in other scientific pursuits, is to assume, initially, the simplest, most easily falsified hypothesis.

At the end of this chapter we give a brief introduction to an easy mathematical method for finding the slope (or rate of change) of simple curves.

When a product has 'price-inelastic' demand any fall in its price will bring about a fall in total revenue. Inelasticity is defined by the range of values from unity to zero, i.e.

$0 < e(p, Q) < 1$ (inelasitic demand condition)

while 'price-elastic' demand is where price increases bring about increases in total revenue, i.e.

$1 < e(p, Q) < \infty$ (elastic demand condition)

'Perfect elasticity' means that a demand curve is infinitely inelastic along its entire length. 'Perfectly inelastic' demand curves are of zero elasticity along their entire length.

When the point elasticity of a demand curve is unity ($e(p, Q) = 1$) a small change in price will bring about an equivalent proportionate change in demand. At this point, therefore, tiny increases or decreases in price will be matched by corresponding decreases or increases in quantity. Because the increase (or decrease) in revenue, caused by the price change, is exactly netted off by the decrease (or increase) in revenue, caused by the quantity change, there will be no alteration in total revenue and this (referring back to Fig. 5.2) can only occur when total revenue is at a maximum.

We can determine the maximum total revenue for a linear demand curve as follows:

$e(p, Q) = 1$ (at maximum total revenue)

then

$$\frac{\Delta Q}{\Delta p} \times \frac{p}{Q} = 1 \tag{5.1}$$

For Almeria, the slope of the demand curve is 0.1, i.e.

$$\frac{\Delta p}{\Delta Q} = 0.1$$

Therefore:

$$\frac{\Delta Q}{\Delta p} = 1/0.1 = 10$$

Substituting in (5.1) above:

$$10 \times \frac{p}{Q} = 1$$

Therefore:

$$\frac{p}{Q} = 0.1 \qquad \text{(at maximum revenue)}$$

or,

$$Q = p/0.1 \tag{5.2}$$

Almeria's demand curve is:

$p = 290 - 0.1 \times Q$

Substituting for Q using Eq. (5.2)

$p = 290 - 0.1 \times p/0.1$

$p = 290 - p$

therefore:

$2p = 290$
$\quad p = £145$

At a price of £145, the demand (Q) is given by rearranging the demand-curve equation:

$p = 290 - 0.1 \times Q$

[handwritten margin notes:]
$p = $ price/unit.
$Q = $ quantity sold.
$e = $ elasticity.
$pq = $ total revenue.

therefore:

$$Q = \frac{290 - p}{0.1}$$

Substituting for p:

$$Q = \frac{290 - 145}{0.1}$$
$$= 1450 \text{ units}$$

Therefore, at maximum revenue, price is £145 and demand 1450 units.

Self test: **Determine the point price elasticity of demand at the following price–quantity points on Almeria's demand curve:**

p (£)	Q (units)
290	0
190	1000
145	1450
115	1750

What does it mean if the demand curve has infinite elasticity along its entire length, i.e. the demand for the product is perfectly elastic?

In a situation where a company faces a perfectly elastic demand curve, the price which the company can obtain for its product is completely independent of the quantity it produces and sells to the market. This state of affairs exists only in perfectly competitive product markets.

Variation of costs with output level

We have noted before that the long-run decision to produce a particular product will commit the firm to a certain level of fixed costs. Because these costs are invariate with the output level chosen they cannot influence the output decision. Such costs are: rent, rates, heating (in so far as it relates to the premises rather than the production process itself), lighting and the salaries of all of those who are not involved directly in production. A graphical representation of this type of cost is shown in Fig. 5.3.

However, certain costs may appear fixed over certain specified ranges of output although these ranges are separated by 'steps' or discontinuities. An example of such a cost is labour charges, where an additional plant or process operator is hired as production passes through fixed points on the increasing range of output. In fact, labour costs exhibit a 'ratchet' effect in that they are stepped going up but appear fixed coming down through the range of output. In other words, hiring labour is often treated and appears as a short-term decision, but firing labour is invariably a

Fig 5.3 Relationship of fixed cost with output

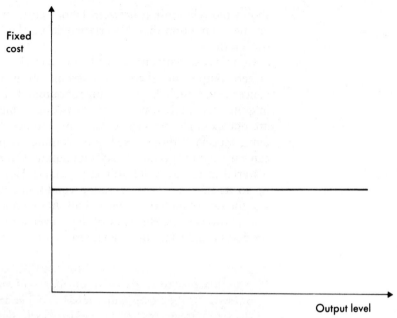

Fig 5.4 Labour costs against output

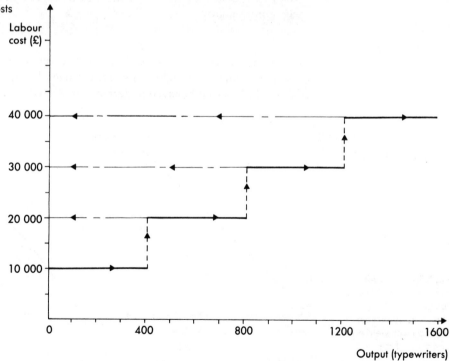

long-run decision given the employment protection for employees in UK law.

For example, Almeria plc requires skilled technicians for the construction of its typewriters. Each engineer can produce 400 typewriters a working year and is paid an average annual salary of £10 000. Figure 5.4

shows the relationship between labour costs and output and is drawn on the assumption that Almeria would not lay off its employees in the short term.

Certain costs vary directly with output level, in that zero cost is incurred at zero output and there is a constant rise in the cost of the resource concerned through the entire range of output. In practice, few costs behave in quite such a tidy way. Material costs (ignoring changes in stock levels) are one example, packaging costs are another. In some production systems, especially those based upon continuous processes, material costs can vary in quite peculiar ways with output. Over initial ranges of output, material costs may well be directly variable. However, as the plant comes up to its most efficient operating conditions, yields may well improve and the rate of material usage fall off. At extremely high operating conditions, however, the efficiency of the conversion of materials into finished products usually falls off and material costs rise rapidly.

> *Note:* Marginal cost is the increase in the cost of a resource brought about by increasing the process output level by just one unit (i.e. a 'marginal' change). Marginal cost can be considered as the slope of the total cost curve at any point.

In Fig. 5.5(*a*) we show a 'well-behaved' variable cost curve, that is one which is linear throughout its entire range of output. In Fig. 5.5(*b*) we show the less well-behaved pattern of variation described above.

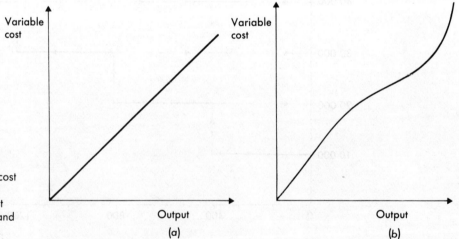

Fig 5.5(a) A 'well behaved' variable cost function
(b) A variable cost function with yield and capacity effects

Certain variable costs have an initial fixed cost which is incurred irrespective of the output level. Sometimes material costs are of this type where a certain quantity of material is required to prime the production process. Many chemical plants have to be primed in this way. Just as a motor-car requires a certain amount of petrol to fill the carburettor before its engine will fire, some chemical plants require a certain level of raw materials in their input system before the reactions can proceed. In Fig. 5.6 we show the typical pattern of behaviour associated with such 'semivariable' costs.

Fig 5.6 Semivariable costs

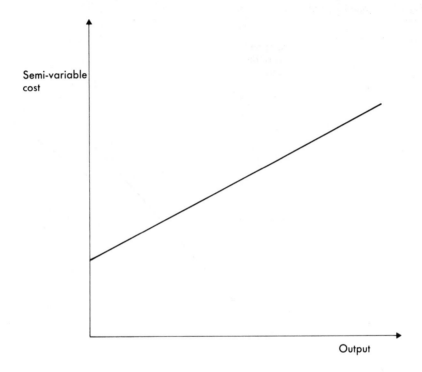

As with fixed costs it is possible to get steps in variable-cost patterns. For example, if a supplier offers a discount on raw materials for deliveries in excess of a certain agreed figure in a given period, then a downward step will occur at that level. In Fig. 5.7 we show an example of a stepped variable cost.

How to estimate cost–output relationships in practice

In order to make decisions concerning output levels, we need to know the current relationship which exists between cost and output for the process concerned. Unfortunately, past costs will not, necessarily, provide a good indication of either current or future cost–output relationships on that particular plant or process. As far as possible, output decisions should be made on the basis of up-to-date estimates of cost; however, in certain circumstances reliance may have to be placed on projections based upon past figures.

In principle, two methods are available to help us estimate the relationship between cost and output:

- Analytically, from the plants' or process's technological characteristics.
- Statistically, from past cost–output data from the plant or process concerned.

Fig 5.7 Stepped variable cost

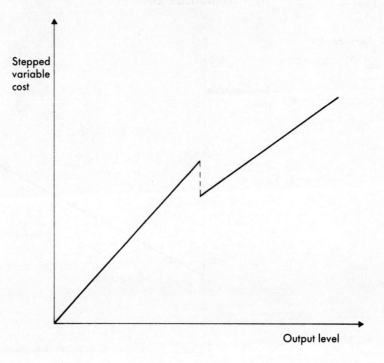

Stepped variable cost

Output level

Analytical process analysis

All physical processes require inputs of raw materials, energy and technical knowledge in order to produce outputs. In many physical systems this conversion of inputs to outputs can be understood with a high degree of accuracy. For example, an engineer in an oil refinery may well be able to predict, with considerable accuracy, the proportions of different types of petroleum spirit which can be 'cracked' from a given type of crude oil. Similarly, a whisky distiller can tell, given a fermented mash of a certain specific gravity, the number of litres of distilled spirit which can be produced. However, because all physical products are susceptible to random fluctuations in performance, the conversion of input to output can only be described in the form of a probability distribution of yields.

A firm's production engineers can usually specify the relevant conversion ratio for input to output on a particular plant or process and can provide estimates of the amount of labour required to operate and control the system. For example, a raw-materials conversion ratio for a chemical plant would be as follows:

$$\text{conversion ratio} = \frac{\text{number of kilograms of raw material}}{\text{number of kilograms of principal output product}}$$

This conversion ratio can be altered to accommodate the situation where some raw material is recovered from the waste effluent during the product's purification stage.

An analytical approach to the problem of determining the relationship between cost and output means that the management accountant must be heavily dependent upon the technical expertise of the firm's engineering staff. However, it is important to appreciate that even the best estimates provided by the engineering staff can be subject to error because of:

- Differences in the quality of raw materials between one batch and another. Even minor variations in the quality of raw materials can have a dramatic impact upon a production system's ability to convert that raw material into final product.

- Variations in the operating procedures of the plant or process. Again, even minor variations in ambient temperatures or even stirring rates in a chemical reactor, for example, can cause major changes in process yields.

- The inherent unpredictability of many natural processes. Often the laws which govern physical processes are probabilistic and so predictions can only be made to certain degrees of confidence.

- The inputs to a particular process and hence the input costs may be dependent upon other variables as well as plant output such as: product quality, labour input, etc.

In many cases the direct examination of a cost–output relationship may be impossible. It may simply be that the manufacturing plant records are insufficiently accurate or that the process has only been attempted at the pilot-plant level and not as yet commissioned on a full-scale plant. In the first case, the management accountant will have to attempt a statistical analysis of the firm's past production records. In the second case, the management accountant may have no alternative but to attempt a similar statistical analysis on the results of any pilot-plant experiments which have been carried out.

Statistical cost analysis

Statistical cost analysis involves the following four steps:

- The collection of past costs of input and output data over as long a period as possible.

- The adjustment of the past data to render them comparable in terms of current input prices.

- The statistical analysis of the collected data into fixed and variable components.

- Determining the degree of confidence which can be placed on the results of the analysis.

Note: If a particular input into a process has an easily ascertained current price (as might well be the case with raw material inputs for example) then we can modify the first two steps above by estimating the relationship of past usages of the input with output and then pricing the input–output relationship at the current price. In the examples worked out subsequently, we will assume that the current price of the inputs cannot be identified easily and that the estimation of that price is part of the exercise.

The collection of past input cost and output data

In order to ensure statistical reliability the largest possible body of comparable data should be collected. For a particular production process a number of sources of data may be available to the management accountant:

- Stock records of inputs and outputs from a particular process.
- Suppliers' price lists and purchasing department records.
- Process log sheets and operator work sheets.
- Cost accounts of raw material or component usages and accounts of process outputs.

In any given situation the management accountant may be forced to use data which are either aggregated (and will need detailed analysis) or are incomplete. In both situations any source of supporting information which can be found will be useful for checking analyses and estimates.

The adjustment of past costs

The accountant's aim, as far as possible, is to create a picture of the current relationship between cost and output. Economists refer to the graphical representation of such a relationship as an 'analytical' cost curve. Such a relationship can be regarded as a cost 'snapshot' of a particular plant's or process's operating potential in that it gives a cost–output relationship over the operating range of output at a particular instant in time.

Three problems can arise with the use of past data:

- The plant's or process's operating procedures may have altered in some way or other which is not obvious from the past cost data. This difficulty can be surmounted by discussion with the firm's technical staff.
- There may have been a step in the input costs at some time in the past brought about by a price rise such as an increase in labour costs following a successful wage claim.

- There may have been a continuous pattern of changing input prices. Specific price inflation affects different input costs in different ways.

> *Note:* Public discussion of inflation normally focuses on the level of the Retail Price Index (RPI), an index published by the government's statistical service. The RPI measures the changes in the price of a 'shopping basket' of consumer goods (hence the term 'retail' index) and does not represent the price changes in industrial costs. Individual companies are subject to specific price changes or specific rates of 'inflation' on their inputs and it is up to the company concerned to devise its own index of input costs. More detailed indices of costs appropriate for particular industrial sectors are also available from the government's Central Statistical Office in the 'Business Monitor' series.

Example: Almeria plc has collected the following costs from its typewriter factory for the last six months of production. We can assume that the costs arise on the last day of the month in question:

	July (£)	August (£)	September (£)	October (£)	November (£)	December (£)
Components	24 455	17 320	27 205	32 440	34 560	41 630
Labour	32 730	22 730	38 500	45 000	47 000	55 500
Variable overheads	9 000	6 250	9 630	11 250	11 750	13 870
Fixed overheads	50 000	50 000	50 000	50 000	50 000	50 000
Total production costs	116 185	96 300	125 335	138 690	143 310	161 000
Output (units)	710	500	900	1 100	1 250	1 150

During our analysis of production costs we discover that the costs of the components have risen during the course of the previous six months at an average rate of 2 per cent per month. In addition, we discover that a 10 per cent wage increase was negotiated for all production staff to take effect from the beginning of September.

Given the facts, as stated above, two adjustments need to be made in order to make all six months' figures comparable. November's component cost figure is based upon purchase prices which are one month out of date. With a 2 per cent monthly increase the November cost, restated in December prices, is:

November component charge = £34 560 × 1.02 = £35 250

October's component cost figure is two months out of date. To make the October figure comparable with November we must raise it by 2 per cent and then by a further 2 per cent to bring it to December prices:

$$\text{October component charge} = £32\,440 \times 1.02 \times 1.02$$
$$= £32\,440 \times 1.02^2$$
$$= £33\,750$$

On the same basis we can revise the remaining component charges for the six-month period as follows:

	Original (£)		Revised (£)
December	41 630	=	41 630
November	34 560	$\times 1.02^1 =$	35 250
October	32 440	$\times 1.02^2 =$	33 750
September	27 205	$\times 1.02^3 =$	28 870
August	17 320	$\times 1.02^4 =$	18 750
July	24 455	$\times 1.02^5 =$	27 000

The wage-rate increase raises a slightly different problem, however, in that the increase affected all wage levels from September onwards. Neither the August nor the July figures contained the increase of 10 per cent in the labour rate. Therefore, to make these two months comparable with the months that follow we should increase their respective labour costs by 10 per cent:

August labour cost = £22 730 × 1.1 = £25 000
July labour cost   = £32 730 × 1.1 = £36 000

Note that with labour costs we are not concerned with a rate of increase as we were with component charges. A rate of increase implies that each month's cost figures are increased by the specified percentage rate. With labour costs we are dealing with a once-for-all rise in the level of labour costs.

Using the corrected component and labour costs we can now create a revised schedule of production costs against output level. But now the month in which the costs arose is irrelevant. We have removed all the timing effects that we know about and are left with a series of production costs (stated in current, December prices).

We have noted that the relationship between cost and output may not, of necessity, be exact and, indeed, if we plot the data below on a graph (see Fig. 5.8) we notice that the points are scattered around what appears to be an upward rising trend.

Schedule of revised production costs:

	Output level					
	710	500	900	1 100	1 250	1 150
Component cost (revised) (£)	27 000	18 750	28 870	33 750	35 250	41 630
Labour cost (revised) (£)	36 000	25 000	38 500	45 000	47 000	55 500
Variable overheads (£)	9 000	6 250	9 630	11 250	11 750	13 870
Fixed overheads (£)	50 000	50 000	50 000	50 000	50 000	50 000
Total production costs (£)	122 000	100 000	127 000	140 000	144 000	161 000

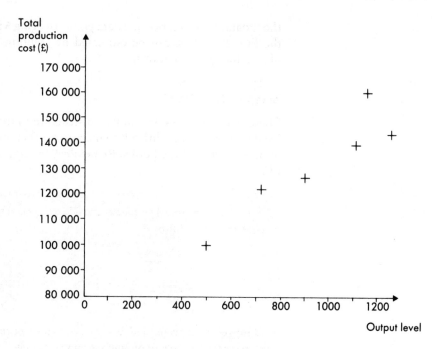

Fig 5.8 Almeria plc—scatter diagram of production cost against output level

The question which now arises is: given that the cost–output data do not fall on a straight line, how do we go about judging the line which best represents the data?

The statistical analysis of past data

In practice, just six data points would not form a particularly promising basis for any form of statistical analysis unless they all clearly fell upon a line or some other smooth function. The greater the degree of dispersion of the points the more data will be required to gain useful results. However, given the data we do have we will now turn to a very simple statistical technique for its analysis.

We will make the simplest assumption possible concerning the relationship between production cost and output, namely that the data fall upon a straight line which can best be described by the relationship:

Production cost =
        fixed cost plus variable cost per unit times the output quantity

which is a relationship of the linear form:

$y = a + bx$

where a is the intercept with the vertical (y) axis (which, in this case, will be an estimate of the fixed cost) and b is the slope of the line relating production cost to quantity (which, in this case, will be an estimate of the variable cost per unit).

The technique of 'linear regression' allows us to convert raw data points on a graph into values of a and b which define the line of best fit for those data. From a series of n data points (n being 6 in Almeria's example), the line of best fit can be estimated by solution of the following pair of simultaneous equations:

$$\Sigma y = na + b\,\Sigma x$$
$$\Sigma(xy) = a\,\Sigma x + b\,\Sigma x^2$$

These two equations are similar in structure to the equations of the line itself and are not too difficult to memorize. Their derivation can be found in most statistical textbooks. Remember, the operator Σ stands for 'sum of'.

> *Note:* Some statistical textbooks provide the general solution of these two equations in the form:
>
> $$a = \frac{\Sigma y\,\Sigma x^2 - \Sigma x\,\Sigma(xy)}{n\,\Sigma x^2 - (\Sigma x)^2}$$
>
> $$b = \frac{n\,\Sigma(xy) - \Sigma x\,\Sigma y}{n\,\Sigma x^2 - (\Sigma x)^2}$$
>
> However, most people find these two equations much more difficult to remember than the pair of simultaneous equations given above.

We can convert the production-cost–output data into a form suitable for inclusion in the two simultaneous equations given above by constructing the following table:

Production cost, y (£)	Output, x	xy	x^2
122 000	710	86 620 000	504 100
100 000	500	50 000 000	250 000
127 000	900	114 300 000	810 000
140 000	1100	154 000 000	1 210 000
144 000	1250	180 000 000	1 562 500
161 000	1150	185 150 000	1 322 500
$\Sigma y = 794\,000$	$\Sigma x = 5610$	$\Sigma(xy) = 770\,070\,000$	$\Sigma x^2 = 5\,659\,100$

Substituting the totals from this table into the two simultaneous equations we have:

$$794\,000 = 6a + 5610b \qquad (5.3)$$
$$770\,070\,000 = 5610a + 5\,659\,100b \qquad (5.4)$$

In order to solve these two equations we need to bring the coefficients of one variable to a common figure so that when one equation is taken from the other one variable drops out. If we multiply Eq. (5.3) by 935 (i.e. 5610/6) we get a revised equation (5.5)

$$742\,390\,000 = 5610a + 5\,245\,350b \qquad (5.5)$$

Equation (5.5) is a transformed version of Eq. (5.3); it expresses the same mathematical relationship as Eq. (5.3) except on a larger scale. If we subtract Eq. (5.5) from Eq. (5.4) we get:

$$770\,070\,000 = 5610a + 5\,659\,100b \tag{5.4}$$
$$742\,390\,000 = 5610a + 5\,245\,350b \tag{5.5}$$
$$\overline{27\,680\,000 = 0 \quad\ + \quad 413\,750b} \tag{5.6}$$

Equation (5.6) when rearranged gives:

$$b = \frac{27\,680\,000}{413\,750}$$
$$= £66.90 \text{ per unit of output}$$

By substituting the value of b (the variable cost per unit) into either Eq. (5.3), (5.4) or (5.5), the value of the fixed costs (a) can be derived.

Using Eq. (5.3):

$$a = \frac{794\,000 - 5610 \times 66.90}{6}$$
$$= £69\,780$$

The result of our analysis is that the production cost–output relationship can be described by the linear relationship:

production cost $= 69\,780 + 66.90 \times$ output quantity

We show this relationship between production cost and output in Fig. 5.9. Note the estimated fixed costs are greater than the fixed costs of

Fig 5.9 Estimated relationship between total production cost and output

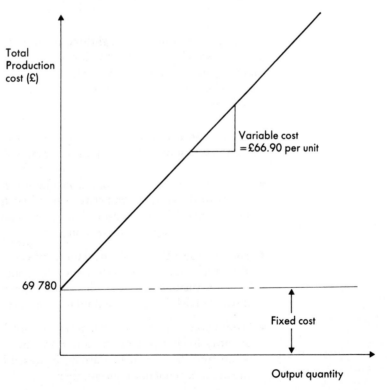

£50 000 specified in the example. This could mean that there is a fixed element in one or more of the other cost classifications. However, with only six observations of the cost–output relationship, our estimation of the overall fixed cost will not be particularly reliable.

Self test: Analysis of Almeria's old cost-accounting records reveals that the production costs for May and June were made up as follows:

	May (£)	June (£)
Component cost	26 117	14 990
Labour cost	36 364	20 450
Variable overhead	10 000	5 625
Fixed overhead	47 000	47 000
Total production cost	119 481	88 065
Output (units)	695	470

The same percentage increase for components applied in May and June as applied to the subsequent six months. There was no extraordinary increase in labour costs in May and June.
   Repeat the analysis of the production-cost–output relationship including the additional data given above.
   Solution clue: 69.85; 67 468.29

Linear regression is a straightforward technique for analysing the relationships which exist between pairs of variables. As we shall see in later chapters linear regression has other uses for the management accountant. For this reason it is important to note some of the limitations of the technique (apart from the presumption that the underlying relationship is linear).

The limitations of linear regression arise from the assumptions upon which the two simultaneous equations (5.3) and (5.4) are based:

- The line of best fit is that one which minimizes the sum of the squared values of the differences between that best-fit line and the individual data points. For this reason, linear regression is often referred to as 'ordinary least-squares regression'.

- The average value of the deviations of each data point from the line of best fit is zero. Obviously some data points will lie above and some lie below the line of best fit; this assumption means that the differences above and below the line should net out to zero.

- Production costs in any given period are solely dependent upon output quantity in that period and any differences between individual data points and the best-fit line are both caused by purely random effects and are independent of one another.

- If the production cost could be measured a large number of times at each possible output quantity (i.e. at each possible x value) then the spread of production costs around the best-fit line would be constant along its entire length.

Given all of these assumptions, one would be forgiven for dismissing the technique as too restrictive. Like all mathematical and statistical techniques, linear regression is only as good as the assumptions which support it. However, in most cost-estimation problems the assumptions given above are unlikely to be too restrictive and the technique of linear regression has the great advantage of removing an element of subjective judgement from cost estimation.

The final stage of regression analysis is that of determining the confidence which can be placed in the results obtained.

Statistical measures of goodness of fit

With any linear regression between two variables the first problem is to identify how well the line of best fit represents the data. We can do this by determining the strength of the relationship between the variables. Two variables which are perfectly correlated with one another would have all of their data points lying along the line of best fit. A statistic called the 'correlation coefficient' (which is symbolized as r) takes the value of one if such a perfect fit exists. If the two variables are positively related (i.e. the slope coefficient has a positive sign) then the correlation coefficient would be plus one given a perfect fit. If, on the other hand, the relationship is negative (as we saw in the relationship between price and demand) then the correlation coefficient for a perfect fit is minus one.

Note: There is only one circumstance where a perfect fit of data points along the best-fit line does not produce a correlation of either plus or minus one. That is when the line of best fit is perfectly flat. In that case, the slope coefficient is zero and there is no relationship between the two variables. Accordingly, the slope coefficient is zero. What type of cost, if regressed against output could give a perfect data fit, with a correlation coefficient of zero?

The correlation coefficient (r) can have any value between plus and minus one. Completely uncorrelated variables have a correlation coefficient of zero. The closer the correlation coefficient is to its extreme value of plus or minus one, the more confident we can be that the relationship between the two variables is dependable and that the line of best fit is a good representation of the data.

The formula for calculating the correlation coefficient is quite simple:

Correlation coefficient
= the slope of the line of best fit multiplied by the ratio of the standard
  deviations of the x and y variable

$$= b \frac{\sigma(x)}{\sigma(y)}$$

where $\sigma(x)$ is the standard deviation of the x variable (output quantity
in Almeria's example) and $\sigma(y)$ is the standard deviation of the y variable
(total production cost in Almeria's example).

The standard deviation of the x variable is given by:

$$\sigma(x) = \sqrt{\left(\frac{\Sigma (x - \Sigma x/n)^2}{n} \right)}$$

$$\sqrt{\left(\frac{(710 - 5610/6)^2 + (500 - 5610/6)^2 + \dots + (1150 - 5610/6)^2}{6} \right)}$$

$$\sqrt{\left(\frac{50\,625 + 189\,225 + \dots + 46\,225}{6} \right)}$$

$$= 262.60$$

Similarly, the standard deviation of the y variable can be calculated:

$$\sigma(y) = \sqrt{\left(\frac{\Sigma (y - \Sigma y/n)^2}{n} \right)}$$

$$= 19\,136.93$$

The correlation coefficient is given by:

$$r = +66.90 \times \frac{262.30}{19\,136.93}$$

$$= +0.917$$

A statistic closely related to the correlation coefficient is the 'coefficient
of statistical determination' or r^2. This statistic is calculated as the square
of the correlation coefficient and represents the proportion of variability
in the independent variable (y) caused by variation in the dependent variable (x).

For Almeria:

$$r^2 = 0.917^2$$
$$= 0.841 \ (= 84.1 \text{ per cent})$$

The correlation coefficient of 0.917 indicates that there is a strong relationship between production cost and output quantity and the coefficient
of statistical determination tells us that 84.1 per cent of the variability
of production cost is explained by changes in output quantity. Therefore,
the remaining 15.9 per cent variation must be attributable to other factors.
For example:

- Step costs may be present in one or more of the cost functions which underlie total production cost. Steps will produce a lowering of the correlation coefficient although their existence may well be quite predictable.

- Random operating variables may be present as discussed above.

> **Self test:** Using the additional 2 months' data for May and June recalculate, for Almeria's management:
>
> **1** The correlation coefficient.
>
> **2** The coefficient of statistical determination.
>
> Also, redraw the relationship between total production cost and output on a graph.
> *Solution clue:* 279.61.

The role of stocks in production planning

Managers often feel uncomfortable with the idea that their output decisions are completely at the mercy of the demand curve for the products they are attempting to sell. In fact, we have oversimplified our discussion to a certain extent. Managers can, in the short term, escape from the constraints of the market demand for their product by creating or reducing stocks. Such stock management is of importance in two situations:

- Where the product concerned is produced by a batch process. Stocks of the finished good can be made at the most efficient level of production for the particular plant involved and then stored until it can be sold at the best price.

- Where there is a significant degree of seasonality in the demand for the particular product. In this situation the output from the production process can be stored (whether it is produced on a batch or continuous process) until the best price can be obtained.

With many products their demand curves change seasonally. For example, in the two months prior to Christmas we would expect an increase in consumer preferences for toys and games relative to other goods. Consequently, we would expect a seasonal shift in the demand curve for these products. A toy manufacturer will, therefore, be concerned with creating sufficient stocks during the production year to satisfy both the normal and the exceptional demand prior to Christmas.

There are costs associated with stock holding, however. Investing resources in stocks means that those resources cannot be used elsewhere. The frequency and size of the production runs will have a significant effect upon the costs of holding stocks. We will consider these, and related issues, in Chapter 8.

Break-even analysis and its application

Break-even analysis is a long-established technique for analysing the output problem. The traditional accounting approach is to assume that price is invariate with output and that costs can be represented as linear relationships with output. A simple example of a break-even curve for a particular process is given in Fig. 5.10. The difference between total cost and revenue at any particular output level can be mapped as a 'profitgram'—see Fig. 5.11.

Fig 5.10 Break-even graph

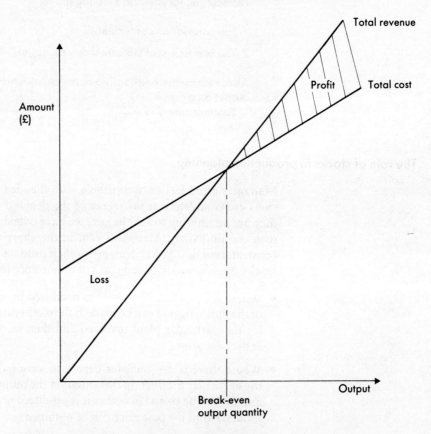

The assumptions of this type of analysis are:

- Increasing profits will be made the greater the output.

- Any production level in excess of that required to break-even is a 'satisfactory' level of output.

An unquestioning approach to the assumption of linearity in cost or revenue behaviour can lead to suboptimal decisions, with an overemphasis on a range of acceptable outputs, and little attention given to the search for an optimal solution. However, it may well be that management is quite prepared to accept the degree of approximation inherent in such a linear analysis because any refinement of the analysis would entail very high and unacceptable search and information processing costs to the firm. Also, it may be that management is of the opinion that, over the firm's likely output range, linearity is a reasonable assumption to make. But, as we shall now show, the assumption of linearity can lead to significant distortions in the decision-making process. Whether the losses which arise from such distortions are offset by the higher information collection and processing costs implied by the type of analysis we are about to describe, is very difficult to say. Some firms, with well-developed management information systems, may be able to collect the additional informa-

Fig 5.11   Profitgram

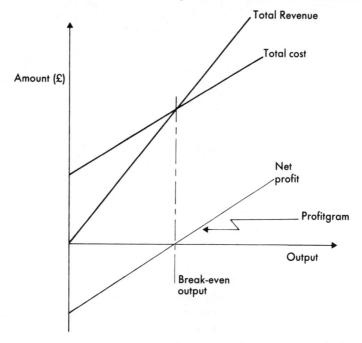

tion at little extra cost. Others may find the cost of obtaining and processing the additional information prohibitively expensive.

The first area of sophistication which can be brought to break-even analysis involves dropping the assumption of linearity in the total revenue function. Consider Almeria's total revenue and total cost curves. The total production cost can be represented by the relationship:

production cost $= 69\,780 + 66.90 \times Q$

and the total revenue function is of the form:

total revenue $= 290Q - 0.1Q^2$

where Q is the output quantity demanded and sold.

We can plot these two functions and their associated profitgram as shown in Fig. 5.12. Unlike the simple break-even analysis illustrated in Fig. 5.10 where a single break-even point was revealed, Fig. 5.12 has two such points. First, a lower break-even point where, for the first time, total revenue exceeds total cost and, second, an upper break-even point where the effect of the declining demand curve has taken total revenue below total cost again.

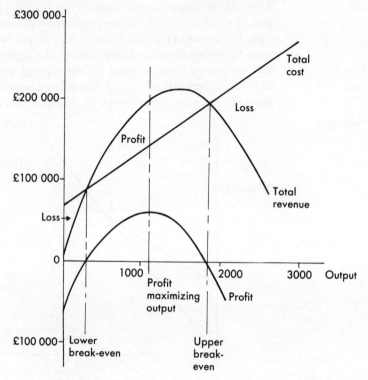

Fig 5.12 Almeria plc—break-even analysis

The profitgram now has a clear maximum, i.e. that point at the top of the profit curve where its slope is zero. At this 'turning point' on the profitgram, the rate of increase in profit following marginal changes in output is zero (that is, marginal profit is zero). This is implied by the statement that the slope of the profitgram is zero at maximum profit. Mathematically, this point of maximum profit is reached when the marginal change in total cost with respect to a marginal change in output (the slope of the cost function at a particular output) is equal to the marginal change of total revenue with respect to a marginal change in output.

Note: Formally, we can establish the position of maximum profit in the following way:

profit (π) = total revenue (TR) − total cost (TC)

The rate of change of profit with respect to output quantity is given by the first differential of profit with respect to quantity which will be zero at maximum profit:

$$\frac{d(\pi)}{dQ} = 0$$

Taking derivatives of the profit function we obtain at maxima:

$$\frac{d(\pi)}{dQ} = \frac{d(TR)}{dQ} - \frac{d(TC)}{dQ} = 0$$

therefore, at maximum profit:

$$\frac{d(TR)}{dQ} = \frac{d(TC)}{dQ}$$

The first differential of total revenue with respect to output quantity we interpret as 'marginal revenue'; the first differential of total cost with respect to revenue as 'marginal cost'. In order to check that the turning point on our profit function is a maximum rather than a minimum we should test to see whether the second derivative has a negative value. This will confirm that we have a maximum rather than a minimum.

To summarize this analysis, we can say that a profit-maximizing producer should set an output level where marginal cost and marginal revenue are equated. In Almeria's example we can easily determine the value of the marginal cost of production. In the case of a linear cost function, marginal cost will be the same as the variable cost per unit.

marginal cost = £66.90

Any additional unit of output incurs an incremental cost of £66.90 for the firm.

Marginal revenue is slightly more complex as it changes with increasing output level. The first differential of Almeria's total revenue function gives:

marginal revenue = $290 - 0.2 \times Q$

At the optimum output, therefore:

marginal cost = marginal revenue
i.e. $66.90 = 290 - 0.2 \times Q$

therefore, by rearrangement:

$$Q = \frac{290 - 66.90}{0.2} = 1115.5 \text{ units}$$

At this level of output profit is:

total profit = total revenue − total cost
$$= (290 \times 1115.5 - 0.1 \times 1115.5^2) - (69\,780 + 66.90 \times 1115.5)$$
$$= £54\,654$$

Marginal analysis of this type presents two problems for practical application:

- The objective of maximization may be inappropriate for the firm (see Chapter 3).

- The calculus technique can only work where the underlying cost and revenue functions are smooth without 'discontinuities'. But discontinuities occur if there are steps in the cost functions or 'kinks' in the revenue functions. In the presence of such discontinuities only a graphical analysis can bring out the full complexities of the problem.

For example, assume that Almeria's fixed costs consist of two elements:

Established fixed costs	£50 000
Fixed component of semivariable cost	£19 780
Total fixed cost	£69 780

However Almeria's management believes that in the future while the variable component of cost will remain the same as at present, the established fixed cost will increase at higher output levels:

Output level (units)	Fixed cost (£)
0– 499	50 000
500– 999	75 000
1000–1499	100 000

In Fig. 5.13 we introduce these steps into the total cost structure. Notice that instead of two break-even points we now have four and, most important of all, a discontinuity has appeared at a lower output level than the profit-maximizing output revealed by our marginal analysis above. The new profitgram shows that profit is maximized at 1000 units. Any increase beyond this output level brings an immediate and dramatic reduction in profit. In addition, the graph reveals a new loss-making area between 500 and 580 units of output.

Our analysis now incorporates two significant improvements over the simple, linear break-even graph. First, we have dispensed with the unrealistic assumption of a linear total-revenue function. Second, we have shown how discontinuities in the basic cost functions can be incorporated into the break-even graph. The introduction of discontinuities into our analysis has highlighted the weakness of simple mathematical methods in that they assume smooth, continuous functions which are mathematically well behaved.

In the next chapter we discuss a further refinement to the break-even analysis described above. In a situation of oligopolistic markets (discussed in the next chapter) it is possible for discontinuities to arise in the total-revenue curve because of a 'kinked' demand curve. Such discontinuities can be added easily to the type of break-even analysis described above.

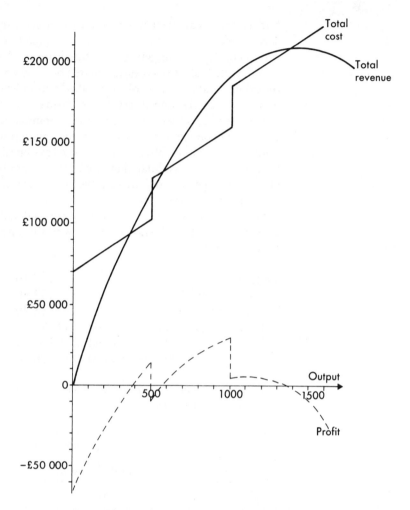

Fig 5.13 Almeria plc—break-even analysis with discontinuities

Note: Some texts discuss the notion of a relevant range of output where linearity of both cost and revenue functions can be assumed. It is certainly true that the simple quadratic total-revenue function can be approximated by a straight line over intermediate ranges of output. You may like to experiment with a ruler on Fig. 5.13. However, the concept of a relevant range cannot surmount the problems of discontinuities. In Almeria's case, for example, the lower and upper break-even points are separated by nearly 1000 units of output and, as Fig. 5.13 shows, most of the interesting problems on the graph lie in that range.

Flexible budgeting and break-even analysis

A break-even graph represents, in diagrammatic form, the possibilities open to management in their output decision-making. With a flexible budget the break-even graph is recast in columnar form usually on a spreadsheet. Indeed, modern computer spreadsheet packages make the process of flexible budgeting very straightforward (see Chapter 14).

A flexible budget is a translation of a break-even graph into a statement of revenue and costs at various specified output levels. These output levels will be set at discrete intervals which may or may not include either the points of break-even or the positions of maximum profit. The purpose of a flexible budget is that it permits the creation of different operational budgets based upon different output-level assumptions. These operational budgets can be consolidated later into the master budget. This procedure allows management to measure the sensitivity of the master budget to different output-level assumptions.

For example, Almeria plc has completed a detailed analysis of its components of total production cost. The variable and fixed costs of production are as follows:

Variable component cost	£25.10
Variable labour charge	£33.40
Variable overheads	£8.40
Total fixed cost (0– 499 units)	£69 780.00
(500– 999 units)	£94 780.00
(1000–1499 units)	£119 780.00

A flexible budget at incremental levels of output of 200 units would then appear as follows:

	Output level						
	200	400	600	800	1 000	1 200	1 400
Total revenue (£)	54 000	100 000	138 000	168 000	190 000	204 000	210 000
Variable component cost (£)	(5 020)	(10 040)	(15 060)	(20 080)	(25 100)	(30 120)	(35 140)
Variable labour charge (£)	(6 680)	(13 360)	(20 040)	(26 720)	(33 400)	(40 080)	(46 760)
Variable overheads (£)	(1 680)	(3 360)	(5 040)	(6 720)	(8 400)	(10 080)	(11 760)
Total fixed cost (£)	(69 780)	(69 780)	(94 780)	(94 780)	(119 780)	(119 780)	(119 780)
Profit/(loss) (£)	(29 160)	(3 460)	3 080	19 700	3 320	3 940	(3 400)

Total revenues have been derived from Almeria's demand curve given the specified output levels.

Note, however, that the flexible budget has lost a lot of the information contained in the original break-even graph although numerical analysis will give more precise results than can be read from a graph. We will discover, in Chapter 9, the usefulness of flexible budgeting as a method of restating budgets under different output assumptions and as a method for determining whether differences between actual and budgeted figures are due to changes in overall output level or due to changes in the efficiency with which resources are used.

Note: If you have access to a computer spreadsheet package such as 'Visicalc', 'Supercalc' or 'Perfect Calc' you may like to recreate the flexible budget for Almeria plc.

Summary

In this chapter we have examined the problems and methods of making short-term output decisions. The choice of output level for a particular process in a given period is an important part of a firm's budgeting procedure. In Fig. 5.14 we summarize the main components of, and influences upon, the output decision as management builds up its operational budgets for short-term output.

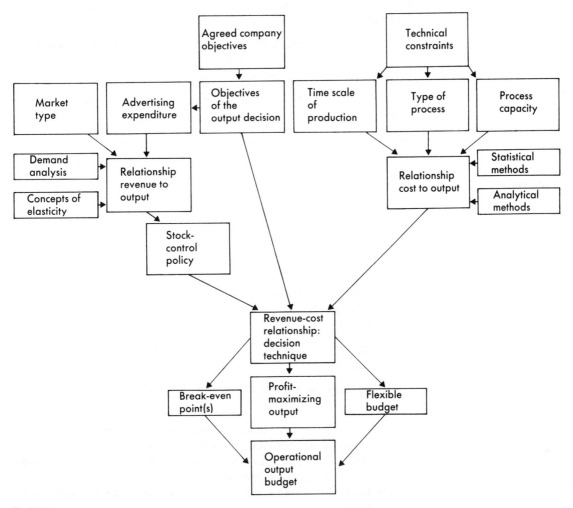

Fig 5.14

Both break-even analysis and marginal techniques have a useful role to play in this area of decision-making. However, it is important to remember that break-even analysis is not an optimizing procedure but is, rather, a graphical portrayal of the consequences of the output possibilities open to management.

Supplementary reading

CARSBERG, B. V., *Economics of Business Decisions*, Penguin, 1975.

PAPPAS, J. L., BRIGHAM, E. F., and SHIPLEY, B., *Managerial Economics* (UK Edn), Holt, Rinehart and Winston, 1983. Especially Chapters 5 and 6.

VICKERS, D., On the economics of break-even, reprinted in Anton, H. R., and Firmin, P. A. (eds), *Contemporary Issues in Cost Accounting*, Houghton Mifflin, 1972.

WILLSON, J. D., Practical applications of cost–volume–profit analysis, reprinted in Anton, H. R., and Firmin, P. A. (eds), *Contemporary Issues in Cost Accounting*, Houghton Mifflin, 1972.

WONNACOTT, R. J., AND WONNACOTT, T. H., *Econometrics*, Wiley, 1970.

WOOD, D., and FILDES, R., *Forecasting for Business*, Longman, 1976.

Questions

1   Sketch the following types of cost–output relationship and give at least one example of a typical cost for each.
   (a) Fixed cost.
   (b) Directly variable cost.
   (c) Semivariable cost.
   (d) Stepped fixed cost.
   (e) Stepped variable cost.
   (f) Ratchet cost.

2   A company faces a demand curve for one of its products which is of the form:

   price per unit = 300 − 0.1 × quantity demanded

   Required:
   (a) Draw a table of (i) price, (ii) quantity, (iii) total revenue, (iv) marginal revenue, and (v) point elasticity of demand at intervals along the demand curve. Identify in your table the point at which total revenue is maximized.
   (b) Comment upon the relevance of a company's demand curve to its output decision.

3 Figure 5.15 shows a break-even graph for a coated paper production process. Identify the following items on the graph:
   (a) Total-revenue function.
   (b) Fixed cost.
   (c) Directly variable cost.
   (d) Semivariable cost.
   (e) Material cost with discounts.
   (f) The points of break even.
   Sketch a profitgram on the break-even curve.

Fig 5.15

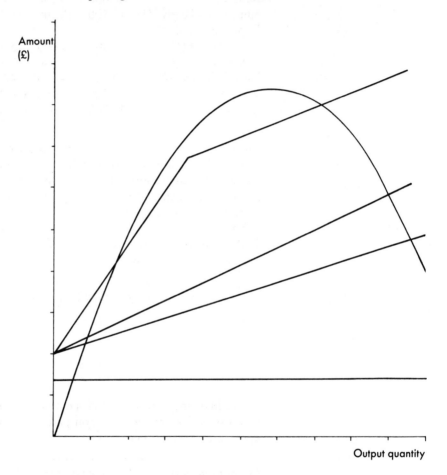

4 Records of catering costs have been kept for the last five years along with the number of cooked meals provided in the Upmarket Polytechnic's refectory. The polytechnic's Refectory Users Consultative Committee has asked for an estimate of the total annual fixed costs and the average variable cost per meal provided (as at 1 January 19X6).
   Wage rates for refectory staff were increased by 10 per cent on 1 January 19X3 and a further 10 per cent was made at the beginning of 19X6. The cost items marked by the asterisk have tended to

increase in line with the Retail Price Index which has averaged 16 per cent per annum over the period.

	Year ended 31 December				
	19X1	19X2	19X3	19X4	19X5
Food* (£)	26 200	70 000	103 000	103 500	119 800
Wages (£)	35 400	82 000	139 000	141 000	162 900
Rent (£)	20 000	20 000	20 000	20 000	20 000
Sundry overheads* (£)	17 500	18 000	18 500	19 000	20 000
Depreciation of equipment (£)	5 000	5 000	5 000	5 000	5 000
Office salaries (£)	6 000	7 000	7 500	8 000	9 000
Heat, light, etc. (£)	4 000	4 500	4 700	4 800	4 800
Sales revenue (£)	120 000	308 000	540 000	510 000	736 000
Meals sold	110 000	300 000	550 000	480 000	680 000

5   The Owen Steel works in Sussex produces steel strip on a continuous process. The molten steel is extruded through dies as it cools from red heat to a dull yellow colour. The steel is then pressed into shape and water quenched. It finally emerges from the process tempered to a light blue colour.

This steel-die process can be operated at any level in the range 10 000–20 000 m of steel strip per production run. The variable and fixed costs are as follows:

	Per metre final product (£)
Iron ore	1.20
Scrap iron	0.25
Energy	1.80
Labour	2.25

A certain quantity of scrap steel is required to prime the process and this costs £8500 irrespective of output. The fixed costs of production apply over certain ranges:

Output (metres)	Fixed cost (£)
0– 4 999	10 000
5 000– 9 999	17 500
10 000–14 999	25 000
15 000–19 999	35 000
20 000–24 999	47 500

Over the range of output specified, the sales revenue is constant at £8.10 per metre.

Required:
(a) Draw a break-even chart for the steel-making process outlined
    above and identify, within the specified range of output, both
    the points of break-even and the profit-maximizing output.
(b) Comment upon the assumptions implicit in break-even analysis
    and discuss the general usefulness of break-even analysis in
    output decision-making.
(c) Construct a flexible budget at 10 000 m output rising to 20 000 m
    in intervals of 2000 m.

6 A company in the mining industry has monitored its average annual
   productivity for a particular class of labour. The average pretax
   earnings per labour hour have also been collected for this class of
   labour. During the course of the latest round of wage negotiations,
   the employees' union has maintained that productivity is unrelated
   to earnings. Management believes otherwise. The relevant figures for
   the previous six years are:

Year to 31 December	Net earnings (£)	Average productivity per labour hour (tons)
19X1	800 500	16.2
19X2	910 100	16.4
19X3	922 000	17.3
19X4	977 000	17.4
19X5	1 050 000	17.7
19X6	1 100 000	17.7

Note the following points:
 (i) Wages have kept pace with the annual rate of increase in the
     Retail Price Index which has averaged 5 per cent over the period.
(ii) There was an additional increase of 5 per cent over the Retail
     Price Index from 1 January 19X4.

Required:
(a) Advise the negotiators on the relationship between annual net
    earnings and average productivity per man hour. Support your
    advice with any statistical techniques which you think
    appropriate.
(b) Discuss the way in which labour costs could be expected to vary
    with output level.

7 A company has derived a demand curve for its product:

$$price = 10\,000 - 4Q$$

From the technical plant specification, the total cost of producing
this product can be expressed by the relationship:

$$total\ cost = 240\,000 + 180Q$$

where Q is the quantity produced. It is assumed, because of the short shelf life of the product, that the quantity produced must be matched with the amount demanded.

Required:

(a) Draw a break-even graph and a profitgram for the above product.
(b) Derive, analytically, the point of optimum output and position this point on your break-even graph.
(c) Comment upon the assumptions implicit in any of the techniques which you have employed in parts (a) and (b) above.

Mathematical note

Any equation relating one variable to another can be expressed upon a graph. For example, quantity produced can be related to profit, to cost or to revenue. The graph will reveal certain things to us. It will show us the point at which the curve relating one variable with another crosses the axes of the graph, it will also give us a visual representation of the rate of change of one variable with the other. The rate of change can be visualized as the slope of the graph at any point.

In Fig. 5.16 we show a total-cost curve. Total cost is the dependent variable (we have plotted it on the y axis of the graph) and output quantity is the independent variable (plotted on the x axis of the graph). Total cost is termed the 'dependent variable' because its value depends upon the quantity produced.

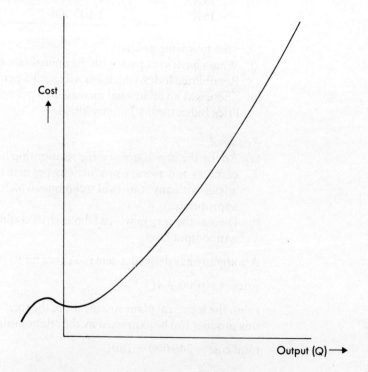

Fig 5.16 A cost curve of function
$C = 2500 + 15Q + 10Q^3$

Cost

Output (Q) →

The cost curve in Fig. 5.16 can be represented by the equation:

$$C = 2500 + 15Q + 10Q^3$$

Notice, as we move through the curve from left to right, that the slope of the curve changes at each point along its length. From the chapter you should now know that the increase in total cost brought about by a small change in output quantity is called the 'marginal cost'. The marginal cost is, therefore, the slope of the total-cost curve at any point and its value will change as we progress along the curve. There is a very simple technique for deriving the equation for the slope of a curve at any point along its length from the basic total-cost equation given above. Written out fully, the total-cost equation above is:

$$C = 2500Q^0 + 15Q^1 + 10Q^3$$

We have included the implied power of each Q term in the equation and given that:

$$Q^0 = 1$$

we have inserted this as the implied Q term after the 2500 (any variable raised to the power zero equals one).

The rules for deriving the equation for the slope of the above curve are:

- Take each term in Q to the right-hand side of the equation and each term in C to the left (this has already been done in this case).

- Take each term on the right-hand side of the equation and multiply the coefficients by the power of the Q variable.
  So:

$$2500 \times 0 = 0$$
$$15 \times 1 = 15$$
$$10 \times 3 = 30$$

These values become the coefficients of the new Q terms on the right-hand side of the slope equation.

- Take each term on the right-hand side of the equation and reduce the power of the Q variable by 1. So:

$$Q^0 \rightarrow Q^{-1}$$
$$Q^1 \rightarrow Q^0 \quad (= 1)$$
$$Q^3 \rightarrow Q^2$$

These become the new Q terms on the right-hand side of the slope equation.

Therefore:

$$\text{slope} = (0 \times Q^{-1}) + (15 \times Q^0) + (30 \times Q^2)$$
$$= 0 + (15 \times 1) + (30 \times Q^2)$$
$$= 15 + 30Q^2$$

Finally, the slope is symbolized as:

$$\frac{dC}{dQ} = \text{slope}$$

dC/dQ is referred to as 'the first differential of C with respect to Q and is the change in C brought about by a very tiny (in fact infinitesimally small) change in the output quantity.

The result of our analysis is that the first differential of cost with respect to quantity (the gradient of the cost curve) changes as Q changes:

$$\frac{dC}{dQ} = 15 + 30Q^2$$

We can do the same type of exercise on all sorts of examples:

Basic equation

$$C = 2500 + 60Q^2 + 3Q^{-2}$$

Add implied terms

$$C = 2500Q^0 + 60Q^2 + 3Q^2$$

Modify coefficients $2500 \times 0 = 0$ $60 \times 2 = 120$ $3 \times -2 = -6$

Modify powers Q^{-1} Q^1 Q^{-3}

Differential

$$\frac{dC}{dQ} = 0 \times Q^{-1} + 120 \times Q^1 + (-6) \times Q^{-3}$$
$$= 120Q - 6Q^{-3}$$

This technique we have shown is an application of the 'chain rule' in the differential calculus. A mathematical text will explain to you how the rule itself is derived, but for all practical purposes the derivation of the rule is unimportant. What matters is that you can successfully apply the rule in any situation.

In the chapter we pointed out an extremely important property of the slope of a curve. That is, the slope of any equation is zero when it is at a maximum, a minimum or a point of inflexion. We show examples of each of these points in Fig. 5.17. At such a turning point on a graph the slope will be zero. For example, if

$$\frac{dC}{dQ} = 15 + 30Q^2$$

at the graph's turning point:

$$15 + 30Q^2 = 0$$

i.e.

$$Q = +0.7071 \text{ and } -0.7071$$

Fig 5.17 Turning points
on a cost curve

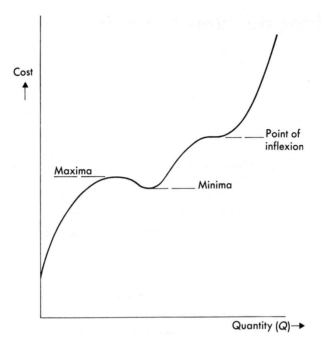

However, without drawing the graph we cannot tell whether these
turning points are maxima, minima or points of inflexion. The calculus
does give us a method of determining the nature of the turning point.
To do this, derive the slope of the slope equation by reapplying the chain
rule to the first differential and see if the 'second differential' is:

negative—maxima,
positive—minima,
zero—point of inflexion.

For example:
Basic equation

$$C = 2500 + 15Q + 10Q^3$$

First differential

$$\frac{dC}{dQ} = 15 + 30Q^2$$

Second differential

$$\frac{d^2C}{dQ^2} = 60Q$$

When $Q = +0.7071$ then d^2C/dQ^2 is positive and we have a minimum
and when $Q = -0.7071$ the second differential is negative and we have
a maximum. Again this is a rule which is derived in many standard
mathematical texts. For our purposes, it only needs to be remembered
and applied.

6 The pricing decision

In this chapter we consider the problems of pricing in different types of markets and the contribution the management accountant can make to the pricing decision.

By the end of this chapter you should understand:

- The role of the market in determining price.
- The problems with simple cost-based pricing procedures.
- How to set the minimum price for a product.
- The problems of setting a price for the sale of a product or service under contract.
- How to determine the market size and type for a particular product.

The pricing decision is the most complex area of short-term decision-making. As we have emphasized before, in most situations the price of a product is determined by factors outside the firm's immediate control. The principal determining factor of price is the supply and demand for the product concerned. More specifically, the following factors all have an important bearing upon the pricing decision:

- The ability of the firm to differentiate in the eyes of its customers its own products from the products of its competitors.

- The advertising and other marketing methods which the firm uses to alter the tastes of its customers.

- The credit facilities and other terms of trade (such as guarantees and after-sales service) which the firm can offer its customers.

- The ability of the firm to minimize its transaction costs in selling its products and its willingness to pass on the cost savings to its customers in the form of lower prices.

The role of the market in determining price

We learn from microeconomic theory that the assumptions of economic rationality on the part of suppliers and consumers lead us, *a priori*, to anticipate a downward sloping relationship between price and demand for a given product. Conversely, we would expect firms to attempt to supply more of a product the higher its price. The supply curve for a particular product should, therefore, represent an upward-sloping relationship between quantity and price. In Fig. 6.1 we show these two relationships superimposed upon one another. p_e is the price and Q_e is the output level for a particular product when its demand and supply are in equilibrium.

Fig 6.1 Supply and demand at equilibrium

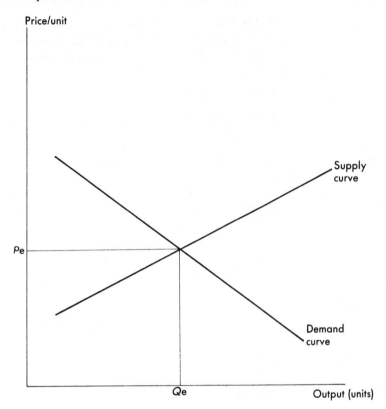

The two curves in Fig. 6.1 represent the supply and demand for a product in the context of its total market. The firm, with which the management accountant is concerned, must judge the degree of control the firm's management holds over the position and slope of the supply curve and the influence it possesses over the slope and position of the product's demand curve.

> *Note:* Each producing firm has its own supply curve and faces a demand curve which represents the prices it can get for the quantity it can sell. Depending on the circumstances (which we will explain later) the individual supply and demand curves may be quite different from those applying to the 'industry' as a whole. The industry supply curve represents the total supply of the product from all producing firms and the industry demand curve represents the total demand for that product in the market.

We can characterize the type of product market which a firm faces according to:

- The number of suppliers in the market.

- The number of buyers or consumers in the market.

- The type of product (i.e. whether it is a uniform commodity, one unit of which cannot be distinguished from another, or whether it is a product which can be given special characteristics which will separate it from the competition).

- The barriers to entry for potential new competitors in the market.

- The degree of discretion which the management of the supplying firm has over the product's price.

In the table below we show the six principal categories of market:

	Number of suppliers	Number of consumers	Barriers to entry	Supplier's discretion over price	Product type
Perfect competition	Many	Many	None	None	Homogeneous
Monopolistic competition	Many	Many	Low	Some	Heterogeneous
Monopoly	One	Many	High	Very high	Homogeneous
Oligopolistic competition	Few	Many	Significant	Considerable	Homogeneous/ heterogeneous
Monopsony	More than one	One	High	Some	Homogeneous
Bilateral monopsony	One	One	High	Some	Homogeneous

The assumption that managers will always attempt to maximize their discretion leads to the consequence that they will seek the greatest degree of monopoly power possible within the markets in which they operate.

In a situation of perfect competition the producing firm is a price taker and, even though the demand for the total supply of the product within the market will be downward sloping, the individual firm will face a flat demand curve where price is independent of output quantity. In this situation the firm can do nothing to affect the price of its product and should set its output level at the point where the increase in total cost incurred through producing one extra unit of output (the product's marginal cost) is equal to marginal revenue which is, in this case, the market price per unit at all output levels.

This analysis of the behaviour of a producer in a perfectly competitive market assumes that producers and consumers are physically very close to one another. In practice, of course, many producers are physically separated from their point of sale, in which case such producers will have to include their transport costs in their marginal cost of production. Similarly, if other transaction costs are incurred (perhaps through the use of middlemen, wholesalers or brokers in the market) then those transaction costs must also be included as part of the cost of production.

The role of the management accountant in a perfect market is constrained to establishing three facts concerning the product:

- The price of the product, which will be in a state of continual change (see Chapter 2).

- The marginal cost of the product concerned.

- Any transaction costs incurred in selling the product.

Management, in its search for some degree of monopoly power, will attempt, as far as possible, to differentiate its product(s) from the competition. In the retail trade, for example, producers often attempt to create a distinction between their products and those of their competitors by some minor physical modification. Such modifications might be achieved through different packaging, brand advertising or any other marketing ploys that the firm can dream up. The firm's intention is to create some sense of brand identification in the consumer's mind which will lead to a situation where higher prices can be charged than would otherwise be the case. The type of market where products are differentiated in minor ways is called 'monopolistic competition'. Naturally, if a producer manages to reap exceptional profits in the short term we would expect competitors to move into the market as the barriers to entry are typically quite low.

A monopolistically competitive firm faces a downward-sloping demand curve for its product although it may be highly price-elastic (remember that in a perfectly competitive market each producer faces a perfectly price-elastic demand curve). Consequently, such a firm faces both a downward-sloping demand curve and a downward-sloping marginal-revenue function, and maximizes its profits when marginal revenue equals marginal cost.

In the short run, a producer in a monopolistically competitive market will be able to take advantage of the benefits of product differentiation and make greater than normal profits (where by 'profit' we mean economic and not accounting profit—see Chapter 4). One strategy for doing this is to reduce output in order to gain a higher price. Indeed, simple economic analysis indicates that the optimizing price–output combination for a firm with a competitive advantage will be set at a lower output than would be the case if that firm were in a perfectly competitive market.

Monopoly is that situation where barriers to entry are so high that potential competitiors are dissuaded from entering a particular market. A monopolistic firm is, effectively, the 'industry' for the supply of the product concerned. Again, as with the two previous market types, the monopolist should set a price–output combination which equates marginal revenue with marginal cost. As with monopolistic competition, the optimal position for a pure monopolist will be at a lower output level than would hold if the product was supplied through the medium of a perfectly competitive market.

Monopolies occur for a number of reasons:

- Because some technical barrier exists which would impose unacceptably high set-up costs for a potential competitor. For example, in the early 1980s the US Government through NASA held a monopoly on satellite-recovery services. At the time, only the USA had the technology in the form of the Space Shuttle to track and recover damaged or off-course satellites. The costs which would be faced by any potential competitor would be prohibitively high even if a viable market for such services could be established.

- Because the government believes (for public policy reasons) that certain products should be supplied by the state or under state control. For example, the government in the UK and in most other countries as well, is a monopoly supplier of defence and policing (although in the latter case certain aspects of police work are available from specialist security firms).

- Because the grant of a patent or copyright has given a producer the legal right to monopoly selling of his or her product. Such a legal monopoly right is usually granted for a fixed number of years only.

- Because certain products or services are held under monopoly control by the government. For example, in the UK the government controls (or has controlled in the past) either directly or through the medium of public corporations such services as telecommunications, the post, gas, electricity and water.

Oligopoly, along with monopolistic competition, forms by far and away the most usual market situation. Oligopoly exists where a few large firms (relative to the market's size) account for a large proportion of the total supply of the product concerned. There may be a large number of smaller firms in the market as well, although they will be price takers and of little significance in the context of the market as a whole. The existence of a small group of large, competing firms makes oligopoly a very interesting market type. Oligopolies are interesting because they permit the possibility of collusion (overt and covert) between the participants and also the possibility of interdependent reactions which have more to do with psychology than economics. It is in oligopolies (and in monopolistically competitive markets to a lesser extent) that competitive action, in the colloquial sense, can be fiercest. In perfect markets, competition is automatic and almost inhuman. Indeed, the great Scottish economist, Adam Smith, referred to such market mechanisms as the 'operation of an invisible hand'. With oligopolies it is just the opposite.

Oligopolies can occur through geographical factors. For example, petrol stations within a particular vicinity can form a small oligopoly for the supply of petrol and other motor products. Many trading situations exist where such localized oligopolies can form. At the other extreme, the clearing banks and the major oil companies have arisen as national oligopolies in the UK.

Two particular phenomena associated with oligopolies, and to a lesser extent monopolistic competition, are relevant to the management accountant. These phenomena are, first, the role of advertising and its effect upon the demand curve for a product and, second, the problem of 'sticky' prices.

The role of advertising and other methods of product promotion

In perfectly competitive and monopolistic markets there is little incentive to advertise. Advertising is principally a marketing technique for the oligopolistic or monopolistically competitive firm. Advertising serves a number of functions:

- It can be used to inform potential consumers of a new product and to give details of the product's price, function and physical characteristics.

- Advertising can be used to alter the shape of the product's demand curve. Usually, advertising will be used to push the demand curve to the right and to make the demand for the product less elastic. A steeper demand curve (i.e. a less elastic demand curve) will give a higher marginal revenue and therefore increase the maximum profit at constant marginal cost. In practice this increased profit will be partly offset by the increased advertising costs so incurred.

- Advertising can be used to create product differentiation by stressing a product's virtues compared with the competition.

- Advertising can be used to create a brand image and brand loyalty. Much advertising is directed at the individual who is already an established customer for the firm's products. Some advertising is also aimed at reducing the 'cognitive dissonance' (see below) of customers after sale. Many people feel uncomfortable after a major purchase and actively seek out reinforcing advertising for the product concerned.

Note: If consumers act according to the rules of economic rationality, we would expect them to forget about the cost of a particular purchase once it had been made. However, in practice, most people find that the purchase of relatively expensive goods can lead to a state of internal conflict as they question whether they have used the money involved in a sensible way. Social psychologists argue that individuals seek means of reducing this internal conflict or 'dissonance' hence the need for reinforcing advertising. In fact we can identify two phases of conflict before and after a decision is made to purchase a particular product. First, there is a phase of predecisional conflict as the consumer attempts to reconcile the conflicting claims upon his or her resources. Second, there is a phase of post-decisional conflict—the cognitive dissonance referred to above—as the individual attempts to subdue the feeling of 'maybe not having done the right thing'. This problem is often made worse because many consumption decisions involve 'hot cognitive processes', i.e. stressful decisions made under some sort of selling pressure.

Fig 6.2 Demand shifts with advertising

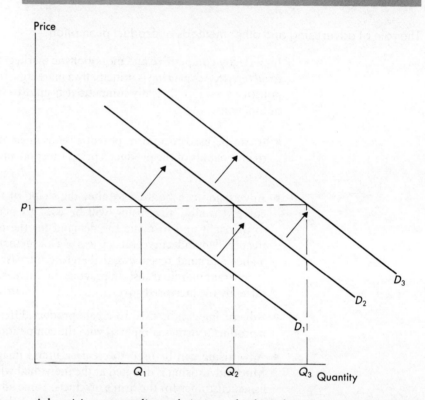

Advertising expenditure brings a further dimension to the price–demand relationship. In Fig. 6.2 we show the effect of different levels of advertising expenditure upon sales and the different demand curves which follow.

The practical analysis of demand relationships can be carried out using historical price–quantity–advertising data and the technique of multiple regression analysis. The details of this technique are beyond the scope of this book. If you are interested in pursuing this topic the further reading at the end of this chapter will be of help.

Sticky prices

The phenomenon of sticky prices is found in oligopolistic markets where there is often considerable resistance to downward movement in prices.

This resistance can be apparent even in the face of changes in demand or government action such as changes in the ease with which credit can be obtained.

To understand the problem of sticky prices, consider the situation of a single oligopolistic competitor who decides, unilaterally, to cut the price of the product concerned. If none of the other competitors were to respond and follow the price decrease the price-cutting competitor might be able to increase both market share and total revenue (although this would depend on the point elasticity of demand facing the price-cutting firm at that point in time). However, it would be unusual for competing firms not to take some form of retaliatory action in order to hold their respective market shares. It is very unlikely that a price-cutting firm would be able to gain a real volume increase from a cut in price; therefore, downward price movements will be along a relatively price-inelastic demand curve.

On the other hand, if our single competitor were, unilaterally, to increase the price of the product concerned, especially if it was a real price increase, i.e. one over and above that justified by the rate of inflation, then the other competitors would be unlikely to follow suit. As a consequence, price increases tend to follow a relatively elastic demand curve. The oligopolistic competitor is faced by two demand curves: one, which is relatively inelastic, governs price reductions and the other, which is relatively elastic, governs price increases. In effect, therefore, the oligopolist faces a 'kinked demand curve', with the kink at the current price–output relationship (Fig. 6.3).

Fig 6.3 'Kinked' demand curve P_0 = the price at which the current sales quantity Q_0 is sold

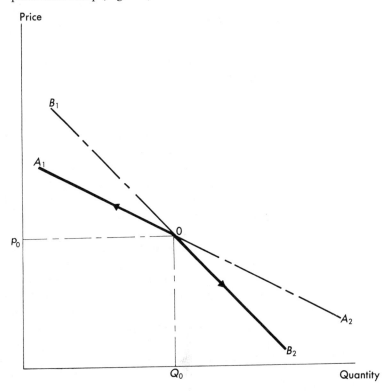

At the producer's current price–quantity relationship downward price movements will be along the section 0, B_2 of demand curve B_1, B_2. Likewise, price increases will be along the more elastic demand curve A_1, A_2. These two demand curves will give rise to two different, intersecting total-revenue curves and, therefore, at the firm's current output level, to a 'mobile discontinuity'. At whatever level the firm chooses to sell its product or service it will face one demand curve for subsequent price decreases and another for subsequent price increases. In other words, the 'kink' in the demand curve will follow price changes as they are made. This discontinuity in the firm's total-revenue function adds a further level of possible sophistication to the break-even analysis developed in the last chapter.

The kinked demand-curve model goes some way toward explaining why some products (such as motor-cars for example) change price infrequently while other products (such as commodities and ordinary shares for example) change price almost by the minute. A number of other models have been developed which attempt to explain how oligopolies behave. Some models are based upon theories of price leadership, where one firm traditionally sets the price and the other competitors follow suit. Other theories assume interdependencies in behaviour as each competitor attempts to take into account the behaviour of other firms in the market.

> **Self test:** The major clearing banks change their base rates in the light of economic events and in the light of one another's behaviour. In addition, they alter their charges on personal accounts in concert with one another. Gather any evidence that you can which supports this behaviour. Is there any bank which consistently appears to be a price leader?

One of the most sophisticated attempts to deal with the problem of oligopolies uses the Theory of Games developed by the two mathematicians von Neumann and Morgenstern. This approach is based upon the idea that in every competitive situation between two or more 'players' each will act in the most rational way. Indeed, it may well be that in certain situations the most rational action will be to deceive the other player by making an irrational choice! In an oligopolistic situation, the game played is, in the terminology of games theory, a 'zero-sum game' where the gains of one competitor will be the loss of the other (assuming, of course, a constant total market). Each competitor can build up a table of payoffs which follow from each possible action it can take given the possible retaliatory move of the opposition. Certain strategies can then be followed which dictate the action the competitor should take. The readings given at the end of this chapter will help you if you wish to pursue this topic.

We will defer discussion of monopsony and bilateral monopsony until we deal with contract pricing later in this chapter.

Problems with simple cost-based pricing procedures

Most firms who survive for any length of time in a competitive market must recognize the impact of their market situation upon the prices they can charge. However, many managers would appear, by their behaviour, to believe that an important component of the pricing decision is the so-called 'full cost of production'. A number of full-costing techniques exist although most are just simple variants of the two main types we will discuss:

- Cost plus pricing.
- Target rate of return pricing.

Cost plus pricing

With cost plus pricing the price of a product is built up from the sum of:

- The variable costs of production.
- A proportion of the firm's long-run costs (which will be fixed in the short term).
- A specified margin which is usually set as a proportion of the total costs derived for the product.

Example: Almeria's monthly production figures for typewriters are as follows:

Variable components cost	£25.10 per unit
Variable labour cost	£33.40 per unit
Variable overheads	£8.40 per unit
	£66.90 per unit
Total labour hours in production	4000 hours
Total fixed cost at a planned output of 800 units	£94 780.00

Almeria's management would like to set its prices at such a level that a 20 per cent profit is made on full cost. It is company policy to allocate fixed overheads on the basis of the labour hours employed in production:

The unit price per typewriter will be made up as follows:

$$\text{cost} \begin{cases} \text{variable cost per unit produced} \\ + \\ \text{fixed cost allocated to each unit produced} \end{cases}$$
$$+$$
$$\text{percentage of fixed plus variable cost per unit}$$
$$=$$
$$\text{price per unit}$$

This technique is straightforward except for the calculation of the fixed-cost allocation per unit. In Almeria's case, management has decided that the appropriate allocation base is the number of labour hours in production. In practice, any base could be used for allocating the fixed overhead charge. Depending upon the circumstances and the nature of the fixed overheads, machine hours used or floor space occupied by the production facility might be more appropriate. With a labour-intensive process, for example, an overhead allocation based upon labour hours employed in production might be deemed most appropriate. On the other hand, a capital-intensive process which uses expensive equipment in production may indicate an allocation based upon machine hours employed in production.

The allocated overhead charge per unit is calculated as follows:

$$\text{fixed overhead charge per unit} = \frac{\text{total fixed overhead to be allocated}}{\text{total labour hours employed in production}} \times \frac{\text{number of labour hours required to produce each unit}}{}$$

which for Almeria gives:

$$\text{fixed overhead charge per unit} = \frac{94780}{4000} \times 5 = \pounds118.48 \text{ per unit}$$

Therefore, the cost per typewriter produced is:

Variable component cost	£25.10
Variable labour cost	£33.40
Variable overhead cost	£8.40
Allocated fixed overhead charge	£118.48
Full production cost	£185.38
Plus mark-up at 20 per cent	£37.07
Price per unit	£222.45

The use of the particular cost-plus formula laid down by Almeria's management gives a price per typewriter of £222.45. Before we consider the implications of this pricing policy, we will outline the method of pricing using target rates of return.

Target rate of return pricing

Example: Upon further consideration, Almeria's management decides that the most appropriate pricing policy would be one which returns, at the targeted monthly output of 800 typewriters, a rate of return on capital employed of 10 per cent per annum. Almeria's total capital employed in its typewriter business is £2 495 000 and the expected total cost of typewriter production for the year is expected to be £1 450 580.

This method of pricing is similar to the cost-plus method outlined above except that the mark-up applied to cost is based upon the desired rate of return on capital employed rather than upon a simple rate applied to cost.

A target rate of return 10 per cent per annum means that on a total capital employed of £2 495 000 a profit of £249 500 must be earned as:

$$\text{rate of return on capital employed} = \frac{\text{annual net profit}}{\text{capital employed}} \times 100$$

therefore:

annual net profit = rate of return on capital employed/100 × capital employed

$$= 0.1 \times 2\,495\,000$$

$$= £249\,500$$

From this we can calculate that on total typewriter production a profit mark-up of 17.2 per cent will be required as:

$$\text{percentage mark-up} = \frac{\text{target profit}}{\text{total production cost}} \times 100$$

$$= \frac{249\,500}{1\,450\,580} \times 100$$

$$= 17.2 \text{ per cent}$$

Using this rate of mark-up we can calculate the price per typewriter as follows:

Variable component cost	£25.10
Variable labour cost	£33.40
Variable overheads	£8.40
Allocated fixed cost	£118.48
Full cost	£185.38
Plus: mark-up to give a 10 per cent rate of return on capital employed, 185.38 × 0.172	£31.89
Price per unit	£217.27

The question which now remains is how do these two pricing systems compare with a pricing policy based upon a knowledge of the firm's demand curve. From the last chapter we know that Almeria's demand curve is given by the formula:

$$p = 290 - 0.1Q$$

where p and Q are the price per unit and the number of units output, respectively.

The demand curve indicates that a planned output of 800 units can be sold at a price of £210 per unit as:

$$p = 290 - 0.1 \times 800$$

$$= £210$$

At this price Almeria will earn a total revenue from sales of:

$$\text{total revenue} = £210 \times 800$$

$$= £168\,000$$

In the table below we compare this result with that obtained using both the cost-plus and the target rate of return formulae.

	Market pricing	Cost-plus	Rate of return
Price per unit (£)	210.00	222.45	217.27
Number sold using the formula:			
$p = 290 - 0.1Q$ (units)	800	675.50	727.30
Total revenue (£)	168 000.00	150 264.97	158 020.47
Total cost of production (£)	148 300 00	139 970.95	143 436.37
Net profit (£)	19 700.00	10 294.02	14 584.10

In each case, the total cost of production is calculated as:

total cost = total unit cost × quantity produced + fixed costs

Using Almeria's demand curve we have calculated the level of output which will be sold at each price. Given the output level and the price it is then a straightforward matter to calculate the total revenue.

Clearly, pricing a product without understanding the reaction of market demand to its price cannot guarantee that the best price will be obtained for a given output level. However, many managers (and management accountants) advocate cost-based pricing techniques, or variants of them, for pricing in practice. A number of reasons can be put forward for this behaviour:

- It is sometimes suggested that it is often impossible to determine the shape of a product's demand curve in the time in which a pricing decision must be made. This argument has particular force in rapidly changing markets such as the fashion industry or the pharmaceutical industry. It may also be that a producer racing to get a new product onto the market before the competition may not be able to draw up a demand curve for the product concerned in the time available.

- Another argument which is often put forward points out that a firm's prices, in the long run, must cover its fixed costs of production or the business will not be viable. However, as we have seen in Almeria's example above, the company would clearly have done better, in the long run, to price the product at the price which would just clear its total production. In fact, we could argue that fixed-formula pricing will lead management to forget the linkage which always exists between pricing and output decisions in practice.

- A more sophisticated argument sometimes put forward claims that fixed-formula pricing is an imperfect attempt to reach the 'economic' price for a product in a competitive environment where zero economic profits will be earned. Full cost, in this case, will include, in a very approximate way, the opportunity cost of all the scarce resources involved in production including those attributable to the entrepreneurial skills of senior management (the allocated fixed cost) and the cost of the capital employed in production (the profit mark-up).

This last argument has some force, in that it may give some economic justification for the fact that many firms who apparently use inferior pricing rules still manage to survive in competitive environments. However, at best, fixed-price formulae can only provide a rough and ready approximation to the price which a company should, in the light of economic theory, charge for its products. Understanding the role of the market in the pricing decision will indicate areas in which new information can be profitably gathered for a particular product. It should focus management's attention upon the relationship between price and output within the context of the firm's product markets.

Setting the minimum price for a product

Up to this point we have discussed the problem of determining the price at which a product will sell and clear the firm's chosen level of production. Analytically, the price–output combination for a producer is found where marginal revenue equals marginal cost, although this rule depends upon rather restrictive assumptions which may not always represent reality. However, the question often arises as to what is the minimum price below which production is no longer worth while. In perfect product markets there is little problem. The perfectly competitive firm cannot expect to make, in the long run, a return in excess of its full opportunity cost of production. An inefficient firm will be forced out of such a market because, in the long term, its opportunity cost of production will exceed its total revenue.

In reality, market perfection rarely exists and where it does it is rarely more than a transient market phenomenon. Market imperfection generally means that some opportunity exists for producers to make economic profits, i.e. some surplus over their full opportunity cost of production. In this situation, the opportunity cost of production represents the minimum threshold price below which production will not be worth while.

In Chapter 3 we outlined a method for determining the opportunity cost of decisions with short-term implications. We defined opportunity cost as the net cash change to the decision-making entity which results from choosing one particular course of action. However, this definition of the opportunity-cost concept only applies to decisions which have short-term consequences. The opportunity cost of a long-term decision must also include the effect of differences in the timing of future cash flows.

No simple short-run criterion exists for establishing a minimum viable price for a product, because the question of product viability is invariably a long-run decision while the pricing decision is governed by short-term market factors.

However, as we shall see, the same argument need not apply where a sale is made under contract. With most contract sales the production implications are often only of a short-term nature.

Pricing contracts

In the introduction to this chapter we introduced two types of market which involved a single buyer. In the first case, where there is more than one seller, we have a 'monopsony'; in the second case, with only one seller, we have a 'bilateral monopsony'. In the first case selling usually proceeds through the submission of tenders which, in most situations, involves the submission of sealed bids. In the second case negotiation proceeds through offer and counteroffer in the light of the seller's perception of the buyer's 'ability to pay' and the buyer's perception of the seller's lowest acceptable price. In Chapter 10 we will discuss the information requirements of this second market type when we consider the needs of management (and employees) in the commonest example of bilateral monopsony—wage bargaining.

Monopsony (where there is a single buyer and more than one seller) occurs in the following situations:

- In central and local government where contracts for public services are offered for tender by potential suppliers. Defence contracts are a particular example of this.

- Where a certain industry is itself under monopoly, or near monopoly control. For example, the railways, postal services and public utilities, such as electricity, gas and water, are nationalized concerns in the UK. Organization of this type act as monopsonist buyers of the specialized goods and services which they require.

- Where a particular individual or firm holds the patent or copyright on a particular product which can be made on its behalf by one or more suppliers.

The usual procedure for supply in a monopsony market is for the monopsonist to publish an invitation to tender. In the case of a local government contract, for example, this invitation may be published in the local and national newspapers. A private firm, on the other hand, may be more selective and publish in a trade journal or magazine or simply write to a number of possible suppliers giving the terms and conditions of supply.

For the specialized product, the supplier must then 'tender' to the buyer, including in the tender the following information:

- A detailed specification of the product to be supplied.

- An estimated delivery date.

- References from previous customers and/or samples of similar work performed by the supplier.

- The full price at which the product will be supplied including any transport costs which the supplier is willing to bear.

- Any credit terms which will be made available to the customer.

The tender documents, when submitted to the buyer, represent a legal offer to sell which will form the basis of the contract between the buyer and seller. The law of contract governs the rights and responsibilities of each party to the contract. The sale of certain items such as land require a written acceptance by the buyer to become legally enforceable. An offer to sell many other types of product can be accepted verbally (although this is not normal practice with commercial contracts).

The buyer will weigh up the conditions of sale before accepting a particular supplier's bid. Rarely, will a buyer accept a bid purely on the grounds that it offers the lowest price. Other factors such as delivery date, the reputation of the supplier, after-sales service and so on are all important.

In a competitive bid situation the various suppliers may have a good idea who their competitors are although there is no obligation on the part of the buyer to reveal such information. In order to set the price each supplier will need to know the following:

- The minimum price at which the product could be sold. As we have discussed before, the opportunity cost of supply is the minimum acceptable price using purely financial criteria. In Chapter 3 we considered the problem of Diego plc which was invited to tender for a contract. That example highlighted the importance of examining the disturbance to the supplier's total cash position if the contract were entered into.

- The bid prices on similar contracts which failed including, if possible, the prices submitted on the bids placed by those competitors who succeeded.

- The likely cost structure of the other firms which are to compete for the contract taking into account any technological advantage they may possess.

Establishing the size and type of product market

An important aspect of the output–pricing decision is the determination of the size of the product's total market available to the firm and the responsiveness of that market to different marketing strategies. A variety of different sources of information are available to the producing firm:

- Published government statistics such as the annual abstract of statistics, the various censuses of production and distribution, the *National Income and Expenditure Blue Book* including the various surveys of household expenditure.

- Statistics of overseas trade and the various publications of the Organization for Economic Cooperation and Development (OECD).

- The Business Monitor series and publications from trade and professional organizations.

- Publications in the fields of market research and general marketing.

Note: Most of the publications mentioned above can be obtained from university and polytechnic libraries as well as from the larger public libraries. Her Majesty's Stationery Office publishes *Government Statistics—A Brief Guide to Sources* which is an invaluable short cut to finding the sources of government information appropriate for a particular task.

The estimation of the potential market size for a given product, especially if the product has a highly specialized use, can be a lengthy and imprecise task. Below we lay out a series of steps which may be useful in those situations where relevant information can be discovered:

1   Identify the product's classification in the light of the available statistics of market segmentation. For example, a producer of video recorders would sell into the market area defined as 'durable consumer goods' reference 63: 'television, radio and musical instruments including repairs' in the *Family Expenditure Survey* published by HMSO.

2   Estimate the total expenditure in the market segment identified in (1) above, splitting the analysis between home and export market sales. Most UK published figures give total domestic expenditure on a particular market segment as a proportion of household income. Published numbers of households within the firm's marketing area and figures of net household income will give an approximate measure of the market expenditure on the class of goods concerned.

3   Identify the proportion of the market segment taken by the particular type of good being produced and its close market substitutes (if any).

4   Analyse the pattern of supply for the product type concerned including the identity and output of the firm's immediate competitors (taking into account the suppliers of any close market substitutes).

Up to this point we have conducted a static analysis of the current market structure for the product concerned. However, the supplier of a new product, or indeed of a product with an established market, would also have to consider ways and means of expanding the market available or creating a new market area (read again the section in Chapter 2 concerned with product life cycles). A variety of marketing strategies are possible including product differentiation and advertising (both of which we have already discussed), altering the pattern of supply through middlemen, wholesalers, etc., changes in credit policy and other terms of trade. In Chapter 8 we will consider the impact of changes in credit policy upon the firm.

Summary

In the last two chapters we have considered the output and pricing decisions for producers in competitive markets. We have shown that these two types of decision are closely related and that price is heavily influenced by the market conditions under which the firm operates. In many respects the problems outlined in these two chapters bring the discipline of management accounting into very close alignment with the microeconomic theories of consumer behaviour and the firm. In this chapter particularly, we have outlined the different market types with which the firm may be faced and the sorts of information which will be relevant in pricing decisions. In addition, we have outlined the problems which face a firm bidding for a contract to supply goods or services to a single buyer. Unfortunately, many of the problems of pricing are unstructured. That is, the accumluated wisdom of management (or textbooks) may be of little use when it comes down to setting the price for a product in a new market context. For this reason effective management decision-making must utilize a variety of different theoretical and practical skills.

Supplementary reading

EDWARDS, R. S., The pricing of manufactured products, reprinted in Carsberg, B. V. and Edey, H. C. (eds), *Modern Financial Management*, Penguin, 1969.

FLOWER, J. F., The case of the profitable bloodhound, reprinted in Carsberg, B. V. and Edey, H. C. (eds), *Modern Financial Management*, Penguin, 1969. This was a famous case where the government forced a defence supplier to pay back money after it had allegedly overpriced when tendering for the supply of a new missile.

PAPPAS, J. L., BRIGHAM, E. F. and SHIPLEY, B., *Managerial Economics* (UK ed), Holt, Rinehart and Winston, 1983. Especially Chapters 5, 6, 11 and 12. Chapter 6 is especially good on the estimation of demand.

SIZER, J., The accountant's contribution to the selling price decision, in Arnold, J., Carsberg, B. and Scapens, R. (eds), *Topics in Management Accounting*, Philip Allan, 1980.

Questions

1 Distinguish between the different types of product market which a firm may face and suggest the types of information the management accountant should produce in each market situation.

2 Discuss the extent to which the structure of a firm will influence its ability to make pricing decisions in different market contexts.

3 Alcala plc is about to launch a new product into the domestic 'do it yourself' market and has just received a report from a team of marketing consultants it had commissioned to examine the problem of the product's price. They have established that:

   1 Customers would be prepared to pay up to £450 for the first units made available by the firm.

   2 Subsequent sales would, on average, reduce the selling price by 1p for each unit sold.

   These figures relate to monthly sales.
   If the product was promoted once per annum at a time just prior to the peak selling Easter period, the firm's demand curve would shift as follows:

   1 The first unit sold in the month would fetch a price of £610.

   2 Subsequent sales would, on average, reduce the price by 0.85p for each unit sold.

   Management request you to consider the following requirements: the process should be operated at a level which, during the 'off season', will produce sufficient to maximize total revenue from sales and that the pre-Easter promotion campaign should offer a 20 per cent discount on the year-round price for the month in which Easter falls.

   Required:
   (a) Draw up a full report for management on the implications of the consultant's advice concerning the market.

   (b) Determine, given management's requirements, the increase in revenue which would result from the Easter sales campaign.

4 You are given the following information concerning a particular product:
   1 The variable cost of production is £16.8 per unit.
   2 Each unit requires 0.5 labour hours and 0.1 machine hours in production.

3 The total annual fixed costs attributable to the factory are
£640 000. During the year 150 000 labour hours and 36 000
machine hours were employed in the factory.
4 The company has a target rate of return on capital employed of
15 per cent per annum. The capital employed is £4 620 000.
5 The factory's products are all physically similar to one another
although they have varying degrees of labour and machine inputs.

The product described above accounts for one-third of the units
produced by the factory, uses 60 000 labour hours and 3960 machine
hours in production.

Required:
(a) Calculate the price which will give the target rate of return when
applied to the 'total' cost per unit produced on three overhead
allocation bases.
(b) Discuss the relative merits of the allocation bases you have used
and comment upon the reasonableness of cost-based pricing
procedures.

5 A friend of yours is considering setting up a factory/shop in a small,
but developing new town. She is primarily interested in producing
and selling women's clothing. The new town has been developed in
a country area near a small village from which the new town has
taken its name. The village is served by a fast train line to London
and it is anticipated that the town will attract some high-technology
industry to the new science park being developed in the area. Over
the next three years the population of the town is likely to expand
to approximately 7500 households in owner-occupied properties.
The average, disposable income of each household is expected to be
1.8 times the national average. Your friend would like to know the
total sales, per annum, which her factory/shop could achieve
assuming no local competition.
   What information would you need to obtain and how would you
go about collecting that information in order to advise your friend?

6 Three years later and your friend (from Question 5) is doing very
well. In broad outline your advice was soundly based and as a result
her business is prosperous and developing rapidly. However, she now
has another problem, a chain of fashion shops has asked her to tender
for the supply of a line of clothes which they will sell under their
own brand label. The production would absorb 20 per cent of her
current capacity which would mean an extension of her current
production facilities in order to cover her current requirements. A
condition of the contract would be that the buying firm would specify
strict conditions on quality control and would hold the right to make
unannounced factory inspections.
   Your friend asks for both your general advice and also to outline
the procedure which she would have to follow in making a tender
for the supply of the clothing.

7 Allocating scarce resources

In previous chapters we have discussed costing the resources used by the firm. In this chapter we discuss the problems of scarcity where inputs into a new production process are in short supply. In a scarcity situation a decision to proceed with a new production run may entail the redeployment of the necessary inputs from some other productive use within the firm.

In this chapter we will examine:

- The problem of reallocating a scarce resource within the firm and costing it in its new use.

- Production planning where a single input into the production process is in short supply.

- The concept of the 'dual' or 'shadow' price and its importance.

- Production planning with more than one input constraint.

- Techniques for handling 'non-ideal' resource allocation problems.

The cost of reallocation

Business managers are often faced with the problem that certain necessary inputs into a particular process are unavailable on the open market. This may be due to simple economic scarcity where, for example, the input in question is unavailable within the firm's planning period. However, in some situations, a resource may be unavailable because of some technological constraint. For instance, an employee who has special experience or skills can be difficult to replace except after a lengthy period of training. Limited storage facilities may also produce problems because, in the short term, the cost of expansion may be prohibitive.

In the long run, all scarcity problems can be overcome. New labour can be recruited and trained, physical plant or equipment can be extended, raw materials can be found from new sources. But in the short run, these possibilities may be unavailable to the firm.

As we have shown in Chapter 3, resources which are used as the consequence of a particular decision entail an opportunity cost. In the situation where a resource is unavailable externally, that is from the open market, the decision to use that resource can only be made if it can be diverted from some existing use within the firm.

The transfer of a resource from one use to another within the firm will not result in the actual expenditure of cash as is the case with resources which can be readily obtained on the open market. Rather, the existing activity on which the resource is currently employed will suffer a loss of net cash contribution (see the Glossary for a definition of 'contribution'). It is this loss of cash contribution which gives rise to the opportunity cost of employing a scarce resource.

For example, Taranto plc is considering bidding for a new contract to produce PXs. However, the production of PXs entails the deployment of specially trained labour which is already employed on another process, 'alpha'. Process alpha currently produces a net cash contribution to the firm of:

Sales revenue		£180 000
Labour costs	£80 000	
Materials	24 000	
Energy costs	20 000	
Variable overheads	32 000	
		156 000
Net cash contribution		£24 000

We assume, and this is a vital assumption for our analysis, that labour, materials and overhead costs are linearly related to output. This means that there is a direct, proportionate relationship between these costs and output.

Ignoring, for the moment, any sales revenues or other costs on eventual PX production, withdrawing labour from alpha production will cause a fall in Taranto's net cash contribution. PX production will require the withdrawal of a eighth of the labour force involved in alpha production.

The loss in net cash contribution to Taranto because of the redeployment of labour is:

	Change (£)
Sales revenue	(22 500)
Labour	—
Materials	3 000
Energy costs	2 500
Variable overheads	4 000
	(13 000)

The assumption of linearity means that sales revenue will fall by one-eighth (a cash loss) and that all of the other costs (except the labour which is still employed) will also fall by one-eighth (a cash saving). Therefore, as a direct consequence of withdrawing labour from alpha production, we see that there is a cash loss on sales revenue, although cash savings are made on materials, energy and overheads. Labour costs remain unchanged as the cash cost to Taranto of employing labour must still be incurred.

Therefore, in a situation of scarcity where a particular resource must be switched from one productive use to another, the full opportunity cost is given by the loss in cash suffered as a direct result of that decision.

In practice, the analysis of cash flows would lead to lengthy and impractical calculations. And, indeed, the firm's information system may not be geared up to produce data in the form required. Using the linearity assumption, the problem can be simplified. The full cash loss (£13 000) in the above example, can be identified as the sum of two components:

1 The market cost of the resource redeployed (or 'external opportunity cost'). In the example above the external opportunity cost of labour $= \frac{1}{8} \times 80\,000 = £10\,000$.

2 The loss in contribution on the process forgone (or 'internal opportunity cost'). In the example above the internal opportunity cost of redeploying labour $= \frac{1}{8} \times 24\,000 = £3000$.

Thus the total opportunity cost (TOC) of using a scarce resource is equal to the sum of the external and internal opportunity cost (EOC + IOC), i.e.

TOC = EOC + IOC

For Taranto, the total opportunity cost of the labour redeployed from alpha production is:

TOC = £10 000 + £3000

$\qquad$ = £13 000

Given, therefore, that the current use of resources generates a cash contribution, a resource which is in short supply will have a total opportunity cost in excess of its market price. Indeed, for a resource which is in short supply, the market price has little meaning in isolation. This additional element of opportunity cost over the market price is the 'internal' opportunity cost which, with the market price, gives the full reallocation cost of the resource in question.

Production planning with a single resource in short supply

The production decision is concerned with allocating the firm's available resources among the various processes which the firm could, potentially, undertake. For a start we will consider a multiproduct firm where the following conditions hold:

- The firm wishes to maximize its cash contribution (the optimization assumption).

- Costs are directly related to output (the linearity assumption).

- There are no joint products. That is, the firm's products are independent of one another, i.e. they are neither complementary nor substitute goods (the independence assumption).

- All processes are perfectly divisible, i.e. small fractions of products can be produced, or small fractions of inputs—such as labour hours or materials—can be utilized (the divisibility assumption).
- There are no hidden costs associated with non-production such as loss of goodwill or market coverage (the completeness assumption).
- All the inputs into the problem are known with certainty (the certainty assumption).

At this stage we will also assume that only a single resource is in short supply. All of the other inputs into the production process can be obtained in any desired amount at their stated market prices. We will also assume that there is a limit to the amount of each product that can be sold given the current level of demand in the market.

We will demonstrate, in due course, the ways in which the various assumptions outlined above can be relaxed. Although the greater the degree of realism we introduce into the methods of solution—or 'algorithms'—the more complex they become.

Example: Taranto plc has six production processes within its plant which (to add a certain classical sophistication) are called alpha, beta, gamma, delta, epsilon and zeta. The production requirements, sales revenue and demand for each product are as specified below:

	Alpha	Beta	Gamma	Delta	Epsilon	Zeta
Sales (price (£)/unit)	22.5	20.0	60.0	30.0	100.0	42.0
Materials (ks/unit)	1	2	4	1	6	5
Labour (labour hours/unit)	0.5	0.25	3.0	1.0	5.0	1.0
Maximum demand (units)	200	300	200	200	200	100

The materials cost is £5 per kilogram and the labour cost is £10 per labour hour. Each process uses the same materials and the same grade of labour. However, due to the special skills required by the labour force, Taranto is limited to a maximum of 1300 labour hours on these particular processes.

The contribution per unit for each of these processes is as follows:

	Alpha (£)	Beta (£)	Gamma (£)	Delta (£)	Epsilon (£)	Zeta (£)
Sales revenue	22.5	20.0	60.0	30.0	100.0)	42.0
Materials	(5.0)	(10.0)	(20.0)	(5.0)	(30.0)	(25.0)
Labour	(5.0)	(2.5)	(30.0)	(10.0)	(50.0)	(10.0)
Net contribution	12.5	7.5	10.0	15.0	20.0	7.0

At first sight it might appear that the best way to solve this problem is to rank the products according to the contribution per unit which they generate:

Ranking	Product	Contribu-tion/unit (£)	Labour hours	Total contribu-tion (£)
1st	Epsilon	20.0	1000	4000
2nd	Delta	15.0	200	3000
3rd	Alpha	12.5	100	2500
			1300	9500

The labour hours used up on each product are calculated by multiplying the number of units produced by the labour requirement per unit. The total contribution for each product is calculated as:

total contribution = number of units produced × contribution per unit

In this production plan, a total contribution of £9500 is earned by producing all the epsilon, delta and alpha which can be sold. The remaining products are not produced.

The weakness of the technique used is that it does not focus on the efficiency of each product in converting the scarce resource into contribution. Because Taranto faces a shortage of labour, its primary concern will be to ensure that labour is used to its maximum efficiency. This line of argument suggests that instead of ranking each product in terms of contribution per unit produced we should rank according to a ratio which reflects the efficiency with which labour is converted into contribution, i.e. our ranking ratio should be:

$$\frac{\text{contribution per unit}}{\text{of scarce resource}} = \frac{\text{contribution per unit}}{\text{units of scarce resource per unit output}}$$

In the case of product 'alpha', half a labour hour is required to produce one unit of output. Therefore, the contribution per unit scarce resource for alpha is:

ranking ratio (alpha) = £12.5/0.5 = £25.0 per labour hour

Ranking all six products by their ranking ratio we obtain:

Ranking	Product	Ranking ratio	Labour hours employed	Total contribu-tion (£)
1st	Beta	30.0	75	2 250
2nd	Alpha	25.0	100	2 500
3rd	Delta	15.0	200	3 000
4th	Zeta	7.0	100	700
5th	Epsilon	4.0	825	3 300
			1300	11 750
6th	Gamma	3.5	(not produced)	

The total contribution for epsilon production is found by dividing the remaining labour hours after completing zeta production by the number of labour hours required to produce each unit. This gives the total units which can be produced $(825/5 = 165)$ which, when multiplied by the contribution per unit, gives the total contribution generated $(165 \times 20 = £3300)$.

The dual or shadow price of a scarce resource

The revised production programme reveals that the use of the same resources can produce an outcome which better satisfies management's objective of maximizing contribution. Given that management finds this programme acceptable, we can then proceed to calculate the value to Taranto of its scarce resource. In the sequence of production priorities, the last (or 'marginal') product is epsilon. Some, but not all, of the demand for epsilon has been met. Consequently, if another labour hour could be found it would increase Taranto's overall contribution by £4, i.e. one-fifth of an extra unit of epsilon could be produced (invoking the 'divisibility' assumption).

The figure of £4 per labour hour represents the marginal benefit which would accrue to Taranto if an extra labour hour could be found or, the contribution loss which would be suffered if, for some reason, Taranto was deprived of a labour hour. This figure of £4 is termed the 'dual' or 'shadow' price of labour. The 'dual' suggests to Taranto that it would be worth paying up to £4 above the current labour rate of £10 per hour (perhaps as an overtime rate) in order to gain extra labour. In terms of net contribution, an overtime rate of £4 per labour hour, for example, would increase the unit cost of epsilon production by £20 per unit which would give a net contribution of exactly zero on the additional units produced.

In our earlier discussion of the cost of redeploying resources from one use to another, we demonstrated that an 'internal opportunity cost' will arise when a given resource is in short supply. In Taranto's case we can see that the figure of £4 represents the contribution which would be foregone if one labour hour was diverted away from the production programme. Withdrawing one hour of labour from epsilon production gives a revised table of total contribution as follows:

Ranking	Product	Ranking ratio	Labour hours employed	Total contribution (£)
1st	Beta	30.0	75	2 250
2nd	Apha	25.0	100	2 500
3rd	Delta	15.0	200	3 000
4th	Zeta	7.0	100	700
5th	Epsilon	4.0	824	3 296
			1299	11 746

The change in contribution following withdrawal of one labour hour
= £11 746 − £11 750 = (£4).

Given that total opportunity cost equals external plus internal opportunity cost, the full opportunity cost of labour is given by the market price of labour (£10 per labour hour) plus the figure of £4 calculated above.

This concept of the contribution per unit on the marginal product is of central importance in production planning. Not only does it indicate the premium which attaches to a given resource—which may be of use in negotiating extra supplies of that resource—it also provides a means of rapidly appraising any new project that may arise after the basic plan has been formulated and accepted.

For example, after deciding to implement its production plan as discussed above, Taranto plc was asked to consider producing 50 units of pi on a special contract. No extra labour is available. The production requirements and sales revenue per unit for pi are as follows:

Sales revenue per unit	£40.0
Materials usage per unit	1.0 kg
Labour usage (hours per unit)	2.0 hours

These production requirements generate a net contribution of £15 per unit produced and sold. Given the shortage of labour, Taranto could introduce pi into its original production plan and rework the solution. As 100 labour hours will be required for pi, Taranto must forgo part of its epsilon production. The original and revised production schedules are as follows:

	Production schedule (original)		Production schedule (including pi)	
	Labour hours	Contribution (£)	Labour hours	Contribution (£)
Beta	75	2 250	75	2 250
Alpha	100	2 500	100	2 500
Delta	200	3 000	200	3 000
Zeta	100	700	100	700
Pi	—	—	100	750
Epsilon	825	3 300	725	2 900
	1 300	11 750	1 300	12 100

The increase in net contribution of £350 indicates that the pi contract should be accepted, even given the depletion in epsilon production.

A more direct route to this answer can be found through the use of the dual price of labour. The figure of £15 per unit net contribution for pi is calculated on the basis of a £10 per hour labour charge. However, if, in assessing the contribution for pi, we include the dual price of labour as part of the overall labour charge we obtain:

Sales revenue per unit		£40.0
Materials cost per unit	£5.0	
Labour cost per unit, $(10 + 4) \times 2$	28.0	
	——	33.0
Increase in contribution per unit		£7.0

Therefore, each unit of pi produced gives a net benefit of £7 over and above that provided by the original marginal product—epsilon. The increase in overall contribution for pi production is:

$$(£7.0 \times 50) = £350$$

which is exactly the result we had before.

One problem with this approach is that it only applies to small changes in the original plan. For example, in Taranto's case any new opportunity which requires more than 825 labour hours would involve forgoing some zeta production with a consequent change in the dual price of labour on the marginal product. Unfortunately, what is a 'small change' is solely dependent upon the circumstances of the case and so no definite rule can be applied.

To summarize:

- An internal opportunity cost will only arise if a particular resource is in short supply.
- If the assumptions of linearity and divisibility apply, the internal opportunity cost is equal to the net cash contribution forgone on the marginal product.
- Marginal alterations to a production plan can be assessed by including the internal opportunity cost (dual price) in the cost of the resource in short supply.

> **Self test:** Rework the Taranto example above assuming free availability of labour, at £10 per hour, but with materials in short supply at 1800 kg. What is the dual price for materials?
> **Solution clue:** The same marginal product as before.

Production planning with several resources in short supply

The single-constraint problem which faced Taranto plc produced some useful insights into the problems of allocating scarce resources between competing uses. In addition, it highlighted an important piece of information: the redeployment or 'internal opportunity cost' of a resource in short supply.

In industry, the more usual problem which occurs is where a number of resources are limited in the short term. The simple solution of allocating resources to production using a ranking ratio, based on contribution per unit of scarce resource, will not work when we are faced with a multiple scarce-resource problem. In order to reach a solution we must turn to a technique which, while being conceptually straightforward, can be computationally very difficult and, given a problem of any real complexity can only be solved with a computer. This technique, which is called 'linear programming' (LP for short), depends, at its simplest level, on the optimization, linearity, independence, divisibility, completeness and certainty assumptions outlined above.

The first stage of LP involves converting a given production problem into a set of linear equations (i.e. ones which are free from power or multiplicative terms). One of these equations describes the objective of the problem (the objective function). The remainder specify the limits which are imposed upon the problem by the scarce resources (the constraints).

Once the problem has been formulated in mathematical terms, the second stage of the LP involves employing a solution technique, or 'algorithm', to identify the production plan which best satisfies the objective function, given the constraints. In this book we will show two solution techniques. The first is a graphical method which, while being straightforward, is limited in its applicability. The second is more general, in that it can handle problems of any complexity, but it is computationally tedious and is only really suitable for computer application. The third and final stage of LP is the interpretation of the output from the solution technique. As we will demonstrate, LP will tell us:

- Which production plan best fulfils management's objectives.
- The dual prices of each of the scarce resources involved.

Fig 7.1 Stages of solving linear programming problems

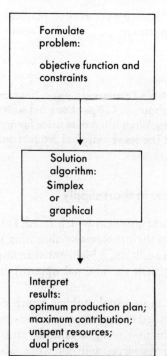

Figure 7.1 shows the three stages of the LP approach to production planning.

To illustrate the LP technique we will examine a problem faced by a small firm concerned with the production of guitar strings. Classical guitarists will know that strings come in packs of six. The top three strings are made from different gauges of single-filament nylon strand. The bottom three strings consist of fine strands of silk wrapped in a spiral of fine wire. All in all, their production is a very skilled process. We will simplify somewhat.

For example, Badajoz plc produces two types of guitar string: 'normal' and 'high' tension. The strings are produced, packed and sold to the trade in boxes of a dozen sets. Badajoz relies upon supplies of single-strand nylon from a major synthetic chemical producer. However, because of the high quality required, only a limited amount can be produced and made available to Badajoz. In addition, the fine silver wire used for making the base strings is also in short supply. Badajoz has 12 fully qualified machine operators available. These operators can work up to 120 hours per month. The relevant monthly financial and production statistics are as follows:

	Normal tension	High tension
Contribution per box	£1.25	£2.00
Usage of silver wire per box	0.20 g	0.40 g
Usage of nylon strand per box	2.00 g	2.00 g
Skilled labour per box	0.60 hours	0.50 hours
Maximum demand	2000 boxes	1500 boxes

At current prices 800 g of silver and 6000 g of nylon strand are available each month. Contribution is net of all labour and materials costs.

Formulating the LP problem

The objective of Badajoz's management is to earn the maximum possible contribution from string production. In fact, LP can deal with either maximization or minimization problems, so it would be possible to handle a problem where management wished to minimize its costs rather than maximize contribution. However, in production planning, contribution maximization is the more common assumption.

The first part of the LP formulation involves converting management's objective of maximizing contribution from production into a mathematical formula expressed in terms of the contribution earned from both types of string.

Because the number of boxes of strings to be produced is an unknown, we specify the production quantity as a variable: Let x be the number of boxes of normal-tension strings produced and y be number of boxes of high-tension strings produced. The total contribution generated through the production process can be expressed as:

total contribution (Z) = contribution per box of normal strings × number of boxes of normal strings produced

+

contribution per box of high-tension strings × number of boxes of high-tension strings produced.

i.e. $Z = 1.25x + 2.00y$

This expression is termed the 'objective function'. You will note that it is a linear expression in terms of three unknowns: the maximum contribution and the output quantities of the two products.

The second part of the LP formulation involves expressing the production constraints in mathematical terms. The first constraint specifies that the total silver usage must be less than, or equal to, 800 g. In addition, we know that the usage of silver on normal strings equals the usage per box produced (which is given) multiplied by the number of boxes of normal strings produced (x). Similarly, for high-tension strings, the total silver usage will equal the usage per box multiplied by the number of boxes of high-tension strings produced (y). Therefore:

$0.20x + 0.40y \leqslant 800$

where the symbol $\leqslant$ means 'less than or equal to'.

Self test: **Which of the following production combinations satisfies the silver constraint:**

	Normal tension (boxes)	High tension (boxes)
1	0	3000
2	1000	1000
3	1000	1500
4	3000	1000

The nylon constraint can be formulated in exactly the same way: i.e. as the sum of the usage of nylon per unit of product multiplied by the numbers of boxes produced. This sum must be less than, or equal to, 6000 g:

$2.0x + 2.0y \leqslant 6000$

The labour constraint, using the same reasoning, is:

$0.60x + 0.50y \leqslant 12 \times 120$ (hours)

i.e. $0.60x + 0.50y \leqslant 1440$

Finally, we note that the total production of normal- and high-tension strings must, in both cases, be greater than or equal to zero (we cannot produce negative amounts), but less than or equal to the maximum number demanded (2000 and 1500 boxes, respectively).

The full formulation of Badajoz's production problem is:

$$1.25x + 2.00y = Z \quad \text{(objective function)}$$

$$0.20x + 0.40y \leqslant 800 \quad \text{(silver constraint)}$$

$$2.00x + 2.00y \leqslant 6000 \quad \text{(nylon constraint)}$$

$$0.60x + 0.50y \leqslant 1440 \quad \text{(labour constraint)}$$

$$x \quad\quad\quad \leqslant 2000 \quad \text{(normal-tension string demand constraint)}$$

$$y \leqslant 1500 \quad \text{(HIgh-tension string demand constraint)}$$

$$x \quad\quad\quad \geqslant 0 \quad \text{(non-negativity constraint)}$$

$$y \geqslant 0 \quad \text{(non-negativity constraint)}$$

Solving the LP problem (graphical method)

As is the case with the objective function, all of the above constraints are in linear form and contain, as unknowns, the number of boxes of normal- and high-tension strings. As we are dealing with only two products, it is a straightforward task to identify, graphically, the full range of production plans which Badajoz could pursue and still meet all of its production constraints. In Fig. 7.2 we show a graph of normal- and high-tension production upon which all of the constraints are drawn as straight lines. Each line represents the position of a constraint at equality, that is, those combinations of x and y which fully utilize the scarce

Fig 7.2 Constraints and feasible region of a linear programme

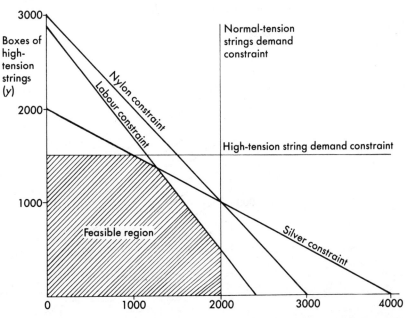

Boxes of normal-tension strings (x)

resource in question. For example, the available silver is fully used (800 g) when:

$$0.20x + 0.40y = 800$$

To draw the line of this particular equation we only need two points:

	Coordinates (x, y)
(i) Point of intersection with y axis ($x = 0$)	0, 2000
(ii) Point of intersection with x axis ($y = 0$)	4000, 0

Any combination of normal- and high-tension string production lying between the origin of the graph and this line will also satisfy this constraint although there will be some silver unused.

When we combine all of the individual constraint lines on a graph (as in Fig. 7.2) a 'feasible' region is defined which contains the set of all possible combinations of x and y which satisfy all of the constraints simultaneously. If a production combination is chosen which lies exactly on a corner or on the edge of the feasible region then the constraint(s) on which it lies will be fully satisfied. Any point which lies outside the feasible region will fail to satisfy one or more constraints and will give values of x and y which cannot be produced given the current availability of resources.

To complete the solution of Badajoz's problem we must determine that production plan which both satisfies the constraints (lies within or on the boundary of the feasible region) and maximizes the value of the objective function. The objective function can be visualized as an indefinite number of straight lines which lie parallel to one another and have a negative slope of 0.625. In Fig. 7.3 we show a number of lines of increasing value of Z.

Fig 7.3 Family of objective functions

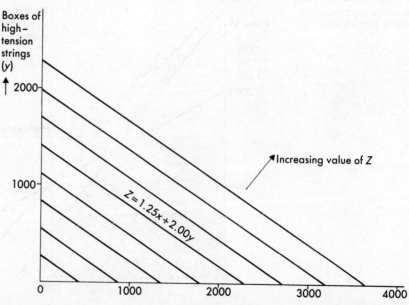

Boxes of high-tension strings (y)

$Z = 1.25x + 2.00y$

Increasing value of Z

Boxes of normal tension strings ⟶ (x)

Note: The objective function:

$$1.25x + 2.00y = Z$$

can be written in the more familiar linear form:

$$y = a + bx$$

(a is the intercept with the y axis and b is the slope), as

$$y = \frac{Z}{2} - \frac{1.25x}{2} = \frac{Z}{2} - 0.625x$$

As we move out from the origin of the graph toward point D on Fig. 7.4 we attain higher values of the objective function. At point D we reach the combination of x and y which satisfies all of the constraints and maximizes the value of the objective function. At that point the objective function intersects the crossover of the silver wire and the labour constraints. We can calculate the value of x and y at this crossover exactly by solving the pair of equalities which represent the limits of these two constraints.

Limit of the silver constraint:

$$0.2x + 0.4y = 800 \qquad (7.1)$$

Limit of the labour constraint:

$$0.6x + 0.5y = 1440 \qquad (7.2)$$

Fig 7.4 Graphical solution to linear programme

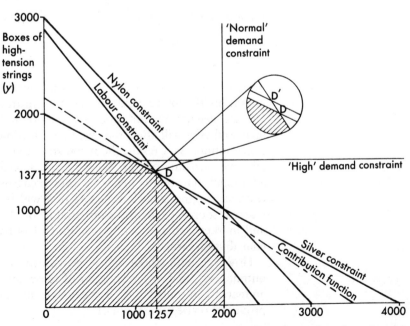

By multiplying Eq. (7.1) by 3 we get:

$$0.6x + 1.2y = 2400 \qquad (7.3)$$

Subtracting Eq. (7.2) from Eq. (7.3) eliminates x and leaves an equation in terms of y only:

$$
\begin{array}{r}
0.6x + 1.2y = 2400 \\
\underline{0.6x + 0.5y = 1440} \\
0x + 0.7y = 960
\end{array}
$$

Therefore

$$y = 960/0.7$$

$$= 1371.43$$

By substituting this value for y in any one of Eqs (7.1)–(7.3) above we can derive a value for x:

Using Eq. (7.3):

$$0.6x + 1.2(1371.43) = 2400$$

Rearranging we find that

$$x = \frac{2400 - 1.2 \times 1371.43}{0.6}$$

$$= 1257.14$$

To summarize our solution to Badajoz's production problem:

normal-tension string production $(x) = 1257.14$ boxes

high-tension string production $(y) \quad = 1371.43$ boxes

and a maximized contribution of:

$$Z = £1.25 \times 1257.14 + £2.00 \times 1371.43 = £4314.29$$

Figure 7.4 also reveals the fact that neither the nylon-strand constraint nor the limits upon demand influence the contribution maximizing output. Neither negotiating for more supplies of nylon, nor advertising for increased sales will affect the overall production level or, therefore, total contribution. As a result, the nylon-strand and the demand constraints all have zero dual prices. Remember that a dual price represents the additional contribution that will be obtained from one more unit of scarce resource, or the contribution loss that will be incurred if one unit of scarce resource is removed from production. In the case of nylon strand and market demand, one unit more or less has no effect on the total contribution earned.

However, both labour and silver wire effectively constrain the overall output level, and any relaxation of these constraints will bring about an increase in contribution. For example, an additional labour hour will produce a revised constraint of:

$$0.60x + 0.50y \leqslant 1441$$

The optimum production point D, will move to D' (see inset, Fig. 7.4). Such fine adjustments to the original plan are difficult with the graphical technique. We can, however, evaluate the dual directly by resolving the two constraints (modified by the addition of the extra labour hour):

The intersection between the two lines:

$0.06x + 0.50y = 1441$ (limit of the revised labour constraint)

$0.20x + 0.40y = 800$ (limit of the original silver wire constraint)

which gives a revised production plan and optimized contribution of:

production of normal-tension strings $= 1260.00$ boxes

production of high-tension strings $= 1370.00$ boxes

total contribution $= £1.25 \times 1260.00 + £2.00 \times 1370.00$

$$= £4315.00$$

The dual price of labour is, therefore:

dual price (labour) $= 4315.00 - 4314.29$

$$= £0.71 \text{ per labour hour}$$

Self test:
 (i) Assuming no alteration in the availability of labour, determine the increase in contribution brought about by an increase in the availability of silver wire by 1 g.
 (ii) Looking at Fig. 7.4, how much extra silver wire would be required before it ceased to limit the production of guitar strings?

 Solution clue: (i) 4.1. (ii) The silver constraint must move to the position of intersection of the labour and 'high' demand constraint.

Solving the LP problem (the Simplex algorithm)

Unfortunately, the graphical technique is only applicable for two-product problems. In order to achieve more general applicability, we must turn to a technique based upon matrix algebra: the 'Simplex' algorithm. Most computer programs use this or a related method for solving LP problems. If you have the optional software disk which goes with this book you will find a program which replicates the procedures we will describe in the next section.

The Simplex algorithm requires little modification to the method of formulating an LP we have already discussed. The only additional step is to convert the various inequalities within the constraints to equalities by introducing a 'slack' variable into each constraint. A slack variable is designed to remove the 'less than' or the 'greater than' from each constraint. For example, the silver-wire constraint in the Badajoz example is:

$$0.20x + 0.40y \leqslant 800$$

By introducing a slack variable (S_1) we can convert this constraint to an equality:

$$0.20x + 0.40y + S_1 = 800$$

S_1 represents the unused silver wire from any production combination (x,y) and can range, given this constraint, from 0 to 800. If x and y are set at zero (the position at the start of the search for an optimum solution) then the value of the slack variable will be equal to the right-hand side of the constraint equation. At optimum, some of the values of the slack variables will be zero indicating that the resources governed by those constraints are fully used up. The remaining slack variables will have positive values representing the quantity of those resources not used.

Introducing a slack variable into each constraint in Badajoz's production problem, we can reformulate the original problem as follows:

$$1.25x + 2.00y \qquad = \quad Z \quad \text{(objective function)}$$

$$0.20x + 0.40y + S_1 = \quad 800 \quad \text{(silver wire)}$$

$$2.00x + 2.00y + S_2 = 6000 \quad \text{(nylon strand)}$$

$$0.60x + 0.50y + S_3 = 1440 \quad \text{(labour)}$$

$$x \qquad\qquad + S_4 = 2000 \quad \text{(normal-tension string demand)}$$

$$y + S_5 = 1500 \quad \text{(high-tension string demand)}$$

With the Simplex algorithm, the non-negativity constraints are automatically dealt with and do not need to be specified.

We have now introduced five new variables into the problem and these, with the original three, make eight variables in a five-equation system. The solution, therefore, requires an iterative procedure where the possible solutions (represented by the turning points on the graph) are tried and tested one by one for optimality.

The steps toward the solution are as follows:

(a) Lay out the coefficients of variables in each constraint in a table of data (called the initial tableau):

	Production		Slack variables					
	x	y	S_1	S_2	S_3	S_4	S_5	Z
(i)	0.2	0.4	1	0	0	0	0	800
(ii)	2.0	2.0	0	1	0	0	0	6000
(iii)	0.6	0.5	0	0	1	0	0	1440
(iv)	1	0	0	0	0	1	0	2000
(v)	0	1*	0	0	0	0	1	1500
(vi)	−1.25	−2.0	0	0	0	0	0	0

Rows (i)–(v) contain the coefficients of the constraints. In addition, each row is controlled by its own slack variable (designated by the coefficient 1 in the respective 'slack' column). Row (vi) is a statement of the objective function as the problem stands at the origin of the graph when the value of overall contribution equals zero, i.e. when:

$$1.25x + 2.00y = 0$$

In order to simplify the procedure we multiply each term in the objective function by -1, which has no effect on the arithmetic sense of the function.

As we saw earlier, when we used the graphical method, when both x and y are zero, all of the constraints are satisfied. In this case, therefore, the origin is a feasible (but obviously not optimal) solution to the problem. This may not always be the case. In some situations the origin is not a feasible solution and certain refinements have to be added to the Simplex algorithm in order to make it work. These refinements are beyond the scope of this book but can be followed up in the readings given at the end of the chapter.

(b) Look along the objective-function row for the value with the highest negative value (-2.0 in this case). This defines what is called the 'pivotal column' (the y column in this case).

(c) Divide every coefficient in the pivotal column into its corresponding element in the Z column:

Row (i) $= 800/0.4 = 2000$

Row (ii) $= 6000/2 = 3000$

Row (iii) $= 1440/0.5 = 2880$

Row (iv) $= 2000/0 = $ infinity

Row (v) $= 1500/1 = 1500$

Select the row which has the lowest value (row (v)). The crossover between this row and the pivotal column defines the 'pivot' which is marked with an asterisk in the initial tableau.

(d) Divide each element in the pivotal row (row (v)) by the pivot. This forms the new row (v) of the second tableau.

(v)	0	1	0	0	0	0	1	1500

In this case row (v) is unchanged but, as we will see later, this is not always the case.

(e) Deduct from, or add to, each of the remaining rows (including the objective-function row) sufficient multiples of the new pivot row (row (v)) to reduce the elements in the pivotal column to zero. Therefore, for row (i) we deduct 0.4 times the new row (v):

Old row (i)	0.2	0.4	1	0	0	0	0	800
Minus 0.4 × new row (v)	-0.4×0	-0.4×1	-0.4×0	-0.4×0	-0.4×0	-0.4×0	-0.4×1	-0.4×1500
Equals new row (i)	0.2	0	1	0	0	0	-0.4	200

Repeat this 'row operation' using appropriate multiples of the remaining rows (e.g. 2 × row (v) for revised row (ii)).

Old row	New row
(i)	$-0.4 \times$ (v) = (i)
(ii)	$-\quad 2 \times$ (v) = (ii)
(iii)	$-0.5 \times$ (v) = (iii)
(iv)	$-\quad 0 \times$ (v) = (iv)
(v)	$+\quad 2 \times$ (v) = (vi)

The revised tableau becomes:

	Production variables		Slack variables					
	x	y	S_1	S_2	S_3	S_4	S_5	Z
(i)	0.2	0	1	0	0	0	-0.4	200
(ii)	2.0	0	0	1	0	0	-2.0	3000
(iii)	0.6	0	0	0	1	0	-0.5	690
(iv)	1	0	0	0	0	1	0	2000
(v)	0	1	0	0	0	0	1	1500
(vi)	-1.25	0	0	0	0	0	2	3000

(f) If any of the elements in the objective-function row remain negative, return with the revised tableau to step (b) and repeat the procedure through to (f). If no negative elements remain, the algorithm has found an optimized solution.

Each iteration (i.e. each repeat of the cycle of steps from (b) to (f)) takes us around to the next turning point of the feasible region. The revised tableau above gives a value for y of 1500 boxes (look down the y column to the 1 and the corresponding element in the Z column is the production quantity). Because the x column has not been cleared by the row operation the value of x remains at zero. The contribution given by this turning point (£3000) is found at the bottom right-hand corner of the tableau. This corresponds to the first turning point of the feasible region in the graphical method (Fig. 7.2).

Because the first element of the revised objective-function row is negative the whole procedure must be repeated and a third tableau created:

	Production variables		Slack variables					
	x	y	S_1	S_2	S_3	S_4	S_5	Z
(i)	1	0	5	0	0	0	-2	1000
(ii)	0	0	-10	1	0	0	2	1000
(iii)	0	0	-3	0	1	0	0.7	90
(iv)	0	0	-5	0	0	1	2	1000
(v)	0	1	0	0	0	0	1	1500
(vi)	0	0	6.25	0	0	0	-0.5	4250

This third tableau represents the second turning point of the feasible region in the graphical solution where:

$$x = 1000 \text{ boxes}$$

$$y = 1500 \text{ boxes}$$

contribution $= (1000 \times 1.25 + 1500 \times 2.0)$

$$= £4250$$

Self test:
 (i) Make sure that you can create the revised tableau.
(ii) The figures in the *Z* column for rows (ii), (iii) and (iv) represent the unused resources. Which ones?

Solution clue: Look for the number of the slack variables heading the column in which the 1 appears in rows (ii), (iii) and (iv).

However, another negative value has appeared in the objective function row, indicating that an optimal solution has not yet been achieved. We repeat the steps (b)–(f) on the revised tableau to create what turns out to be our final tableau:

	Production variables		*Slack variables*					
	x	y	S_1	S_2	S_3	S_4	S_5	Z
(i)	1	0	−3.57	0	2.86	0	0	1257.14
(ii)	0	0	−1.43	1	−2.86	0	0	742.86
(iii)	0	0	−4.29	0	1.43	0	1	128.57
(iv)	0	0	3.57	0	−2.86	1	0	742.86
(v)	0	1	4.29	0	−1.43	0	0	1371.43
(vi)	0	0	4.105	0	0.715	0	0	4314.29

Looking down the x and y columns for the 'ones', we can identify those rows which contain the production quantities for normal- and high-tension strings, respectively:

Row (i)   Normal-tension strings (x) 1257.14 boxes
Row (v)   High-tension strings (y) 1371.43 boxes

with a total, optimized contribution of £4314.29 (in the lower right-hand corner). As an added bonus, we find that the slack-variable columns give the dual prices in row (vi):

Silver wire (S_1) £4.105 per gramme
Nylon strand (S_2) 0
Labour (S_3) £0.715 per labour hour
Normal demand (S_4) 0
High demand (S_5) 0

In addition, we can also identify the unused resources in the optimal plan by going down the slack-variable columns which have zero duals (S_2, S_4 and S_5) until we reach the number one and reading off the corresponding value in the Z column.

S_1	Nylon strand unused	742.86 boxes
S_4	Unsatisfied 'normal' demand	742.86 boxes
S_5	Unsatisfied 'high' demand	128.57 boxes

We have achieved with the Simplex algorithm all that we did with the graphical method and, in addition, we have discovered the magnitude of the unused resources. We have also achieved greater generality in our analysis but at the expense of greater computational difficulty.

> *Computer application:* If you have a copy of the supporting software disk for this book or access to a computer with an LP package enter the Badajoz production problem and check our results with the output from the computer. Try changing the variables in the problem (one by one) and see what happens.

Non-ideal production problems

Many of the production problems which are encountered in the course of business decision-making can be solved with the Simplex algorithm outlined above. However, on occasions problems are met which either cannot be solved directly using LP or present us with serious problems in interpreting the results.

We can identify two main problem areas:

- Where the assumptions of the LP model are violated.

- Where the solution is degenerate.

Violation of the assumptions

Variants of the LP model have been devised to deal with some of the principal assumptions. We will not discuss these variants in great detail in this book (the reference to the book by Salkin and Kornbluth at the end of this chapter will help you if you wish to pursue this topic further), but here are some pointers:

1 The linearity assumption, when violated in a particular problem, can be avoided by the use of a linear approximation technique. For example, a non-linear contribution function can be segmented and treated as a number of short, linear sections. Of course, the greater the number of sections the better the approximation but the greater the computational complexity.

2 The independence assumption can be surmounted, in some cases, by restating the objective function using logarithms. This will convert any multiplicative terms to simple linear functions. However, in practice, considerable interpretive skills are required to restate such problems in a form suitable for LP analysis.

3 The divisibility assumption can be a serious problem when we are dealing with essentially indivisible products. British Petroleum would not thank their corporate planners if they proposed the construction of a fraction of an oil rig! In some situations, however, the divisibility assumption may be a good enough approximation for the problem in hand. Integer programming methods, which produce integer solutions, have been developed although, until recently, lack of the necessary computer facilities has inhibited their more general acceptance in business.

4 The uncertainty assumption presents some of the most complex theoretical problems in LP and, indeed, in management accounting in general. The simplest method for examining problems of uncertainty is through a sensitivity analysis which examines the changes in the output from an LP which result from small variations in the inputs.

5 The maximizing assumption is the only behavioural assumption in the simple LP model outlined above. However, as we discussed in Chapters 1 and 2, managers may not consider contribution maximization to be their most appropriate goal—especially if the completeness assumption is violated. It may be that a given LP solution indicates that only a small proportion of the firm's current product lines should be continued. In such a situation managers may wish to see the results which would be produced at a suboptimal, but still satisfactory, contribution level. One technique for dealing with this type of problem is called 'goal programming'. Goal programming is a simple extension of the basic LP model, where the objective function is specified in terms of minimizing the deviations from a preset target contribution or some other goal. The goal chosen may be set as a break-even point or as a positive, fixed level of contribution. The further reading (especially that by Dunn and Ramsing) given at the end of this chapter will help develop your understanding of this technique.

Degeneracy

Degeneracy can occur in production planning where management, over a period of time, attempts to relax those constraints which limit the level of production and, therefore, the level of contribution which can be earned. In the Badajoz problem, production is constrained by the availability of silver and labour. Naturally, management will place the highest priority on relaxing those constraints because, by doing so, higher levels of production and hence cash contribution can be achieved. However, a point will arise when nylon strand becomes a third constraint upon the problem. When this occurs, the problem is said to be 'degenerate'.

In the Badajoz problem, the dual price was interpreted as the increase in contribution which would arise through a marginal relaxation of one of the two binding constraints. Unfortunately, if more than two constraints bind the optimal solution, the relaxation of a single constraint will have no effect on the overall solution whatsoever. However, the converse is not true. If one unit of a binding constraint is withdrawn from the optimal plan, contribution will fall. In other words, the dual price for each resource has become 'one sided'.

> *Self test:* Resolve Badajoz's problem (either graphically or with the Simplex algorithm) assuming that the nylon strand available has fallen to 5317.14 g.

If nylon strand had also been a binding constraint in the Badajoz problem, then the feasible region shown in Fig. 7.2 would have a triple crossover point at the optimal solution (see Fig. 7.5(a)). A marginal release of either the labour, silver-wire or nylon-strand constraint would leave the solution just as it was before (Fig. 7.5(b)). But the withdrawal of a unit of any one of these three constraints would serve to 'close in' the feasible region thereby reducing the overall contribution (Fig. 7.5(c)).

Unfortunately, degeneracy is a common difficulty in many production problems especially after a period of time, when managers have been working at relaxing their externally imposed production constraints. Suddenly, they may find that more than two constraints have become critical and that the dual prices cannot help them to determine which of the binding constraints should be relaxed next.

The LP program included in the software suite which accompanies this book will warn you if a problem turns out to be degenerate.

Summary

In this chapter we have developed our analysis of the production decision to the point where we can solve problems involving many products and many constraints. By using LP we can determine the ideal production combinations and, by using the dual prices, find the maximum prices we should be prepared to pay in order to gain extra supplies of scarce resources. We concluded our discussion by indicating the major problems associated with the use of the LP techniques and the contribution mathematical methods can make in surmounting them.

Supplementary reading

DEV, S., Linear programming dual prices in management accounting and their interpretation, *Accounting and Business Research*, Winter 1978

DEV, S., Linear programmng and production planning, in Arnold, J., Carsberg, B. and Scapens, R. (eds), *Topics in Management Accounting*, Philip Allan, 1980

Fig 7.5 Degenerate
solutions in linear
programming

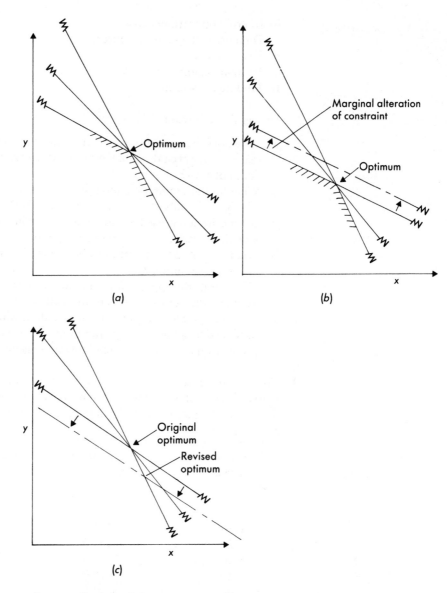

(a)

(b)

(c)

DUNN, R. A. and RAMSING, K. D., *Management Science—A Practical
Approach to Decision-Making*, Collier Macmillan, 1981

HEARD, W. J., Linear programming without tears, *Management
Accounting*, December 1982

SALKIN, G. and KORNBLUTH, J., *Linear Programming and Financial
Planning*, Accountancy Age, 1973

Questions

1   Define the following terms:

   (a) An algorithm.

(b) Internal opportunity cost.
(c) Dual price of a scarce resource.
(d) Degeneracy.
(e) Feasible region.
(f) Binding constraint.

2 Answer the following:

(a) Why does the opportunity cost of a scarce resource include its market price even though, temporarily, a market for that resource does not exist?
(b) What limits are imposed upon the size of a production problem which can be solved by the graphical method?
(c) What criterion is used to rank items of production when only a single scarce resource is in short supply?
(d) What output-market type must be assumed in formulating a linear programming?
(e) What limits the applicability of dual prices as a means of assessing the merits of alterations to an existing production plan?
(f) Why does degeneracy limit the information which can be produced by a linear programme and why is it possible that all production processes may tend toward degeneracy over time?

3 Torre produces seven products each of which requires use of a raw material called anisrot. The contribution per unit, maximum annual demand and quantity of raw material required per unit of product are as follows:

Product	Contribution per unit (£)	Maximum annual demand (units)	Quantity of anisrot per unit (kg)
A	2.40	6 000	2
B	1.60	2 000	2
C	4.20	2 500	5
D	5.00	10 000	10
E	2.20	7 000	1
F	6.00	6 500	3
G	1.50	7 700	1

Torre does not maintain stocks of either finished products or raw materials.

Required:
(a) Calculate the optimal annual production plan for Torre assuming:
1 that anisrot is available in unlimited quantities at its market price of £6.25 per kilogram,
2 that only 50 000 kg of anisrot are available per annum at the market price.

(b) Calculate the maximum price which Torre would be prepared to pay for extra supplies of the raw material required on the assumption that only 50 000 kg are available at the price of £6.25 per kilogram.

(c) Discuss the economic significance of your answers to (a) and (b) above.

4   Solea produces corn and potatoes on his 240-acre West Country farm. Corn and potatoes yield a contribution of £4 and £3 per ton, respectively. One acre of land is required to produce ½ ton of corn or one ton of potatoes. For seed sowing 140 man hours are available. One man working for one hour can sow four acres of corn or one acre of potatoes.

Required:
(a) Calculate the optimal acreage of potatoes and corn and the cash contribution which will result. (Use both the graphical and the Simplex methods).

(b) Derive the dual prices of labour and land and comment on the significance of the figures you derive.

(c) Comment upon the usefulness of mathematical modelling in production planning.

5   Nerja plc is finalizing its production budgets for the month ending 29 February 19X4. On one particular production facility, using one specialist machine, it produces three products coded AXX1, AXX2 and AXX3. Each product has certain constraints imposed by production and demand. The products have a very short shelf life and must be dispatched to customers on completion.

The contribution, production requirements and demand constraints for each product are as follows:

	AXX1	AXX2	AXX3
Contribution per unit produced (£)	15.00	9.45	20.20
Plant operators' time per unit produced (hours)	0.60	0.35	0.75
Machine time per unit produced (hours)	0.10	0.15	0.08
Spun gold mesh produced by rare-metals division (grams per unit)	2.20	0.00	3.10
Spun copper mesh produced by rare-metals division (grams per unit)	0.00	5.00	0.00
Maximum demand (units)	1500.00	2000.00	1750.00

The constraints imposed upon production are as follows:

Plant operators' time (without overtime)	2000 hours
Machine time	650 hours

Spun gold mesh	6000 g
Spun copper mesh	8000 g

Required:

(a) Formulate Nerja's problem as a linear programme and derive:

  1 The maximum, feasible contribution which can be earned by production.

  2 The optimal production quantities of each product.

  3 The dual prices of each scarce resource and of each product demanded.

  4 The quantities of unused resources and the unfulfilled demand (if any) for each product.

(b) Linear programming makes a number of highly restrictive assumptions concerning the objectives of management and the nature of the production process. Discuss the extent to which these assumptions restrict the linear-programming method and the ways in which they can be overcome.

(c) On the assumption that management proceeds to relax its binding constraints over the next production period and that the remainder of the production specification remains as it is, identify the first point at which degeneracy will occur.

8 The control of short-term working capital ————

In this chapter we consider a particular aspect of control, namely the control of short-term working capital. We will, first, examine the nature of control and why it can be regarded as a decision-making activity. We will then move on to an examination, in this chapter, of the problems of controlling short-term working capital. The next chapter extends the story when we examine the problems of cost control and the control of production processes. As with other aspects of decision-making we will be concerned with providing relevant information for those managers who are making control decisions.

Our chapter outline is as follows:

- The general problems of short-term control.
- The different varieties of control systems.
- The control of debtors and the importance of a planned credit policy.
- The methods of controlling stocks and the problems of stock valuation.
- The general problems of controlling cash.

General problems of short-term control

Many of the ideas that have shaped our understanding of the concept of control have come from other disciplines, notably electronics and communications. Over the years management scientists have seen the relevance of the insights provided by electronics, communications and, especially, the theory of electronic control systems for the control of business organizations.

A control system is a structured decision system where managers use past and predicted data about a process to control its behaviour. The problems of control are an integral part of the decisions which managers take in order to operate their business. We will not, therefore, treat the problem of control as an isolated topic on its own, but as one aspect of the decision-making theme of this book.

The very idea of control presupposes that information concerning a system's performance will be acted upon and decisions made on the basis of any deviations from what was anticipated. Firms collect actual costs from their production processes and compare those costs with the budgets set up for that aspect of the firm's activity. The deviations of actual costs from budget provide management with some of the information it needs to make the control decisions necessary to keep the firm on its budgeted course.

Therefore, for our purposes, we can define control as:

• A process of reactive decision-making concerned with maintaining the performance of the firm or any of its component parts as close as possible to the targets set by management.

In Fig. 8.1 we present, diagrammatically, the basic elements of the control procedure.

Fig 8.1 Closed loop control

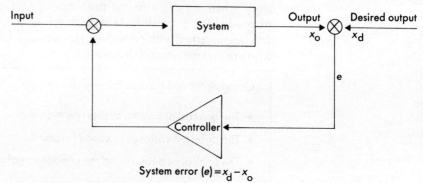

System error $(e) = x_d - x_o$

In Chapter 2 we depicted the firm as an input–output system where resources (labour, capital, hard factors and managerial skills) are converted into outputs in the form of cash surpluses, products and services. In this chapter we expand that simple input–output model to include its control elements.

The type of control system shown in Fig. 8.1 includes a closed 'feedback' loop where the system's actual and desired output (x_o and x_d, respectively) are compared and 'fed back' into the input stage in order to correct the system's performance. Such control may be automatic in that the error signal is used directly, perhaps through the intervention of some mechanical controller, to alter the level of input into the system. An example of this would be a flow meter monitoring the rate at which a chemical flows into a reactor vessel. Deviations in flow rate from that set on the meter would cause a valve to open or shut as the case may be. In such a system, control is entirely automatic and does not rely on any human intervention in the system.

Alternatively, the control may be non-automatic where disparities between actual and desired output are acted upon by some individual only if they exceed certain acceptable tolerances in system behaviour. For example, a driver operating the throttle of his or her car does not continuously monitor the speed of the vehicle in order to keep its speed exactly in line with what is intended. In this case, control is both intermittent and discretionary.

Within the firm, control operaties at a variety of levels. At some levels, control may be highly automated using continuous monitoring systems; at other levels, control may be non-automatic and at the discretion of the manager. For convenience we can classify business control systems into three levels. These levels correspond to the levels of managerial responsibility discussed in Chapter 1.

Class of control	Level of management	Degree of automation	Examples of control within control class
Strategic	Senior/upper middle	None	Control of the consequences of the firm's long-term decisions, such as finance and investment, labour relations, resource utilization and maintenance.
Tactical	Upper/lower middle	Some	Control of the consequences of short-term decisions concerning the conversion of the firm's factors of production into physical outputs or services and cash; in particular the control of short-term resources—stocks, cash balances and debtors.
Operational	Operational	High	Control of the physical processes within the firm such as production systems and stock-handling systems.

There are two important general problems associated with the control of all systems:

- The problem of noise.
- The problem of the speed of control.

The problem of noise

The output from all systems consists of two parts:

- A 'systematic' component which results from the predictable behaviour of the system as it converts inputs into outputs.
- An 'unsystematic' component, often called randon 'noise', which arises from unknown, and therefore unpredictable, aspects of the system's operating characteristics.

For example, a chemical plant producing a particular chemical may find that the output of the chemical concerned is contaminated by a number of unwanted by-products which are caused by randon fluctuations in the operating conditions of the plant. The performance of the system is measured in terms of the output and purity of the required chemical, and the plant engineers will attempt to control and measure the performance of the process in terms of those variables. The output of the required chemical can be thought of as the systematic component of the plant process whilst the output of by-products can be looked upon as 'noise'.

In the natural sciences, laboratory conditions facilitate the control of random elements which can be effectively eliminated from the performance of the system under observation. Laboratories permit experimentation where the only component of the system output is systematic. However, such control is very difficult in most social science and business situations where a very difficult mixture of systematic and non-systematic elements can occur in any data collected. For example, as noted in Chapter 5, total production cost is principally related to output quantity and this cost–output relationship can be regarded as the production system's systematic component. However, other quite unpredictable variables, such as contamination in one of the input materials (for example), may disturb this relationship between cost and output. Indeed, not only are such random disturbances difficult to predict prior to the production run, they are also very difficult to identify after the production run is over.

Many of the statistical methods employed in management accounting are primarily concerned with the problem of separating systematic from unsystematic performance. In fact, you have already met a good example of such a method when we examined the use of linear regression as a method of cost estimation. The technique of linear regression gives us a method of determining the relationship between one variable and another. In our cost–output study in Chapter 5, cost was deemed to be systematically dependent upon output level while the other variables which could affect the control of production were regarded as noise and accounted for in the error term of the regression.

The problem of the speed of control

The effectiveness of control is dependent on, first, the right action being taken to correct a system and, second, that action being taken quickly enough to prevent overreaction and consequential loss of control. Many systems have a natural variability (sales levels may fluctuate with the seasons, for example), other systems have a tendency to correct themselves to some equilibrium state (many economic markets exhibit this property). If the actions taken to control such systems are mistimed then the effect can be to exacerbate the fluctuations and make matters worse. A skidding car can provide, for the driver and passengers, an unpleasant illustration of this phenomenon. If, as the vehicle begins to stray from its line, the driver overcorrects, a worse skid in the opposite direction will result and it is only a matter of seconds before the driver's frantic efforts to regain control will put the car into a spin. Similarly, a firm which tries to counteract a temporary depression in the market for its products by the use of advertising may, if that action is too late, find itself with demand well in excess of its capacity when the advertising takes effect.

In managerial control situations, the effects described above can usually be avoided by improving the rate at which the system's performance is monitored. The more quickly information is obtained from (say) a firm's markets, the more quickly management can take the necessary action to change its output levels and advertising policy.

Varieties of control systems

Both automatic and non-automatic control systems can be classified into three separate categories:

- Feedback control.
- Feedforward control.
- Feedback/feedforward or 'hybridized' control.

Feedback control

We showed a diagram of feedback control in Fig. 8.1 where the error signal given by the differences between planned and actual output were fed back into the controller to produce changes in the inputs of the system.

Fig 8.2 Feedback stock control

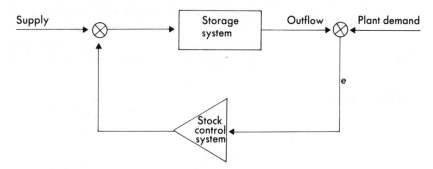

In Fig. 8.2 we show how feedback can be used to control a stock system. The principal problem with feedback control arises because the control data (the error signal) are derived from the output stage and are, therefore, intrinsically out of date. The idea behind feedforward control is designed to get around this problem.

Feedforward control

With feedforward control the inputs into a system are monitored in order to predict potential disturbances in its operating characteristics. If such disturbances can be successfully predicted then they can often be counteracted. The trick, of course, is to have reliable means of predicting the operating characteristics of the system concerned when input disturbances occur.

A feedforward, stock-control system linked to a production process would entail monitoring the quality of the raw material arrivals in order to predict variables such as rejection rates and yields on conversion of those raw materials into finished goods. These predictions of rejection rates and yields, allied with predictions of future plant demand, can give a greater degree of system control. In Fig. 8.3 we show the structure of such a feedforward system.

Fig 8.3 Feedforward control

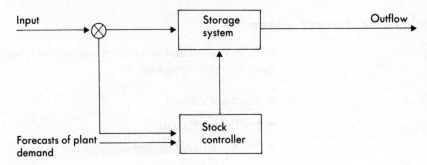

Feedback/feedforward control

Feedback/feedforward control attempts to obtain the best aspects of both types of control system described above. In Fig. 8.4 we show a stock-control system designed upon these lines. The feedback element compares the outflow of stock from the system with the actual production demand. Any discrepancies are fed back into either the input stage (thus changing the levels of new orders) or into the stock-handling system itself in order to speed up the rate at which orders from production are processed.

Fig 8.4 Feedback–feedforward control

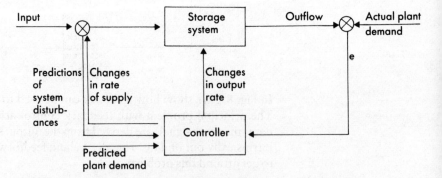

The feedforward element works in two ways. The first is by monitoring the quality of material stock as it is received from suppliers. These quality-control data can then be used to predict changes in production requirements caused by alterations in the raw material quality. Second, by predicting future production levels in order to match stock holdings with likely usages of the materials concerned.

A high degree of automation in the types of control system we have described can be very expensive. Indeed, fully automated stock-control/ordering systems are still a rarity in industry. However, in many control situations the required response rate of the system under consideration is not fast enough to justify the cost of automation. The closer we get to the strategic levels of decision-making within the firm, the less effective automation will, in any event, become.

In the remainder of this chapter we will consider three areas of tactical, short-term control. These are:

- The control of the firm's debtor balances through the use of credit-control techniques.

- The control of stocks through the use of simple, mathematical optimization techniques.

- The control of cash flow.

We are, therefore, concerned with the control of the three main subdivisions of working capital which appear in the typical company balance sheet as 'current assets'. They are termed current assets because they are either cash, or potentially realizable assets held for conversion into cash in the short term.

When a company invests in current assets such as debtors and stocks it uses up cash. The use of this cash entails a cost to the firm in that it forgoes the opportunity of investing that cash in other ways and earning the returns which would result from those alternative investments. This forgone return is the opportunity cost of capital tied up in current assets. In principle, the way we calculate the opportunity cost of capital is much the same as for any other resources although we will defer discussion of the mechanics of such calculations until Chapter 12. Suffice it to say at this stage that the only difference between costing capital and any other resource is that the cost of capital is expressed as a percentage rate of interest rather than as a money sum per unit or per labour hour.

Control of debtors

Apart from the retail sector of the economy and the so-called illicit 'black economy', most selling by firms and by individuals is on credit. A credit sale means that the firm invoices its customers at the point of sale and requests payment within so many days or weeks of that date. The firm may offer a discount (usually expressed as a percentage of the sale price) for prompt payment, although some of its customers will still delay payment for as long as possible and, indeed, may not pay at all.

The rate at which debtors pay their bills can have a dramatic effect upon a firm's cash flow and hence its liquidity. To illustrate this we will consider the case of Mr Montoya. Mr Montoya had been in business for six months. During that period his transactions were as follows:

1st January—purchase of equipment	£3 000
Sales per month from January to March	£5 600
Sales per month from April to June	£15 200

Annual rent (payable quarterly in advance)   £1 200
General overheads per month (paid in cash)   £700

The gross profit percentage on sales during the period was 25 per cent of the value of sales. Throughout the period Mr Montoya planned his purchases of materials to match his production requirements exactly. He also kept to the normal practice within the industry of paying for purchases one month after the date of their receipt. However, he has allowed his debtors two months' credit. His equipment is expected to last five years. He financed the business out of his own resources. On the basis of monthly profit and loss accounts Mr Montoya would appear to be doing rather well:

| | | Monthly profit | |
		January to March	April to June
Sales		£5 600	£15 200
less: Cost of goods sold			
(75 per cent)		4 200	11 400
Gross profit (25 per cent)		1 400	3 800
less: Rent	£100		£100
Overheads	700		700
Depreciation	50	850	50	850
Net profit		£550	£2 950

These figures might lead Mr Montoya to believe that he could withdraw £550 per month from the business in the period January to March and £2950 per month in the period April to June for his own personal use. However, the position looks somewhat different when we examine the monthly cash flows of the business over the six-month period.

	January (£)	February (£)	March (£)	April (£)	May (£)	June (£)
Equipment	(3 000)					
Sales (cash received)			5 600	5 600	5 600	15 200
Purchases (cash payments)*		(4 200)	(4 200)	(4 200)	(11 400)	(11 400)
Rent	(300)			(300)		
Overheads	(700)	(700)	(700)	(700)	(700)	(700)
Monthly cash flow	(4 000)	(4 900)	700	400	(6 500)	3 100
Cumulative cash flow	(4 000)	(8 900)	(8 200)	(7 800)	(14 300)	(11 200)

* Because there is, on average, a zero change in stock level from month to month, the difference between sales and gross profit is accounted for entirely by purchases.

This statement of cash flow highlights Mr Montoya's difficulty. Even taking account of his immediate payments of cash for equipment, rent and overheads (which means he starts his business with a cash deficit),

Mr Montoya's situation is made much worse because of the time lag between payment of creditors and the cash receipts from sales.

Clearly, Mr Montoya's problems are exacerbated by his expansion of trade in April. Indeed, an adverse credit gap (the average time difference between settling creditors and receiving payment from debtors) will always cause a transfer of cash resources into debtor balances in a situation of expanding markets. The reverse is true in a situation of contracting markets.

For example, Mr Montoya would like to know how his cash flow position will alter over the subsequent four months assuming: (i) he holds his sales level constant, (ii) he increases his sales by 10 per cent per month or (iii) he decreases his sales by 10 per cent per month.

Statement of monthly cash flow

		July (£)	August (£)	September (£)	October (£)
(i)	Assuming constant sales				
	Sales	15 200	15 200	15 200	15 200
	Purchases	(11 400)	(11 400)	(11 400)	(11 400)
	Rent	(300)			(300)
	Overheads	(700)	(700)	(700)	(700)
	Net cash flow	2 800	3 100	3 100	2 800
	Cumulative cash flow	(8 400)	(5 300)	(2 200)	600
(ii)	Assuming 10 per cent sales increase				
	Sales	15 200	15 200	16 720	18 392
	Purchases	(11 400)	(12 540)	(13 794)	(15 173)
	Rent	(300)			(300)
	Overheads	(700)	(700)	(700)	(700)
	Net cash flow	2 800	1 960	2 226	2 219
	Cumulative cash flow	(8 400)	(6 440)	(4 214)	(1 995)
(iii)	Assuming 10 per cent sales decrease				
	Sales	15 200	15 200	13 680	12 312
	Purchases	(11 400)	(10 260)	(9 234)	(8 311)
	Rent	(300)			(300)
	Overheads	(700)	(700)	(700)	(700)
	Net cash flow	2 800	4 240	3 746	3 001
	Cumulative cash flow	(8 400)	(4 160)	(414)	2 587

In situation (ii) Mr Montoya's adverse credit gap means that the cash return from sales is being received after payments have to be made for the purchases necessary to create those sales.

But, in situation (iii), the decrease in Mr Montoya's sales has an effect on cash flow to creditors (for purchases) in August while the corresponding decline in sales revenue does not feed through until September. The reduction in the amount paid to creditors in August helps boost cash flows in that month because the cash receipts from debtors are still coming in at their old level.

The policy implications which arise from the study of Mr Montoya's problem is that he should attempt to improve his liquidity by closing his credit gap rather than by cutting his sales. However, if there was no possibility of improvement in his credit gap he may be forced to cut back on his production and sales to improve his liquidity.

The control of an adverse credit gap entails:

- Monitoring the time taken by customers to pay their debts (by means of a debtor 'ageing' analysis).

- The control of the level of debtors by:
  1 Improved reminder and collection systems.
  2 Offering discounts for early payment.
  3 Improved credit control.

In Fig. 8.5 we show the basic structure of a debt-control system.

Fig 8.5   Debtor-control system

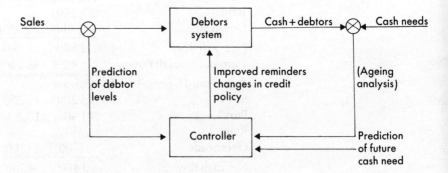

Debtor ageing analysis

During the course of time a firm will gather a list of outstanding debts which will lengthen and contract over the firm's selling seasons. A simple test can be conducted on a firm's outstanding debts to determine their average age. Assuming a constant rate of sales during the year, the debtor turnover ratio (expressed in days) will give a rough-and-ready guide to the average age of debts. This ratio is calculated at a given time using the formula:

$$debtor\ turnover\ ratio = \frac{total\ outstanding\ debts}{annual\ sales} \times 365$$

This ratio gives the average age in days of a firm's debtors although it cannot reveal the structure of the debtors' list. Similarly, the average time taken by the firm to pay its debts to its suppliers (its liabilities) can be estimated using the ratio:

$$creditor\ turnover\ ratio = \frac{total\ outstanding\ creditors}{annual\ purchases} \times 365$$

Depending upon the business in which a firm is engaged some debtors' accounts may be very large, while others may be very small. Clearly, if the resources the firm can devote to retrieving its debts is limited, it will pay to attend to the large balances as a matter of priority while leaving the smaller accounts to some more automatic debtor-control system.

The first stage in analysing the structure of a firm's debtor listing is to create a cumulative ranking of the outstanding balances and to plot the resultant ranking against the number of individual debts held. A certain group of debts (group A in Fig. 8.6) will account for the largest proportion of outstanding debts while being few in number. An intermediate group of balances (group B) will represent a large number of medium to small debts, while the final group (group C) will consist of a much larger number of very small accounts.

Group A debts involve the largest cash amounts and the firm may well consider it appropriate to devote every possible effort to recovering these debts as quickly as possible. The majority of these debts will have arisen for the simple reason that they are the balances on the accounts of the firm's largest customers. Some, however, may have arisen because the firm has continued to supply a customer with a poor payment record

Fig 8.6 A-B-C- analysis. Group A is two-thirds of total value of debtor balances. Group B is two-thirds of remaining balances. The actual grouping will depend on the steepness of the curve in practice

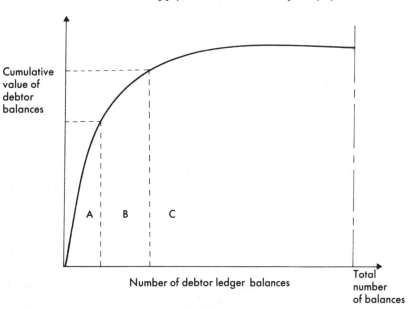

and a large outstanding balance has arisen as a result. Naturally, it should be this second class of debts which are the target of the firm's initial efforts.

The intermediate range of debts, while being important in the sense that the firm would not want them to default, are not of sufficient size to warrant a significant commitment of managerial time to their collection. The final range of debts will be for such trivial amounts that the cost of pursuing them may well be higher than the loss of interest resulting from the delay in their payment.

Once a listing of outstanding debtors in order of size has been compiled, the age of each outstanding debt can be analysed by month, week or even day, depending upon the nature of the business. Using the A–B–C analysis described above, the listing can be partitioned into three groups. In the table below we show part of a simple debtor ageing analysis with the proportion of debt held (as a percentage) in each month to the total appended underneath.

Account number	Account name	Total (£)	Dec. (£)	Nov. (£)	Oct. (£)	Sept. (£)	Aug. (£)
J.134.006	Julio plc	15 360		12 100	500	2 760	
J.125.007	Carlos plc	14 150	7 000				7 000
J.134.001	Ramon plc	10 250			10 250		
S.138.006	Joachim plc	9 000		9 000			
⋮	⋮	⋮	⋮	⋮	⋮	⋮	⋮
S.134.112	Martin plc	25					25
S.134.119	Barnabe, M.	12					12
Total		243 560	112 110	51 000	44 700	15 890	18 700
Proportion (per cent)		100	46	21	18.4	6.5	8.1

Given a total sales figure for the year of (say) £1 778 000, the debtor turnover ratio is:

$$\text{debtor turnover ratio} = \frac{243\,560}{1\,778\,000} \times 365$$

$$= 50 \text{ days}$$

The methods used to speed up the collection of debts vary from industry to industry. Indeed, in some cases firms sell their debts (just like any other assets) to financial institutions which specialize in this form of 'debt factoring' business. Other firms employ specialist debt-collection agencies who take over the problem of following up bad debts. The most common method for reducing the average age of unpaid debtor accounts (apart from sending frequent reminders and statements or withdrawing credit facilities for delinquent customers) is by offering discounts for early payment. It is a fairly straightforward matter to evaluate the benefit (or loss) which will follow from a change in credit policy.

For example, Mr Moron's credit sales now stand at a constant value of £20 000 per month and are expected to stay at this level indefinitely. Mr Moron is considering introducing a 2.5 per cent discount on the sale price of his goods for payment within one month. At the moment 25 per cent of debtors pay within one month, 50 per cent within two months and the remainder within three months. As a result of the change in credit policy, Mr Moron hopes that 80 per cent will pay within the first month, 10 per cent in the second month and the remainder in the third month. Mr Moron's opportunity cost of capital is 2 per cent per month (for more on the opportunity cost of capital see Chapter 12).

The first stage in the analysis of a credit policy change, such as that proposed by Mr Moron, is to analyse the change in cash flows from sales which will result. Obviously, in a steady-state situation, with no change in sales level and with no bad debts, the cash received each month will equal the monthly sales figure. In each month 25 per cent of the cash received will relate to sales made three months before, 50 per cent of the cash received will relate to sales made two months before and the remaining 25 per cent comes from the previous month.

In the first month, operating the new policy, Mr Moron will receive outstanding debts of £5000 and £10 000, respectively, from sales made two and three months previously. In addition he will also receive 80 per cent of the sales made in the previous month less the discount of 2.5 per cent:

$$\text{Receipts under new policy in month } t_1 = £20\,000 \times 0.8 \times 0.975 = £15\,600$$

In the second month of operation under the new policy Mr Moron will receive cash receipts of: £5000 from three months previously (under the old policy), £2000 from two months previously (the first month under the new system) and £15 600 from the previous month (as calculated above). The pattern of cash flows will emerge as shown below.

As you can see, the disturbance caused by the change in credit policy occurs in the month following the change and disappears from the system two months later. In this case the net effect has been to produce two cash gains in t_1 and t_2 which are paid for by the cash loss thereafter of £400 per month.

The second stage in the analysis of this change in credit policy is to determine its net effect on Mr Moron's wealth using the discounting procedure discussed in Chapter 3. You will note that the perpetuity of £400 per annum which runs from t_3 is discounted in two stages. The perpetuity summation formula derived in the appendix to Chapter 3 will bring the cash flows back to a present value at t_2 (i.e. one year prior to the start of the perpetuity). This 'present value' at t_2 must then be brought to t_0 by discounting at the rate of 2 per cent over the intervening 2 months.

The monthly rate of 2 per cent gives an annual rate of:

$$\text{Equivalent annual rate} = (1 + i)^{12}$$
$$= (1 + 0.02)^{12}$$
$$= 26.8 \text{ per cent}$$

	t_0 (£)	t_1 (£)	t_2 (£)	t_3 (£)	t_4 (£)	t_5 (£)	t_6 (£)
				Month number			
Original policy:							
Cash receipts	20 000	20 000	20 000	20 000	20 000	20 000	20 000
Revised policy:							
Receipts from:							
t_{-3} sales	5 000						
t_{-2} sales	10 000	5 000					
t_{-1} sales	5 000	10 000	5 000				
t_0 sales		15 600	2 000	2 000			
t_1 sales			15 600	2 000	2 000		
t_2 sales				15 600	2 000	2 000	
t_3 sales					15 600	2 000	2 000
t_4 sales						15 600	2 000
t_5 sales							15 600
Total cash receipts	20 000	30 600	22 600	19 600	19 600	19 600	19 600
Change in cash flow	0	10 600	2 600	(400)	(400)	(400)	(400)
Discount rate		1.02	1.02^2				
Perpetuity					0.02		
Present values:							
t_0	0						
t_1	10 392						
t_2	2 499						
			20 000				
			1.02^2				
t^3 (perpetuity)	(19 223)						
Net present value	(6 332)						

Even at this opportunity cost of capital the switch in credit policy is not worth while. Indeed, in practice the policy of offering general discounts can be a very expensive way of improving short-term liquidity.

Self test: **Repeat Mr Moron's analysis assuming:**

1 **The discount rate offered to customers is set at (a) 1 per cent per month, (b) 3 per cent per month.**

2 The discount rate of 2.5 per cent per month is withdrawn after 2 months (i.e. in t_2) and that the original pattern of payments re-emerges.

3 The discount rate of 2.5 per cent brings all payments in within 1 month.

Solution clue: (i(a)) −26 168, (i(b)) 174.07; (ii) −245.89; (iii) −9311.8.

Control of stocks

Figure 8.7 shows a combined feedback/feedforward control system for either raw materials or finished stocks. As with debtor control, discussed in the previous section, a company attempting to control its stock may feel it appropriate to focus attention upon its most expensive lines, while keeping moderately large reserves of stocks of its cheaper items. For example, a television manufacturer may wish to optimize his holding of colour tubes, while keeping, at the same time, a very large stock of cabinet screws! As with debtor analysis performed in the last section an A–B–C analysis of stock can be an effective tool for identifying those items which require the highest degree of control (see Fig. 8.8).

Fig 8.7 The control of stocks

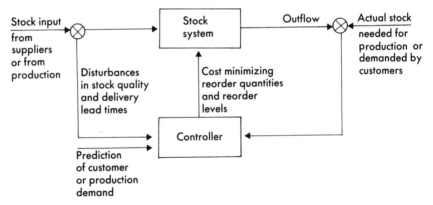

As can be seen from Fig. 8.7 the control of stocks involves the following stages:

- Predicting the future usages of stocks.

- Monitoring the actual usages of stock.

- Monitoring the actual cost of reordering stock.

- Monitoring the time taken for stock to be delivered or produced (the supply or production 'lead time').

We will assume, as a natural extension of the managerial objectives discussed in Chapter 1, that an optimal stock policy will be one which minimizes the overall cash cost of holding stock. Given a particular level of demand (from production for raw materials or from customers for finished stocks) the cost of holding stock will be a trade-off between two conflicting factors:

• The fixed cost of reordering.

• The opportunity cost of the capital invested in stock.

Fig 8.8 A-B-C stock analysis. Group A is two-thirds of total stock value. Group B is two-thirds of remainder

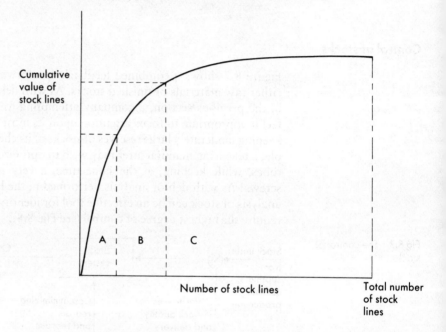

A certain fixed cost will be incurred each time stock is reordered. In the case of raw materials purchased from suppliers the reorder cost is the cost of placing the order plus any fixed transport costs which may be incurred. In the case of replenishing finished stocks from production this fixed cost of reordering will be the set-up cost for the production facility and any other fixed administrative charges which might be incurred. We will assume that the cost of warehouse space is fixed with respect to the range of stock levels which could be held.

The more often stock is reordered from suppliers or requisitioned from production the greater will be the sum of the fixed reorder costs during a given period. On the other hand, the higher the average stock levels maintained by the firm, the less frequently stock must be reordered and, therefore, the lower will be the fixed reorder costs incurred during the period.

When a firm ties up its working capital in the form of stock it forgoes the opportunity of using that capital in other ways. As a result, capital locked up in stock holding has an opportunity cost associated with it, and the higher the average level of stock held, the higher this opportunity cost of capital will be.

In order to minimize overall annual stock-holding costs management can adopt one or both of the following strategies:

- Reduce the fixed cost of each reorder to the lowest possible level (which will permit lower average stock levels to be held with a consequent lowering of the opportunity cost of capital invested in stock).

- Given a particular fixed cost of each reorder, optimize the average level of stock holding so that the total cost of holding stock over a period (fixed reorder cost plus the opportunity cost of capital) is minimized.

The second strategy is subservient to the first in that, given the lowest possible reorder cost, the overall cost of stock holding can then be minimized. Lower reorder costs mean that the firm can operate with a lower level of stocks (whether they be raw material or finished goods stocks) with more reorders during the particular period. Indeed, a logical extension of this would be that suppliers, for example, would be making many small deliveries during a day which were exactly matched to the firm's production requirements and that little or no raw-material stock need be held with the consequent avoidance of the cost of warehouse facilities and all of the other associated costs of holding stock.

Matching and optimizing supply, production and deliveries requires a total production management philosophy which is only now being adopted by some UK and US firms. Japanese firms, on the other hand, deliberately follow a philosophy of carefully planned and designed total production systems. For example, Toyota (Japan) has only one hour's worth of back-up stocks while Ford (USA) has three weeks. Small stock levels require efficient and predictable production systems while large stock levels can protect an inefficient and unpredictable production system from collapse.

Note: For an interesting and thoughtful analysis of the problems of Western manufacturing in the light of the Japanese experience read Robert S. Kaplan's article cited at the end of this chapter. Kaplan's article also poses many questions for management accountants in the way they monitor the performance of their firms.

The technique of minimizing overall costs given a particular level of fixed reorder cost is reasonably straightforward. In Fig. 8.9 we show a simplified diagram of how stocks vary through time.

The reorder quantity is the predetermined amount which a firm reorders whenever its stocks fall below a certain 'reorder level'. The lower the reorder quantity, the lower will be the average level of stock holding by the firm. To control stocks we need two items of information:

• The reorder quantity which minimizes the cost of holding stock given a particular fixed cost of reordering and a given opportunity cost of capital.

• The reorder level which once passed indicates to the stock controller that fresh stock must be ordered. Stock must be reordered at the point where sufficient stock remains to sustain production (for raw materials) or satisfy customers (for finished stocks) over the time between order and delivery—which is normally termed the 'lead time'.

Fig 8.9 Stock movements through time

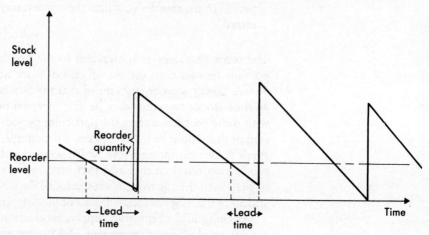

Setting reorder quantities and reorder levels

As noted above, the cost of holding stock consists of two elements: one which varies directly with, and one which varies directly against, the sizes of the batches ordered. Figure 8.10 shows the pattern of these two costs against batch size for a given period of time (we will assume a

Fig 8.10 Total cost of holding stock

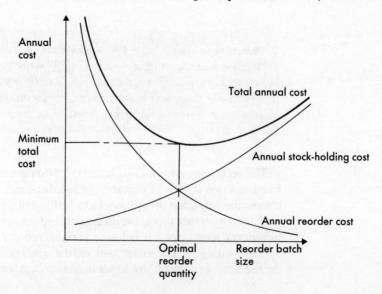

year although in some applications it may be a month, week or even a day).

If the firm reorders a set amount (Q) of a particular stock line every time the recorded stock level falls below the reorder level then the average holding of stock (assuming an even rate of usage between deliveries) will be given by:

average stock holding $= Q/2$

Over the year the overall cost of holding this stock will be given by the following formula:

annual cost of holding stock $= iQV/2$

where i is the opportunity cost of the capital tied up in stock (expressed as an interest rate) and V is the value per unit of stock. In this case stock should be valued at its replacement cost or current buying-in price plus any variable transport costs or other variable transaction costs incurred.

During the course of a year if D is the annual usage or demand for the stock item then the number of reorders during the year will be given by:

$$\text{number of reorders} = \frac{\text{annual usage of or demand for stock item}}{\text{reorder quantity}}$$
$$= D/Q$$

Now, if F is the fixed administrative cost incurred in setting up each order then:

annual costs of reordering $= DF/Q$

Combining these two formulae we obtain an equation for the total cost which is shown graphically in Fig. 8.10 above:

$$\text{total annual stock-holding cost} = \frac{iQV}{2} + \frac{DF}{Q}$$

A formula for the minimum overall cost can be obtained by differentiating the above formula with respect to the reorder quantity (Q) and setting the resultant differential to zero:

$$\frac{d(\text{TAC})}{dQ} = \frac{iV}{2} - \frac{DF}{Q^2} = 0$$

where TAC is the total annual cost of holding stock.

By rearrangement of this formula we can find the reorder quantity which will give the minimum total annual cost of holding the stock line:

$$Q = \sqrt{\left(\frac{2DF}{iV}\right)}$$

For example, Marchena's annual demand for a dangerous industrial chemical called Olic Acid is expected to be 16 000 kg in the coming year.

Each kilogram will cost £10 (including variable transport costs) and Marchena's opportunity cost of capital is 12 per cent per annum. The fixed reorder cost is £200 per order and this includes a fixed handling charge by British Rail. The average lead time for delivery of stock is 18 days and the firm has found that an average of an extra 10 days' supply is sufficient to cover the risk of stock-out. Marchena uses Olic Acid on a continuous production process.

The optimal order quantity for Olic Acid can be found by substituting the relevant data into the reorder quantity formula:

$$Q = \sqrt{\left(\frac{2 \times 16\,000 \times 200}{0.12 \times 10} \right)}$$

$$= 2309\,\text{kg (to the nearest kilogram)}$$

The reorder level is determined by two sorts of uncertainty:

- Uncertainty in the length of the lead time (i.e. a delay by a supplier, for example, could lead to 'stock-out').

- Uncertainty in the usage of stock during the lead time period (i.e. excess usage could also lead to 'stock-out').

The firm must decide, given the nature of its business, how much of this uncertainty it wishes to protect itself against when setting the reorder level. The reorder level will consist of two components:

- The level of remaining stock required to cover the expected lead time.

- The additional amount of stock required as a 'buffer' against running out of stock.

The lead-time demand can be calculated as follows:

$$\text{average lead-time demand} = \frac{\dfrac{\text{annual demand}}{\text{for stock item}} \times \dfrac{\text{average lead}}{\text{time (days)}}}{365}$$

$$= \frac{DL}{365}$$

Using the data in Marchena's example we can estimate the average lead-time demand as:

$$\text{average lead-time demand} = \frac{16\,000 \times 18}{365}$$

$$= 789\,\text{kg}$$

The buffer stock required is equivalent to 10 days' supply (managements assessment based upon historical evidence of delivery lead times). We can calculate this figure in exactly the same way as the average lead-time demand:

$$\text{buffer stock} = \frac{16\,000 \times 10}{365}$$

$$= 438 \, \text{kg}$$

The reorder level (ROL) is equal to the sum of the average lead-time demand plus the buffer stock, i.e.

$$\text{ROL} = 789 + 438$$

$$= 1227 \, \text{kg}$$

The reorder level specifies the level of stock at which the firm places its reorder quantity. In a continuous process such as that operated by Marchena, running out of stock could be disastrous. Equipment would have to be shut down, cleaned and reprimed when new stock becomes available—all of which could be very expensive. However, in other production situations a firm may be able to operate with lower buffer stocks and hence lower reorder levels, provided that some other process could take up the spare production capacity in the event of the necessary stocks running out.

The benefits of quantity discounts

Using the total annual stock-holding cost formula, given above, it is possible to calculate whether a quantity discount offered by a supplier is worth while. To do this we compare the total annual cost of holding the stock line without the discount against the total annual cost with the discount. We assume, for the first calculation, that the company uses the optimal reorder quantity as specified by the optimal reorder quantity formula; for the second calculation we use the reorder quantity required to earn the discount.

For example, Marchena's supplier is prepared to offer a 5 per cent discount for all orders of 2750 kg or more. The total annual stock-holding cost formula was:

$$\text{TAC} = \frac{iQV}{2} + \frac{DF}{Q}$$

At the optimal reorder quantity of 2309 kg the total annual cost is given as:

$$\text{TAC} = \frac{0.12 \times 2309 \times 10}{2} + \frac{16\,000 \times 200}{2309}$$

$$= £2771 \text{ per annum}$$

At the discounted order quantity of 2750 kg the total annual stock holding cost is given by:

$$\text{TAC} = \frac{0.12 \times 2750 \times 9.5}{2} + \frac{16\,000 \times 200}{2750}$$

$$= £2731 \text{ per annum}$$

The effect of the discount is marginally favourable as it reduces the total annual cost by £40.

> **Self test:** Determine whether a 3 per cent discount is worth while for orders in excess of 2500 kg.
> **Solution clue:** Almost the same answer as with 5 per cent on orders in excess of 2750 kg.

Two-bin stock-holding systems

The method of stock control outlined above lends itself quite naturally to a very simple, and effective, physical control system known as the 'two-bin system'. The stock is held in two containers or 'bins'; the first is filled to the reorder level and the second is filled with the remainder of the reorder quantity.

Withdrawals from stock are made from the second container and as soon as it is emptied a new order is raised. Withdrawals are then made from the first, reserve container, until the new stock is delivered. Before the new delivery arrives the contents of the reserve container should be transferred to the second container (to avoid build up of obsolete stock). When the new stock is delivered, the reserve container is filled first and any remainder then added to the old stock in the second container. With automatic feed containers such a dual container system as we have described may be too costly. It that is the case, the stock controllers will either have to take frequent measurements of stock level or fit some automatic level meter.

The valuation of stock

Raw-material stocks can be valued in one of two ways:

* On the basis of current market value.

* On the basis of the original cost of purchase.

For all normal decision-making purposes the first is the only relevant valuation basis if 'current market value' is the same as the opportunity cost of the stock item in use. We discussed the opportunity-cost concept in detail in Chapter 3. However, in practice, stock is usually valued on the basis of one of several original-cost valuation methods. There can be some important reasons why this type of valuation basis is used even though it is strictly irrelevant for decision-making purposes:

* The taxation authorities specify that stock should be valued using the original cost of purchase.

- The rate of turnover of certain stock may be so fast that there is no significant difference between the historical and the current market value of that stock.

- Historical cost is still the main basis for preparing accounts for external users.

- A historical-cost valuation basis may be necessary for financial control purposes. If stock is valued at its original cost it should be possible for the firm to reconcile its cash payments for raw materials during the year with the original cost of the stock used during the year and the difference between the opening and closing stock values.

The last point may be of considerable importance to a firm in determining stock wastages and losses and in keeping a check on cash movements.

We will discuss three bases for historical-cost stock valuation:

- First in first out (FIFO).

- Last in first out (LIFO).

- Average cost.

During the course of a firm's financial year its stock movements can be described as in Fig. 8.11.

Fig 8.11 Stock movements during the accounting year

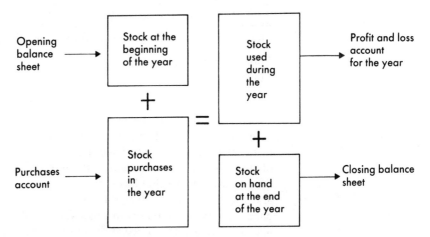

The first in first out system assumes that stock purchased first is used first leaving stock acquired last on hand at the end of the year. Note that this stock flow is only an assumption for stock-valuation purposes and need not necessarily coincide with physical stock flows.

For example, Marchena plc purchased a chemical 'alpha-sludge' in six batches during the course of a year. The purchases and usages were as follows:

	Purchases (tons)	Purchase price per ton (£)	Total cost (£)	Usage (tons)
1 January	1 800	4.50	8 100	
15 January				900
28 February	2 240	4.50	10 080	
3 March				2 000
31 April	1 000	4.60	4 600	
27 August	3 250	4.80	15 763	
29 August				2 590
28 September	1 100	5.00	5 500	
13 October				1 400
28 December	2 000	5.25	10 500	
30 December				1 500
	11 390		54 543	8 390

There was no stock of alpha-sludge at the beginning of the year; 3000 tons of the chemical were in stock at the end of the year.

Using a FIFO basis, the 8390 tons of stock which were used during the year would be valued as follows:

1 800 tons at £4.50 per ton	£8 100
2 240 tons at £4.50 per ton	£10 080
1 000 tons at £4.60 per ton	£4 600
3 250 tons at £4.85 per ton	£15 763
100 tons at £5.00 per ton	£500
8 390 Total cost of used stock	£39 043

The remaining stock at the end of the year is valued as follows:

1 000 tons at £5.00 per ton	£5 000
2 000 tons at £5.25 per ton	£10 500
Total stock value at year end	£15 500 (FIFO)

The last in first out system assumes that stock used at any particular point in time is valued on the basis that it was the most recently purchased. In order to use the LIFO basis we need to know the pattern of usage of stock so that we can identify the most recent price applicable at the time of use. On a LIFO basis, therefore, we would value the stock used and the stock on hand at the end of the year as shown on the next page. Follow the numbers through very carefully. Note that any usages in a given period are valued at the most recent price available.

Under the LIFO basis of stock valuation:

The value of stock used in the period	£40 442
The value of stock on hand at 31 December	£14 101
Total	£54 543

The difficulty with the LIFO method is that each usage must be valued according to the prices attaching to the latest arrivals. On 30 October, for example, stock of 1400 tons was used which was valued at £5 for the first 110 tons (the latest arrival) and at £4.85 for the remaining 300

	Valuation	Value of stock used (£)	Balance of stock (£)
1 January	$1\,800 \times 4.50$		8 100
15 January	$(900) \times 4.50$	4 050	
28 February	$2\,240 \times 4.50 + 900 \times 4.50$		14 130
3 March	$(2\,000) \times 4.50$	9 000	
	$240 \times 4.50 + 900 \times 4.50$		5 130
31 April	$1\,000 \times 4.60 + 240 \times 4.50$		
	900×4.50		9 730
27 August	$3\,250 \times 4.85 + 1\,000 \times 4.60$		
	$+\quad 240 \times 4.50 + 900 \times 4.50$		24 593
29 August	$(2\,590) \times 4.85$	12 562	
	$660 \times 4.85 + 1\,000 \times 4.60$		
	$+\quad 240 \times 4.50 + 900 \times 4.50$		12 931
28 September	$1\,100 \times 5.00 + 660 \times 4.85$		
	$+\quad 1\,000 \times 4.60 + 1\,140 \times 4.50$		18 431
30 October	$(1\,100) \times 5.00 + (300) \times 4.85$	6 955	
	$360 \times 4.85 + 1\,000 \times 4.60$		
	$+\,1\,140 \times 4.50$		11 476
28 December	$2\,000 \times 5.25 + 360 \times 4.85$		
	$+\quad 1\,000 \times 4.60 + 1\,140 \times 4.50$		21 976
30 December	$(1\,500) \times 5.25$	7 875	
	$500 \times 5.25 + 360 \times 4.85$		
	$+\quad 1\,000 \times 4.60 + 1\,140 \times 4.50$		14 101
	Value of stock used	40 442	

tons which was deemed to have arrived (for valuation purposes) on 27 August. Unlike the FIFO method, the use of the LIFO method entails keeping a precise account of the movements of stock in and out of the stock account and the prices at which purchases are made.

The average stock method prices stock withdrawals at the average cost of stock on hand prior to the withdrawal:

	Purchases (tons) (i)	Price (£) (ii)	Withdrawals (tons) (iii)	Balance (tons) (iv)	Average (£) (v)	Balance value (£) (vi)	Value of stock used (£) (vii)
1 January	1 800	4.50		1 800	4.500	8 100	
15 January			900	900	4.500	4 050	4 050
28 February	2 240	4.50		3 140	4.500	14 130	
3 March			2 000	1 140	4.500	5 130	9 000
31 April	1 000	4.60		2 140	4.547	9 730	
27 August	3 250	4.85		5 390	4.730	25 493	
29 August			2 590	2 800	4.730	13 244	12 250
28 September	1 100	5.00		3 900	4.806	18 744	
30 October			1 400	2 500	4.806	12 015	6 729
28 December	2 000	5.25		4 500	5.003	22 515	
30 December			1 500	3 000	5.003	15 009	7 505
			8 390				39 534

Purchases (i) are added to the balance of stock (iv) in tons and priced at their input price (ii) for addition to the stock value (vi). The average cost (v) is computed by dividing the stock value (vi) by the balance in tons. The average cost is then used to price withdrawals from stock as they occur.

We can now summarize these three valuation methods as follows:

	FIFO (£)	LIFO (£)	Average cost (£)
Cost of stock (as shown in the profit and loss account)	39 043	40 442	39 534
Valuation of stock on hand (as shown in the balance sheet)	15 500	14 101	15 009
Total cost of stock purchases	54 543	54 543	54 543

The FIFO system uses the most recent cost as its valuation base for year-end stock, but out-of-date costs for the valuation of stock consumed during the year. In a situation of rising costs, therefore, the value of stock in the balance sheet will approximate current cost (because the most recent purchase prices of stock are used) while the cost of stock in the profit and loss account will be at a lower value. Because accounting profit is given as sales revenue less the cost of the resources used (including stock consumed in production) FIFO will tend to overstate that profit in a period of rising prices. Exactly the reverse holds for the LIFO system which uses a closer approximation to current cost in computing the profit and loss account figures.

Of the three methods LIFO charges the closest to the current cost in calculating profit but shows an undervalued closing stock figure in the balance sheet. The average-cost method combines the advantages and disadvantages of both FIFO and LIFO in that in a situation of rising prices it tends to overstate both accounting profit and understate the current value of stock held at the balance-sheet date. However, all three systems suffer from the disadvantage that the numbers they produce, while being objectively verifiable, have no economic significance as all three involve the aggregation of costs acquired at different points in time.

Control of cash

In most firms cash is not held for its own sake, as an item of stock (banks are, of course, an important exception to this). For most firms cash is a 'residual' of its operations and the amount held at any point in time will vary as trading activity varies. We have already described how the timing of payments from debtors and to creditors can strongly influence cash flow. Some other important influences upon cash flow are:

- The seasonality of a firm's trading pattern. With most consumer goods peak demand comes in the pre-Christmas season; with travel services there is usually a peak in demand in early spring; in the energy-supply industry demand is at its highest in the winter months. We would normally expect to find the peak in cash flows following behind the peak in demand. The actual lag between demand, sale and cash inflow will depend upon the firm's terms of trade.

- There may be seasonal elements in a firm's cash outflows which are quite independent of the cycle of demand. For example:
    (i) Seasonal office and plant heating bills.
    (ii) Fixed interest charges on debt capital.
    (iii) Profit taxes which are paid to the Inland Revenue at the time specified by law.
    (iv) Dividends to investors.

All of these items, and more, will form part of any cash budget. If the firm has high seasonality in its cash budget it may well benefit from diversification into areas of operation which will help to smooth its cash flows from one month to another.

In Fig. 8.12 we show the annual cash-flow profile of a business which specializes in summer holidays to the Costa del Sol. Its cash position

Fig 8.12 Cash flow potential of diversification

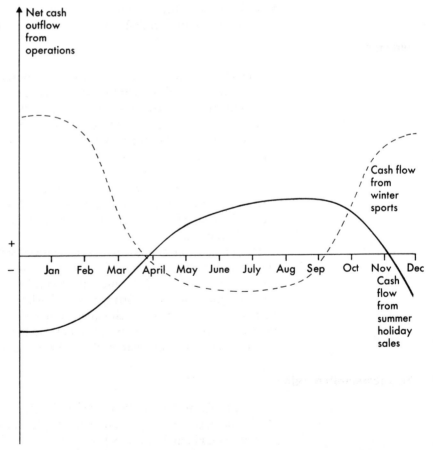

is shown by the heavy, continuous line on the graph. Naturally, a company such as this would do well to diversify its business interests in the winter sports market although there may well be problems setting up in such a new market with different hotels, venues, etc. If successful, the winter sports business would produce cash flows as shown by the dotted line. The overall effect will be, of course, to diversify away some of the variability associated with the single line of business.

In general, cash flows can be controlled by a mixture of the following methods:

- Altering the incidence of payments, where management has some control over its timing (dividends and bonus payments are good examples of this).

- Seeking the most favourable credit policies.

- Optimizing the holding of stocks and work in progress.

- Making sure that cash does not lie idle for any length of time. It may be that short-term cash surpluses can be placed on deposit with a bank or in some other short-term investment.

- Seeking diversification into new areas which complement the firm's existing pattern of cash flows.

Summary

In this chapter we have examined three important areas of short-term control: the control of debtors, stocks and cash which, taken together, represent the three most important classes of current assets.

We have noted that the holding of current assets involves an investment of cash which implies an opportunity cost associated with the capital used. We have seen how this opportunity cost of capital influences decisions concerning the optimal holding of stock and the merits of particular discount policies to encourage speedier repayments by debtors.

We have also noted the problems associated with different credit policies and the liquidity problems that can arise through inadequate control of terms of credit.

Throughout our analysis we have deployed simple mathematical and statistical techniques to model the real situations we are attempting to control. Naturally, real business problems are much more subtle and complex than we have portrayed in this chapter. However, much can be done with the simple techniques outlined in this chapter and where they are insufficient for the problem in hand the additional readings suggested at the end of this chapter should help to supplement them.

Supplementary reading

AMEY, L. R., and EGGINTON, D. A., Stock control models, in Arnold, J., Carsberg, B., and Scapens, R. (eds), *Topics in Management Accounting*, Philip Allan, 1980

ANNAN, T., Effective stock control procedures, *Management Accounting*, November 1981

KAPLAN, R. S., Measuring manufacturing performance: a new challenge for management accounting research, *Accounting Review*, October 1983.

LORANGE, P., and SCOTT MORTON, M. S., A framework for management control systems, in R. H. Chenhall *et al.* (eds), *The Organizational Context of Management Accounting*, Pitman, 1981.

Questions

1 Describe, using diagrams if necessary, and supply one example of each:

   (a) Feedback control.
   (b) Feedforward control.
   (c) Hybrid or feedback/feedforward control.

2 Seville produces coated paper and is attempting to optimize its holding of its principal raw material, rolls of paper. Each roll is purchased at a price of £125 excluding variable freightage of £2 per roll. The fixed freightage for each order is £45 and Seville estimates that its fixed cost of ordering is £25 per order. Its annual usage of the paper is budgeted for next year at 12 000 rolls although its usage could vary by 5 per cent either way. Seville's opportunity cost of capital is 12 per cent per annum. Delivery from date of order is guaranteed at 10 days.

   Required:
   (a) Determine the reorder quantity on the basis that 12 000 rolls will be required during the coming year.
   (b) Determine the reorder level given the uncertainty in the usage and assuming that management wants to avoid the possibility of stock-out.
   (c) Assuming an annual usage of 12 000 rolls, determine whether a discount of 2.5 per cent on the invoiced cost (excluding freightage) would be worth while for orders in excess of 350 rolls.
   (d) Calculate the minimum acceptable discount for orders in excess of (i) 350 rolls and (ii) 400 rolls.
   (e) Discuss the nature of the assumptions implied by the simple two-cost component, reorder quantity model.

3 Martin plc is valuing its stock of 'sludge-nuts' at the end of June 19X5. There was no stock in hand at the beginning of the month. During the month the following purchases and issues from stock were made:

	Purchases (bags)	Purchase price per bag (£)	Issues (bags)
1 June	10	100	
4 June			5
7 June	20	110	
12 June			15
15 June	12	112	
22 June			8
24 June	10	116	
27 June			9

Required:

(a) Determine the end of month stock value using (i) FIFO, (ii) LIFO and (iii) the average-stock method of valuation.

(b) Comment upon the advantages and disadvantages of the three methods of valuing stock.

4   The monthly projections for a small electronics components manufacturer are as follows.

Sales revenue currently stands at £7800 per month and is expected to expand at 1 per cent per month into the indefinite future. This is the average rate of expansion which the firm has enjoyed over the previous six months. The firm's debtors pay up as follows: one-third within one month, half within two months and the remainder within three months.

The company has enjoyed a gross profit margin of 25 per cent on monthly sales over the past year and has tried to keep its inventory constant at a very low level. The company's suppliers require payment within one month. They can enforce this condition of trade because of the high demand for microelectronic components.

The company's management is considering a 1.5 per cent discount on the invoiced value of goods if payment is received within one month. It believes that this will ensure that 50 per cent of the firm's debtors pay within the month and that half the remainder will pay at the end of the second month and the rest at the end of the third month.

Assume all cash receipts and payments occur on the last day of the month and that the company's cost of capital is 0.8 per cent per month.

Required:

(a) Create a projected cash budget for sales less purchases over the next six months, and show the effect on that cash budget if the change in credit policy is implemented.

(b) Calculate whether the change in credit policy is worth while given the firm's cost of capital.

(c) Discuss the problems of maintaining liquidity in a situation of expanding trade.

5   Zambra plc wishes to prepare a budget for the production and sale of one of its products, the Mora, for the coming three years. Current financial statistics for Mora production are as follows:

Variable cost per Mora:

Raw materials	£15.00
Labour	£10.00
Variable overheads	£5.00

Selling price per Mora	£55.00
Output quantity per annum	8 000.00 Moras
Fixed overheads per annum	£45 000.00

Fixed overheads can only be avoided if production is discontinued. The expected rates of cost increases are:

Raw materials	10 per cent per annum
Labour	15 per cent per annum
Variable overheads	6 per cent per annum
Fixed overheads	3 per cent per annum

Zambra sells all of the Moras it can produce at the planned selling price. Because the Mora has an extremely short shelf life, no stocks are maintained.

Required:

(a) Draw up a projected budget for the next 3 years on the assumption that (i) output is held constant and (ii) the current net profit margin (ratio of net profit to sales revenue) remains constant.

(b) Outline the difficulties in controlling the cash resources of a firm and the ways in which they can be overcome.

9 Cost control

In this chapter we consider the purpose of collecting costs within the firm. In particular, we consider various techniques for costing production processes in order to give an insight into their use for decision-making purposes. We then return to a problem we have considered before—the issue of overhead allocation and its relevance for decision-making. We will present some of the justifications which have been advanced for the common practice of including fixed overheads in decision-making procedures. Finally, we examine the technique of variance analysis whereby actual costs can be compared with budgeted figures and relevant control information produced.

> By the end of this chapter you should have an understanding of:
>
> - The purpose of cost accounting within the firm.
> - The techniques of costing different production systems.
> - The purpose of fixed overhead allocation within the firm.
> - The methods of variance analysis and its use in management control.

Purpose of the cost-accounting function within the firm

At the beginning of the last chapter we discussed the concept of control. The principal objective of the cost-accounting function within the firm is to measure and record the costs of operating different processes and to compare those costs with the preset cost targets set by management. In this sense, cost accounting is a very important instrument of control within the firm. To serve their purpose, the costs which are collected do not have to be of any general value in the decision-making processes of the firm, although there are obvious benefits if they are. The major value of such costs lies in their role of monitoring the performance of the system being controlled and their ability to be consistently compared with the planned targets set by management.

The danger with cost accounting arises if managers come to believe that the cost data are automatically suited for general decision-making purposes. It may be that cost-accounting data (which are past data) can be converted to estimates of future costs which would be useful for decision-making purposes. But, as we have said before, this is not the primary purpose of cost accounting which is to monitor the cost behaviour of production and other systems in order that control decisions can be made.

Cost accounting is one part of the overall management-accounting activity of the firm. Its primary function is one of providing data for the control decision but it may have an additional purpose of providing 'off the peg' data which can be converted into information for other decision-making purposes at some later point in time. Within this context, cost accounting can be seen as a part of the more general activity of management accounting. As we outlined in Chapter 1, the wider brief of management accounting is to provide information 'made to measure' for all sorts of management decisions in addition to those exclusively concerned with control.

In this chapter we will examine two of the cost accountant's most important tasks: first, the measurement of costs for production control and, second, the techniques for identifying the possible causes of differences between actual and planned (budgeted) costs. We will also discuss how and why fixed overheads are often included in the cost-accounting process.

Techniques of costing different production systems

As we have noted before, all production systems can be described, at the highest level of generality, as processes for the conversion of inputs into outputs. For many decision situations this level of generality is all that is necessary, because we happen to be concerned with the overall characteristics of a system rather than with the precise detail of its operation. However, because cost accounting is concerned with monitoring detailed system performance it must match the complexities of the system concerned. Two problems immediately arise: the identification of those aspects of production which attract specific costs and the time scale of any particular process.

In any production system there are certain physical positions where resources are applied to the system. Materials may be brought together or some labour or managerial activity may occur. For example, a car-body paint shop would be a point within a car production system where materials (car bodies, paint, pickling acid, etc.) and other resources (labour, scientific and managerial skills) are brought together as a production activity. Cost accountants call such a position a 'cost centre' because, even though the activity does not attract revenue directly, it does attract costs which can be identified and recorded.

The planning of a firm's financial activities will include major cost items such as materials, various variable and fixed overheads, labour, scientific, technical and managerial skills. These overall costs arise through the consolidation of individual elements of cost (the costs of specific items of materials, specific grades of labour, etc.) which are incurred in the various cost centres within the firm. In Fig. 9.1 we show, in outline, the consolidation of the various elements of cost into the overall cost of a particular process.

Fig 9.1 The collection of costs from cost centres

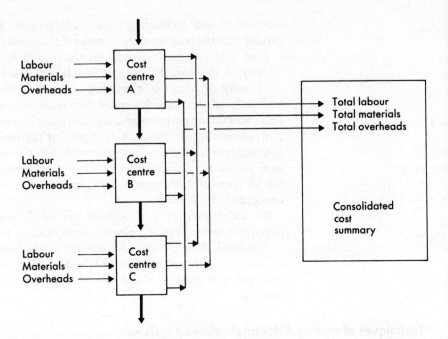

For example, one particular cost element may be the usage of electricity for the electrolytic coating of car bodies. The cost element is, therefore, the metered usage of electricity on that particular aspect of production. The cost centre concerned is the car-body paint shop and the basic cost classification is variable overheads (factory power).

The following factors can influence the selection of cost centres:

- The precision with which costs can be attributed to the process concerned.

- Whether the costs attributable to a proposed cost centre can be controlled at that point in the production process.

- Whether the costs collected through a proposed cost centre can be directly related to some aspect of the centre's performance.

With respect to the last point, the usage of electricity by a car-body paint shop could be related to the following aspects of performance:

- The throughput of car bodies. We would expect the usage of electricity to be directly related to the number of bodies treated.

- The thickness of the electrolytic deposit on the body parts treated. The required thickness will have been laid down in the production design specification.

- The quality of the cleaning and any other pretreatment which has been carried out on the car bodies.

- The quality of the steel and hence the electrical conductivity of the particular batch of bodies being treated.

Certain of the factors outlined above will be under the control of the operators and foremen working in the paint shop. Other factors, however, may be related to other parts of the production process or, indeed, as in the last factor mentioned, to the skill of the firm's purchasing department.

> **Self test:** Identify the cost centre in which you either work or study. If you are a student your department or scheme may be the cost centre in which you work. List out the main costs which you think your cost centre is responsible for. Do the costs, as collected, give any information on the performance of your cost centre?

It is one of the cost accountant's tasks to form an opinion on the relationship between cost and cost centre and the degree to which variations in the costs concerned can be attributed to a given activity.

The second problem in costing production processes concerns the length of time over which production occurs. If the production time is longer than the time period over which control is to be exercised then the system is essentially a continuous one. In this situation the production system must be 'notionally' stopped so that the costs incurred in a particular period can be measured. If, on the other hand, production takes place over a shorter time period than that required for control purposes then no such artificial stops are necessary. In the next section we will examine this problem in much more detail. We will look at the two basic types of production system:

- Process costing (continuous-time production processes).
- Job costing (discrete-time production processes).

Process costing

Continuous production systems which do not have convenient breaks in their production runs present problems for the cost accountant in the assignment of costs. These problems arise because, at any point in time, a certain amount of production will still be in progress. For example, a motor-car production line will always contain a certain number of cars that are only partly completed.

A continuous production process will begin each period with a particular stock of work in progress. During the course of the production period, this initial stock of work in progress will be completed, followed by further units which will be both started and finished. In addition, at the end of the period there will be some units in production which have been started but remain uncompleted. The problem we have in establishing a cost per unit during the production period is that we can only identify the number of units fully completed. Some will be incomplete although they will have consumed certain raw materials and other resources. It is the cost accountant's job to establish the cost of those units completed during the period and the cost incurred on uncompleted units remaining at the end.

Example: Peteneras plc operates a continuous production process for the manufacture of one type of standard electronic component. Only four cost categories are involved (of course, in practice, there will be many more than this): materials, labour, power and other variable overheads. The cost of each month's production and the value of the work in progress are calculated for budgeting purposes. The components are produced on a continuous production line with monthly periods of account.

At the beginning of period 9, 15 units were in various stages of completion on the production line. On average, each unit had 80 per cent of its materials in place, and 50 per cent of the labour required to build each unit had been applied. In addition, 30 per cent of the necessary power and 40 per cent of the necessary variable overheads had been applied (on average) to each unit.

The opening work in progress had been valued at the end of the preceding period at:

	Valuation of work in progress (period 8)
Materials	£600
Labour	£525
Power	£135
Variable overheads	£480
	£1 740

During the course of the period 250 units were completed including the sets in progress at the beginning of the period. During period 9 the following costs were incurred:

Materials	£13 475
Labour	£17 640
Power	£8 085
Variable overheads	£19 600
	£58 800

At the end of the period 20 units were in progress. Their average degree of completion was as follows:

Proportion complete—materials	50 per cent
Proportion complete—labour	30 per cent
Proportion complete—power	25 per cent
Proportion complete—overheads	10 per cent

In Fig. 9.2 we show the degree of completion of each element of the production process.

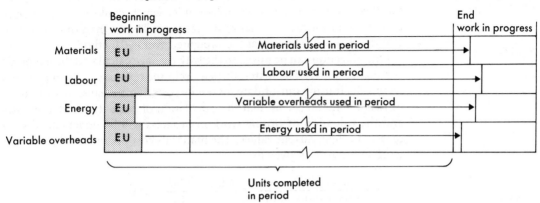

Fig 9.2 Degree of completion of production

Taking materials as the first element of cost, the work in progress at the beginning of the period consisted of 15 units which were 80 per cent complete as far as materials were concerned. This is equivalent to saying that these materials could have produced 12 (i.e. 0.8×15) complete units. For the purposes of this illustration we will assume that materials are homogenous, although in practice materials would consist of many different components. During the period of production, after finishing the work in progress, a further 235 units ($250 - 15$) were both started and completed in the period. In this, and indeed in any period, the work schedule is as follows:

- Complete the opening work in progress.

- Produce units which will be both started and completed within the period.

- Start the closing work in progress (WIP).

The final work in progress of 20 units is only 50 per cent complete with respect to materials. This is equivalent to ten fully completed units. To summarize:

Materials flow

	Equivalent complete units	Cost (£)
Opening work in progress (WIP) (15×0.8)	12	600
Completion of opening WIP (15×0.2)	3	
New units completed (235×1.0)	235	
Closing WIP (20×0.5)	10	13 475
Total equivalent units	260	
Total materials costs		14 075

The cost per equivalent unit produced $= £14\,075/260 = £54.13$

The equivalent unit of production is a very useful measure for partly finished products. The equivalent units produced in a period represent the theoretical number of complete units which could have been fully completed given the material resources used. The method of calculation employed above is known as the 'weighted average' method.

One objection can be raised to the way we have calculated the materials cost figure above. The materials tied up in the opening work in progress were valued using out-of-date materials costs. This means, in a situation of rising material prices, that the calculation of current period unit costs and the valuation of closing work in progress will be undervalued with respect to their current values. The materials cost per unit of the opening work in progress is given by:

$$\frac{\text{(cost of materials in opening WIP)}}{\text{equivalent units in progress}} = \frac{(600)}{12} = £50$$

The materials purchased during the period (£13 475) effectively completed the equivalent of 248 units giving a materials cost of £54.33 per unit (excluding, for the moment, the opening work in progress, which used prior period materials). The weighted-average valuation procedure, where the work in progress brought forward from the previous period is valued at the costs ruling in that period, implies that £50 is relevant for inclusion as part of the unit materials cost to be applied in the current period (period 9). On the other hand, it can be argued that the materials component of opening work in progress should be excluded when calculating the unit cost. A revised calculation procedure, excluding the value of the opening work in progress, will change the materials cost per unit charges from £54.13 (as above) to £54.33. This second method is referred to as the 'first in, first out' (FIFO) valuation method.

To summarize:

	Units	Weighted-average cost (£)	Units	FIFO (£)
Opening WIP	12	600.00	—	—
Completion of opening WIP	3		3	
New units completed	235	13 475.00	235	13 475.00
Closing WIP	10		10	
Total equivalent units	260		248	
Total materials cost		14 075.00		13 475.00
Materials cost per equivalent unit		54.13		54.33

We can repeat these calculations for the labour component of production. The only difference in this case is that the opening and closing work in progress are, respectively, 50 and 30 per cent complete as far as their labour input is concerned.

Self test: In all of the calculations which follow, do the alternative calculation using the FIFO procedure described above. Your answers will not come out very different to those produced by the weighted-average procedure—can you see why? Under what conditions would you expect the results to be significantly different?

The calculation of the labour cost per unit, using the weighted-average cost valuation procedure and assigning an opening work in progress of (0.5×15) 7.5 equivalent complete units, gives:

	Units	Weighted average (£)
Opening WIP	7.5	525.00
Completion of opening WIP	7.5	
New units completed	235.0	17 640.00
Closing WIP (20×0.3)	6.0	
Total equivalent units	256.0	
Total labour cost		18 165.00
Labour cost per equivalent unit		70.96

Using exactly the same procedure we can calculate the unit power cost and the unit variable overheads as follows:

	Units	Weighted average (£)
Power		
Opening WIP	4.5	135.00
Completion of opening WIP	10.5	
New units completed	235.0	8 085.00
Closing WIP (20×0.25)	5.0	
Total equivalent units	255.0	
Total cost of power		8 220.00
Power cost per equivalent unit		32.24
Overheads		
Opening WIP	6.0	480.00
Completion of opening WIP	9.0	
New units completed	235.0	19 600.00
Closing WIP (20×0.1)	2.0	
Total equivalent units	252.0	
Total variable overheads		20 080.00
Variable overheads per equivalent unit		79.68

We can summarize these results into a final statement of unit cost:

	Unit cost (£)
Materials	54.13
Labour	70.96
Power	32.24
Variable overheads	79.68
	237.01

If you have followed the details of our workings and have calculated the corresponding figures using the FIFO method we described before, you should be able to see how the difference between the methods has arisen although you may be wondering why we bothered, given that the actual differences are so small. In most situations, what we have found is quite typical because:

- Work in progress at the beginning of a period is usually quite small in relation to the month's total production.

- The specific price changes for individual resources are unlikely to be significant over the period of production.

However, on occasions, the difference between the two methods may be significant and the question arises as to which is the superior method of valuing work in progress. The more appropriate question, however, is 'significant for what?' If the aim of the costing procedure is simply to ensure adequate control of the resources devoted to production, then the answer to the question is that method which most simply relates cost figures to the resources being controlled. In most circumstances, because the weighted-average method relates costs to the normal flow of resources, it is probably the better of the two. However, if the firm concerned is seeking to use the costs obtained in other areas of decision-making, such as pricing or output, then the answer to the question posed is neither; in such situations the opportunity cost of the resource concerned should be used. To restate a point we have made before, the information required for general decision-making is quite different from that required for the purposes of control. Neither of the methods shown above uses current buying prices; nor do they necessarily reflect opportunity costs.

Once the schedule of unit cost has been calculated it is a reasonably straightforward matter to evaluate the total cost of the period's completed production, including the prior period's work in progress which is finished off. We will complete our calculations using the weighted-average method.

The cost of production during month 9 is as follows:

Materials cost (250 × £54.13)	£13 532.50
Labour cost (250 × £70.96)	£17 740.00
Power cost (250 × £32.24)	£8 060.00
Variable overheards (250 × £79.68)	£19 920.00
Total cost of production (period 9)	£59 252.50

The valuation of work in progress is calculated in exactly the same way, except that instead of using the number of units produced (250) we use the number of equivalent units in progress at the end of the period.

The valuation of work in progress at the end of the period is:

Materials component (10 × £54.13)	£541.30
Labour component (6 × £70.96)	£425.76
Power component (5 × £32.24)	£161.20
Overhead component (2 × £79.68)	£159.36
Cost of work in progress	£1287.62

Self test: Repeat the exercise we have carried out for Peteneras assuming no opening work in progress and 250 units were started and completed in the period. Calculate the cost of the period's production and the cost of the work in progress to be carried forward to period 10.
   Solution clue: £229.26

Job costing

Job costing, where it can be appropriately employed, is much simpler than process costing in that the costing procedure itself can be matched to the actual physical process of production. However, job costing presents many more data-handling, collation and control problems than process costing.

Job costing can be applied to a wide range of different production systems. For example:

- A car-repair shop.

- The production of custom-built furniture.

- A production run to print a book (like this one for example).

- A chemical produced on a batch process.

All of these processes can be regarded as discrete 'jobs' in that the time scale of the costing process has a definite beginning and end.

The core document in a job-costing system is the job card (or job sheet), one of which is assigned to each job or task performed by the particular production or service facility concerned. The job card records all cost elements charged to a particular job: materials withdrawn from stock, labour used, other services applied and, in many cases, a fixed charge for the use of the machinery and other fixed facilities. The job cards, once completed, can then be consolidated onto master job sheets which give the break down of different elements of cost applied to the particular aspect of production in a day.

In order to illustrate this type of costing we will describe the procedures which might be operated by a large car-repair shop.

When a motor-car is brought into a workshop, a set of multicopy stationery is opened up. One part of this stationery eventually becomes the customer's invoice and another part acts as the job card. When the car comes to his or her workstation the mechanic will perform any diagnostic checks necessary and then proceed with the repairs and/or service. As the job proceeds the mechanic will withdraw from stores the necessary spare parts: plugs, oil, lubricants, points, etc. Each withdrawal from the stores entails two entries:

- A credit entry on a stock card showing the part withdrawn and any other details specified by the company's stock accounting system.

- A corresponding entry on the job card showing the item used on the job (this would form the corresponding debit entry).

Similarly, the engineer's time on the job would be shown by two entries: one on his daily (or weekly) time sheet and one on the job card for the particular repair or service. In Fig. 9.3 we show the entries which would be made on the motor-repair job sheet.

Job-costing procedures, of necessity, revolve around the job card. In

Fig 9.3 Consolidation of cost elements through a job card

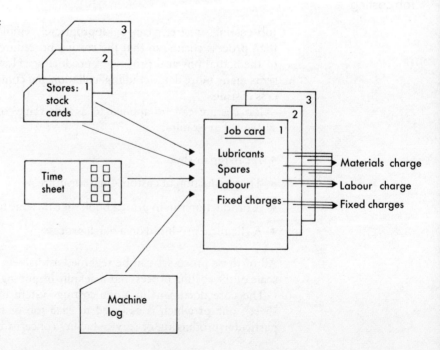

modern accounting systems the cost elements on the job card can be encoded and entered into a computerized cost analysis system, perhaps through a computer terminal located at the workstation concerned. However, no matter how a card is actually entered up it must be intelligible and readily usable by the operator involved (such as the mechanic above). In addition, a good job card should disrupt the flow of work as little as possible and, indeed, should be designed, wherever possible, to enhance the production process. In our car-repair shop example an ideal job card might also include a checklist of the jobs to be performed as well as clearly identifiable cost classifications.

In Fig. 9.4 we suggest a layout for a car-repair or service job card. You will notice that we also include a Value Added Tax (VAT) column into which will be entered the VAT component of any items used.

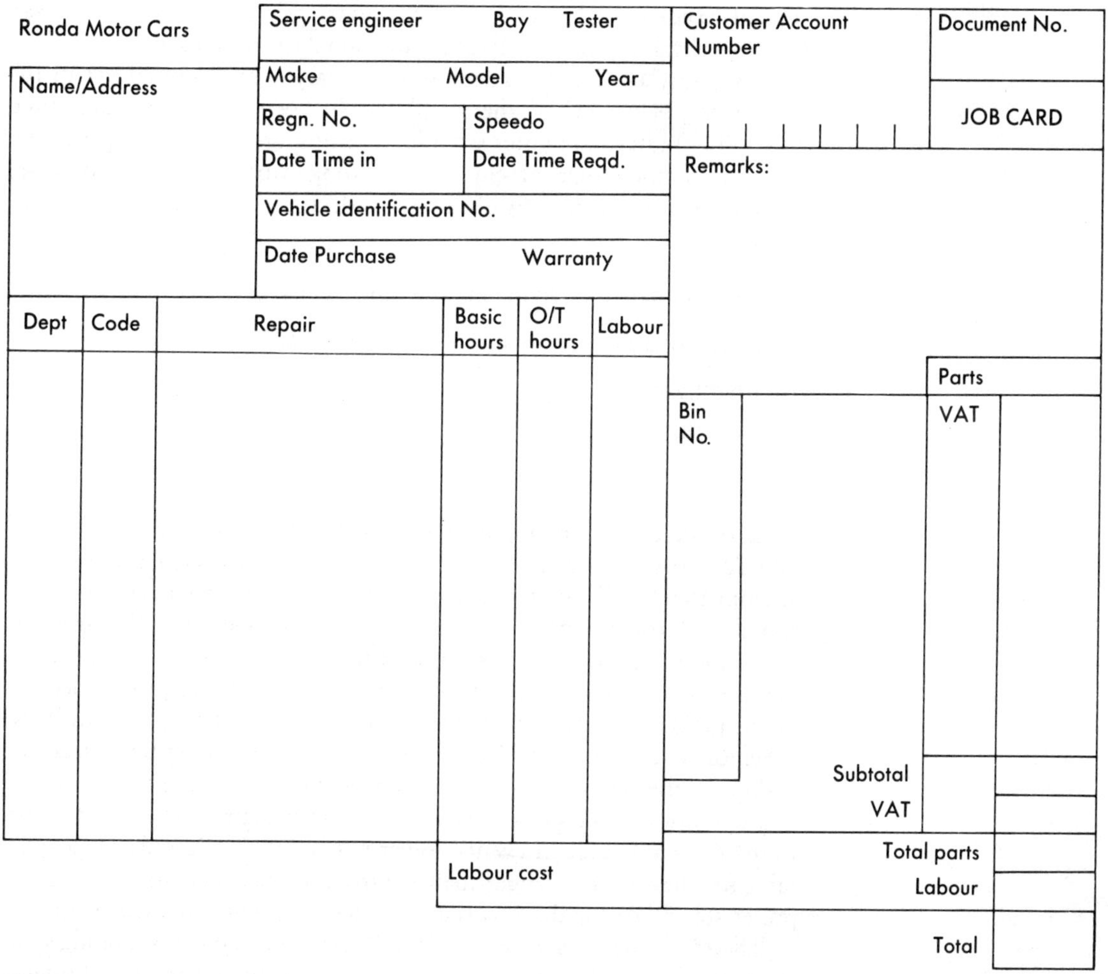

Fig 9.4 Motor-repair job card

> *Self test:* Design a job card for the construction of a pine, refectory-
> style table by a craftsman carpenter in a company specializing in
> custom-built pine furniture. Use your imagination!

Purpose of fixed-overhead allocation

In Chapter 6 we commented on the use of cost-based pricing procedures
which involve the inclusion of some charge for the fixed resources of
the firm—a fixed overhead allocation in other words. In this section we
will examine some of the reasons which might explain why fixed costs
are allocated to production processes by companies which in all other
respects appear to conform to the axioms of economic rationality. We
will then outline some of the techniques for allocating or 'absorbing'
fixed costs into production activities. Finally, we will round off our discussion of fixed-cost allocation with a salutary tale of a farmer who used
fixed-overhead allocations in his production decision-making.

As we saw in Chapter 5, many costs vary with output level in the
short term. Nevertheless, there will also be costs which are committed
and will not alter, no matter what level of output is produced, providing
it is within the range of current operating capacity. These costs are
incurred as a result of a firm's long-run decision to produce. Such costs
include:

- Costs of financing (dividends and interest charges).

- Salaries of administrative and supervisory staff.

- Other head office expenditure.

- Fixed charges of the production facility—rent, rates and standing
  charges for utilities such as gas and electricity.

None of these costs are opportunity costs for the firm's short-run production decisions, as we explained in Chapter 3. However, many firms do
attempt to relate fixed overheads to production through a variety of allocation or 'absorption' procedures. As we shall see later, the arbitrary
allocation of fixed overheads can lead to bad decisions being made. The
question which remains is whether, in a control context, the procedure
can be justified. One argument in support of this practice goes as follows.

Senior management is largely responsible for the long-term decision-
making of the firm while lower management is responsible for the tactical
and operational decisions of selling, purchasing, production and so on.
In the normal course of events, lower managers should only be accoun-
table for the variables under their control and their performance against
preset standards for those variables. However, senior management may
well 'load' the performance criteria of lower management by adding some
element of cost (the so-called fixed costs) into their operating budgets.
In this way, the standards of performance for lower levels of management

are raised to cover the costs which result from the consequences of senior management's decisions. It may well be that senior management will offer some additional compensation (in the form of increased salary, bonuses or even shares in the business) for the higher demands placed upon the performance of lower management.

The allocation of fixed overheads can be viewed, therefore, as the spreading of senior-management-related costs throughout the organization where they become part of the control criteria for lower management.

Another argument which is often put forward is that the allocation of fixed overheads is a very imperfect attempt to allocate the internal opportunity costs of scarce senior management time and scarce fixed resources (such as plant and equipment) to a firm's production activities. This argument is the same as that advanced in Chapter 6 in defence of fixed formula pricing although we are now identifying the internal opportunity cost with the cost of senior managerial time and other fixed resources. The difficulty with this argument is that the very arbitrary allocation of fixed overheads is unlikely to lead to any better decisions than those made using unadjusted costs.

Fixed overheads are usually allocated using the following formula:

$$\frac{\text{fixed-overhead}}{\text{allocation rate}} = \frac{\text{total fixed}}{\text{overheads}} \times \frac{\text{units of measurement base used in production}}{\text{total units of measurement base}}$$

The base for allocating fixed overheads could be any of the following:

- The number of units of final production.

- The number of labour hours employed in production.

- The number of machine hours employed in production.

- The cost of materials employed in a particular process.

- The total wages allocated to a particular aspect of production.

For example, Martin plc produces 16 000 units of Bolero for sale per month. Each Bolero sells for £5 per unit. The statistics for total factory production (of all products) and Bolero production are shown below:

	Bolero production		Factory production	
Total production (units)	16 000			
Sales revenue (£)		80 000		725 000
Materials usage (kg)	10 000		73 000	
Material cost per unit (£)		0.5		0.8
Labour usage (hours)	1 250		31 680	
Labour rate per hour (£)		10.0		9.0
Machine hours	240		2 700	

The total fixed overheads for the factory as a whole are £110 000.

The production of Bolero amounts to 16 000 units with a sales value of £80 000. An allocation of fixed overheads to Bolero production on the basis of sales value would be as follows:

$$\text{overhead charge to Bolero production} = £110\,000 \times \frac{80\,000}{725\,000}$$

$$= £12\,138$$

$$= £0.759 \text{ per unit produced}$$

This exercise can be conducted on a number of different bases:

	Base					
	Value of production	Materials usage	Materials value	Labour hours	Labour cost	Machine hours
Allocation ratio	$\dfrac{80\,000}{725\,000}$	$\dfrac{10\,000}{73\,000}$	$\dfrac{5\,000}{58\,400}$	$\dfrac{1\,250}{31\,680}$	$\dfrac{12\,500}{285\,120}$	$\dfrac{240}{2\,700}$
Total fixed overheads (£)	110 000	110 000	110 000	110 000	110 000	110 000
Allocated overhead (£)	12 138	15 068	9 418	4 340	4 822	9 778
Charge (£) per unit produced	0.759	0.942	0.589	0.271	0.301	0.611

As you can see each allocation base has produced a different charge per unit produced for fixed overheads which will, ultimately, lead to a different total unit cost. The basis of apportionment is purely arbitrary, although there may be some sense in the argument that apportionment should be on the basis of that aspect of production which most influences the level of fixed overheads. On this basis, rent and rates could perhaps be allocated according to the floor area used in production while supervisors' wages, for example, could be allocated according to labour hours employed. However, no matter what allocation basis is chosen, the inclusion of fixed overheads into decision-making can distort the relative costs and benefits of the various alternatives available. In order to demonstrate this point we tell the story of Farmer Joe.

Farmer Joe has a fixed-acreage farm with facilities to produce wheat, corn, chickens and pigs. To make our point, and to avoid confusion with other issues, we will assume that any labour not required for production can be laid off and that production facilities (including land) are not interchangeable.

Farmer Joe earns a net cash contribution as a result of his annual production as follows (net cash contribution is calculated after the deduction of labour costs):

	Wheat	Corn	Chickens	Pigs
Net cash contribution	£5000	£2600	£1000	£2000
Labour hours required to produce	1500	900	600	900

The total anticipated fixed costs associated with running the farm and the farmhouse during the year are £7800.

Farmer Joe is reviewing his situation after he has been told by his 'financial adviser' that chicken production is not worth while as it does not cover its fair proportion of fixed overheads. The total labour devoted to the farm is 3900 hours per annum. Therefore, the proportion of the total overheads attributable to chicken farming is:

$$\text{allocated overhead (chickens)} = £7800 \times 600/3900$$

$$= £1200$$

The same calculation for each product produces a profit and loss account for each as follows:

	Wheat (£)	Corn (£)	Chickens (£)	Pigs (£)
Net cash contribution	5000	2600	1000	2000
Allocated fixed costs	3000	1800	1200	1800
Net profit/(loss)	2000	800	(200)	200

Farmer Joe wonders what would be the logical consequence of following his financial adviser's advice. If chicken production is stopped, the farm will still have to bear the full overheads of £7800 although on a reduced labour base of 3300 labour hours—assuming that the labour devoted to chicken production is laid off. We can now repeat the above calculations on the three remaining products:

	Wheat (£)	Corn (£)	Pigs (£)
Net cash contribution	5000	2600	2000
Allocated fixed costs	3545	2127	2127
Net profit/(loss)	1455	473	(127)

We have calculated the allocated fixed overheads to wheat production, for example, as follows:

$$\text{fixed overheads allocated to wheat production} = \frac{1500}{3300} \times £7800$$

$$= £3545$$

On the basis of the revised net profit or loss figures, it would now appear that pig production is no longer worth while. Perhaps using the same argument as before, pig production should be stopped. But if pig production is stopped, what then? This story does not have a happy ending!

The inclusion of fixed overheads into the decision has provided a performance target for each product. This has the result of deflecting attention from choosing the cash-maximizing alternative (i.e. producing all products in the absence of any better alternatives) to deciding which is the least worth while of the four products if the resources needed for its production could be diverted to a better use.

Farmer Joe's problem clearly highlights the dangers of including fixed overheads as part of the cost of production in that it blurs the distinction between two types of decision-making. First, the decision concerning production, where the allocation procedure may lead to the non-production of worthwhile products, and, second, the setting of performance targets, where it is intended to reflect (albeit inaccurately) the internal opportunity cost of managerial resources in the costing of individual processes.

Note: A team of academic accountants argued that the National Coal Board allocated fixed overheads to its cost per ton of coal lifted from the ground. At one pit in particular, which the Coal Board claimed could only produce coal at a loss of £6.20 per ton, a closure notice was served and the coal strike of 1984 started. Analysis of the Coal Board accounts suggested that approximately 23 per cent of the cost attributed to the colliery concerned was due to central Coal Board costs. If these non-attributable costs were added back, the colliery concerned appeared to make a cash contribution of up to £5.45 per ton depending upon the assumptions made. The National Coal Board claimed that (a) the figures were wrong and (b) that the publicly quoted profit figures were only used to justify decisions made on other grounds! (See the reference at the end of this chapter to the article by Berry *et al.* in *Accountancy.*)

Variance analysis

The collection of actual production costs and revenues will inevitably yield discrepancies when compared with the preset budgeted costs and revenues. We call such discrepancies cost or revenue 'variances' and it is an important part of management's work to identify the reasons why such variances have occurred even when they are favourable. In this section we will discuss the simple numerical methods which are at the cost accountant's disposal for identifying variances.

Price and volume variances

We have already discussed the idea in Chapter 4 that short-term decisions are usually governed by activity or quantity variables. Total revenue is the product of price per unit and quantity and total cost is the product of cost per unit and quantity. Therefore, part of every variance between actual and budgeted total revenue or cost will be due to a change in the price or cost per unit, while the remainder will be due to a change in quantity sold or used.

For example, the materials used in producing a particular product were budgeted to be 23 000 kg at £13.00 per kilogram. The actual usage was 27 000 kg at £14.00 per kilogram. It had been planned to produce 17 000 units of final product although in the event 18 000 units were produced.

> *Note:* Many firms establish 'standard costs' for various aspects of their production. These standard costs may reflect what is expected on technical grounds or in terms of what is feasible, given the current operating conditions and work practices within the production facility. Standard cost per unit can be applied to planned output levels to derive budgeted costs. In this example we will assume that all of the unit costs used to produce budgeted figures are in fact standard costs.

The variance between total budgeted and total actual material cost can be found as follows:

Actual materials cost $(27\,000 \times £14.00)$	£378 000
Budgeted materials cost $(23\,000 \times £13.00)$	£299 000
'Crude' materials cost variance	£79 000 (A)

The (A) indicates that the variance is adverse in that actual cost exceeds budgeted cost. Favourable variances are designated (F).

The crude cost variance can be split into three components:

- A unit cost or 'price' variance caused by the change in the buying price per unit of the resource.

- A materials usage or 'volume' variance caused by the difference between the budgeted and the actual quantity used.

- A joint price/quantity variance which is, by convention, assigned to the price variance.

To illustrate how these three variances arise we show, on a graph (Fig. 9.5), the budgeted and actual unit costs and the budgeted and actual quantities of materials. The total actual materials cost is given by the area of the larger rectangle, i.e. actual cost per unit times actual quantity $(AP \times AQ)$. The smaller rectangle gives the total budgeted cost, i.e. budgeted cost per unit times budgeted quantity $(BP \times BQ)$.

The total variance is given by the area of the border of the two rectangles, the horizontal portion $(AP - BP) \times BQ$ being the price variance; the vertical portion $(AQ - BQ) \times BP$ being the volume variance and the small corner portion $(AP - BP) \times (AQ - BQ)$ being the joint variance. Given the numbers in the example these three variances are:

$$
\begin{aligned}
\text{unit cost or price variance} &= (AP - BP) \times BQ \\
&= (14.00 - 13.00) \times 23\,000 \\
&= £23\,000\text{(A)}
\end{aligned}
$$

$$
\begin{aligned}
\text{volume or usage variance} &= (AQ - BQ) \times BP \\
&= (27\,000 - 23\,000) \times 13.00 \\
&= £52\,000\text{(A)}
\end{aligned}
$$

$$
\begin{aligned}
\text{joint variance} &= (AP - BP) \times (AQ - BQ) \\
&= (14.00 - 13.00) \times (27\,000 - 23\,000) \\
&= £4000\text{(A)}
\end{aligned}
$$

Because the actual cost per unit of materials and the actual usages both exceed the budgeted values all three variances are adverse. When attempting to determine whether variances are adverse or favourable it is often

Fig 9.5 First-level vacancies

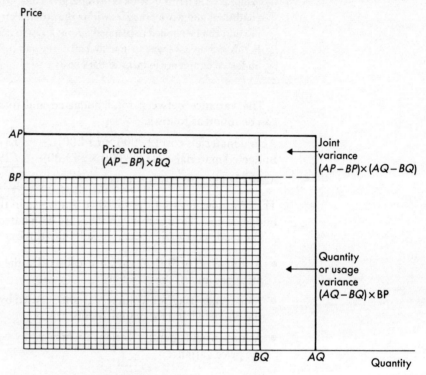

easier to ignore the sign and to make the choice by inspection. With costs, actual figures in excess of budget give adverse variances, while the reverse is true for revenue items.

The sum of the three variances calculated above gives the 'crude' material variance of £79 000(A). Traditional variance analysis assigns the joint variance to the price variance. Following this convention the revised formulae for the price and volume variance are as follows:

price variance (including joint variance) $= (AP - BP) \times AQ$

volume variance $= (AQ - BQ) \times BP$

The price variance now represents the entire area of the upper rectangle in Fig. 9.5.

Using this revised price variance formula we obtain a variance of £27 000(A) as:

$$(AP - BP) \times AQ = (14.00 - 13.00) \times 27\,000$$

$$= £27\,000(A)$$

An adverse price variance on materials indicates that any investigation should be directed toward the company's purchasing department. An adverse variance in the unit price for materials could arise for any number of reasons including:

- A price increase has been imposed for materials of the same quality as those previously supplied.

- The purchasing department has taken a higher quality product which may well reveal itself in a favourable volume variance.

- The company may not have taken advantage of discounts for early payment.

The adverse quantity variance, on the other hand, directs attention toward the production department, although we are not yet in a position to say how much of the increase in material usage was due to the higher than expected output of final product and how much was due to changes in the efficiency of use of the material.

Efficiency and activity variances

The original budget was set on the presupposition that 17 000 units of final product would be produced. However, an actual final output of 18 000 units was achieved. At this level of output we would have anticipated a materials usage (on budget) of 24 353 kg, calculated as follows:

$$\text{revised usage} = \text{original budgeted usage} \times \frac{\text{actual final output}}{\text{budgeted final output}}$$

$$= 23\,000 \times \frac{18\,000}{17\,000}$$

$$= 24\,353\,\text{kg}$$

This revised usage is sometimes referred to as the 'flexed' usage or quantity (FQ). Note the usefulness here of the flexible budgeting concept discussed in Chapter 5. A flexible budget, especially when the basic budget is on computer, should be able to yield these flexed usages as soon as the actual output is known.

The original variance on materials usage can now be separated into two components:

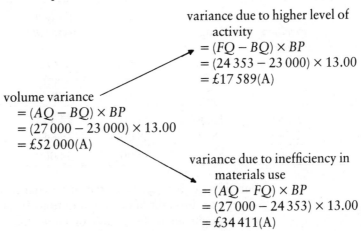

variance due to higher level of activity
$= (FQ - BQ) \times BP$
$= (24\,353 - 23\,000) \times 13.00$
$= £17\,589(A)$

volume variance
$= (AQ - BQ) \times BP$
$= (27\,000 - 23\,000) \times 13.00$
$= £52\,000(A)$

variance due to inefficiency in materials use
$= (AQ - FQ) \times BP$
$= (27\,000 - 24\,353) \times 13.00$
$= £34\,411(A)$

Therefore:

volume variance = activity variance + (in)efficiency variance
i.e. £52 000(A) = £17 589(A) + £34 411(A)

Clearly, the adverse activity variance is not the fault of the production department but can be accounted for by the increase in overall production activity. However, the inefficiency variance may well be attributable to the production department although the greater than anticipated usage of material may simply be due to an overoptimistic budget being set in the first instance.

Self test: Using the same procedure as described above calculate the variances on labour cost for the same product.

	Budget	Actual
Labour hours used	2100	2000
Wage rate per hour	£10	£12

Calculate the 'crude' labour variance, the labour price (wage rate) variance, the labour usage (volume) variance and the activity and labour efficiency variance. Can you suggest reasons why the variances may have occurred?
   Solution clue: 3000, 4000, 1000, 1235(A).

Mix and yield variances

When more than one material is used to produce a given product and the proportions of the materials can be altered by chance or by design then it is useful to identify the part of the (in)efficiency variance which has been caused by alterations in the mix of the two (or more) materials and the part which has been caused by differences in the efficiency with which each material is converted into final product (the individual material's yield variance).

Using the last example for one material and introducing a second material into the analysis we have:

Material	Specified usage per unit output (kg) (1)	Budget price per kilogram (£) (2)	Budget usage at budget output (kg) (3)	Budget usage at actual output (kg) (4)	Actual usage (kg) (5)	Budget mix at actual usage (kg) (6)
A	1.353	13.00	23 000	24 353	27 000	26 609
B	1.647	8.00	28 000	29 647	32 000	32 391
	3.000		51 000	54 000	59 000	59 000

Our objective is to split the efficiency variance for each product produced into a part brought about by variations in the mix of materials and a part brought about by poorer or better than expected material yields.

As we are working on components of the usage or volume variance everything is based on budget price per kilogram of the material concerned. To explain the method behind this calculation we will go through the above columns one by one.

Column 1 This is the technical specification for mixing materials into final product (given). Three kilograms of materials in the specified mix will, under ideal conditions, yield one unit of final product.

Column 2 These are the budget unit prices of each material.

Column 3 This column gives the budgeted material usage based upon the specified mix from column 1 and the budgeted output of final product of 17 000 units (i.e. $1.353 \times 17\,000 = 23\,000$ and $1.647 \times 17\,000 = 28\,000$).

Column 4 At an actual output of 18 000 units we would expect a budgeted usage of materials:

A: $1.353 \times 18\,000 = 24\,353\,\text{kg}$
B: $1.647 \times 18\,000 = 29\,647\,\text{kg}$

The activity variance for each material can be calculated by deducting column 3 from column 4 and multiplying the resultant variance in usage by the budget price.

Column 5 Gives the actual usage.

Column 6 This column gives the budgeted mix we would have expected on a total actual usage of the two materials of 59 000 kg:

$$\text{material A usage} = \frac{1.353}{3.000} \times 59\,000 = 26\,609\,\text{kg}$$

$$\text{material B usage} = \frac{1.647}{3.000} \times 59\,000 = 32\,391\,\text{kg}$$

The difference between actual usage and the budgeted mix (column 5 − column 6) gives the mix variance when priced at the budgeted price. The remainder of the difference between the actual and budgeted usage at the actual output is the yield variance (column 6 − column 4).

To summarize, the efficiency variance can be split into mix and yield variances as follows:

	Efficiency variance (col. 5 − col. 4) × budget price		Mix variance (col. 5 − col. 6) × budget price		Yield variance (col. 6 − col. 4) × budget price
A:	$(27\,000 - 24\,353) \times 13.00$ $= £34\,411(\text{A})$	=	$(27\,000 - 26\,609) \times 13.00$ $= £5083(\text{A})$	+	$(26\,609 - 24\,353) \times 13.00$ $= £29\,328(\text{A})$
B:	$(32\,000 - 29\,647) \times 8.00$ $= £18\,824(\text{A})$		$(32\,000 - 32\,391) \times 8.00$ $= £3128(\text{F})$		$(32\,391 - 29\,647) \times 8.00$ $= £21\,952(\text{A})$

The mix variance indicates the extent to which the technically specified mix has been met in production. With material A the mix variance is adverse; i.e. more material A was used than was anticipated given a total materials usage of 59 000 kg. With material B the reverse is true, as we would expect. The yield variance indicates the level of efficiency in production and immediately draws attention to the operating conditions under which production has been undertaken.

Mix and yield variances can be calculated on any joint, interdependent factors of production: different grades of labour, energy and materials, the number of labour and machine hours, respectively. The only constraint, when examining joint factors of production, is that the units of activity are comparable for the factors concerned. Material usages in kilograms can be compared with one another but labour (where the usage is in hours) and materials cannot.

Overhead variances

Traditional variance-analysis techniques assume that fixed overheads are included in the unit costing procedures and attempt to identify those parts of the overhead under- or overabsorption which can be attributed to variances in the allocation base. For example, if a particular class of fixed overhead has been apportioned on a labour-hour basis then a greater usage of labour hours during a production period will lead to an overallocation (or overabsorption) of overheads in the period. Similarly, an underabsorption will occur if less labour hours are used than planned. However, the efficiency and activity variances on labour impart all the information we need to know concerning that factor of production. The fact that a particular fixed element has been included in the unit labour cost (which is what the allocation procedure is about) tells us nothing more about the long-term ability of production to cover overheads.

The more serious problem with fixed-overhead allocation is that it treats as variable a cost element which is fixed in the short run. Fixed-overhead allocation and fixed-overhead variances are only relevant if bonuses or other side payments made to lower-level managers are related to the recovery of fixed overheads in production. Nevertheless many firms do apply fixed-overhead allocation procedures and then attempt to attribute variances to the over- or underabsorption which may occur.

Example: Overheads are allocated at a rate of £5 per labour hour. The budgeted labour usage is 2100 hours, at a budgeted labour rate of £10 per hour. The actual labour usage was 2000 hours at an actual rate of £12 per hour. The actual production was 18 000 units compared with the budgeted production of 17 000 units. Given the allocation rate of £5 per labour hour we can calculate the level of fixed overheads which management expects to recover from production as follows:

total overheads to be absorbed is £5 × 2100 = £10 500

You should have calculated the wage rate and labour usage variances in the last self-test exercise:

total wage-rate (price) variance $= (12.00 - 10.00) \times 2000$
$$= £4000(A)$$

labour-usage (volume) variance $= (2000 - 2100) \times 10.00$
$$= £1000(F)$$

As fixed overheads are allocated on the usage of labour hours, we can easily see the level of underabsorption in the period:

actual labour hours × budgeted absorption rate
$$= 2000 \times £5 = £10\,000$$
budgeted labour hours × budgeted absorption rate
$$= 2100 \times £5 = £10\,500$$
underabsorption of fixed overheads in the period $= \quad £500$

We could, if we wished, split this underabsorption into the part caused by changes in production activity (cf. activity variance) and the part caused by changes in the level of production efficiency (cf. the efficiency variance). To do this we first calculate the activity and efficiency variances on the budgeted labour hours and then apply the absorption rate to obtain the corresponding overhead variances.

Budgeted labour hours at actual (rather than budgeted) output $\left(\dfrac{18\,000}{17\,000} \times 2\,100\right)$	2224
Budget labour hours	2100
Activity variance in hours	124
Activity variance at the budgeted wage rate of £10 per hour	£1240(A)
Actual labour hours	2000
Budgeted labour hours at actual output	2224
Efficiency variance in hours	224
Efficiency variance at the budgeted wage rate of £10 per hour	£2240(F)

The overhead activity and the efficiency variances (in hours) can be derived using the overhead absorption rates:

overhead activity variance $(124 \times £5.00)$	£620(A)
overhead efficiency variance $(224 \times £5.00)$	£1120(F)

Therefore, the greater than expected efficiency in the use of labour has led to an underabsorption of overheads which has been partly offset by the increase in production activity.

Sales variances

As with materials, labour and other variable costs total sales revenue variances can be split into volume and price effects. The formulae to use are exactly the same as those we derived earlier for price and volume variances:

price variance = (actual price − budget price) × actual quantity sold
volume variance = (actual quantity − budget quantity) × actual price

Because sales revenue volume variance is determined by sales (or activity) level it is impossible to split this variance in the way we did for materials and labour. However, it is possible to determine how much of the price variance can be attributed to suboptimal pricing given a particular level of production and a known demand curve.

For example, given an actual level of production (which was all sold) of 18 000 units compared with a budgeted production and sales figure of 17 000 units, determine the element of price variance due to marketing (in)efficiency and the element due to market conditions.

The actual and budgeted selling prices were £28 per unit and £30 per unit, respectively. The demand curve for the product was expected to be:

$$p = 40.5 - 0.000\,62 \times Q$$

where p is the price per unit sold and Q is the quantity demanded.

With an actual sales volume of 18 000 units we would anticipate a price of £29.34 per unit as:

$$40.5 - 0.000\,62 \times 18\,000 = £29.34$$

$$
\begin{aligned}
\text{crude sales revenue variance} &= (AP \times AQ) - (BP \times BQ) \\
&= (28 \times 18\,000) - (30 \times 17\,000) \\
&= £6000(A)
\end{aligned}
$$

$$
\begin{aligned}
\text{price variance} \quad &= (AP - BP) \times AQ \\
&= (28 - 30) \times 18\,000 \\
&= £36\,000(A)
\end{aligned}
$$

$$
\begin{aligned}
\text{volume variance} &= (AQ - BQ) \times BP \\
&= (18\,000 - 17\,000) \times 30 \\
&= £30\,000(F)
\end{aligned}
$$

Note the reversal in the way we assign adverse and favourable to the variances we have calculated. In the case of revenue items increases in price and volume are regarded as favourable to the firm contrary to the situation with cost variances.

The price variance can be split into two components:

demand specific variance = (£29.34 − 30) × 18 000
                        = £11 880(A)

price variance
= £36 000(A)

marketing variance due to underpricing
= (28 − 29.34) × 18 000
= £24 120(A)

The interpretation of these variances is dependent upon the following assumptions:

- The original demand curve accurately represents prevailing demand conditions.

- There is no alteration in the position of the demand curve during the production period.

- The original price has been correctly set for the level of output planned.

Given these assumptions the marketing and demand variances can only, at best, indicate the possible causes of the overall sales revenue variance. We can now collect all of the variances we have discussed in this chapter into a variance 'tree'. See Fig. 9.6.

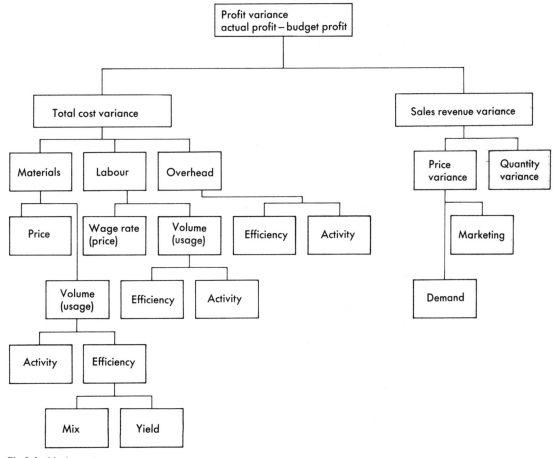

Fig 9.6 Variance tree

In practice, not all of these variances can be calculated in all instances. Many firms which use standard costing procedures only extract price and volume variances and others adapt the concepts presented here to their own particular information structures and reporting systems. Do not be surprised, therefore, if you fail to meet the variance-analysis system described here in practice.

Controllable and non-controllable variances

Variances of all types can be classified into two groups: controllable and non-controllable. Controllable variances are ones which come under direct management influence, for example:

- The usages of resources on processes.
- The level of production activity.
- The cost of labour and certain overheads.

Other costs are not directly controllable:

- Suppliers' prices.
- The final market price of the product (which is subject to market influences).

The investigation of variances can be a very expensive process for management in terms of both time and the resources required to identify and explain their causes. 'Management by exception' is a name given to the process where, following the establishment of a range of acceptable variances, management only pursues those variances which lie outside the range. In practice, the magnitude of the range will depend upon the degree of control which management either wishes to have or feels that it can impose upon the system. It also depends upon the degree of slack which can be tolerated in the production or selling system. An effective management by exception system relies on periodic management reports which:

- Provide a comparison between actual and budgeted figures and show the variances for each expenditure and revenue item reconciled to the variance of actual with budgeted profit or loss.
- Flag those variances which exceed the ranges of acceptability specified by management.

Wherever possible the cost accountant should provide a commentary on the exceptional variances which have arisen during a period and give the results of any preliminary investigations which have been conducted to establish their causes.

Self test: To help you understand the mechanics of variance analysis we have collected all the data laid out in the variance-analysis section of this chapter and added some other bits and pieces to make it more exciting. Your task is to extract, using the techniques we have outlined above, all of the information you can in the form of a management report. Make sure that all your variances reconcile with one another.

	Actual		Budget	
	Quantity	Price (cost per unit) (£)	Quantity	Price (cost per unit) (£)
Sales and production level	18 000 units	28.00	17 000 units	30.00
Material A	27 000 kg	14.00	23 000 kg	13.00
Material B	32 000 kg	13.00	28 000 kg	8.00
Labour (semiskilled)	2 000 hours	12.00	2 100 hours	10.00
Labour (unskilled)	600 hours	8.00	550 hours	8.00
Overheads (variable with output)		2.00		1.50
Fixed overheads (allocated on semiskilled labour hours)		16.00 (per hour)		15.00 (per hour)

The relationship between price and quantity demanded is given by:

$$p = 40.5 - 0.000\,62 \times Q$$

Management policy is to investigate all variances which differ from budget by more than 2 per cent.

Summary

In this rather formidable chapter we have taken a broad look at the work of the cost accountant whose task it is to collect the cost and revenue data from the production and selling activities of the firm and transform them into data suitable for the control decision. We looked first of all at two principal types of production system—the job and continuous-process production systems. We then examined the way such systems could be controlled through cost collection and processing. Finally, we addressed ourselves to the problem of variance analysis and the control of actual costs against their preset budgetary targets. In line with the decision-making dimension of this text we have considered the relevance of cost data for specific decisions. We have also outlined the dangers of confusing the effects of long-term decision-making with the immediate effects of short-term decision-making by incorporating fixed costs into production decisions.

Supplementary reading

BERRY, T., *et al.*, NCB accounts—a mine of misinformation, *Accountancy*, January 1985

BROMWICH, M., Standard costing for planning and control, in Arnold, J., Carsberg, B. and Scapens, R. (eds), *Topics in Management Accounting*, Philip Allan, 1980

DEMSKI, J. S., Analysing the effectiveness of the traditional standard cost variance model, in Solomons, D. (ed.), *Studies in Cost Analysis*, Sweet & Maxwell, 1968

SMITH, A. F., Overhead variance analysis—as simple as ABC, *Management Accounting*, October 1982

SOLOMONS, D., Flexible budgets and the analysis of overhead variances, reprinted in Anton, H. R., and Firmin, P. A. (eds), *Contemporary Issues in Cost Accounting*, Houghton Mifflin, 1972

YOUNG, A. X., The management accountant and variance analysis, *Management Accounting*, July/August 1981

Questions

1   Define the role of the cost accountant and explain how it differs from the role of the management accountant.

2   Briefly outline the meaning of the following cost-accounting terms:

  (a) Cost centre.
  (b) Overhead allocation.
  (c) Weighted-average process costing.
  (d) Job card.
  (e) Efficiency variance.
  (f) Controllable and uncontrollable variances.

3   Ramon Industrial (Chemicals) plc started up continuous production on its trinitrotoluene plant at the beginning of the month of January. The costs of production in the month of January were as follows:

Toluene (raw material)	£18 000
Nitric acid (raw material)	£6 500
Labour	£7 800
Energy costs	£6 600
Other variable production costs	£4 000
	£42 900

Of the final product 10 000 kg were produced during the month and 1000 kg were still in progress. Mr Ken Tucky, the plant manager, believes that the state of completion of the work in progress is as follows:

Toluene	Complete
Nitric acid	Half complete
Labour	Two-thirds complete
Energy	One-third complete
Other variable costs	Half complete

Required:
  (a) Calculate the unit cost of trinitrotoluene during the the month's production.
  (b) Value the work in progress at the end of the month.
  (c) Comment on the use of process costing in corporate decison-making.

4 The budgeted and actual sales revenue and labour costs for a particular process are as follows:

Sales revenue:
Actual price per unit	£65.00
Budgeted price per unit	£60.00
Actual quantity produced	12 000 tons
Budgeted quantity produced	15 000 tons

Labour costs:
Actual labour rate per hour	£10.50
Budgeted labour rate per hour	£12.00
Actual labour hours employed in production	8400 hours
Budgeted labour hours employed in production	8200 hours

Required:
  (a) Caculate the labour wage rate, the labour usage, the labour efficiency and the activity variances for the above process and comment upon the figures you have produced.
  (b) Comment upon the usefulness of variance analysis as a technique of management control.

5 Lorca plc produces Garcias among other things. Lorca's manufacturing director believes that the production of Garcias is no longer viable although, under pressure from the marketing director, she is prepared to conduct an investigation into this product's profitability. Toward this end the manufacturing director has decided to analyse the differences between actual and budgeted sales and production for Garcias for the year ended 31 December 19X2.
   Financial figures, abstracted from the company's annual management reports, are as follows:

	Actual	Flexible budget
Sales of Garcias (units)	7 000.00	7 000.00
Unit sales price (£)	24.00	24.00
Raw materials used (kg)	36 810.00	35 000.00
Cost per kilogram (£)	0.58	0.60
Labour hours employed	15 000.00	14 000.00
Cost per hour (£)	4.10	4.00
Fixed overheads (£)	88 500.00	85 400.00

Stock levels were unchanged during the year. The fixed overheads are directly attributable to Garcia production although they are only fixed over the range 6000–10 000 units.

Required:
(a) Prepare a statement showing the actual and budgeted profits for the year ended 31 December 19X2.
(b) Calculate the price and efficiency variances for both labour and materials.
(c) The company's master budget had specified sales of 9000 units. Calculate the variance which would appear to be attributable to the marketing function for the shortfall in sales volume.
(d) What comments can you make about the figures you have prepared in (a) to (c) above?

6   Two materials are used in a chemical cracking operation. The output of final refined product, budgeted at 145 000 kg, was 8 per cent down on budget. The usages (budgeted and actual) and the budgeted cost per unit of each material were as follows:

	Budget usage (kg)	Actual usage (kg)	Budget price (kg)
Material A	90 000	87 000	24
Material B	65 000	65 000	38

Required:
(a) Draft a report for management identifying, as far as possible, the differences between actual and budgeted figures for the production period.
(b) What do you understand by the term management by exception?

10 The distribution of surplus

A major and often politically sensitive aspect of the management account-ant's work involves the preparation of information for the distribution decision. The distribution decision is concerned with the allocation of the firm's surplus between the various interest groups within the firm. In this chapter we develop the concept of 'value added' that we introduced in Chapter 2 and examine, in some detail, the concept of 'ability to pay'.

By the end of this chapter we will have examined the following points:

- An introduction to the distribution decision.
- The relevance of traditional statements of account for the distribution decision.
- The process of wage negotiation and wage bargaining.
- The concepts of 'ability to pay' and 'value added'.
- The dividend decision.

Introduction to the distribution decision

In this chapter we turn our attention to the distribution decision which is an extremely sensitive aspect of managerial decision-making. This sensitivity arises because it involves, overtly, the exercise of the central feature of managerial power; namely, the power to control the distribu-tion of the firm's surplus.

Traditionally, the material discussed in this chapter has been regarded as the province of the financial accountant because financial accounts are often used as an important input into (and justification for) the distri-bution decisions made by management.

The financial accountant is primarily concerned with the preparation of accounting information for interest groups outside the firm who do not have day-to-day access to the firm's information system. As a result, financial accounts are a partial summary of the affairs of the organization over a period of time. Further, financial-accounting information is based upon a number of conventions and standards of accounting practice which are meant to facilitate the interpretation of that information by external users. However, because managers often use financial accounts for their distribution decisions (or, at least, look to see what impact those decisions will have on the financial accounts) we will spend some time examining the conventions under which the accounts are prepared.

To a certain extent the role of the management accountant is to 'complete the picture' for management, by providing other relevant financial information not provided in the financial accounts and even, on occasions, to reinterpret the financial-accounting information in the context of the needs of those user groups for whom it was not originally intended.

You will remember that we have depicted the firm as a coalition of different interest groups: management, investors, employees plus their unions, suppliers, customers, government, etc. Each of these groups will, to a certain extent, have conflicting aims and, therefore, conflicting claims upon the firm's resources. Each of these groups (and even subgroups within these groups) will negotiate overtly and covertly in order to achieve their aims.

However, much of the difficulty with the distribution decision results from the fact that different interest groups may have quite different views on who has the primary claim upon the firm's surplus and, indeed, how that surplus should be calculated.

In order to explore the difficulties of the distribution decision we will briefly examine how the concepts or surplus, profit and value added relate to each other.

In Fig. 10.1 the outer circle represents the total revenue of the organization which comes from the sale of products and services for cash and on credit. Credit sales produce the debtor balances which appear in the balance sheet as current assets and which are normally turned into cash very quickly. The resources earned from sales are used, in the first instance, to pay for the materials needed to produce products for sale. The remainder (represented by the first inner circle) is the firm's 'value added'.

This value added is used to pay the other contractual commitments of the firm—agreed wages and salaries, interest payments on debts, fees for services rendered, etc. This leaves a remainder, distributable at management's discretion, which we term the 'cash surplus'. Part of this cash surplus will go in tax payments which depend, in part, on the way in which the remainder of the surplus is distributed. For example, if management decides to use some of the firm's cash surplus to increase the bonuses payable to its employees, those bonus payments (because they are a tax deductible expense) will reduce the overall tax liability. Taxation, in the short term has, therefore, both a mandatory and a discretionary element and so it overlaps both inner circles.

The remainder of the cash surplus can be distributed at the discretion of management. Accounting profit does not exactly correspond with cash surplus, however, because of the different conventions under which it is calculated and because of the inclusion of certain non-cash items such as depreciation, accruals and prepayments. The shaded overlap region in Fig. 10.1 defines the area which is potentially distributable to shareholders in any given period.

In the majority of Western economies, the profit or 'earnings' shown in the financial accounts of a firm is legally deemed to belong to the equity capital holders. In addition, because the managers of a firm are deemed to be the agents of the shareholders, they are expected to use the firm's cash surplus to maximize the shareholders' wealth. Most managers would take this to mean that they should use the cash surplus generated by the firm's operations to maximize the value of the firm and that this can, in certain circumstances, be best achieved by, for example, paying increased wages and thus buying better relations with the workforce.

Fig 10.1 The distribution of surplus

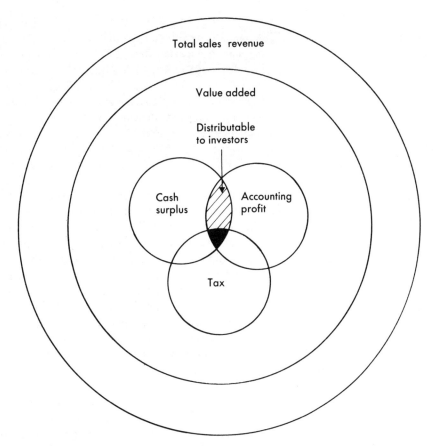

As we shall point out in Chapter 12, while the holders of equity capital have a share in the legal ownership of the firm, in the larger public companies such ownership is purely formal and has little real significance. The individual equity investors in such companies have very little effective control and often very little contact with their companies. In fact only a small proportion of investors take advantage of their right to attend and vote at company meetings or to examine their company's registers and other public documents.

The principal benefit received by the equity investor from his or her shareholding is the cash dividends received from the company and any appreciation of the cash value of the shares held. A share is, therefore, a cash-generating asset for the investor. In Chapter 12 we will discuss, in more detail, the factors which govern the return that an individual investor earns on a particular shareholding. For the moment we can make the point that the most important determinant in deciding the value of a share is its cash-generating ability (in the form of dividends and future sale proceeds) and that the element of control which the investor holds over the company is unlikely to influence this valuation, one way or the other.

> *Note:* In recent years the so-called 'institutional' investors have become particularly important in the UK share market. Institutional investors include the pension funds, the insurance companies, unit trusts and other organizations who use equity shareholdings as a means of investment. Because such institutional investors tend to have larger holdings in particular companies than individual shareholders they can exert a much greater influence over the firm's (and more particularly, management's) behaviour.

Even though equity investors are regarded as the legal owners of a firm and consequently the ultimate owners of any cash surplus, they do not have to bear the full consequences of any losses which are made. In normal circumstances shareholder's maximum liability is limited to the nominal value of the capital invested by that individual.

Figure 10.2 shows, in the context of the financial accounts of a business, how various interest groups impact upon a company's profit and loss account and how the profits may actually be distributed by way of dividends or retained on the investors' behalf within the firm.

You may remember that in Chapter 4 we compared a typical corporate budgeting system with a traditional line management organization (see Figs 4.4 and 2.3). We also commented upon the fact that in the majority of firms their accounting systems feed into the final profit and loss account, balance sheet and source and application of funds statement. Taken together, these three documents form the principal financial statements of the directors' accountability to their firm's investors. The emphasis placed upon these statutory documents of managerial accountability can lead to two implicit objectives being assumed by senior management:

- The surplus available for distribution should be maximized.

- The costs of the firm, which represent payments to other interest groups, should be minimized.

The traditional framework of accounting implicitly supports the view that equity investors 'own' all that remains after a firm has paid off the other interest groups, and that the labour force is an input factor which should be used at the highest level of productivity in order to achieve the lowest cost. It is unlikely that the labour interest group within a firm will regard the traditional accounting statements as an unbiased representation of the firm's obligations.

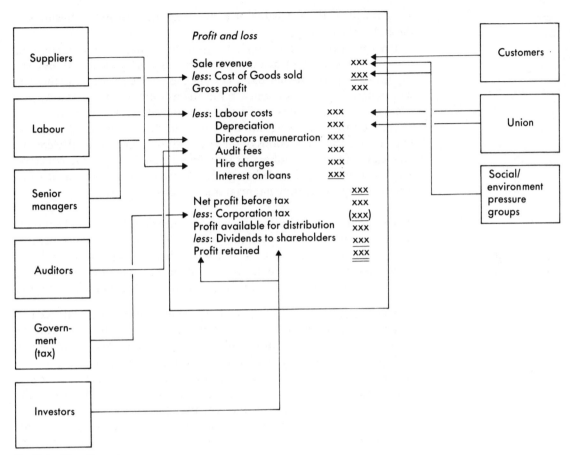

Fig 10.2 The effect of various groups upon income

In their negotiations with management, employees (or their union representatives) will seek information which assists their decision-making. Indeed, in some circumstances the provision of such information may well be one of the issues of the negotiation procedure. Consequently, the management accountant could be required to collect and report information specifically for employees.

In the next section of this chapter we will discuss the relevance of the traditional statements of account for the distribution decision and the objections which the employees or their unions may raise to the figures presented.

Traditional statements of account

Many accountants call the profit and loss account an 'income' statement and the balance sheet a 'statement of affairs'. This is because the profit and loss account indicates the income attributable to the firm's owners over the period in question and because the balance sheet should give a statement of the net value of their assets invested in the business at the end of the period.

The net value of a company's assets at the beginning of an accounting period (which we will assumed to be a year) is equal to the owner's capital or 'equity' at that date. During the course of the year the firm will undertake activities which result in cash inflows and outflows and changes in the amounts owed to or by outsiders. These transactions, as they occur, will bring about changes in the net assets of the firm. In recording the transactions of the year and compiling the final accounts, financial accountants adhere to four fundamental accounting concepts. These concepts are intended to guide the accountant's judgement when different ways of treating financial transactions are possible:

- The 'going concern' concept which assumes that the firm will continue its existence into the indefinite future. This is of importance because the value of the assets of a firm which is being wound up and sold piecemeal is likely to be much lower than the value of the same assets in a firm which plans to continue its operation into the indefinite future.

- The 'accruals' concept or 'matching principle' where costs and revenues are matched to the period in which they are incurred. It is this principle which distinguishes a profit and loss account from a statement of cash flow. The latter only records cash received or paid during a period whereas a profit and loss account shows the costs and revenues attributable to the period. For example, if a company has not paid its electricity bill for the final quarter of the year then the full year's charge would be shown in the profit and loss account with a liability for the final quarter shown as outstanding in the balance sheet at the end of the year.

- The 'consistency' concept where the accountant attempts to maintain the same bases for presenting financial information from one period to the next. This is done in order to make the accounts comparable between accounting periods.

- The 'prudence' concept whereby the accountant will only recognize revenues when they are actually realized either in the form of cash or in the form of a contractually committed debtor.

The financial accountant has great latitude in the interpretation of these concepts and, given the multitude of bases on which income figures can be calculated, is able to produce financial statements to reflect any one of a wide range of positions which management may choose to adopt.

In any bargaining situation between management and other groups, the financial accounts may well be represented as a definitive statement of the financial health of the business. Indeed, the words 'profitability', 'economic', 'financial health', etc., are often bandied about in public debate concerning wage negotiations as though such terms represented objectively verifiable aspects of a firm's position. A number of questions can always be raised concerning the level of distributable income the financial accounts purport to show:

- To what extent have receipts been brought into account and to what extent have they been reduced by an overzealous application of the prudence concept?

- Have the costs attributable to an accounting period been reasonably allocated and valued in terms of an agreed definition of the concept of cost?

- Have reserves been created for the protection or even the increase of the equity capital which represents an undisclosed increase in shareholder wealth at the expense of other interest groups?

- To what extent do depreciation charges represent an attempt to reinvest in capital equipment or an attempt to reduce distributable profit? Increasing the annual depreciation charge on plant and equipment will reduce accounting profit and could convey an impression to the labour negotiators of declining performance.

- Has there been any alteration in the measurement of income which is designed to present a different impression of the firm's affairs to that which held before?

To summarize, the traditional, financial accounts are the primary statements of management's accountability to their shareholders. As such the financial accounts, and the resultant concepts of 'earnings' and 'profit', present the financial performance of the firm in a particular way:

- The financial accounts measure performance in terms of the profit which is available to the firm's shareholders who are only one of many interest groups within the firm.

- The financial accounts present a figure which is implicitly viewed as a measure of the firm's ability to distribute to investors.

However, accounting information can be presented in other ways which are, perhaps, less biased in the perspective they offer to the negotiating interest groups within the firm.

The wage negotiating process

In this section we will examine the process by which managers and employees (or more usually their unions) negotiate. Negotiation has been classified into four subprocesses all or some of which may occur in an actual negotiating situation.

- Negotiation can be about establishing a common agreement on the 'share out' of the total surplus which the firm is able to distribute between the various interest groups.

- Negotiation can be about the solution of common problems held by both parties and would be designed to increase the firm's total ability to pay.

- Negotiation can also be designed to change the attitude of the various parties toward one another and to the relative merits of their respective claims.

- Negotiation can also be centred around achieving consensus within each of the negotiating groups.

Accounting information can have a different role to play in each of these negotiating subprocesses. In the first case each party in the negotiating process will attempt to present information in a way which enhances their particular negotiating position.

Self test: Taking any recent or current industrial dispute with which you are aware attempt to identify from published sources the types of negotiation which have been pursued by the parties to the dispute. In addition, note whether any appeal has been made to financial-accounting information and what arguments have been conducted as to the role of that information in the negotiation process.

In the second case the accounting information may well be designed to elicit the consequences of the negotiating process and will itself be prepared in an agreed format. In the third case accounting information may fulfil an important function in shaping the attitudes of participants in the negotiating process, and in the fourth case the information may be used to reform or strengthen attitudes and opinions in those supporting the negotiating process.

We can view the wage-negotiating process as a conflict situation where labour and management form beliefs about the other's position and act upon those beliefs in order to achieve their aims. On the labour side the negotiators will form an opinion about:

- The ability of the firm to pay a wage claim and thus the maximum amount which could be conceded by management. This will be the target wage claim which the union negotiators will have in mind although, invariably, they will table a demand which is in excess of this target.

- The minimum wage award which will satisfy the labour force on whose behalf they are negotiating (this will form the negotiators' resistance point).

On the other hand, management will assess:

- The maximum claim which the company could meet and this upper resistance point would be defined by their perception of the company's ability to pay.

- Their target settlement which will almost certainly be higher than their initial offer.

- The minimum which they believe the labour force are likely to accept.

This description of the negotiating process was first modelled by two writers called Walton and McKersie. Their model can be represented diagrammatically as in Fig. 10.3.

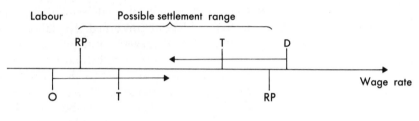

Fig 10.3 Initial position in wage bargaining
RP—resistance point;
T—target settlement;
D—labour demand;
O—management initial offer. Arrow indicates movement of perceptions

The relationship between the two parties' perceptions defines the area in which negotiation will proceed. Labour will attempt to change management's beliefs concerning the company's ability to pay the wage claim and management will attempt to convince the labour negotiators that their beliefs are unrealistic. The difference between both parties' resistance points defines the range within which a possible settlement could be achieved. In Fig. 10.3 both parties are well informed and their respective targets have been set close to the other's resistance point. In this sort of situation negotiation should quickly produce a settlement as management talk down the labour side's demand and the labour side, in its turn, talks up management's offer until a consensus is achieved (Fig. 10.4).

In Fig. 10.3 the initiating conditions are favourably disposed toward an early settlement. But in the case shown in Fig. 10.5 both parties have

Fig 10.4 Position at settlement
RP—resistance point;
T—target settlement;
D—labour demand;
O—management initial offer. Arrow indicates movement of perceptions

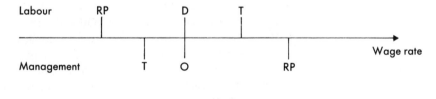

Fig 10.5 Wide range with no initial settlement possible
RP—resistance point;
T—target settlement;
D—labour demand;
O—management initial offer. Arrow indicates movement of perceptions

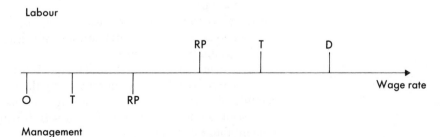

quite different perceptions and no range of settlement exists. In this case both sides will adopt strategies in order to alter the other's belief:

- Both parties in this 'distributive' type of bargaining will produce information which supports their case and highlights the weaknesses of the other's. Arguments will be put and information presented by both sides in order to convince the other of the firm's ability to pay the wage claim.

- Claim and counterclaim will be made about the market for the particular type of labour concerned. The labour negotiators will attempt to establish the comparative rate paid by other firms for the same type of labour. The reasoning behind this claim being 1 that labour has an opportunity cost which is the current market rate for labour of the type under discussion, 2 that the current market rate is, indeed, the firm's opportunity cost of labour and 3 that the firm should regard this opportunity cost as the minimum acceptable rate. If there is no directly comparable market for the type of labour concerned, the negotiators will try to force comparisons with other workers of roughly equivalent skills.

- Both parties will attempt to alter the other's perceptions of their 'commitment' to the demand or offer that they have made. This may result in some form of industrial action by either party (work to rules, strikes, lockouts, etc.).

Both parties in this and in any other bargaining situation will attempt to establish their view of the firm's ability to pay the wage claim. We will now examine some of the ways in which an estimate of a firm's ability to pay could be arrived at.

Measuring ability to pay and the concept of value added

The concept of 'ability to pay' is clearly fundamental to the wage-bargaining process, although there is considerable debate as to how it should be measured. For the reasons we outlined in the first section of this chapter, the concept of profit is unlikely to form an acceptable basis of measurement for both parties in the negotiation process. The profit and loss account presupposes a hierarchy of priority in the distribution process where the investor group is the sole claimant on all the firm's surplus after the other groups have been paid the minimum necessary to satisfy their requirements.

Any ability to pay measure must go back one stage in the distribution process and examine the situation prior to any distribution to the principal interest groups within the firm.

A statement of 'value added' outlines the distribution of the value added to the materials and services purchased by the firm from outside. In the example of such a statement below, we show how the value added to the cost of goods sold and other services is distributed between a firm's different interest groups:

Statement of value added

Turnover for the period		£120 000
less: Cost of goods sold	£42 000	
Other services	7 500	
		49 500
Value added		£70 500
Applied as follows:		
To pay employees		£50 000
To pay the providers of capital:		
Dividends	6 000	
Interest on loan	2 000	
		8 000
To pay government:		
Taxes		4 000
For the maintenance of capital:		
Depreciation	6 000	
Profits retained	2 500	
		8 500
Value added		£70 500

Self test: The figures shown in the value-added statement above can be recast in profit and loss form as follows:

Profit and loss statement

		£120 000
Turnover for the period		42 000
less: Cost of goods		78 000
Gross profit	7 500	
less: Other services	50 000	
Wage costs	6 000	
Depreciation	2 000	
Interest on loan	—	65 500
		12 500
Net profit before tax		4 000
less: Taxation		8 500
Profit available for distribution		6 000
less: Dividends paid to equity shareholders		£2 500
Profit retained		

Check that you can see how the same figures as those presented in the value-added statement have been rearranged and consider to what extent the profit and loss account gives a different impression of the affairs of the business.

> Take any set of company accounts that you can find which show both a profit and loss account as well as a statement of value added. Compare the two statements and identify the accounting conventions which have been used in their presentation. Does the value-added statement contain any information not contained elsewhere in the accounts? (N.B. Redland plc usually publish a particularly clear profit and loss and value-added statement.)

Even though a value-added statement contains very similar information to a profit and loss account it puts a completely different perspective on the figures presented. In a value-added statement, the value added by the business is shown as available for distribution to the principal interest groups, the profits retained are presented as part of the maintenance of capital along with depreciation. Dividends take their place alongside interest paid to other suppliers of long-term capital and the cost of labour is shown as one of the distributions.

It can be objected that taxation is a cost and should not be deemed to be a distribution of the value added of a business. The answer to this is that the level of taxation depends, in part, upon the distributions made to labour and to lenders of fixed-term capital and has, therefore, a discretionary element. For this reason taxation is usually shown alongside payments to other groups.

We can depict the value-added statement as a pie chart (Fig. 10.6) and this is one way it is shown in the employee's reports produced by many British companies.

Within the context of the value-added statement, a measure of the firm's ability to pay revolves around two issues:

- The current distribution of value added between the various interest groups.

- The increase in value added anticipated in the following periods.

For example, in the case of the company whose value-added statement is shown above, turnover and costs of goods sold are expected to rise by 10 per cent over the next year while the cost of other services is expected to rise by 6 per cent. The projected increase in value added is, therefore:

Turnover (£120 000 × 1.10)		£132 000
less: Cost of goods sold (£42 000 × 1.10)	£46 200	
Other services (£7500 × 1.06)	7 950	
		54 150
Value added for next period		£77 850
Value added for current period		70 500
Increase in value added		£7 350

The projected increase in value added (£7350) provides the basis for determining the firm's ability to pay in the next accounting period.

However, the estimate of ability to pay made above is only the first stage in the wage-negotiation process. The negotiators may wish to open

Fig 10.6 Pie chart representation of value added

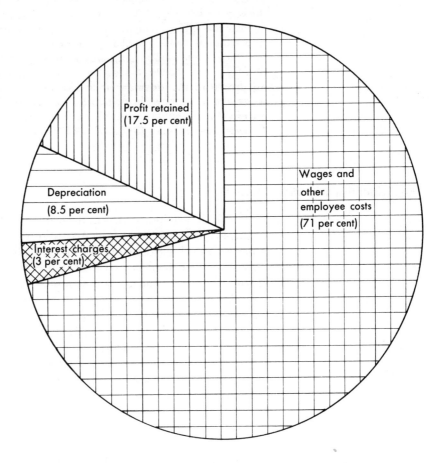

Profit retained
(17.5 per cent)

Depreciation
(8.5 per cent)

Interest charges
(3 per cent)

Wages and other employee costs
(71 per cent)

up the debate on the way in which the value added is split up between the various interest groups as well as the way in which the projected increase in value added should be distributed. All of these areas of negotiation can be supported by the management accountant's estimates of their effect upon the financial performance of the firm.

Finally, any determination of a firm's ability to pay must also recognize the problems of liquidity, especially in the short term. Increased labour charges will affect the firm's projected cash budget and, where productivity deals are involved, the management accountant will have to make projections of future labour costs on the basis of the assumed levels of future production. New pay deals invariably require a complete revision of a firm's budgets for the coming year or an explicit recognition of the changed position when variances are calculated during the period.

Self test: A company had originally budgeted a labour rate of £11.50 per hour for its production workers. The planned labour hours for a quarter had been set at 218 000 hours on the basis of an output of 8230 units of production. On the first day of the final quarter of the year a new wage deal was negotiated giving a 5 per cent increase in basic rates. The actual hourly rate was, as expected, 5 per cent above that planned. Actual output for the quarter was 8 per cent up on budget while labour usage was up by only 2000 hours. As the quarter concerned was the last one of the year, a revised budget was not produced. Management would like the effect of the increased wage rate to be shown in the quarterly exception report. Calculate the effect of the wage deal on the variances concerned.
Solution clue: 5110.83(A); 23 000(A); 177 560(F).

The dividend-distribution decision

According to the traditional view of the firm, the shareholder is the owner of the surplus generated by the firm. According to this view, in an economically perfect world, the directors of a firm should not concern themselves about the level of dividend payment. Once the costs of the firm have been paid, the firm's management should invest all surplus cash in any investments which have a positive net present value when discounted at the firm's opportunity cost of capital (we will explain these concepts much more fully in Chapters 12 and 13 although you have already come across the notion of net present value in Chapter 3). Only when the firm has undertaken all its worthwhile investment opportunities should it distribute any remaining cash to its shareholders. In this view of the world the owners will appreciate that the management is acting to increase the value of the firm by investing all surpluses in worthwhile projects and that they can realize the increase in their wealth by borrowing against the firm's security in the capital market.

Of course, the world is not perfect and there are a number of reasons why a firm's directors would wish to make dividend payments and, indeed, want to increase them year by year:

- There is a belief that the value of a company's shares are responsive to changes in dividends and that a drop in dividends in any particular year will be detrimental to the firm's share price.

- Under UK law trustees who are governed by the Trustee Investment Act (1961) are not permitted to invest in companies who fail to declare an annual dividend.

- Institutional investors who rely upon company dividends for their own short-term liquidity (e.g. in order to make payments on pension funds) will take a very serious view of a firm which permits wide swings in its dividend payments.

- The directors of the company and its employees may well also be shareholders and will have a vested interest in the maintenance of dividends.

Unlike the labour group within a firm, the outside shareholders do not have a formal negotiating forum for claiming higher distributions and can only register a real protest at the annual general meeting of the firm or by selling their shares. In the final analysis, the management of a firm will only pay the level of dividends necessary to maintain the value of the firm's equity shares and hence the ability of the firm to raise new capital in the market when necessary. At this point the dividend decision begins to become part of the financing decision—an area which we will examine in much more detail in Chapter 12.

Summary

In this chapter we have examined the way that two types of distribution decision are made. We have explicitly considered the role of traditional accounting information in the wage-distribution decision and especially how it can be used in management/labour negotiations. We suggest that the traditional form of profit and loss account gives a particular and selective view of the status of labour costs and that other forms of account, such as the value-added statement, give a less slanted view of a firm's performance. Finally, we considered some of the factors which influence the dividend-distribution decision.

Supplementary reading

ACCOUNTING STANDARDS STEERING COMMITTEE, *The Corporate Report*, The Institute of Chartered Accountants in England and Wales, 1975

COOPER, D. and ESSEX, S., Accounting information and employee decision making, *Accounting, Organizations and Society*, 1977, pp. 201–217

FOLEY, B. J. and MAUNDERS, K. T., *Accounting Information Disclosure and Collective Bargaining*, Macmillan, 1977

SOLOMONS, D., Economic and accounting concepts of income, in Parker, R. H. and Harcourt, G. C., *Readings in the Concept and Measurement of Income*, Cambridge University Press, 1969

Questions

1   Discuss the extent to which a management accountant should be prepared to produce accounting information which is designed to support the position of shareholders in opposition to employees.

2 A company has produced the following detailed profit and loss account:

Sales revenue		£877 000
less: Cost of goods sold	£199 500	
Direct labour	416 000	
		615 500
Gross profit		261,500
less: Depreciation	66 000	
Interest on long-term loan	24 000	
Director's emoluments	38 400	
Auditor's remuneration	2 400	
		130 800
Profit before taxation		130 700
less: Corporation tax		54 894
Profit after tax		75 806
First and final ordinary dividend for the year		28 000
Profit transferred to reserves		£47 806

Required:

(a) Convert the statement of profit and loss shown into a statement of value added.

(b) What additional information would you require in order to interpret the significance of the profit and loss account shown above and the statement of value added which you have produced.

3 What are the different types of wage negotiation which employees can enter into with management? To what extent can accounting information inform or obstruct the progress of these different types of wage negotiation.

4 A manufacturing company has decided to introduce a new, microcomputer-controlled, robotic assembly line. The union negotiators have protested that this is an attempt by management to increase profitability for the investors at the expense of the workforce and as a result have called for a work to rule in the factory. The company had hoped to increase production through the assembly line. Discuss the difficulties in resolving this type of industrial dispute.

Part 3 Accounting for long-term decisions ───────

11 Uncertainty and long-term decision-making ———

In this chapter we consider the problems of risk and uncertainty in decision-making and how risk can be reduced. After examining some simple problems of risk measurement we then move on to a brief introduction to the areas of long-term decision-making considered in the next two chapters of this book.

An outline of the topics in this chapter is as follows:

- **The concept of decision risk and how it is measured.**
- **Strategies for the reduction of risk and uncertainty.**
- **The general nature of long-term decisions.**

Risk and uncertainty in decision-making

The notion of rational decision-making presupposes the idea that future outcomes, measured in terms of their cash effects upon the firm, can be identified and measured. If we happen to be in the happy but unlikely position of possessing complete information on all the economic processes surrounding a particular decision then we should be able to predict the future with complete certainty providing, of course, that we accept the assumption that all social and economic events are causally linked to one another. However, we rarely possess complete information in this sense and so we are forced to consider the uncertainty attached to the outcomes of our actions.

With outcomes which are very close in time to a particular decision the link between cause and effect can be quite clear. However, the more remote the outcome the less clear the linkages between action and consequence become and the greater the degree of uncertainty with which the decision-maker must contend. In addition, outcomes over which management have some control and/or some prior experience will be less uncertain than where the opposite is the case.

The uncertainty of an outcome can be attributed to four sources:

- The time lag between decision and outcome.
- The degree of management's control over the outcomes in question.
- The complexity of the relationships between the variables which impinge upon the decision.

• The experience of similar decision situations possessed by management.

In some situations management may have accumulated sufficient past experience of a particular type of decision to enable them to predict, with a considerable degree of certainty, the likelihood of certain events occurring. Life-insurance companies regularly predict the life expectancy of particular individuals when assessing premiums for life-insurance policies. They can do this by virtue of the large amounts of data which they

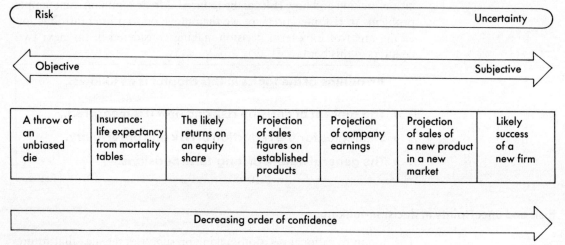

Fig 11.1   The risk–uncertainty spectrum

have collected over the years and compiled into their actuarial tables of life expectancy. In other situations, management may find itself in a situation where it has acquired little or no past experience of a particular type of decision and must rely upon subjective judgement in order to make decisions. For example, an entrepreneur setting up a new business, or an existing company entering into a new market, may have very little experience upon which to base their decisions.

The insurance company, which uses the results of a large number of similar events as a basis for estimating the probabilities of particular events occurring, is in what we call a 'risk' situation. At the other extreme, a company trying to take decisions without any prior knowledge, and purely on the basis of subjective estimates, is in an 'uncertainty' situation.

The words 'risk' and 'uncertainty' denote opposite ends of the objectivity–subjectivity spectrum. In Fig. 11.1 we show this risk–uncertainty spectrum with examples of decision-making situations which lie within it.

We can use the statistical concept of probability to assess the likelihood of an event occurring in both risk and uncertainty situations. In risk situations we can use objective probabilities to make statistical predictions, while in uncertainty situations we use probabilities as subjective measures of likelihood.

Note: There is much argument among statisticians about whether or not it is valid to use probabilities in the uncertainty situation. The problem is that the statistical rules for using probabilities have been developed on the presupposition that a reliable distribution of probabilities of an event occurring can be drawn up before it occurs (see below for an example). This is not possible with the uncertainty situation, and the question is whether the rules for manipulating probabilities can be extended into a context of uncertainty. Our view is that they can, but only with great care. It is important not to attach a spurious level of accuracy or reliability to figures calculated on the basis of subjective probabilities.

Probabilities are represented on a scale from 0 to 1 (or sometimes on the equivalent percentage scale of 0–100 per cent). Completely certain outcomes have a probability of 1 of occurring. Absolutely impossible situations have a probability of 0 of occurring. In Fig. 11.2 we show the scale of probabilities from 0 to 1 with some suggestions of appropriate situations and their probability of occurring.

In all decision situations a range or 'set' of possible outcomes exists and each outcome has its own probability of occurring.

To give an example from the short-term decision-making area, consider Marchena plc, which uses a raw material, Olic Acid, in its production processes. The material is bought from a supplier who produces Olic Acid as a by-product from another process. Because the production runs which produce Olic Acid follow a monthly cycle the supplier cannot

Fig 11.2 The scale of probabilities

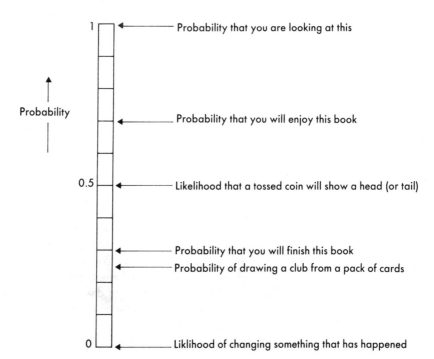

guarantee delivery on any particular day but only within 28 days of order. Marchena's purchasing department has kept a note of the order to delivery time (the 'lead time') for the last 400 orders (more than one order may be placed within a particular calendar month).

They have noted that no delivery has ever been made within 10 days of order. The purchasing department's figures are summarized in the table below:

Number of days from order	Number of deliveries*	Number of days from order	Number of deliveries*
10	0	19	59
11	1	20	46
12	4	21	31
13	9	22	18
14	18	23	9
15	31	24	4
16	46	25	1
17	59	26	0
18	64	27	0

* Total number of deliveries = 400.

By dividing the number of deliveries on a given day by the total number of orders (400) we can estimate the probability of a delivery being made on a particular day.

Number of days from order	Probability of delivery	Number of days from order	Probability of delivery
10	0	19	0.1475
11	0.0025	20	0.1150
12	0.0100	21	0.0775
13	0.0225	22	0.0450
14	0.0450	23	0.0225
15	0.0775	24	0.0100
16	0.1150	25	0.0025
17	0.1475	26	0
18	0.1600	27	0

The total probability of delivery within 28 days is exactly 1.00.

In Fig. 11.3 we show the probabilities calculated above in the form of a line chart. The y axis carries the measure of probability and the horizontal x axis represents the variable of interest to us which is, in this case, the number of days to delivery. The dotted line which connects the top of each line (whose heights represent the probability of deliveries being made on that number of days after the order) forms a bell-shaped curve which we call a 'continuous probability distribution'.

The shape we have drawn in Fig. 11.3 closely approximates an ideal type of curve known to statisticians as a 'normal probability distribution'.

Fig 11.3 Probability of deliveries

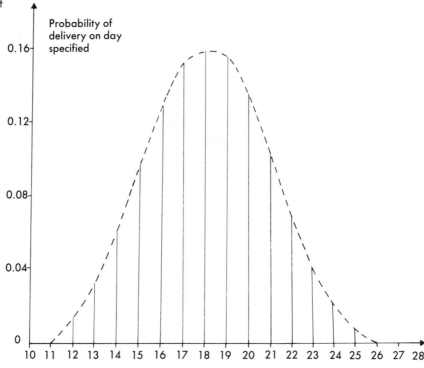

The height of the curve above the x axis at any point gives the probability of that x value occurring. Many social, economic and physical systems generate variables which appear to be close approximations of the normal distribution. For example, the height of males (and the height of females as a separate group) in the population are distributed normally, so are the returns generated by ordinary shares. Many more examples can be found.

Note: The normal distribution is an ideal case, continuous probability distribution which appears to be representative of many different economic, social and physical variables. Marchena's data are unusual in that they produce a very close approximation to the normal distribution. One would be very unlikely to find such a close match with real data although in many instances, with all sorts of different random variables, the normal distribution does provide a good approximation to the actual data.

The curve of the normal distribution can be drawn using the following formula:

$$p_i = \frac{1}{\sqrt{2\pi\sigma^2}} \, e^{-1/2(x_i - \mu)^2/\sigma^2}$$

where p_i is the probability of x_i occurring, σ is the standard deviation (see below), μ the mean of the distribution, π is a constant 3.1416 and e is a constant 2.7183.

Only two values need to be known in order to draw a normal distribution and they are its mean value and its standard deviation. Once these two values are known the value of p can be obtained by taking any value of x and substituting it into the above equation. If this is done a sufficient number of times and the results drawn on a graph the normal curve will emerge.

As we have noted above only two items of information are needed to describe a normal distribution: its mean and its standard deviation.

For Marchena's problem the mean is given by:

mean (number of days from delivery to order)

= the sum of: each value of the x variable multiplied by its respective probability

In mathematical notation this becomes:

$$\mu = \sum_{i=1}^{n} (p_i x_i)$$

where:

μ is the mean value. This is often called the 'expected value' of the variable x and is sometimes symbolized as $E(x_i)$.

p_i is the probability of 'observing' any one of the n possible values of x_i. In this case $n = 16$.

x_i is the probabilistic variable under consideration. In this example it is the number of days from order to delivery.

$\sum_{i=1}^{n}$ is a mathematical symbol which means 'the sum of' the range of values which immediately follow it. The range of values to be summed is given by the values above and below the Greek letter sigma. Therefore, in Marchena's example the summation sign indicates that we have to add n (=16) values together to get the mean value. Symbols such as the summation sign which denote a particular arithmetic or mathematical operation are called 'operators'. This sign is, therefore, the 'summation operator'.

Therefore, the mean number of days to delivery is given by:

$\mu = 0 \times 10 + 0.0025 \times 11 + 0.01 \times 12 + 0.0225 \times 13 + 0.045 \times 14 +$
$\dots + 0.0250 \times 25 + 0 \times 26 + 0 \times 27$
$= 18$ days

The standard deviation gives a measure of the 'spread' or standard width of the normal distribution. Because the true normal distribution has infinitely long tails it is impossible to measure its full width—indeed, the normal distribution has infinite width! The standard deviation measures the width of the distribution which encloses approximately 68 per cent of the total area under the curve.

The standard deviation of a normal distribution is given by:

$$\sigma = \sqrt{\sum_{i=1}^{n} p_i(x_i - \mu)^2}$$

where the notation is the same as that specified for the mean.

To calculate the standard deviation we deduct the mean number of days (μ) from each possible day. This gives the deviation of each day from the mean. Each deviation is then squared and multiplied by its respective probability. The square root of the sum of the resultant values gives the standard deviation. Normally, if we take the square root of any number we get two answers or 'roots', one plus and the other minus. However, the standard deviation is defined in terms of the absolute value of the deviation from the mean, i.e. for Marchena:

$$\sigma = \{0 \times (10 - 18)^2 + 0.0025 \times (11 - 18)^2 + 0.01 \times (12 - 18)^2$$
$$+ \ldots + 0.0025 \times (25 - 18)^2 + 0 \times (26 - 18)^2 + 0 \times (27 - 18)^2\}^{1/2}$$
$$= 2.478$$

Notice that we have used the power $1/2$ to denote the square root of the term in the brackets.

The distribution of delivery times for Marchena can now be represented by the graph shown in Fig. 11.4.

Fig 11.4 Normal approximation to distribution of delivery times

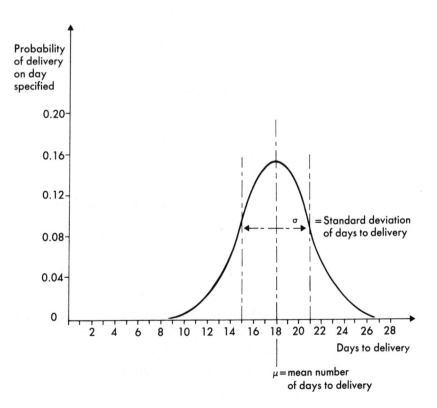

Note: The variance of a normal distribution is equal to the standard deviation squared, i.e. it is calculated as above except that the square root is not taken. Computationally, the variance is an easier figure to calculate: however, it has less meaning as a measure of spread, as it is measured in squared units of the decision variable concerned.

The probability with which an outcome occurs measures the risk attached to that outcome. Given a range of possible outcomes which approximate to the normal distribution (as in Marchena's example) the mean or expected value of the distribution gives the most likely outcome (i.e the outcome with the highest probability). The standard deviation measures the variability of possible outcomes around the mean value and is a measure of the risk attached to the distribution as a whole.

To understand this point, consider the following example: Nino is a brewer of real ale and is investigating alternative bottling machines for installation in his brewery. Two machines have been short-listed. Both machines can fill and top bottles of the type Nino uses. Each bottle is labelled as containing 500 ml and each machine can be calibrated to fill to this level. However, like all filling machines inaccuracies do occur even though, on average, over a large number of fills, the machine will inject the calibrated 500 ml.

Sample trials with both types of machine have indicated that one machine (machine A), when calibrated to 500 ml, gives a mean fill of 500 ml with a standard deviation of 5 ml from the mean. The other machine (machine B) gives a mean fill of 500 ml with a standard deviation of 10 ml. The legal minimum on a bottle with a stated capacity of 500 ml is 492 ml. In Fig. 11.5 we show the distributions of filling performance for both machines.

With machine B the probability of filling bottles at or below the legal minimum is greater than that for machine A. Therefore, the risk of unacceptable fills is higher with machine B than with machine A. Distribution B has a greater risk than distribution A and this risk is reflected in the magnitude of the standard deviation.

To summarize these points on risk and uncertainty:

- Risk and uncertainty arise through our imperfect attempts to predict the future.

- We use probabilities to measure the risk or uncertainty attaching to a particular outcome.

- If a range of alternative outcomes is possible then the mean or expected value will give the most likely outcome.

- If a range of alternative outcomes is normally distributed then the standard deviation gives a measure of the risk or uncertainty attaching to that outcome.

Fig 11.5 Distributions of filling performance

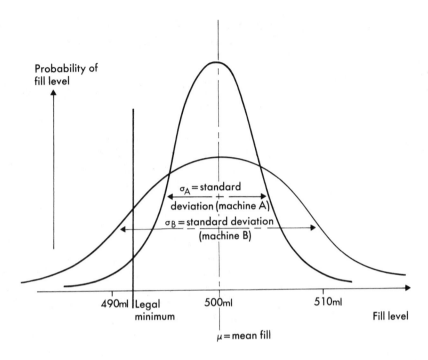

Probability of fill level

σ_A = standard deviation (machine A)

σ_B = standard deviation (machine B)

490ml | Legal minimum   500ml   510ml

Fill level

μ = mean fill

Self test: **The long-run operating history of a chemical plant has shown that weekly wastage of materials (expressed at the current buying-in price) is as follows:**

Number of weeks	Wastage (£)	Number of weeks	Wastage (£)
5	0–10	38	40.01–50
17	10.01–20	18	50.01–60
40	20.01–30	10	60.01–70
53	30.01–40	0	>70

Individual weekly wastages are expressed in ranges: £0–10, £10.01–20 and so on. Take the midpoint of the range as the representative value of x. Compute the mean value of wastage cost and its standard deviation.
    Solution clue: **35.55; 13.4.**

Strategies for the reduction of risk and uncertainty

When managers perceive that following a particular course of action entails accepting risky outcomes they will attempt to quantify and minimize that risk as far as possible. In the last section we saw how the risk attaching to a particular outcome can be measured, making the implicit assumption that the variability of the recorded values of a particular variable is a reliable indicator of future risk. There are, however, a number of strategies management can follow in order to minimize the level of risk:

• It can seek further information about the relationship between particular decisions and their consequences. For example, if a company decides to alter the price of its product it may believe that there is a level of uncertainty concerning the amount it will sell. To a certain extent market research can reduce that uncertainty and, indeed, may be able to quantify the situation in terms of a range of possible sales levels with probabilities attached to them.

• It may attempt to insure against the possibility of undesirable outcomes (i.e. outcomes lower than the mean or expected value). For example, if a company perceives that a new production facility increases the risk of fire at a particular plant it may decide to cover that increased risk by taking out extra fire-insurance cover. Similarly, if an investor sells shares he or she does not possess (a 'short sale') in the hope of earning a profit on an immediate fall in share price, that investor can insure against the possibility of an increase in share price by buying a 'call option'. A 'call option' represents a right to purchase the shares at a stated price at a specified future date. The risk of an increase in share price, which would entail buying back the shares at a loss, is covered by the option. Reducing risk in this way is often called 'hedging', hence the term 'hedging one's bets'.

• Finally, management can reduce risk by 'diversification'. When several outcomes are put together, their combined risk is not always a linear addition of their individual risks. The combined risk may be greater or less than a simple combination of their risks depending on the circumstances. When management takes combinations of decisions in order to obtain outcomes which reduce risk overall it is said to be following a 'diversification strategy'. We will examine this important method of risk management in the next chapter.

General nature of long-term decisions

In Chapter 4 we outlined the general features of short-run decisions and in so doing also touched upon the crucial characteristics of long-run decisions. We will reiterate some of the points we made in Chapter 4 here for those of you who have decided to study the problems of short-term decision-making before moving on to the long-term decision-making chapters of this book.

All short-run decisions presume some prior long-run decision. An output decision presumes a production decision and so forth. Conversely, a long-run decision assumes a certain set of feasible short-run decisions which will arise as a consequence of that long-run decision being made. We can make a certain number of points about long-run decisions which separate them from short-run decisions:

- The range of costs which will be changed as a result of a long-run decision is much wider than those which will be influenced by the consequential short-run decisions. This is just an extension of the idea that in the very long run no costs are fixed.

- Long-run decisions affect a number of future periods (where period is defined as the time span covered by the short-run decision-making period). As a result the changes in wealth caused by the long-run decision are likely to involve timing effects. If you are unsure of this idea, refer back to Chapter 3.

- Because the difference in time between decision and consequence is much greater in long-run decisions than in short-run decisions, the problems of uncertainty become more difficult. Much of the theory and practice of long-run decision-making is concerned with the problem of handling risk and uncertainty.

In Fig. 11.6 we show the sequence of financial decisions made by a typical firm.

The first decision in any period relates to the amount of the cash resources, available in that period, which should be devoted to immediate expenditure and the amount which should be used for investment. Investment can be regarded as the deferral of current consumption expenditure in order to generate future cash returns. The question then arises as to the worthwhileness of the possible investment projects a firm can under-

Fig 11.6 Sequence of corporate decisions

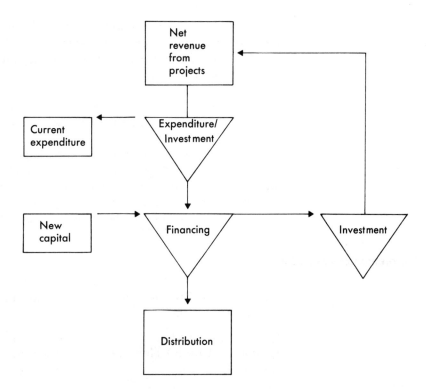

take. In theory, following the ideas developed in Chapter 3, a firm should invest in all investment projects which yield a positive net present value (more on this in Chapter 13). If the firm has insufficient cash resources to accept all worthwhile investment projects it should seek to raise extra finance on the capital market. We will examine the merits of the various types of finance available to a firm in the next chapter. Finally, as we noted in the last chapter, any residual cash remaining after the investment decisions have been made should be returned to the shareholders as a dividend distribution.

If the managers of the firm were to act entirely in the best interests of their shareholders they might well follow the sequence of decisions suggested by Fig. 11.6. However, as we indicated in the last chapter, many other factors will influence the decisions managers must make about the distribution of the firm's cash resources. Unfortunately, the methods of long-term decision-making which have been developed by financial theorists have largely ignored the problems posed by such a wider view of the responsibilities of company managers. In the two chapters which follow we will draw heavily upon the ideas developed in the finance literature assuming that managers are primarily concerned with maximizing the wealth of their shareholders. We will, where appropriate, point out the limitiations of this approach to prescribing long-term decision-making practice.

Summary

In this chapter we have considered the problem of measuring risk and uncertainty which is a problem germane to both short- and long-term decision-making. We have shown how probabilities can be used in the measurement of the risk or uncertainty attaching to a particular outcome and how the standard deviation can be used to measure the risk or uncertainty attaching to a range of outcomes. Finally, we have made some introductory remarks concerning the nature of long-term decision-making.

In the next chapter we will examine the problem of raising finance and how a company's general business risk is reflected in the cost which attaches to the capital it uses for investment purposes. In Chapter 13 we will extend the cost of capital concept developed in the next chapter into an explicit discussion of the problems of investment decision-making.

Supplementary reading

HERTZ, D. B., Risk analysis in capital investment, *Harvard Business Review*, **42** (1), 1964.

PAPPAS, J. L., BRIGHAM, E. F., and SHIPLEY, B., *Managerial Economics* (UK edn), Holt, Rinehart and Winston, 1983, Especially Chapter 4.

Questions

1 Readings were taken from the distributions of weekly returns for a pair of securities:

Security A		Security B	
Probability of return	Percentage return	Probability of return	Percentage return
0.015	0.011	0.001	0.020
0.018	0.015	0.008	0.025
0.045	0.019	0.025	0.030
0.085	0.023	0.082	0.035
0.110	0.027	0.260	0.040
0.189	0.031	0.300	0.045
0.190	0.035	0.189	0.050
0.124	0.039	0.081	0.055
0.080	0.043	0.045	0.060
0.065	0.047	0.007	0.065
0.049	0.051	0.002	0.070
0.020	0.055		
0.010	0.059		

Required:
(a) Draw the two distributions above on a sheet of graph paper using the same axes for both.
(b) Calculate the mean, standard deviation and variance of the two distributions.
(c) Determine which of the two distributions has the greatest standard deviation per unit of mean.
(d) Define the concept of risk and uncertainty and outline how probability measures can assist in their measurement.

2 Outline the features which distinguish long-run decisions from short-run decisions. To what extent does this distinction represent reality or an arbitrary classification for the purposes of analytical convenience?

12 The financing decision

The management accountant's function with respect to the firm's capital covers two important and interrelated areas. First, the identification of the cheapest source of finance (the financing decision) and, second, the evaluation of the competing uses for that finance (the investment decision). The linking factor in both these decision areas is the costing of different souces of finance to the firm.

In the chapter we consider the principal sources of finance for the firm. We examine the characteristic features of the market for capital funds and discuss the relative merits of different types of finance. Drawing upon the concept of risk discussed in the last chapter, we will demonstrate the methods which the management accountant can employ in costing the firm's capital resources.

In this chapter we will examine:

- The function of the capital market in the supply of capital funds.
- The function and operation of the stock exchange.
- The economic characteristics of the stock exchange.
- The advantages and disadvantages of different types of finance.
- The concept of 'gearing' and financial risk.
- The costing of the firm's capital resources.
- The optimal proportions of different types of finance within the firm's capital structure.

Supply of capital and the role of the capital market

In Chapter 2 we said that capital is one of the primary resources needed for production. Capital is traded in the capital market in the form of financial securities. A financial security is any item which is a transferable store of wealth. A share certificate is a capital-market security as it can be sold by its holder to anyone who wishes to purchase it. Indeed, any item can act as a capital-market security provided it can be used as a store of wealth. For example, fine wines held with a view to future sale, rather than for consumption, can be regarded as a capital-market security. The trading in capital-market securities makes up the capital market and it is to this market that firms have to go in order to raise new finance.

Any firm requiring capital for investment can obtain that capital in one of two ways:

- By selling an ownership stake in the business for cash. Ownership of a part of a business is termed a 'share'. As we noted in Chapter 2, firms are under no obligation to return the funds which they realize through the sale of their shares and are not under any compulsion to pay a dividend. The point to note here is that the shareholder-investor is not 'lending' money to the firm. The shareholder is purchasing a legal claim to part of the business and, therefore, to part of the surplus which the firm may generate.

- By borrowing money either indefinitely or for a fixed term. In the case of fixed-term loans, the borrowing must be repaid at the due date of redemption and the agreed rate of interest must be paid when it falls due. In essence, borrowing money is like a hire agreement where the article hired is a capital sum and the rental is the interest paid.

Later in this chapter we will consider these two sources of finance in more detail.

A capital market exists to bring together savers, who may not have any direct productive investment opportunities open to them, and firms who have the investment opportunities but lack the necessary funds to undertake them. A firm seeking funds for investment raises new money through what is often termed the 'primary capital market'. However, investing firms typically require funds for the long term, while individual savers generally require a degree of liquidity to finance their changing patterns of consumption. This conflict between the long-term needs of firms and the short-term requirements of their investors has given rise to a 'secondary capital market' where share and loan certificates are traded independently of the companies in which they are held.

Self test: Obtain the accounts of a large public company and identify its principal sources of finance. To what extent is it funded by equity capital or by debt capital? Has the firm raised any new finance during the previous year? If so, can you find any reasons why the money was required and why the firm chose to raise it in the way it did?

In Fig. 12.1 we show, as a circular flow, the movement of cash between firms and individual investors. Firms use their cash resources in productive investment opportunities, in investment in working capital (stocks, debtors and short-term cash balances) and in interest and dividend payments (which we call capital charges). These capital charges represent the reward to the individual investors for their investment in the firm concerned. You will also note in Fig. 12.1 that in the link between investors and firms, intermediaries called 'underwriters' may intervene. These underwriters, who are usually financial institutions such as merchant banks, assist in the acquisition of new funds by guaranteeing the uptake of a new share issue by investors.

As far as companies are concerned, the capital market is represented by all possible sources of funds which are available to them. For large public limited companies the range of sources of new funds is very wide

Fig 12.1 The capital cycle

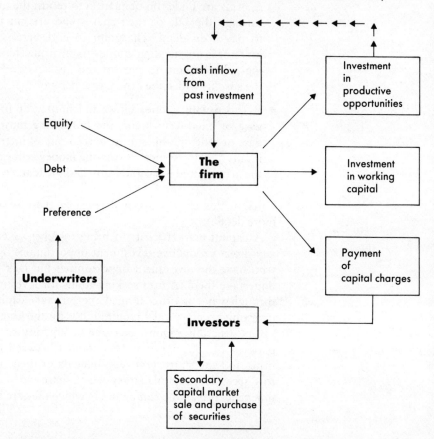

indeed. The banks and other financial institutions as well as private and institutional investors all provide finance for such companies. For small, private limited companies and other small firms the range of possible sources of finance is much smaller. Private limited companies, for instance, do not have access to finance through the stock market and would also find it very difficult to raise long-term loans from the major financial institutions. Such companies normally have to rely on the personal resources of their owners, managers and bank finance. However, no matter how large or small the firm concerned, the rate of return (in the form of interest or dividends), which will be required by the suppliers of the finance, is governed by the following factors:

- The degree of risk which the supplier perceives is attached to either the payment of interest or dividends or to the repayment of the original invested capital.

- The rate of change in the supplier's purchasing power (which in general terms is called 'inflation') and the degree of uncertainty which attaches to that rate of change.

- The rate of return which the supplier of finance can earn on equivalent investments elsewhere. As we shall see later, equivalence in this context can be taken to mean 'investments of equivalent risk'.

Function and operation of the stock market

The focus of the secondary capital market in the UK is the London Stock Exchange where share and debt stock are traded. Similar institutions exist in all of the major financial centres in the world. The London Stock

Fig 12.2 Capital issues in the United Kingdom

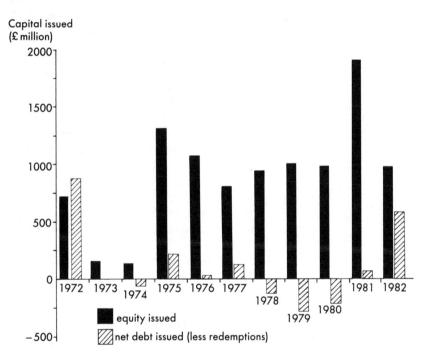

Exchange is not only an important secondary market but it also serves as an important primary market where public limited companies can raise new finance.

In Fig. 12.2 we show the issues of capital made through the London Stock Exchange to British industry and commerce over the years 1972–82.

The London Stock Exchange is unusual in that it has a two-tier trading system of 'jobbers' and 'brokers'. Individuals and institutions wishing to deal in securities must buy and sell through a broker. Brokers then buy or sell on behalf of their clients (and on their own behalf) with the 'stall-holders' of the exchange—the jobbers. It is the jobbers who make the market in any security by setting the price which they believe will balance its supply and its demand.

> *Note:* The Council of the London Stock Exchange is proposing that the two-tier trading system should be done away with and the role of brokers and jobbers merged. This will bring the Exchange into line with other exchanges around the world. It may also help to reduce the concentration of dealing power in the hands of the very few, large jobbing firms who dominate the market.

Jobbers are not permitted to deal directly with the public so they must make their money in one of two ways:

● By making a 'turn', i.e. taking the difference between the price at which they buy and the price at which they sell securities. In this respect they are just like any other second-hand dealer.

● By making profits on their 'short-term positions' in particular securities. If a jobber oversells a particular security, i.e. sells more than he or she possesses, the excess sales can be covered by purchases at a later date. Sometimes the jobber may find it advantageous to be oversold on a particular security at the close of business on a particular day and to buy enough of that security the following morning to cover the oversold position. As a result, the jobber will make a profit if there has been a drop in price of the security concerned. The reverse can also occur if the jobber buys in more securities than he or she has sold in a particular day and then realizes a profit following a rise in price. In the first case the jobber is said to have sold 'short' and in the second case to have bought 'long'.

Other investors, apart from jobbers, can also deal speculatively in a security in the way described above. Because the London Stock Exchange operates on the basis of 14-day trading periods, it is possible to buy and sell securities within a period and only account to the broker for any difference when the account is settled.

In Fig. 12.3 we show a trading period on the London Stock Exchange and how a speculative profit or gain may be made. You will notice in Fig. 12.3 that both purchases and sales of the security in question are

Fig 12.3 A 'bull' transaction within one account

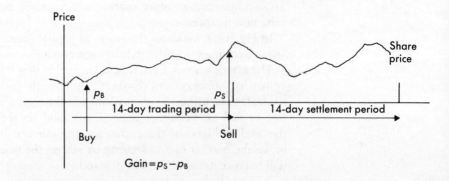

made within the one trading period. It is quite typical for there to be a sudden reversal in the movement of a security's price just before the account end. Such reversals are caused by speculators taking their profits. Indeed, such price reversals are often described by commentators, in the press and elsewhere, as being caused by 'profit taking' or sometimes as technical 'rallies' or 'declines'.

Of course, the success of such speculative transactions depends upon the accurate prediction of future price movements and the ability of the speculator to sustain quite severe losses.

We can identify two motives which predominate in the investment decision-making of individuals:

- An 'income motive', where the security is purchased for the cash which it will generate, for the holder, in the form of interest or dividends and for the potential capital gain which the security may achieve. Investors with an income motive usually spend time establishing the economic quality of the security concerned, particularly in respect of its ability to yield future cash flows.

- A 'speculative motive', where investors trade against anticipated price changes in particular securities in order to make short-term capital gains. In this case the investor is less concerned with the ability of the security to generate future cash returns than with the reactions of other investors to changing events.

There is considerable debate as to the desirability or otherwise of speculative activity in the stock exchanges. What can be said, however, is that speculation in a particular security can reinforce a price trend although there is no real evidence to suggest that speculators can make abnormal gains (a term we will define later) from their transactions.

Economic characteristics of the stock market

Although the influence of speculators can be most spectacular in their effect upon prices in the short term, the more important question concerns the degree to which the stock market can be said to be competitively perfect and information efficient in the longer term. This is an important issue for firms who wish to ensure that their stocks and shares are correctly priced by the market. This, as we shall see later, is an important consideration when a firm is attempting to cost its capital resources or raise new finance.

> *Self test:* Revise the conditions required for any market to be perfectly competitive (see Chapter 2). To what extent is free and speedy access to information a necessary prerequisite for a perfect market?

A market in an individual security is said to be perfectly competitive if:

- Individual traders in the market are unable to influence the price of a particular share through their own transactions. This will only occur if there are a large number of shares spread amongst a large number of investors.

- There are no transaction costs or capital taxes which would make small transactions unprofitable and eliminate the possibility of investors taking small profit-making opportunities.

- There are no 'barriers to entry' to the market either in the form of tansaction costs, as mentioned above, or in the form of institutional constraints on those who wish to trade.

- There is costless access to information about the market and about individual securities for both actual and potential investors.

In fact, all of these conditions are violated to a greater or lesser degree in the real capital market, although it is an open question whether the imperfections which do exist substantially affect the efficiency with which capital funds are allocated by the market. Certainly, on the London Stock Exchange, the concentration of the market in the hands of a very few jobbing firms in recent years has brought about a situation where individual jobbers can trade so as to 'make markets' in individual securities and can impose severe transactions costs upon the market. Indeed, the levels of transactions costs which are imposed by brokers themselves are often sufficient to nullify the gains which can be made on small portfolios. In addition, the existence of Capital Gains Tax also adds a substantial imperfection to the market.

However, the more important problem with which we have to deal is the efficiency with which the stock market translates new information about particular companies into changes in security prices. When we say that the stock market is perfectly efficient we are saying that the prices of all securities traded in that market respond instantly to any new items of information.

More precisely, a perfectly efficient market with respect to a single item of information (an information signal) about a security, would be one where the price of that security jumped instantaneously from the already existing price to the price which would have existed had the market known about the information signal all along. In Fig. 12.4 we

Fig 12.4 Degrees of market efficiency.
p_0 = equilibrium price in absence of information;
p_e = price which would have ruled if entire market knew of information;
t_0 = time of arrival of information to market

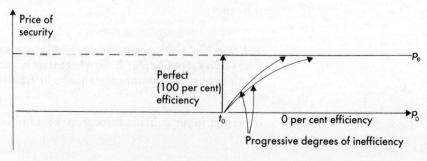

show this diagrammatically. If the price of a security does not respond to new, economically significant information about the company concerned then the market in that security is completely inefficient. However, in practice, the efficiency of the market for individual securities will lie somewhere between these two extremes, as shown in Fig. 12.4.

> *Note:* It is quite possible that a stock market may be efficient with respect to individual information signals about a particular security but not about others. We can only say that the market as a whole is completely efficient if all traded security prices react instantaneously to new information.

A considerable amount of research, much of which is highly technical, has been done into the efficiency of the stock markets in both the USA and the UK. Most of this work has been done on the efficiency of the market with respect to the pricing of equity shares which are usually more actively traded than loan stocks. In general, the following conclusions can be drawn from this voluminous research literature:

1 Prices of shares in these markets fully reflect all past information. In other words, the current price of a given share faithfully represents the value which market traders have placed upon that share given the information which has already been disclosed about the company concerned. A moment's thought will show that the corollary of this is that past price information concerning a share cannot be used to predict its future price movements as the current price is a fair valuation based upon all that is known concerning that share. Given the absence of any new information concerning a share the only movements which will occur in its price will be random effects caused by traders buying and selling for other reasons than the arrival of new information. Many statistical studies have been done on the behaviour of share prices over time and the general conclusion is that share prices do appear to move randomly. When the market is efficient with respect to past information it is said to be 'weak-form' efficient.

2 The prices of shares in the UK and USA stock markets do appear to adjust extremely rapidly to the economic content of information which is made publicly available. Indeed, evidence would suggest that it is nigh on impossible to make excess gains from investment in shares by combing the press for tips, reading company accounts and other handouts or, indeed, taking the advice of a stockbroker! In fact there is evidence to suggest the market appears to predict future information signals and 'discount' the economic content of certain types of information many months before it is actually released. A market which is perfectly efficient with respect to publicly available information is said to be 'semistrong form' efficient.

3 Finally, it may well be possible to use privately available or 'insider' information to make excess gains through share dealing on the UK or

USA stock exchanges. However, few investors are likely to confess to such sources of information and hence the proposition that the market is efficient in this 'strong form' is extremely difficult to prove. It does appear, however, that investors who are most likely to have access to such private information (if it could be obtained) do not systematically produce better than average returns for the funds on whose behalf they deal. Such investors are the highly professional dealers who specialize in particular investments on behalf of institutions such as pension funds, unit-trust companies, insurance companies and so on. A recent study showed that no UK unit trust or pension fund had managed to out-perform, over the long term, what one would expect from a randomly drawn portfolio of equivalent risk. This leads us to the rather weak conclusion that even those investors who we would expect, through their expertise, could gain access to generally unavailable information, cannot convert that expertise into consistently better results than can be obtained from a random selection of shares.

Advantages and disadvantages of different types of finance

We have already distinguished between equity and debt finance in Chapter 2. In this section we will consider the various types of finance which are available within these two subdivisions and the relative merits of each type will be discussed. Certain types of finance, such as preference shares and convertible loans, have some of the properties of equity capital and some of the properties of debt capital. A detailed consideration of these hybrid securities is beyond the scope of this book.

Equity finance

Both public and private companies raise equity finance by issuing 'ordinary shares' (called 'common stock' in the USA). It is normal in the UK to attach a nominal value to each ordinary share (usually 25p, 50p or £1). This figure has no real significance, as ordinary shares are invariably issued to the market at much higher figures per share than the nominal value. The excess is termed the 'share premium'. Furthermore, the nominal value has no significance for the price at which any given share is traded. The only time that the nominal value of a share matters is if the share's market value falls below its nominal value. In this case the company would not be able to raise new equity finance of the same type, as it would entail issuing shares at a discount which is illegal under UK company law.

Raising equity by an issue of ordinary shares can be accomplished in a number of ways:

By a prospectus issue

With a prospectus issue the company concerned (which must be a public limited company) invites applications for its shares from the general public. The invitation to subscribe for shares must be accompanied by a 'prospectus' which is a document designed to advertise the affairs of the company in a prescribed fashion to prospective investors. The contents of the prospectus are prescribed by the Companies Acts (1948, 1967 and 1981) and, for those companies issuing shares through the London Stock Exchange, by the Stock Exchange 'Yellow Book'—*Admission of Securities to Listing*. The principal legal requirements are that the prospectus should contain a five-year financial history, a statement of the directors' financial interests in the company and certain other information concerning the issuing company's financial affairs.

By an offer for sale

With an offer for sale an independent institution takes up the shares to be issued and then administers the sale of those shares on behalf of the public limited company concerned. In 1983 the British Government privatized British Aerospace (which had been a nationalized concern) as a part of its programme of selling off the profitable parts of British industry in public ownership. The offer was made as an 'offer for sale' of 100 million ordinary shares of nominal value 50p at a price of 150p per share. The administrating agent who made the 'offer for sale' itself was the merchant bank Kleinwort Benson Ltd. The 'offer for sale' document, in such a situation, is deemed to be the prospectus and it must present the same information as that required for a prospectus under the Companies Acts and the Stock Exchange regulations.

In addition, several companies (including Kleinwort Benson) underwrote the issue of the British Aerospace shares. That is, they agreed (for a commission) to take up any shares not taken up by the public. Such an 'underwriting agreement' is an important guarantee to a company (or to the government in the peculiar circumstances of the British Aerospace flotation) that it will be able to obtain its full financial requirements from the issue. However, the costs of underwriting commission can be very high, thus, substantially raising the costs of obtaining this type of finance.

By a rights issue

With a rights issue a company's existing shareholders are offered new shares in proportion to their current holdings. The offer can often be very attractive to shareholders, as the new shares are usually offered at a considerable discount on the existing share's current market price. With a rights issue the company will send to its shareholders a 'revocable letter of allotment' for the shares being offered which the individual concerned (or any individual to whom the shareholder sells the letter of allotment) must accept within a specified period of time. These letters of allotment have value in their own right if the shares are being issued at a discount on the current market price. The holder of the letter can sell it on the market as it represents an option on the shares on offer.

By an open offer

This is similar to a rights issue except that existing shareholders may apply for any number of shares irrespective of their current holding. This method is not particularly popular apart from very small privately owned companies where the offer is put out to family members and close friends who are shareholders already.

In Fig. 12.5 we show, in diagrammatic form, the various ways in which shares can be issued. All of these methods of raising finance can be very

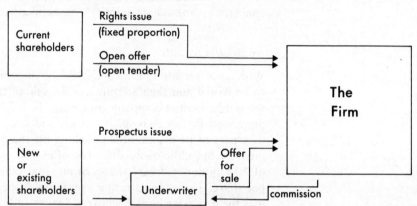

Fig 12.5 Methods of raising new equity capital

costly to the company, especially when the amounts of finance being sought are relatively small. The costs of administering a share issue can be high, especially for an offer to the general public where a large number of individual investors may be involved. On top of this, the yield of cash from a share issue can be significantly reduced if underwriting commission must be deducted. For this reason, of all the possible ways for raising equity finance which exist, rights issues have been the most popular with companies in the UK.

However, the full cost of equity capital to a firm will depend upon other factors apart from the cost of actually raising funds. Most importantly, the company must consider the 'opportunity cost' of equity finance—a concept we will consider later in this chapter.

Debt finance

The other main form of finance is debt or loan finance. Debt finance can be broadly categorized into either redeemable (where the company promises to repay the capital sum to its debt holders at a given future date) or irredeemable (where no such promise is made). In addition, debt can be either secured or unsecured. A debt is secured where the firm 'pledges' or 'mortgages' part of its real assets (usually land or buildings but stocks are sometimes used with short-term debt) to the lender. If the company fails to honour the conditions of its debt contract, perhaps by not paying interest or not repaying capital on the due date, then the lenders of secured debt have the right to foreclose and sell the pledged or mortgaged assets forming their security to settle their claim.

In Fig. 12.6 we show the notes to the 1983 accounts of Redland plc.

Loans and bank overdrafts

Secured loans		1982/83 (£ millions)	1981/82 (£ millions)
Redland PLC	6¼% Redeemable Debenture Stock 1980/85	0.2	0.2
	6¼% Redeemable Debenture Stock 1988/93	1.3	1.3
	7½% Redeemable Debenture Stock 1990/95	3.0	3.0
		4.5	4.5
Subsidiaries	Bank loans	3.4	3.4
	Other loans	5.7	4.8
Total secured loans		13.6	12.7

Unsecured loans			
Redland PLC	Bank loans	15.4	2.1
	Bank overdrafts	0.4	0.6
		15.8	2.7
Subsidiaries	10% Redeemable Debenture Stock 1981/91	1.0	0.9
	9½% Guaranteed Bonds 1991*	13.5	12.6
	Bills discounted	31.5	27.5
	Bank loans	7.4	4.3
	Bank overdrafts	9.5	9.3
	Other loans	4.9	5.3
Total unsecured loans		83.6	62.6
Total loans and overdrafts		97.2	75.3

At 26 March 1983 ultimate repayment of the loan capital and overdrafts of £97.2 million is analysed as follows:

Repayable:	Bank loans, bills discounted and overdrafts (£ millions)	Other borrowings (£ millions)	Total (£ millions)
Bank loans and overdrafts—due within 1 year	10.6	0.6	11.2
Between 2 and 5 years	8.8	0.5	9.3
5 years or more	48.2	28.5	76.7
	67.6	29.6	97.2

*The 9½% Guaranteed Bonds 1991 are unconditionally and irrevocably guaranteed by Redland PLC.

Fig 12.6 Notes to Redland plc accounts showing debt capital

Public limited companies can issue loan stock in just the same way as they issue shares, i.e. through a stock exchange. In such cases, the formal procedure for the issue of debt is very similar to that for equity. A prospectus must be published and the issue can be underwritten. It is normal for such publicly subscribed debt to be issued in nominal £100 units. In the case of debt, the nominal value is usually the issue value and will be the amount repaid to the debt holder on redemption. The nominal value of a stock is usually referred to as its 'par' value and this is the amount upon which interest payments are calculated.

For smaller companies, the more usual sources of debt finance are the clearing banks, merchant banks, company directors (and their relatives) and government-financed loan schemes for small businesses. Unfortunately, the latter tend to change with the Chancellor of the Exchequer, if not more frequently! One such is the 'Government Loan Guarantee Scheme'. With this scheme certain financial institutions, including the clearing banks, offer loans to existing and new businesses which are guaranteed by the government. Normally, the maximum loan which can be taken under this scheme is £75 000 with a 2–7 year repayment term. Because the loan is guaranteed the financial institutions offering the loans can offer them at a lower rate than would otherwise be the case.

> *Note:* The terms of Government Loan Guarantee Schemes change regularly. The main clearing banks can provide up-to-date details of the scheme on request.

The great advantage of these sources of finance for small businesses is that they do not require the degree of disclosure required for debt issued to the public, although banks do require a very full statement of a client company's affairs and prospects.

Bank lending has, historically, been for medium- or short-term finance rather than for the longer term. This is now changing, however, as the banking sector has responded to criticism of its somewhat conservative lending policies levied against it by, among other, the Wilson Committee Report on City Institutions.

Bank lending comes in one of two forms:

- A loan, usually for a fixed term, bearing interest at some agreed rate above the Inter-Bank Base Rate. For a very low-risk company, the premium above base rate may be as low as 1 to 1.5 per cent. Unlike a redeemable debenture raised through the market, bank borrowing is normally repaid on a schedule of instalments rather than in a final lump sum.

- Through an overdraft, which may be for an agreed or for an indefinite term. An overdraft simply allows a business to spend over the balance on its bank current account. The rate of interest on overdraft accounts is much higher than for equivalent sums borrowed on fixed loan. The banks have the right to call in an overdraft at any point in time, that is to ask for the overdrawn customer to bring the account into immediate credit.

> *Note:* Debt has one important advantage over equity finance, namely the tax deductibility of the interest payments (this only applies to company debt). Because debt interest is a contractually fixed charge, which cannot be avoided, it is regarded just like any other cost for tax purposes. In other words, tax is levied on profits after debt interest has been deducted. Because distributions to other shareholders are at the discretion of management they are not regarded as a cost for tax purposes. We will discuss the sense in which such payments are regarded as a cost later in this chapter.

The concept of 'gearing' and financial risk

The introduction of debt into a firm's capital is called 'gearing' in the UK and 'leverage' in the USA. The gearing ratio measures the proportion of debt in a firm's capital structure and is given by the formula:

$$\text{historic gearing} = \frac{\text{book value of all debt plus overdrafts not covered by cash balances in hand}}{\text{book value of all equity including retained earnings and provision for deferred taxation}} \times 100$$

$$\text{market gearing} = \frac{\text{market value of all outstanding debt plus overdrafts not covered by cash in hand}}{\text{market value of all equity shares}} \times 100$$

Sometimes the denominator of each of the above ratios is taken as the sum of the debt (as given by the numerator) plus the equity (as given by the denominator).

In Fig. 12.7 we show the gearing of Redland plc.

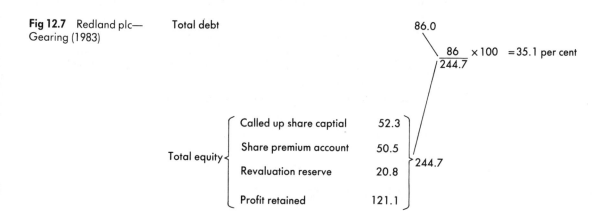

Fig 12.7 Redland plc— Gearing (1983)

Total debt   86.0

$\dfrac{86}{244.7} \times 100 = 35.1$ per cent

Total equity
- Called up share capital   52.3
- Share premium account   50.5
- Revaluation reserve   20.8
- Profit retained   121.1

244.7

Although debt is often cheaper to raise than equity (and, some would argue, it has a cheaper long-run cost as well) it does have one significant disadvantage. Because debt involves a contractual commitment on the part of the lender to pay interest and repay capital on the due date the penalties for default are high.

If a company fails to pay a dividend on equity, all that is likely to happen is that its share price will decline as disgruntled investors sell their shares. There may also be some rather technical problems as a company's shares could lose their status under the Trustees Investment Act 1961 which defines the conditions which a company must fulfil before public trustees can use it as a means of investment. However, none of these consequences are likely to threaten the immediate survival of the business.

On the other hand, non-payment of debt interest is a serious matter in that the majority of industrial and commercial loan agreements give the lenders the right to appoint a receiver in such circumstances to manage the affairs of the company on their behalf. The appointment of a receiver is usually the precursor of either corporate bankruptcy (where the company is forced into 'liquidation') or the sale of a substantial part (or even the whole) of the company in order to redeem its debts.

The additional risk brought about by gearing arises by virtue of the power of foreclosure on the part of lenders. We call the risk 'financial risk' as opposed to the normal 'business risk' which the company faces through its operations.

In order to quantify and understand the concept of financial risk consider two companies, A and B, the first of which is financed entirely by equity and the second which has a geared capital structure. Both companies earn an average of £100 000 per annum and both have a standard deviation on their earnings of plus or minus £40 000. Both companies distribute their earnings in full, A to its equity shareholders and B to both its debt and equity investors. Company B pays interest of £30 000 per annum to service its debt capital.

In Fig. 12.8 we show the distribution of earnings for both companies. In order to get a relative measure of the risk (as both companies have different average after-interest returns) we will use a standardized measure of risk. As we outlined in Chapter 11, risk can be measured by the standard deviation of the relevant variable. However, a problem arises when we try to compare two or more distributions with widely different mean values. To avoid this difficulty, standardized risk measures the amount of risk (measured in pounds sterling of standard deviation) per pound sterling of average value.

Standardized risk (Z) = standard deviation per unit of mean

For company A
$$Z = \frac{40\,000}{100\,000}$$
$$= 0.4$$

Fig 12.8 Earnings risk
increase through gearing

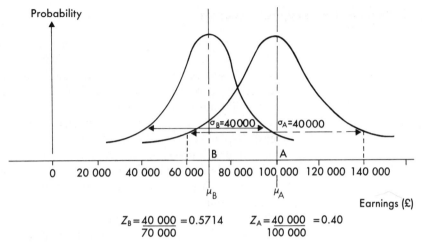

$$Z_B = \frac{40\,000}{70\,000} = 0.5714 \qquad Z_A = \frac{40\,000}{100\,000} = 0.40$$

For company B

$$Z = \frac{40\,000}{70\,000}$$

$$= 0.5714$$

Therefore, company B has relatively more risk (measured in standardized units of risk) than company A. This extra risk has been brought about by the higher level of gearing in company B as compared with company A.

Intuitively, this means that the more highly geared a company becomes, the greater the chance that a poor year's trading performance will leave it in a situation where its debt interest cannot be paid and the consequent possibility that a receiver will be appointed. Although gearing can be a source of trouble in poor trading situations, in good times the equity shareholders, in a geared firm, will earn higher equity returns as the full benefit of the increased earnings will accrue to their smaller equity base compared with the ungeared firm.

High levels of gearing can be especially dangerous where the rate of interest is not fixed but can vary with changing economic circumstances (as is usually the case with bank loans). Nationally, a dramatic example of this danger materialized when the British Government attempted to reduce the money supply by pushing up interest rates in 1980–81. As a result debt became very expensive and many small companies (as well as some larger ones), who were competitive in every other way, were forced out of business. Furthermore, because the increased interest payments consumed a greater proportion of company value added (see Chapter 10) less resources were available for labour and thus companies were forced to lay off employees in order to survive.

> *Self test:* Discuss the gearing concept in relation to your own personal finances. What should be included as part of your own debt finance? Try and estimate your own personal gearing ratio.

Costing the firms's capital resources

In Chapter 3 the concept of 'opportunity cost' was introduced to describe the impact on current and future cash balances of the decision to use scarce resources such as labour and materials. Capital can also be considered as a productive resource as well, and in most respects its treatment is just like any other resource.

To assess the opportunity cost of capital we must establish the net cash loss to a firm when it decides to use up capital on a particular investment (a project). This cash loss is not measured in absolute terms when applied to capital, as was the case with other resources, but rather in terms of a percentage rate of the capital used up. However, as with other resources, the opportunity cost of capital is dependent upon its nearest available alternative use.

If a firm has capital which is surplus to its requirements, its opportunity cost of capital will be the higher of (i) the best available rate of interest on external investment (say, on a short-term deposit) and (ii) the rate which its equity investors can earn on their best alternative investment (of equivalent risk). We assume that, if the managers of a firm have no further use for the capital funds at their disposal and cannot earn a rate of return on external investment in excess of the return their inves-

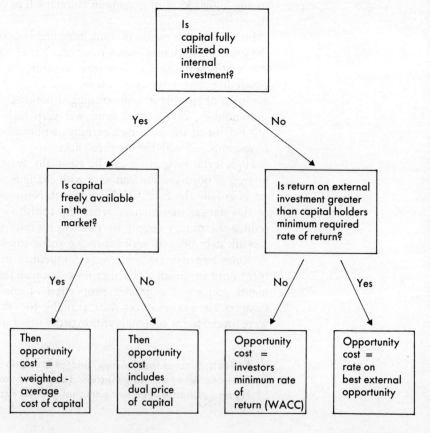

Fig 12.9 The opportunity cost of capital

tors can earn elsewhere, they will distribute those surplus funds to their shareholders. The rate of return which a firm's investors can obtain on their best alternative investment opportunity (of equivalent risk) is deemed to be their minimum required rate of return on their investment in the firm (we will clarify this notion a little later in this chapter).

If, however, a firm is currently fully utilizing the capital within its business then the decision to use up more capital on further projects will mean that new capital funds will have to be raised from the market. This follows on from the idea in Chapter 3 that when a decision is made to consume a useful resource, the cash loss to the firm is the replacement cost of that resource. With capital its 'replacement cost' will be the minimum rate of return (in the form of dividends and interest) the firm will have to pay in order to attract new capital funds in its current gearing ratio.

> *Note:* We always assume that a firm will keep its financing decisions separate from its investment (project selection) decisions. In this way the company can avoid the situation of accepting (relatively) poor investment opportunities at one point in time because finance is cheap while rejecting much better opportunities later because finance has become expensive.
>
> When costing the capital required for a particular investment we assume that the firm will finance the project in its current gearing ratio. By doing this the firm is able to assess the merits of the investment project independently of its capital structure.
>
> Consequently, we take the average cost of capital for the firm in its current gearing ratio rather than the rate of interest on its cheapest available source of finance.

On occasions a firm may find itself in need of capital which cannot be obtained on the open market. In such a situation of 'capital rationing', as it is usually called, the firm will have to redeploy its existing capital internally. As a consequence, the capital used will have an internal opportunity cost as well as an external opportunity cost (see Chapter 7). We will discuss the concept of the internal opportunity cost or 'dual price' of capital in the next chapter of this book.

In order to decide between the alternative bases for determining the opportunity cost of capital we have constructed a diagram (Fig. 12.9) which is very similar to that shown in Chapter 3 (Fig. 3.1).

We will now consider how the external opportunity cost of capital can be determined when:

- The firm is financed solely through equity.

- The firm is financed solely by debt.

- The firm has a geared capital structure.

In this book we will consider the most usual circumstances where the investor's minimum rate of return determines the opportunity cost of capital.

The pure equity firm

If a pure equity firm wishes to replenish the capital used up in investment, it must offer to potential new investors a rate of return equal to, or in excess of, the minimum acceptable rate, in the market, for equity shares of the same risk class.

For this purpose 'return' is defined as the capital gain on a share plus its dividend yield, i.e.

$$\text{return} = \frac{p_1 - p_0}{p_0} + \frac{d_0}{p_0}$$

$$= \frac{p_1 - p_0 + d_0}{p_0}$$

where p_1 is the price at the end of a given period of time, p_0 is the price at the beginning of the period and d_0 is any dividend declared in the period.

> *Note:* The period we choose for calculating the return on an equity share can be any length of time we wish. For example, daily, weekly, monthly or annual returns can be calculated. If sufficient (say) weekly returns are calculated then an average weekly return can be calculated also. Note that there is an inverse ratio between the return and beginning period price p_0; i.e. the higher the price p_0, the lower the return (all other things being equal).

For example, the shares of Montoya plc were quoted at the following prices (per share):

1 January 19X3	160p
31 January 19X3	166p

A dividend of 10p per share was paid in the month of January. The return on Montoya's shares in January were as follows:

$$\text{return} = \frac{166 - 160 + 10}{160}$$

$$= 16/160$$

$$= 0.1 \text{ (or 10 per cent)}$$

This figure is the return over one month. However, we often prefer to show returns annualized, that is, how they would be if the same monthly return was achieved over each month during the year and the equivalent annual return produced. Because the returns are compounded, the equivalent annual return, given a monthly return figure (r) expressed as a decimal, is:

annual return $= (1 + r)^{12} - 1$

therefore:

annual return $= (1 + 0.1)^{12} - 1$
$= 3.1384 - 1$
$= 2.1384$ (213.84 per cent)

In this case a relatively small increase in price, combined with a dividend payment, appears to give a very large annual return. However, in practice, the share's performance in other months is unlikely to be so good and the net effect, over the year, will be a much lower annual return.

On the basis of a series of (say) monthly return figures the investor will form an 'expectation' of what the average rate of monthly return should be on those shares in the future. If that expected return is high enough the investor will consider buying. Conversely, if the expected rate is lower than the investor's minimum required rate of return the investor will not buy the shares concerned and, indeed, should sell those shares which he or she possesses at that point in time. It would be very difficult for a firm to determine the minimum rate of return which investors, within the market place, require for its shares by going and asking them. The only real way to find the appropriate rate is to infer it from their buying and selling behaviour on the basis of some simple assumptions concerning investor rationality.

The model we present below, for estimating the minimum rate of return required by investors, is based upon the axioms of rational economic man plus the following assumptions:

● Investors hold individual shares in well-diversified portfolios.

● Investors are only concerned about the average rate of return that they can earn on their investments and the riskiness of that return (as measured by the standard deviation of returns).

● There are no transaction costs or taxes which will prevent the prices of individual shares reaching equilibrium.

● Investors have free access to all information concerning the shares in question.

The theory of investor behaviour, at the heart of the model described below, suggests that investors can best evaluate the performance of their share holdings by comparing them with some 'yardstick' of performance. In theory this yardstick is the average return and risk of all possible securities in the capital market combined together into a giant, representative portfolio. In practice the performance of this market portfolio is approximated by the performance of a broadly based stock market index (the level of which can be taken to be the price of a portfolio of the shares contained in the index). Such an index could be the *Financial Times*' Actuaries All Share Index.

The model we will use relates the expected return on an individual share to the following:

- The return an investor would expect from an investment in a completely risk-free security—the risk-free rate of return.

- The extra element of return needed to induce an investor to bear the risk entailed in holding the share concerned—the risk premium.

The risk premium is measured by comparison with the index of market performance. If movements in the periodic returns of the individual share are a perfect reflection of movements in the returns of the market portfolio (as shown by changes in the market index) then that share has the same risk as the market. As a result, investors will expect the same average return from that share as from the market portfolio.

More precisely, these two components (the risk-free rate and the risk premium) can be expressed by a simple formula which explains the expected rate of return on a security when the supply and demand for that security are in equilibrium.

Expected return on security (i) = risk-free rate of interest
$+ \beta \times$ (expected return on the market portfolio $-$ risk-free rate of interest)

β is the market risk loading factor for security i which we will explain in detail below.

The formula above when put into mathematical form is:

$$\Sigma (r_i) = R + \beta_i [\Sigma (r_m) - R]$$

This model is known in the theory of finance as the Capital Asset Pricing Model (CAPM). It is no exaggeration to say that this is one of the most important models in the theory of finance and has been shown to be remarkably robust at explaining the average return earned on shares and other securities.

If a share has a return which is exactly as risky as the market (i.e. where the share returns move up and down exactly in line with movements in the index) then that share's β value will be exactly 1. In this case investors will expect to earn exactly the same level of return on the share as they could earn by holding a portfolio containing all the shares in the market.

The value of β for a given share tells us how volatile the returns on that share are in comparison with the returns on the market portfolio. Once we know the value of β for a firm's shares we can then predict the expected return that share should earn given a value for the expected return on the market portfolio and the risk-free rate of interest.

Therefore:
if $\beta = 1$ then the security is exactly as risky as the market;
if $\beta > 1$ then the security is more risky than the market;
if $\beta < 1$ then the security is less risky than the market.

In Fig. 12.10 we show this relationship between the return which can be expected on a share and the market risk loading factor, β. In practice

β values for individual shares are calculated using linear-regression techniques on the shares' past returns against the returns of the market index. In the UK values of β for British shares can be obtained from the London Business School's Risk Measurement Service which is revised and published quarterly.

Fig 12.10 Expected return on a security against market risk

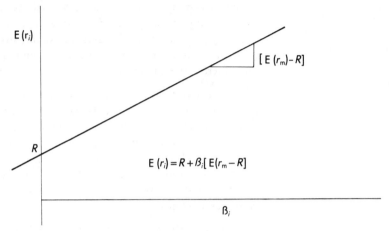

In order to see how the CAPM can be used to estimate the minimum required rate of return on an equity share consider the following example:

On average the return on a broadly based market index is 14 per cent per annum and the return on 90-day government 'tap' stock (the nearest thing to a risk-free rate of interest) is 8 per cent per annum. Determine the minimum rate of return on a share which has (i) 20 per cent more risk, (ii) 20 per cent less risk and (iii) the same risk as the market.

Case (i)—20 per cent more risk means that $\beta = 1.2$:

$$\text{expected return} = 0.08 + 1.2 \times (0.14 - 0.08)$$
$$= 0.152 \,(= 15.2 \text{ per cent per annum})$$

Case (ii)—20 per cent less risk means that $\beta = 0.8$:

$$\text{expected return} = 0.08 + 0.8 \times (0.14 - 0.08)$$
$$= 0.128 \,(= 12.8 \text{ per cent per annum})$$

Case (iii)—the same risk means that $\beta = 1.0$:
$$\text{expected return} = 0.08 + 1.0 \times (0.14 - 0.08)$$
$$= 0.14 \,(= 14.0 \text{ per cent per annum})$$

Self test: Repeat the calculations above for:

1 $\beta = 1.4$,

2 zero risk,

3 $\beta = 0.5$

and plot a graph of expected return from the CAPM against the value of β (put β on the horizontal axis).

There are three points to note about this discussion of the equity rate of return and the nature of risk:

- The only variable which relates to the individual firm is the β factor. The β value for an individual share measures the response of that security to change in market-wide conditions. β is, therefore, an indication of the part of the security's overall variability of returns which is caused by market-wide influences such as changes in interest rates, exchange rates, government fiscal and monetary policies, etc. All of these factors will affect the security's price and hence its return.

- The expected return of a security such as a share is linearly related to the β value. In the last self-test exercise you should have obtained a graph which looked like that shown in Fig. 12.10. Because expected return is inversely related to price we can say that any security which has a return above the line in Fig. 12.10 is underpriced and any security which has a return below the line is overpriced. The theory of the CAPM suggests that, at equilibrium, all securities have returns which lie somewhere along the line.

- If an investor holds a widely diversified portfolio, the most crucial consideration concerning an ordinary share is how that security performs in relation to the total market. In fact, the 'averaging' process which occurs when shares are combined into portfolios tends to eliminate the effect of the risk which is caused by factors peculiar to the individual firms rather than to the market as a whole. The only component of a securities risk which appears in the risk of a well-diversified portfolio is its market risk, i.e. the risk caused by market-wide rather

Fig 12.11   Risk benefits from diversification

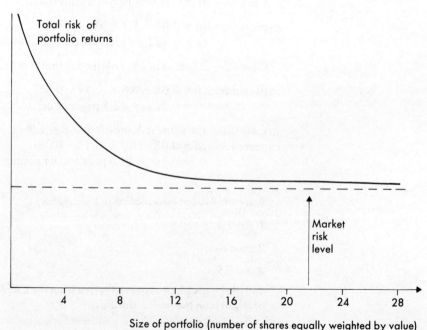

than firm-specific factors. That part of a security's overall risk which is caused by general market influences is often referred to as 'systematic risk'. Firm-specific risk, on the other hand, is referred to as 'unsystematic risk'. In Fig. 12.11 we show how diversification reduces the risk of a portfolio. The graph in Fig. 12.11 is based upon empirical studies which show that as the size of a portfolio is increased (in terms of the number of securities contained within it) so its risk decreases.

Notice that the total risk does not fall to zero but tails down to a constant value. This constant value is the level of market or systematic risk. Obviously, if a portfolio was diversified continuously it would eventually come to resemble the market portfolio and would then possess a level of risk very close to that of the market portfolio itself.

Note: It is a very theoretical point, but you may be wondering why we say that the risk would be 'very close' to the risk of the market portfolio, rather than having exactly that level of risk. The market portfolio is a portfolio containing all securities in the market in such a proportion that its risk is at a minimum for the level of return $\Sigma\,(r_m)$ generated. Any portfolio which we could put together would be unlikely to be balanced quite so perfectly. However, the discrepancy between the risk/return performance of our widely diversified portfolio and that of the market portfolio is likely to be very tiny and well within the range of measurement error in any event.

What is surprising is that the empirical evidence indicates that the benefits of risk reduction through increased diversification are mostly gained by the time fifteen or so securities have been added into the portfolio. Building portfolios of larger size just wastes transaction costs such as management costs, brokerage fees and so forth. This is true no matter how much is invested, in value terms, in the portfolio.

The pure-debt firm

In principle, every company must have an ownership interest. However, it is possible that a firm could acquire so much debt that it is effectively fully geared. Also, with many small, private companies the shareholding is restricted to a few controlling individuals who would not consider expansion of the firm's equity capital in any event.

If a firm's debt finance comes solely from bank lending the opportunity cost of its capital is the current rate of interest required to obtain new funds. In this case the rate is likely to be that which a bank would charge upon a new loan.

If, on the other hand, the debt had been raised on the market through the issue of loan stock then the opportunity cost of capital would be the rate of interest which the company would have to offer to the market on a new issue in order for it to be fully taken up. Where a loan stock is freely traded in the capital market it is reasonably easy to establish this rate. This is the situation which we will consider first.

Let us examine two cases: (i) where the loan stock is irredeemable and (ii) where it is redeemable.

The cost of irredeemable loan stock

We will assume that when investors value loan stock they discount cash receipts they expect from that loan at their required rate of return for stock of that type. On average, therefore,

$$\text{market value} = \frac{I}{(1+r)^1} + \frac{I}{(1+r)^2} + \frac{I}{(1+r)^3} + \frac{I}{(1+r)^4} + \dots$$

where r is the minimum required rate of return for this type of loan stock and I is the interest paid per unit of stock (i.e. the 'coupon' or 'nominal' rate).

This type of formula is a perpetual geometric progression which simplifies to:

$$\text{market value} = \frac{I}{r}$$

(*Note:* the solution of this type of progression was discussed in the appendix to Chapter 3).

Example: A firm's quoted loan stock has a coupon rate of interest of 10 per cent per annum and a market value of £86.00 per cent (which is a way of saying '£86 per £100 nominal stock unit').

Therefore:

$$\text{market value} = £86.00 = 10/r$$

Rearranging, the implied value of r, the minimum required rate of return, is given by:

$$r = 10/86$$
$$= 0.1163 \ (= 11.63 \text{ per cent})$$

This means that if the firm wished to issue new loan capital it would have to offer a coupon rate of at least 11.63 per cent per annum in order to induce investors to take up the new stock at its par value of £100 per unit.

> *Note:* The formula given above assumes that the investor has to wait one complete period before receiving his or her first interest payment. Such a model is, therefore, an 'ex-div' valuation model; i.e. the market valuation is computed on the basis that a payment of interest (I) has just been made and that no more interest will be received until the end of the period. A 'cum-div' valuation model, which assumes an immediate payment of interest, is of the form:
>
> $$\text{market value} = I + \frac{I}{r}$$

The cost of redeemable loan stock

In this case interest payments will be received up to the date of redemption whereupon repayment of the original amount will be made. Therefore, the market value of this type of stock is given by:

$$\text{market value (ex-div)} = \frac{I}{(1+r)^1} + \frac{I}{(1+r)^2} + \ldots + \frac{100+I)}{(1+r)^n}$$

where n is the number of years which must elapse until redemption.

For example, consider a firm with 10 per cent redeemable loan stock which has a market value of £86.00 per cent. The firm has agreed in the loan deed to redeem the loan in four years' time at par.

Therefore:

$$86.00 = \frac{10}{(1+r)^1} + \frac{10}{(1+r)^2} + \frac{10}{(1+r)^3} + \frac{110}{(1+r)^4}$$

We now have to find the value of r which satisfies the above equation. The easiest way of doing this is by substituting increasing values of r into the equation and plotting these values of r against the resultant market value. Where the graph cuts through the value of £86 we have, at the crossover point, the minimum required rate of return for this type of loan stock.

Fig 12.12 Estimation of cost of debt

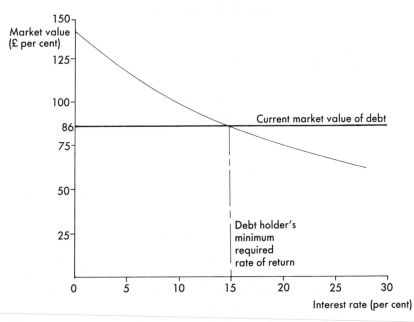

In Fig. 12.12 we have drawn the graph of the above equation. The value of r is 15 per cent at the market value of £86.

In some situations a firm's loan stock may not have a recognized market value because it is not traded on the open market. There are two ways in which an approximation to the opportunity cost of debt capital can be derived:

- By obtaining estimates from merchant banks and other long-term lenders of the appropriate rate for new borrowing given the firm's size and current level of gearing.

- By using the market value of an equivalent government gilt-edged security. The gilt-edged security used for comparison purposes should have the same nominal rate of interest and redemption date as the loan stock concerned. The prices of government gilt-edged securities can be obtained from the daily publication of security prices in the *Financial Times* or other quality newspapers in the UK.

The cost of capital in a geared firm

We are now in a position to calculate the average return which must be offered to a firm's investors where it has both equity and debt in its capital structure. The opportunity cost of each type of capital is calculated as described above. The average rate is then calculated by weighting each type of capital according to the relative proportions of each type in the firm's capital structure. The proportion (w) of each capital type is calculated as the ratio of the market value of that capital type to the total market value of all the firm's capital.

For example, consider a firm which has three components of capital in its capital structure:

Equity shares:
   1 000 000 ordinary shares, market value 270p each, opportunity cost 18 per cent per annum.

Redeemable loan stock:
   12 000 £100 units, market value £86 per cent, opportunity cost 15 per cent per annum.

Irredeemable loan stock:
   50 000 £100 units, market value £90 per cent, opportunity cost 16 per cent per annum.

The total market value and the proportion of each type of capital in the firm's capital structure is given below:

Security	Total market value
Equity	1 000 000 × 270p = £2 700 000
Redeemable debt	12 000 × £86 = £1 032 000
Irredeemable debt	50 000 × £90 = £4 500 000
Total capital value	£8 232 000

The weighting (w) of each component is, therefore:
Equity shares

$$w_e = \frac{2\,700\,000}{8\,232\,000} = 0.328$$

Redeemable debt

$$w_d = \frac{1\,032\,000}{8\,232\,000} = 0.125$$

Irredeemable debt

$$w_{irr} = \frac{4\,500\,000}{8\,232\,000} = 0.547$$

Note that the sum of the weights is 1.

The weighted average cost of capital (WACC) for this firm is given by:

$$\begin{aligned}
WACC &= w_e \times r_e + w_d \times r_d + w_{irr} \times r_{irr} \\
&= 0.328 \times 0.18 + 0.125 \times 0.15 + 0.547 \times 0.16 \\
&= 0.1653 \; (= 16.53 \text{ per cent})
\end{aligned}$$

We conclude that this firm would need to pay its investors and lenders an average rate of 16.53 per cent. To its equity investors (who account for 32.8 per cent of the total) it will pay 18 per cent, similarly it will pay the appropriate rate to the other two classes of capital subscriber in their respective proportions. On average, the rate of 16.53 per cent is the minimum rate which investors and lenders would require to provide further finance for the company. In the next chapter we will consider in some detail how a company should use the weighted average cost of capital in its investment decision-making.

Optimal gearing

The fact that debt finance usually has a lower opportunity cost of capital than equity finance may seem to suggest that a firm should gear itself up as quickly as possible thus reducing its overall cost of capital. However, very high gearing can bring about high levels of financial risk and this would mean that equity investors would require a higher return as compensation for the extra risk they have to bear.

When a company increases its gearing there is a shift in risk from one class of capital investor (the debt holders) to another (the shareholders). One view, put forward by two theorists in this field—Modigliani and Miller—is that the capital market is perfectly efficient in the way it allocates the appropriate level of return to a given level of risk. In other words the lower return required by debt holders for the lower risk of holding debt is exactly counterbalanced by the extra return required by the equity investors for holding the increased financial risk. In Modigliani and Miller's view, if there are no taxation benefits in holding debt, then a firm's weighted average cost of capital will remain constant as the firm increases its level of gearing. Therefore, in their view, there is no optimal level of gearing.

Another view is that the capital market is not perfectly efficient in the way it allocates return to holders of different levels of risk. This 'traditional' view is that up to a 'reasonable' level of gearing increased financial risk is not as great as the reduced levels of return required by debt holders. Up to a certain point, therefore, increased levels of gearing bring about a reduction in a firm's weighted average cost of capital. However, beyond a certain point, the increased return required by equity investors as compensation for the higher levels of financial risk which accrue with very high gearing, exceed the cost savings associated with holding debt. As a result the net effect is that the weighted average cost of capital will rise again. In Fig. 12.13 we show these two views in graphical form.

Fig 12.13 The relationship of cost of capital to gearing

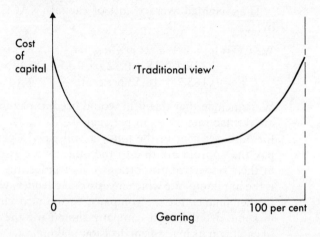

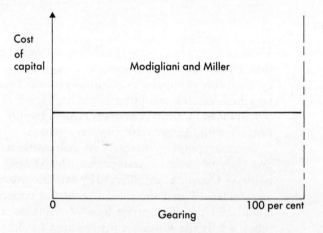

Because the weighted average cost of capital is inversely related to the market value of a firm it follows, if the traditional view is correct, that alterations in gearing will cause alterations in the value of the firm. In other words, if a level of gearing can be found which minimizes a firm's cost of capital then that level of gearing must also be the position at which the firm's total capital value is maximized. Modigliani and Miller's view, on the other hand, is that the value of a firm is solely dependent upon its business performance and the level of business risk which it faces. Altering the financing of a firm will have no effect upon its valuation.

There is a lot of debate concerning these two views. The weight of theoretical development in capital-market research leans toward supporting the views of Modigliani and Miller. There is very little conclusive empirical evidence either way, however, and certainly insufficient evidence to warrant an extensive search by individual firms for an optimal level of gearing.

The argument about the advisability of one level of gearing *vis-à-vis* another does not alter the fact that different classes of investor will require different rates of return depending upon the type of capital they hold in the firm and the financial risk which they have to bear. Therefore, it is still necessary to calculate the weighted average cost of capital of the firm even though, accepting Modigliani and Miller's view, this rate is unlikely to alter significantly over the full range of gearing.

Summary

In this chapter we have examined the different sources of finance which are available to a firm and their relative advantages and disadvantages. This material forms an important background to the financing decisions made by firms and a necessary precursor to our study of investment decision-making in the next chapter.

Different types of finance have different costs depending upon the risk associated with them. We defined the opportunity cost of capital as the minimum rate of return which a firm must offer to the market in order to raise new capital to replace that used in investment. Only in exceptional circumstances will this 'replacement cost' of capital not be its opportunity cost. We then developed these ideas to consider the opportunity cost of capital for a geared firm, i.e. a firm financed by a mixture of equity and debt capital. Finally, we discussed whether an optimal level of gearing exists at which a firm's opportunity cost of capital is at a minimum. We concluded that even though the empirical research is not conclusive, the weight of theoretical research is against the proposition that alterations in gearing can influence a firm's weighted average cost of capital and hence its market value.

Supplementary reading

ARDITTI, F. D., The weighted average cost of capital: some questions on its definition, interpretation and use, *Journal of Finance*, September 1973.

BEAVER, W. H., *Financial Reporting: An Accounting Revolution*, Prentice Hall, 1981. Chapters 5 and 6 are especially good.

FAMA, E., Efficient capital markets: a review of theory and empirical work, *Journal of Finance*, May 1970.

LONDON BUSINESS SCHOOL, *Risk Measurement service*, published quarterly. The introduction and appendices give an excellent introduction to the use of the capital asset pricing model in investment management.

MODIGLIANI, F., and MILLER, M. H., The cost of capital, corporation finance and the theory of investment, *American Economic Review*, June 1958.

RYAN, R. J., The discount rate problem in capital budgeting, *Terotechnica*, **1**, 1979. A superb article by a master of the genre!

VASICEK, O. A., and McQUOWN, J. A., The efficient market model, *Financial Analysts Journal*, September–October 1972.

Questions

1   Explain what you understand by the following terms:
    (a) The capital market.
    (b) A security.
    (c) The primary and secondary capital markets.
    (d) Capital-market efficiency.

2   Define the concept of the opportunity cost of capital. To what extent can the opportunity cost of capital be likened to the opportunity cost of any other resource?

3   The minimum, average required rate of return for a firm's investors is estimated to be 12 per cent per annum. Forty per cent of the market value of the firm's capital is attributable to the equity investors and the balance to debt holders. The equity investors require 4 per cent more return than the debt holders. The firm wishes to finance a new project by a 10 per cent increase in its debt capital.
    Assume:
    1 The new issue will not disturb the market value of the firm's existing debt.
    2 The new debt will hold its market value at par.
    3 The market gearing ratio for the firm will rise to 0.65 following the new debt issue.
    4 There will be an increase in the premium which equity investors require over debt holders to 5 per cent.

    Required:
    (a) On the assumption that the firm's overall cost of capital is constant through all levels of gearing, calculate the cost of equity, debt and the weighted-average cost of capital to the firm before and after the issue.
    (b) Explain the significance of all the assumptions outlined in this question.

4   Ventas has just heard about the capital asset pricing model and is extremely anxious to use the model in his portfolio management

decisions. He has found the following estimates of β for the following four companies:

	β
Fama	1.35
Fisher	1.00
Jensen	0.00
Roll	0.51

The return on short-dated government stocks is 0.002 per cent per month and the estimated market return is expected to be 0.01 per cent per month.

Ventas believes he can predict the way the market will move in the near future and he generally tailors his investment strategy to anticipated market conditions.

(a) Plot the annual expected return for each security against its β value.
(b) What will be the return on a portfolio of these four securities which bears 10 per cent more risk than the market?
(c) Which of the four securities would Ventas invest in if he expected: 1 a sudden rise in the market and 2 a sudden fall in the market.

5 What do you understand by the concepts of 'systematic' (or 'market') and 'unsystematic' risk? What effect does diversification have on these two types of risk?

13 The investment decision

As we pointed out in Chapter 11, long-term decisions entail consequences which occur at different points in time. However, in order to decide between alternative courses of action, the financial effects of each course of action must be evaluated and reduced to some common measurement base so that comparisons can be made. In this chapter we discuss the techniques for making such comparisons between the different productive investments which are open to management.

> By the end of this chapter you should have an understanding of:
>
> - The nature of investment decisions.
>
> - The usefulness of the net-present-value technique for comparing investments.
>
> - Some other methods available for making investment decisions and their relative merits.
>
> - The difficulties of choosing between projects when capital is in short supply.
>
> - Some general problems faced by management in their investment decision-making.

The nature of investment decisions

By now you should be familiar with the idea that investment entails giving up current cash balances in the hope of earning future cash flows. In Chapter 3 we outlined how an individual decision-maker can convert expected future cash flows into an estimate of current wealth by discounting the future cash flows using his or her 'marginal rate of time preference' for cash.

In practice, we can characterize the typical investment decision as a five-stage process:

- An opportunity identification stage where new production projects are identified following an analysis of some commercial opportunity or the recognition of some production problem.

- A development stage where the anticipated outcomes from the project are evaluated and cash-flow projections made.

- A selection stage where a choice is made between those opportunities which are available to the firm.

● An implementation stage where the capital expenditure is made, any appropriate construction work undertaken and the process commenced.

● A post-project audit stage where the project's actual performance is monitored and compared with the projected cash flows.

These five stages can be superimposed upon the stages of the investments overall life which we depict in Fig. 13.1.

Fig 13.1 Life cycle of an investment project

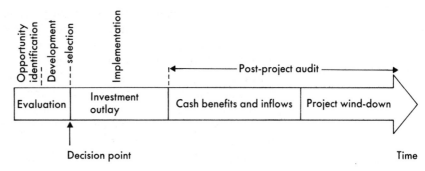

Fig 13.2 Project cash flow profiles

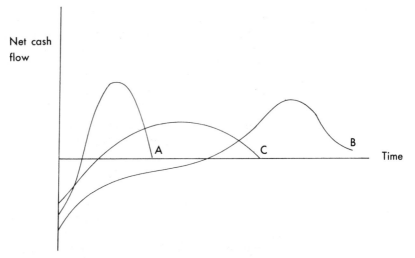

The process from project evaluation to project wind-down is referred to as the project 'life cycle'. The actual decision concerning the investment of capital may well occur quite a way through the evaluation phase of the project and, by this time, a considerable part of the evaluation expenditure may well have been made. This evaluation expenditure will then be a sunk cost with respect to the decision.

In principle, all capital-investment projects can be evaluated by deducting the necessary investment outlay from the present value of the future cash flows generated by the project. In Fig. 13.2 we show a graph which typifies the types of cash-flow profile we can expect from investment.

Investment A is a project of very short-term duration with an immediate return on the capital invested. An example of this type of project would be a short-term construction project where funds are invested in development, design and the purchase of capital equipment which is followed by cash inflows over a relatively short time period (say 1–4 years). Projects like this are regarded as investment decisions only when the timing effects upon future cash flows are likely to be significant. At the other extreme we have projects such as B in Fig. 13.2 where there is a considerable time lag between investment and the return of cash surpluses. Examples of this type of project can be found in the aerospace and energy-supply industries.

However, the majority of investment projects fall between these two extremes. For example, a firm setting up a new plant to produce a widely used chemical compound would expect to earn cash surpluses within a reasonable time of the commissioning of the plant and would hope that those surpluses could be sustained for a substantial period of time before the plant had to be taken out of service.

Generally speaking, the capital investment and operating costs entailed in the production of completely new market products are larger than that required for the production of more mature products. The reasons for this are as follows:

- New products often entail new production technologies which are themselves expensive. However, as competing manufacturers enter the market the increased demand for the necessary production equipment will bring down its price.

- With completely new products the technology of production may not be optimized and this means that the new producers have to bear the costs associated with this suboptimality—costs which will not have to be borne by later entrants to the market.

- Quality control and performance measures may well be difficult to establish with new products where their technology of production is still in its infancy. As a result the new producer will have to bear the additional costs of production which will be incurred.

Considerations such as these have led to a view which is very common among managers in manufacturing industry that it is often best to be second into a new market.

Below we give some examples of common long-term investment decisions within industry:

- Investment in the expansion of current production facilities.

- Investment for entrance into new product markets.

- Investment in the maintenance and replacement of existing plant and machinery.

- Investment in long-term advertising campaigns and in research and development.

- Investment in administrative facilities.

- Investment in 'human capital' through training, education, etc.

The area of investment decision-making is particularly complex in that choices have to be made on the basis of projected outcomes which may be very uncertain. It is also true that in highly competitive (technologically and economically) industrial environments worthwhile investment projects are very hard to find. Naturally, if such projects were easy to find there would be far fewer company failures than there are! In such highly competitive environments most projects will have net present values of approximately zero as firms compete away their technological and economic advantages and hence their potential for earning excess profits.

The net-present-value technique

In Chapter 3 we considered the problem of Mr Paco. We discovered that the present value of his expected net cash flows, when discounted at his marginal rate of time preference, represented the actual increase in his disposable wealth. We also described how Mr Paco could finance his current spending by borrowing from a bank the present value of his future cash flows. Those cash flows could then be used to pay off his borrowing. However, the possibility of doing this only exists in a situation of a perfect money market where:

- A single market rate of interest exists for both borrowing and lending.

- An individual can borrow or lend any amount of money at the market rate of interest.

- There are no transaction costs or taxes, i.e. the market is 'frictionless'.

- There is perfect certainty concerning future cash flows.

If these conditions hold, the net present value of the future cash flows which accrue to an individual represent an absolute increase in wealth which that individual can use for immediate consumption if he or she so desires.

But when we move to corporate investment decision-making additional difficulties arise. As firms are made up of a diverse set of interest groups it may well not be appropriate to extend a model for individual decision-making directly into the corporate environment. However, even assuming a situation where the sole objective of a firm is to maximize the wealth of its investors, there are a number of difficulties involved in using simple present-value techniques. Initially, we will examine the usefulness and difficulties of net-present-value techniques assuming the objective of shareholder supremacy. Later, we will discuss the wider problems associated with the net-present-value model once we assume more realistic objectives for the firm.

The net-present-value model states that for an individual investor a project will only be acceptable if it increases his or her current wealth, i.e.

$$W_f - W_0 \geqslant 0$$

where:

W_f is the present value of the future receivable net cash flows generated by the investment. As we have stated above, the present value of these future cash flows represents the increment of current wealth which accrues to the investor once the investment's potential is recognized.

W_0 is the current wealth given up to undertake the investment. We sometimes talk about this amount as the investment 'outlay'.

For example, an investment entailing an outlay of £25 000 followed by net cash returns of £12 500 over 3 years could be evaluated as follows. We will assume a marginal rate of time preference for the investor of 10 per cent per annum.

	t_0	t_1	t_2	t_3
Cash inflows		£12 500	£12 500	£12 500
Discount factor		$1/1.1^1$	$1/1.1^2$	$1/1.1^3$
Present value:				
t_1	£11 364			
t_2	£10 331			
t_3	£9 391			
Present value of cash inflows, $W_f =$	£31 086			
Cash outlay, $W_0 =$	£25 000			
Net present value	£6 085			

This project increases the investor's wealth by the net present value of £6085. Any project such as this with a positive net present value would be worth while to the investor.

> **Self test:** Demonstrate that the above investor can borrow the full amount of his wealth invested in the project from a bank in a perfect money market and use the project cash flows to repay the loan (see Chapter 3).
> **Solution clue:** 0.

The main technical problem to be resolved before we can apply this technique directly to a firm's investment decisions concerns the nature of the discount rate. Because a firm may have a large number of share-holders, the discount rate of interest must offer a rate of return which will satisfy the marginal rates of time preference of all those individuals. The discount rate, therefore, should be equivalent to the average marginal rate of time preference for the firm's investors. In the light of our discussion in the last chapter, this average rate is the same as the opportunity cost of equity capital. Accordingly, the opportunity cost of equity capital will be the appropriate discount rate for a pure equity firm. In a geared firm, however, the discount rate should offer a return which will satisfy all types of investor (equity and debt) within the firm. Therefore, the weighted-average cost of capital will be the appropriate discount rate for such a firm.

If the market value of a firm is a perfect reflection of the total wealth invested within the firm then, given perfect access to information on the part of investors, the acceptance of a new project by the firm's management should bring about an increase in the market value of the firm equal to the project's net present value. In this situation the secondary capital market will fulfil the role of a perfect money market bank as the investor can realize the increase in wealth following the project's acceptance by judicious selling of his or her investment for cash. This assumes, of course, that the stock market is, itself, competitively efficient.

As you can see the validity of the net-present-value model as a measure of project worth is hedged around by a number of assumptions which we would not expect to be realized in reality. Over the last 30 years considerable theoretical developments have been made in the area of investment appraisal although the practical application of these developments has been very difficult. However, discounting methods based upon the simple net-present-value model described above are widely used in industry. But the limitations of these methods and the restrictiveness of the underlying assumptions do not seem to be widely recognized.

In order to discuss the problems of investment appraisal we will set up an example which we will use as the basis of our discussion throughout the remainder of this chapter. This is an extensive problem employing a number of data manipulation techniques. The numbers are not easy ... so study the problem carefully.

Martinez plc is considering the construction of a chemical plant to produce a staple product used widely in the chemical industry called alpha-nievene. The production process is continuous and the expected life of the plant is five years. The plant capacity will be 65 000 tons in the first year, but this will rise by 10 per cent per annum over the following two years before levelling off at a constant capacity for the remainder of the plant's life.

The selling price of alpha-nievene is currently £100 per ton and this is expected to rise by 8 per cent per annum over the plant's life. The total market for the product currently stands at 550 000 tons per annum, which is rising by 5 per cent per annum. Martinez expects to hold its market share of 10 per cent into the indefinite future. The raw-material cost is £30 per ton bought in, and the expected conversion ratio is 0.7

tons of finished chemical for every ton of raw-material input. Raw-material costs are expected to rise at a rate of 12 per cent per annum over the life of the project.

While output is rising, labour costs are expected to be directly related to output. The wage rate is currently £25 per ton of finished product and this rate is expected to increase by 6 per cent per annum. Half of the labour force committed to this project are on the permanent establishment and will have to be replaced by direct recruitment. Half of these permanent staff have special skills and their redeployment from other activities within the firm will bring about a loss of £75 000 contribution in the first year. The newly recruited staff should have acquired the necessary skills after their first year of employment. The remainder of the staff necessary for this project will be recruited on short-term contracts.

Current energy costs for the chemical process are £6 per ton produced and are expected to rise by 5 per cent per annum.

The firm depreciates its plant and equipment on a straight-line basis over its expected life. Development and pilot-plant experimentation have already incurred costs of £80 000. The capital cost of the plant is £6 250 000 which will be spent immediately and the plant will be commissioned and fully operational for the current production year. The plant will be scrapped and dismantled at the end of its life at a net cost of £30 000. All cash flows, except the immediate capital outlay, can be assumed to be incurred at the end of the year in question.

Martinez would like to plan on the basis of full capacity operation each year with any final stock balances being sold in the sixth year. Martinez has an opportunity cost of capital of 10 per cent per annum. The Retail Price Index is expected to continue growing at 4 per cent per annum over the indefinite future.

This example is primarily concerned with the problem of projecting cash flows and the correct application of the various investment appraisal models. Our first task is to project the cash flows which occur beyond the decision point ignoring any costs and revenues which do not alter with the decision.

> *Self test:* Make a list of those cost types which are normally regarded as irrelevant for decision-making. Refer back to Chapter 3 for the answer.

Each item of information given above was expressed in terms of current quantities or prices. Using the expected rates of change for each item the future cash flows can be estimated as shown in Fig. 13.3.

Plant capacity has been set at 65 000 tons for the first year of operation and then expanded by 10 per cent in each of the following two years:

year t_1 = 65 000 tons
year t_2 = 65 000 × 1.1 = 71 500 tons
year t_3 = 65 000 × 1.1^2 = 78 650 tons

		Year						
	0	1	2	3	4	5	6	Total
Plant capacity (tons)		65 000	71 500	78 650	78 650	78 650	78 650	372 450
Demand (tons)		55 000	57 750	60 638	63 669	66 853		303 910
Actual sales (tons)		55 000	57 750	60 638	63 669	66 853	68 540	68 540
Price per unit	100	108	117	126	136	147	159	
Total revenue		5 940 000	6 735 960	7 638 579	8 662 148	9 822 876	10 876 481	
Materials cost		3 120 000	3 843 840	4 735 611	5 303 884	5 940 350		
Labour cost:								
Internal opportunity cost		75 000						
Wages cost		1 722 500	2 008 435	2 341 835	2 482 346	2 631 285		
Energy costs		409 500	472 972	546 283	573 597	602 277		
Scrap costs							(30 000)	
Total cost		5 327 000	6 325 247	7 623 729	8 359 827	9 173 914	30 000	
Net contribution		613 000	410 713	14 849	302 321	648 962	10 846 481	
Discount factor (10 per cent)	1.000	0.9091	0.8264	0.7513	0.6830	0.6209	0.5645	
Discounted cash flow		557 273	339 432	11 157	206 489	402 955	6 122 556	7 639 861
Capital cost	6 250 000							6 250 000
Net Present Value	6 250 000							1 389 861
Real cash flows	6 250 000	589 423	379 727	13 201	258 425	533 400	8 572 132	
Discounted cash flow (at 5.77 per cent)	6 250 000	557 273	339 432	11 157	206 489	402 955	6 122 556	1 389 861

Fig 13.3   Statement of project cash flows

In years t_4 and t_5 the capacity will remain constant at 78 650 tons.

Martinez's share of the annual demand for alpha-nievene is expected to be 10 per cent of a total market which is rising by 5 per cent per annum. The demand in the first three years of the project can be estimated as follows:

year $t_1 = 550\,000 \times 0.1$ $= 55\,000$ tons

year $t_2 = 550\,000 \times 0.1 \times 1.05 = 57\,750$ tons

year $t_3 = 550\,000 \times 0.1 \times 1.05^2 = 60\,638$ tons

Demand for each of the remaining years of the project is calculated in a similar fashion.

The firm's actual sales of alpha-nievene in each of the five years of the project will be the lower of demand and plant capacity. The total production throughout the life of the project is expected to be 372 450 tons while the actual sales will be 303 910 (see Fig. 13.3). Given that management operate at full capacity throughout the life of the project and clear the remaining stocks of chemical in the sixth year we can project a figure for sales of 68 540 tons for that year.

The sale price per ton has been compounded from its current price of £100 per ton at the rate of 8 per cent per annum. This figure is then multiplied by the projected sales figure to obtain an estimate of total revenue. The same procedure has been applied to the materials cost per ton except that with materials a yield ratio of 0.7 must be applied to the material price and the resultant figure multiplied by the estimated production rather than sales. Therefore, in the first year material costs are given by:

materials $t_1 = $ £30/0.7 × 1.12 × 65 000

$= $ £3 120 000

A yield ratio of 0.7 means that 0.7 tons of alpha-nievene are produced from one ton of raw material input. Therefore, we divide the material cost per ton by 0.7 in order to determine the cost of the materials required to produce one ton of final product.

Labour costs are calculated on the basis of expected production although in the first year we also include the internal opportunity cost incurred through redeployment of labour with special skills. Because the labour force on the permanent establishment must be replaced the cost of their replacement is an opportunity cost of production. We assume that the rate of £25 per ton of finished product is also appropriate for the replacement labour.

Current energy costs are increased by the specified rate of 5 per cent per annum.

As we noted in Chapter 3, depreciation is not a true economic cost because it is independent of any decision concerning the machinery to which it relates. However, the cost of scrapping the plant at the end of its life is a true cash change to the firm brought about by the investment decision. Therefore, the cost of scrapping the plant has been applied as a cost in year t_6 of the project. The costs incurred for project development are sunk costs at the point at which the decision is made. No matter what choice is made, the development costs and pilot-plant expenses have already been incurred and cannot be recovered.

In Fig. 13.3 we deduct the total opportunity costs of production from total revenues in each year, to give a projected estimate of the annual net cash contribution generated by the project. Because the net cash contribution earned each year represents the cash change brought about as a direct consequence of the decision to invest, it represents a direct change in the investors' future anticipated cash stream. Further, all of these cash changes are expressed in the actual money values appropriate for the years in which they arise. We discount these anticipated money cash flows at the opportunity cost of capital (10 per cent), in the usual way, to get the net present value of the project.

As the project has a positive net present value it is acceptable to the firm.

Self test: A 5 per cent shareholder in Martinez plc has protested to the firm's management about this level of investment. She would much prefer the funds to be distributed immediately. She can borrow or lend money at a rate of 10 per cent per annum and her bank manager is prepared to lend her any amount that she might want. What is her best course of action? Support your advice with the relevant figures.

A second way of handling a series of future net cash flows when prices are rising is to restate them in current prices. For example, in Martinez's example the first cash flow of £613 000 represents money receivable in one year's time. It is possible to calculate the sum of money which, at the purchasing power of time t_0, will buy the same basket of goods as that future cash flow. We can calculate the current purchasing power equivalent or 'real' value of a future cash flow by discounting the future cash sum over the number of years concerned at the rate of inflation:

Year	Future money cash flow (£)	Discount at inflation rate	Future money cash flow expressed in real terms (£)
1	613 000	$1/1.04$	589 423
2	410 713	$1/1.04^2$	379 727
.	.	.	.
.	.	.	.
.	.	.	.
6	10 846 481	$1/1.04^6$	8 572 132

In Fig. 13.3 we show the series of real cash flows for all of the years of the project. It should be reasonably easy to see that if we have converted the money cash flows to their equivalent value expressed in current prices the rate of discount required to calculate the net present value should not be the same as that used to discount the money cash flows. The rate of 10 per cent used previously represents the rate of return required by investors in an inflationary environment. However, if the effect of that inflation has been eliminated from the net cash flows which those investors will receive then the appropriate rate of discount should also have the inflationary element removed.

You should now know that a discount rate of 10 per cent implies that £1 is the present value of £1.10 receivable in one year. However, the real value of £1.10 receivable in one year (i.e. the sum of money which will buy the same basket of goods in current prices as £1.10 will buy in one year's time) is obtained by discounting the £1.10 at the rate of inflation: i.e.

the real equivalent to a money discount rate of 10 per cent $= 1.10/1.04$
$$= 1.0577$$

Note, the rate is not simply the difference between 10 and 4 per cent!

If we use this real rate of discount to discount the real cash flows we arrive at exactly the same answer as we had with the money analysis, namely a project net present value of £1 389 861.

We have shown this second method of analysis because many industrial managers do prefer to think, and make projections, in terms of current prices. A study, conducted in the UK in the mid 1970s, suggested that managers in industry do, however, attempt to discount real cash flows using discount rates incorporating a return for the inflationary expectations of investors (the money rate). This is wrong, and if discounting procedures are an important component of senior management's decision-making then this mistake will lead to systematic underinvestment in the firms concerned.

> *Self test:* Discount the real cash flows in Fig. 13.3 at the money rate. What effect does this have on the viability of the project?
> *Solution clue:* The net present value should be much reduced.

At the end of this chapter we provide a reference to the study cited above (Carsberg and Hope, 1976).

To summarize, we can make the following assertions concerning the benefits of the net-present-value technique for investment appraisal:

- In a world of perfect money markets the net present value of a project represents the absolute increase in the wealth of the firm's investors.
- On the assumption that a firm's investment capital is not in short supply (which is implicit in the perfection assumptions) then the net-present-value rule is extremely easy to apply. All the decision-maker need do is determine whether a single number (the project's net present value) is positive or negative.

The net-present-value rule has given us a simple means of structuring a complex and, what appeared to be, a very unstructured decision situation. It is for this reason that managers are often prepared to follow this rule, and decision rules like it, even when the assumptions supporting them are not satisfied in practice. However, the reliability of decision-making techniques such as the net-present-value rule are largely dependent upon the quality of the forecasting procedures employed to estimate the future cash flows. A decision rule can only ever be as good as the forecasted information on which it is used.

Other methods of investment appraisal

In one respect or other all of the techniques which we will outline in the following section are deficient in some respect when compared with the net-present-value rule. However, all of the techniques outlined below are popular in practice and we will suggest some reasons why this may be so.

The internal rate of return criterion

The internal rate of return of an investment project is that rate of discount which sets the project's net present value to zero. If a project has an outlay A_0 and net cash inflows of A_1, A_2 to A_n, where n is the number of years the project is expected to run, then the internal rate of return is the value of i which satisfies the following equation:

$$-A_0 + \frac{A_1}{(1+i)^1} + \frac{A_2}{(1+i)^2} + \ldots + \frac{A_n}{(1+i)^n} = 0$$

If the value of i is greater than the firm's opportunity cost of capital then the project is acceptable.

Given Martinez' problem the internal rate of return of the project is given by the solution of the following equation:

$$-6\,250\,000 + \frac{613\,000}{(1+i)^1} + \frac{410\,713}{(1+i)^2} + \frac{14\,849}{(1+i)^3}$$
$$+ \frac{302\,321}{(1+i)^4} + \frac{648\,962}{(1+i)^5} + \frac{10\,846\,481}{(1+i)^6} = 0$$

It is extremely difficult to solve such equations directly, indeed, it is difficult enough even when the length of the project is only two years and a quadratic equation is involved. The easiest way of arriving at a solution to the above equation is to graph the net present values obtained using a range of discount rates. Below we show the net present values obtained using a range of discount rates:

Rate of discount (per cent)	Net present value (£)
0	6 586 326
4	4 096 307
8	2 180 511
10	1 389 860
12	690 842
16	(479 009)

Clearly, a zero net present value will be obtained for this project if a discount rate of between 12 per cent and 16 per cent is used. In fact, as Fig. 13.4 shows, the internal rate of return is approximately 13.4 per cent. As the internal rate of return for the project is in excess of 10 per cent (the firm's opportunity cost of capital), the project is acceptable.

Fig 13.4 Graph of net present value against discount rate

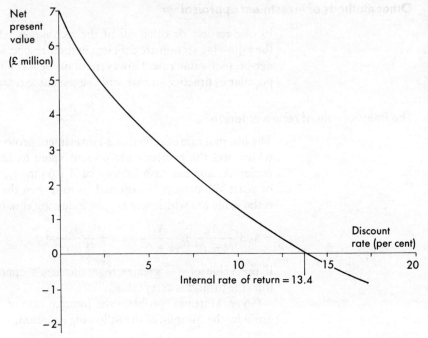

There are a number of reasons why the internal rate of return criterion can give misleading results compared with those obtained using the net-present-value rule.

First, for a project with an unusual pattern of cash flows (i.e. ones where some of the future cash flows are negative) the internal rate of return may have more than one value. This is because equations such as the six-term discounting formula given above can have a number of solutions. Even an equation for a two-year project which will, therefore, contain a squared term (to give a quadratic equation) can have two answers or 'roots'.

Second, because the internal rate of return measure is a percentage, it does not give an absolute measure of a project's worth as does net present value, but rather gives a relative measure of return against outlay. Other things being equal, therefore, internal rate of return will favour projects with small rather than large outlays. For example, consider the following two, mutually exclusive, projects:

	t_0	t_1	t_2
Project (i) net cash flow	−£100 000	£70 000	£80 000
Project (ii) net cash flow	−£20 000	£19 000	£18 000

The net present value of the two projects (assuming the investor has an opportunity cost of capital of 10 per cent per annum) are as follows:

$$\text{NPV (i)} = -100\,000 + \frac{70\,000}{1+i} + \frac{80\,000}{(1+i)^2} = +29\,752$$

and

$$\text{NPV (ii)} = -20\,000 + \frac{19\,000}{1+i} + \frac{18\,000}{(1+i)^2} = +12\,148$$

Project (i) has the greater net present value and under the assumptions required for the net present value to be valid will bring about the greater increase in the investor's wealth. However, the internal rate of return criterion ranks project (ii) over project (i):

Project (i) internal rate of return = 31.05 per cent
Project (ii) internal rate of return = 53.60 per cent

Fig 13.5 Internal rate of return against net present value

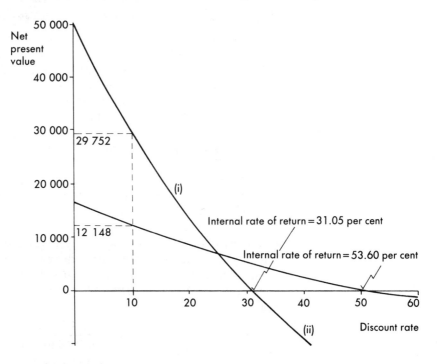

The graphs of net present value against interest rate are shown in Fig. 13.5. As we can see, because the investor's cost of capital is less than the interest rate at the crossover point, the internal rate of return and the net present value criteria disagree on the relative ranking of the two projects although both projects are acceptable in themselves.

The net-present-value rule is regarded as the safest guide in the situation where a choice has to be made between two or more mutually exclusive investment projects.

The payback criterion

With new projects managers often wish to know how quickly the original cash investment will be repaid by the anticipated future cash flows. In a situation of perfect money markets this question is irrelevant because in such markets it is assumed that the investing firm has access to an unlimited supply of funds which it can use to fund any project which has a positive net present value. Sadly, the real world is not perfect and lending institutions often question how quickly an investment can be repaid. Lenders normally attribute a higher degree of risk to long-term projects than they do to short-term projects and will assess the appropriate rate of interest to charge on the loan accordingly. The payback period on any project is, therefore, an important piece of negotiating information.

In Martinez' case we can calculate the payback period on both the money and the discounted cash flows:

Year	Cash flow (£)	Cumulative cash flow (£)	Discounted cash flow (£)	Cumulative discounted cash flow (£)
0	(6 250 000)	(6 250 000)	(6 250 000)	(6 250 000)
1	613 000	(5 637 000)	557 273	(5 692 727)
2	410 713	(5 226 287)	339 432	(5 353 295)
3	14 849	(5 211 438)	11 157	(5 342 138)
4	302 321	(4 909 117)	206 489	(5 135 649)
5	648 962	(4 260 155)	402 955	(4 732 694)
6	10 846 481	6 586 326	6 122 556	1 389 862

The above analysis shows that this project will only finish repaying its initial investment in the sixth year when the accumulated stocks are finally sold off. The payback period (for both money and discounted cash flows) can be calculated exactly as follows. The payback period lies somewhere in the sixth year on both the money and discounted cash-flow basis. Taking the money cash flows first, the proportion of the cash balance outstanding at the end of the fifth year (£4 270 155) to the amount paid back in the sixth year (£10 846 481) gives the payback time in the sixth year:

$$\text{payback in money cash flows} = 5 + \frac{4\,270\,155}{10\,846\,481}$$

$$= 5.394 \text{ years (5 years 4.72 months)}$$

Similarly:

$$\text{payback in discounted cash flows} = 5 + \frac{4\,732\,694}{6\,122\,556}$$

$$= 5.773 \text{ years (5 years 9.28 months)}$$

The problem with payback based upon the money cash flows is that it ignores the opportunity cost of the capital used to fund the investment and emphasizes the benefits of short-term projects with immediate positive cash flows. Payback can also be misleading in that it ignores any cash flows (positive or negative) which occur after the payback period irrespective of the magnitude of those later flows.

Discounted payback surmounts the principal deficiency of simple money payback in that it does incorporate the opportunity cost capital. However, like the internal rate of return criterion discounted payback may not give the same advice as the net-present-value rule when a choice has to be made between mutually exclusive projects. This is because the payback criterion ignores the magnitude of any cash flows which arise subsequent to the payback period. For example, consider the projects (i) and (ii) discussed above. Their discounted paybacks, given a discount rate of 10 per cent, are as follows:

	Project (i)			Project (ii)		
Year	Cash flow (£)	Discounted cash flow (£)	Cumulative cash flow (£)	Cash flow (£)	Discounted cash flow (£)	Cumulative cash flow (£)
0	(100 000)	(100 000)	(100 000)	(20 000)	(20 000)	(20 000)
1	70 000	63 636	(36 364)	19 000	17 273	(2 727)
2	80 000	66 116	29 752	18 000	14 876	12 149

discounted payback for project

$$(i) = 1 + \frac{36\,364}{66\,116} = 1.55 \text{ years}$$

discounted payback for project

$$(ii) = 1 + \frac{2727}{14\,876} = 1.18 \text{ years}$$

As with the internal rate of return criterion, discounted payback has favoured the project with the lower net present value. However, with the payback criterion it is not the magnitude of the outlays which is important, but the speed with which they are paid back.

Given the unreliability of the payback criterion, even in its discounted form, one may wonder why it is as widely used as it is. We conclude our discussion of payback by advancing the following reasons for its popularity:

- Lending institutions often place a premium on projects which can be repaid quickly. Indeed, the main clearing banks lend primarily to short- or medium-term borrowers. For this reason, any investing firm which seeks funds from institutions like the banks must be aware of the payback period on its proposed projects.

- Where capital funds are in short supply and the future is highly uncertain projects promising quick cash returns will be highly favoured by firms.

- Managers are often judged according to the returns which are generated by the projects they have initiated. This, coupled with the fact that many managers perceive that they may never see the full fruits of their company's long-term investments, means that there will be a bias in managerial choice toward short payback projects.

The accounting rate of return

It is quite a common practice in investment appraisal to determine the effect a project will have on the company's accounts. Such effects are generally measured by a project's accounting rate of return. Naturally, because senior managers are judged in terms of their performance, as revealed by their firm's financial accounts, they will pay particular attention to this measure of project viability even though other criteria may lead to better decision-making overall. We define the accounting rate of return as:

$$ARR = \frac{\text{average annual profits generated by the project}}{\text{average investment over project life}}$$

Unlike the appraisal methods discussed up until now, the accounting rate of return is based upon measures of profit rather than cash flow. This has the effect of introducing non-cash costs such as depreciation into the calculation. For projects (i) and (ii) above, assuming straight-line depreciation over the investment life, we can calculate the accounting rate of return as follows:

$$ARR = \frac{\text{average annual cash flows less depreciation}}{\text{average investment in project}}$$

The annual depreciation charge for each project is as follows:

$$\text{project (i) depreciation} = \frac{100\,000}{2} = £50\,000$$

$$\text{project (ii) depreciation} = \frac{20\,000}{2} = £10\,000$$

Therefore,

$$ARR\ (i) = \frac{((70\,000 - 50\,000) + (80\,000 - 50\,000))/2}{(100\,000 + 0)/2}$$

$$= 0.5\ (50\ \text{per cent) for project (i)}$$

$$ARR(ii) = \frac{((19\,000 - 10\,000) + (18\,000 - 10\,000))/2}{(20\,000 + 0)/2}$$

$$= 0.85\ (85\ \text{per cent) for project (ii)}$$

Note that the average capital investment is taken by averaging the value of the asset at the beginning and at the end of its life.

Again, we can note the same problem with accounting rate of return as was found by the internal rate of return measure discussed earlier.

Both methods are measured relative to the investment outlay and this has the effect of favouring the smaller of the two projects. In addition, accounting rate of return suffers from the fact that it ignores the cost of financing the capital investment and includes non-cash costs such as depreciation which are arbitrarily defined.

> **Self test:** Calculate the accounting rate of return for Martinez' project. Note that you will have to deduct the annual depreciation charge from the first five years' cash flows before averaging over the six-year period.
> **Solution clue:** In excess of 350 per cent.

Choosing between projects when capital funds are scarce

It may well be that in any particular period a firm may experience a short-term shortage of investment funds which restricts the range of investment projects which it can adopt. There may be a number of reasons why such a 'capital rationing' problem may arise. However, such rationing problems can usually be overcome if worthwhile investments are available. Of course, the problem can be more pronounced for smaller companies who generally do not have the wide range of financial sources open to larger companies. In this book we will only consider the case where capital is rationed for one period.

Consider a firm that has a range of projects with the following cash flows and net present values when discounted at the firm's opportunity cost of capital of 10 per cent:

	Cash flows (£)					Net present value (£)
Project	t_0	t_1	t_2	t_3	t_4	
A	(46 000)	5 000	21 780	26 620	17 855	8 740
B	(24 000)	4 100	14 250	10 648	7 987	4 959
C	(10 500)	5 100	4 599	3 250	2 854	2 328
D	(13 000)	650	3 980	8 225	6 280	1 349

We will assume that the company can scale down each project by any factor it wishes although the magnitudes of the cash flows shown are the maximum size of project permissible. We also know that the company is limited to £50 000 of investable funds.

Our first reaction may be to accept the project which gives the largest positive net present value—project A in this case—and to invest the remaining £4000 in project B. However, you may remember that in Chapter 7 we considered an analogous problem where a company had a single limiting scarce resource. In Chapter 7 we discovered that contribution could be maximized by choosing those projects which were most efficient at converting scarce resource into contribution. In this case we are not seeking to maximize contribution *per se* but rather to maximize net present value. We can achieve this objective by ranking the projects according to the ratio of net present value to unit of capital outlay:

Project	NPV/£ outlay	Outlay (£)	NPV (£)
C	$\frac{2328}{10\,500} = 0.2217$	10 500	2 328
B	$\frac{4959}{24\,000} = 0.2066$	24 000	4 959
A	$\frac{8740}{46\,000} = 0.1900$	15 500	2 945
Net present value on an investment of		£50 000 =	10 232

Projects not included in investment plan:

Project	NPV/£ outlay	Outlay (£)	NPV (£)
A	$\frac{8740}{46\,000} = 0.190$	30 500	5 795
D	$\frac{1349}{13\,000} = 0.1037$	13 000	1 349

Note that only part of project A has been accepted. We calculated the appropriate proportion as follows:

$$\text{proportion of A accepted} = \frac{\text{cash remaining for the marginal project}}{\text{outlay required for the marginal project}}$$

$$= \frac{15\,500}{46\,000} = 0.337$$

The net present value of this proportion of project A is:

$$\text{proportion of A's NPV} = 0.337 \times 8740 = £2945$$

> ***Self test:*** **Estimate the internal rate of return for each of the four projects above (use the graphical method demonstrated earlier in this chapter). Does ranking the four projects by their internal rate of return give the same result as we obtained above?**

If an extra £1 of capital is obtained in t_0 the net present value of the firm would rise by £0.19, as this extra £1 would be invested in the marginal project, namely project A. Similarly, if £1 had to be diverted from this set of projects to some other use then the total net present value would fall by £0.19. The dual price or internal opportunity cost of capital to this firm is, therefore, £0.19 per £1 or 19 per cent. The total opportunity cost of the firm's capital is:

$$\text{total opportunity cost} = \text{external opportunity cost}$$
$$+ \text{ internal opportunity cost}$$
$$= 0.10 + 0.19$$
$$= 0.29 \ (29 \text{ per cent})$$

This firm should be prepared to pay up to 29 per cent per annum for the remaining £30 500 required to exhaust project A and then 20.37 per cent (0.10 + 0.1037) for the additional funds required for project D.

> *Note:* At this point we have drawn together the opportunity-cost concept for all scarce resources: for hard factors and labour in Chapters 3 and 7 and for capital in this chapter and the last. In all cases we have identified the external and the internal component of the opportunity cost. We do not in this book explore the use of linear programming for problems of capital rationing in more than one period. If you wish to pursue this topic, references are provided at the end of this chapter.

General problems of capital investment

We conclude this chapter with some general remarks about the problems of investment faced by management.

1   The effectiveness of the methods outlined above depend upon a number of assumptions about how the capital market operates and about the efficiency with which information concerning new projects is transmitted to the market. We have already pointed out that discounting procedures depend upon a number of highly restrictive assumptions about the capital market. We should also note that the net-present-value method depends upon a specific notion of the value of the firm; namely the capital-market valuation. This valuation relies upon the market appreciating that a new investment project is being undertaken and agrees with management's projections of the future cash flows.

The difficulty is that management is unlikely to disclose publicly its projections of cash flows for a new project. Further, the company's published accounts provide a picture of what has passed rather than of what is to come. As a result of this, even if the firm's investors appreciated that a new investment was under way, they would not have access to the necessary information to revalue the firm and might, indeed, react adversely if they observed inexplicably negative cash flows in the early years of a project.

These rather pessimistic comments lead us to the conclusion that management will be biased against any investment project which, even for a period, happens to be a drain on a firm's cash flow and reported earnings.

2   The general level of uncertainty which managers feel will undoubtedly affect their investment decision-making attitudes. Changes in government macroeconomic policy, for example, can radically influence the environment in which investment decisions are made. Money market interest rates, as we have observed before, feed through into a company's opportunity cost of capital, and sudden changes in interest rates can turn otherwise viable investments into liabilities. Changes in taxation policy can also have a profound effect on the viability of projects. We have not discussed the impact of taxation on investment appraisal in this book but it is not hard to see that if government changes the basis upon which tax reliefs and Corporation Tax are calculated this will disturb even the most carefully laid investment plans.

3   Finally, new investment often brings problems with employees especially if the investment is not designed to increase the firm's productivity as a whole but rather to get the same level of production with less labour. Union negotiators may well put the point that this is really just an attempt by the owners of capital to appropriate more of the surplus value from labour. In other words, if management views labour just as a cost to the minimized by whatever means available it is unlikely to meet a favourable response from its employees' representatives. If, on the other hand, the new investment is designed to increase the productivity of the firm overall, the labour negotiators will want to see a fair proportion of the resultant value added being passed on to the labour force in the form of higher wage benefits.

This brings us back to the point we made in Chapter 1. The role of managers is to negotiate and settle conflict between the various interest groups within the firm. New investment projects inevitably give rise to new claims from the various groups within the firm and it is management's task to respond to these claims in the light of the information made available to them.

Summary

In this chapter we have considered a number of techniques for analysing the value of new investment projects to a firm. The validity of individual techniques relies upon the rigour and consistency with which they treat the available information and the limitations of the assumptions upon which they are based. We have argued that the net-present-value method, of all the techniques considered in this chapter, is the one which most clearly measures the increment in wealth which will accrue to an individual or firm as a result of the decision to adopt a particular project. However, the net-present-value method does rest upon a number of assumptions which are unlikely to fully hold in practice. In particular, the net-present-value method cannot be used to rank projects in a capital-rationing situation but must be modified to account for the relative efficiency with which a given project converts capital expenditure into increased wealth. Finally, we have made some observations on the general problems which face managers in investment decision-making and, especially, to throw some light on the reasons why managers prefer projects which recoup their capital outlay quickly rather than others which do not.

Supplementary reading

BREARLEY, R., and MYERS, S., *Principles of Corporate Finance*, McGraw-Hill, 1981. An excellent textbook which expands upon the topics covered in the last two chapters.

CARSBERG, B., and HOPE, A., *Business Investment Decisions under Inflation*, The Institute of Chartered Accountants, 1976. A remarkable little book which suggests one reason for the chronic underinvestment in manufacturing industry in the UK.

HIRSHLEIFER, J., On the theory of optimal investment decisions, *Journal of Political Economy*, October 1958.

MILLS, R., More effective use of npv in investment appraisal, *Management Accounting*, 1983.

PAPPAS, J. L., BRIGHAM, E. F., and SHIPLEY, B., *Managerial Economics* (UK edn), Holt, Rinehart and Winston, 1983. Especially Chapter 14.

Questions

1   Outline the assumptions necessary for net present value to measure the increase in wealth which accrues to an investor as a result of accepting an investment project.

2   Tonas Ltd produces Pacos in bulk. It is considering the installation of a new plant which would produce 10 000 Pacos per annum. The initial outlay would be £10 000, payable immediately. The plant is expected to have a life of three years and a zero scrap value at the end of that time. The following additional information is also available:

    1 The selling price per Paco is £1.50 during the first year rising by 8 per cent per annum thereafter.
    2 The labour cost on the new plant is £3500 for the first year increasing at 15 per cent thereafter.
    3 Other costs associated with the new plant are £7000 for the first year increasing at 20 per cent per annum thereafter.

The current inflation rate is 10 per cent per annum. Tonas's opportunity cost of capital is 3 per cent per annum in real terms.

Required:
(a) Evaluate the above project in both real and money terms.
(b) Discuss the problems involved in handling inflation in project appraisal.

3   Melchor plc is considering the following two, mutually exclusive projects:

	t_0	t_1	t_2	t_3
Net cash flow (A)	−£4 000	£3 000	£2 000	£2 000
Net cash flow (B)	−£140 000	£70 000	£30 000	£80 000

Melchor has a cost of capital of 10 per cent per annum.

Required:
(a) Calculate the net present value and estimate the internal rate of return for each project and state (giving reasons) which one should be accepted.
(b) Estimate, to the nearest month, the payback period for each project.
(c) Comment upon the usefulness of the payback criterion in investment appraisal.

4   A chemical company is considering an investment in a short-term project to produce Burcolene, a wonder substance which fails to react with any known chemical. The production process is expected to operate for five years before the plant would become unsafe to use. The capital investment is £1.25 million in the first year and the net cash flows from the project would be £0.4 million per annum over the remaining five years of the project. At the end of the fifth year the plant would be dismantled and scrapped, the scrap proceeds just covering the dismantling costs incurred.

The company pays tax on its net cash flows (less tax allowances) at an average rate of 45 per cent per annum. The company is allowed to deduct from its cash flows an allowance for the capital expenditure of one-fifth of the capital cost in each of the five years of the project's life. The tax payment is made one year after the liability for tax is incurred.

Required:
(a) Determine whether the above project is viable assuming an opportunity cost of capital of 10 per cent per annum.
(b) Calculate the payback period and the discounted payback period for the above project.
(c) Outline some of the difficulties which managers face in making long-term decisions.

5 Nueva plc is a company in the fashion industry faced with a short-term
   capital shortage. It is considering the following projects for investment
   in the next twelve months (in £'000):

Project	t_0	t_1	t_2	t_3	t_4	t_5
A	(160)	(200)	450	150	(50)	—
B	(50)	(550)	—	670	300	40
C	(2000)	1200	1700	300	—	—
D	(1000)	(500)	1000	1000	1000	—
E	(700)	(700)	100	1600	—	(50)
F	(3000)	4000	—	—	—	—
G	(300)	—	500	—	—	—

The capital available is limited to £2.0 million in the first year after
which funds will be freely available. Additional funds may be
available in the first year at considerably higher rates of interest. Due
to the nature of the industry, early market entry is vital and,
consequently, investment in new projects cannot be delayed.

   Assume the company's opportunity cost of capital is 10 per cent
per annum and that all projects are perfectly divisible.

Required:
(a) Calculate the net present value of each of the above projects and
    advise the company on their acceptability.
(b) Determine which of the above projects should be accepted and
    the dual price of capital in year 1.

Part 4 Conclusions

14 Management information systems and management accounting

In previous chapters of this book we have studied the problems of management accounting as part of the decision support system of the firm. In this chapter we broaden the context and look at management accounting as part of the firm's overall management information system. The design and management of management information systems themselves has been revolutionized by the advent of cheap digital microcomputers. This new technology has wide implications for management accounting not only as a way of controlling and manipulating information but also in its communication throughout the organization. This is the Information Technology revolution.

In this chapter we will consider the following topics:

- The contribution of new technology to management information systems.

- The nature of 'management information systems and technology'.

- Specific examples of the impact of information technology on corporate decision-making in the areas of:
  1 Management control decisions and management by exception.
  2 Tactical, production decision-making.
  3 Strategic, investment decision-making.

- The development of the 'silicon office'.

The technological revolution

Much has been written about the so-called technological revolution and the impact which modern microcomputer technology will have upon the lives of individuals and the operation of business. Since the early 1970s the relationship between the cost of hardware and the cost of software has dramatically altered. Developments in microtechnology have brought about a situation where the cost of microprocessors (the logic unit within a computer) and the cost of memory have fallen by a factor of ten every three years. In Fig. 14.1 we show the reducing cost of hardware since 1970.

Three factors have worked together to bring about this technological revolution:

- The reduction in the cost of hardware (measured in terms of units of memory capacity).

- An expansion in the sophistication of the programs which can be handled by modern computers.

- A reduction in the cost of maintaining software through the advent of more 'user-friendly', self-documenting, high-level computer languages for the software designer.

Fig 14.1 The reducing cost of microelectronic circuits

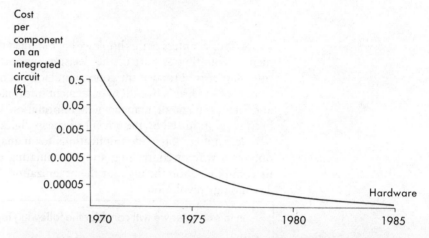

Note: A digital microcomputer is controlled by a microprocessor. The microprocessor can only work on instructions and data which are presented to it in byte-size chunks of binary numbers. A computer's memory can be likened to a stack of such bytes which the processor can access at any point. The more powerful the processor, the higher the stack of bytes it can deal with and, generally, the faster it can perform its operations on those memory locations.

The lowest-level languages which can be used to program a microprocessor have a one to one correspondence between the instructions and the binary code which the microprocessor understands. In higher-level languages, such as BASIC, Pascal, Modula 2, etc., readily understood words and symbols are converted into many machine instructions. These languages are, therefore, more accessible to the programmer than the low-level, 'assembly' languages.

The new business computers of the 1980s have the following characteristics:

- They are extremely small. A mainframe computer of the early 1970s would have filled a large, air-conditioned room. An equivalent minicomputer of the mid 1970s would have occupied a smaller room and today a microcomputer of the same power as that mainframe weighs less than 10 kg and can operate from a desk top.

- They can perform a number of concurrent activities, i.e. processing, printing, file handling and communication can all happen together.

- They can be networked together to form multiaccess systems with access to large, hard disk, storage devices.

In Fig. 14.2 we show the structure of a modern microcomputer.

Fig 14.2   A modern microcomputer

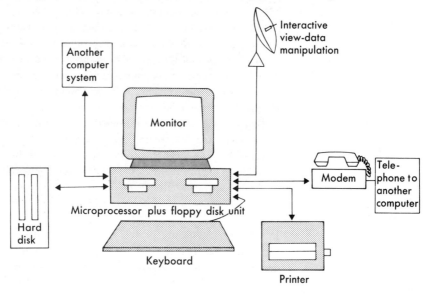

The characteristics outlined above have taken the business computer away from its earlier role as a data processor toward being part of a firm's electronic communications and decision support system. This has had three notable effects upon corporate decision-making:

- The speed with which information can be produced and acted upon has increased rapidly. This has the effect of reducing the comparative disadvantage of formal, bureaucratic organizations in rapidly changing environments (see Chapter 2).

- Management are able to see the results of their decisions much more rapidly. Nowhere is this better exemplified than in the foreign-exchange markets where dealing decisions are rapidly carried out and their effects realized.

- Greater diagnostic skills can be brought to bear on routine decision-making through the rapid development of 'expert systems'. This enhances the possibilities for delegation of decision-making within management not only from senior to lower levels but also from managers who possess specialist skills to those who do not.

Note: An 'expert system' is a computer program whose primary function is to make decisions on the basis of information supplied to it and to provide the user with judgements based upon those decisions. An expert system consists of two components: a 'shell' and a 'knowledge base'. The 'shell' contains the decision-making routines which permit the program to evaluate the attributes of a particular decision situation using certain judgement rules. The 'knowledge base' contains the appropriate information on decision attributes and outcomes.

Expert systems have been used in a number of applications including the routine diagnosis of illness, helicopter maintenance and the diagnosis of computer faults. Expert-system shells are now commercially available which can support any knowlege base that a human expert can supply. In addition, such systems can be programmed to explain the route which they have taken in arriving at a particular conclusion. Most types of structured decision situations, which previously required expert analysis, can, in principle, be replaced by an expert system. Indeed, it is quite possible that many of the routine decisions made by management will be made, in the future, by computerized expert systems with management accountants maintaining and updating the appropriate knowledge bases.

In Chapter 2 we interpreted the role of management accounting within a contingency framework. At one level management accounting is concerned with the provision of information as an input into the specialist (differentiated) activities of the firm. At another level management accounting is concerned with aiding management in their efforts to control the organization through the provision of rules and procedures. In terms of the contingency framework outlined in Chapter 2, the early use of computers was, predominantly, in the support of the specialist functions within the firm, notably, general accounting and payroll.

More recent developments in management information systems have opened up the possibility of using computers as part of the integrative, control functions of management. Unfortunately, it does seem to be true that many computerized control systems were designed in the context of, and to support, a purely formal hierarchy of relationships within the organizations concerned. This has often been done at the cost of weakening the informal systems of relationships which enable the firm to overcome the dysfunctional aspects of its structure. The problem arose because of the once prevalent belief amongst system designers that one single, ideal, prototype management information system existed. The only difficulty was in finding the ideal system. The modern theory of organizations has shown us that there is not a single, ideal organizational structure for all firms in all environments and this is equally true of management information systems.

The nature of management information systems and technology

Within a hierarchical structure we can depict a management information system as in Fig. 14.3. Data in the form of signals from the firm's external environment are processed by the lowest levels in the hierarchy and fed up through the various organizational levels.

Each level of management in the hierarchy acts upon those data transforming them into information for use by higher levels or acting upon them by making decisions at the level concerned. Data, as they are received

Fig 14.3 Communications through managerial structure

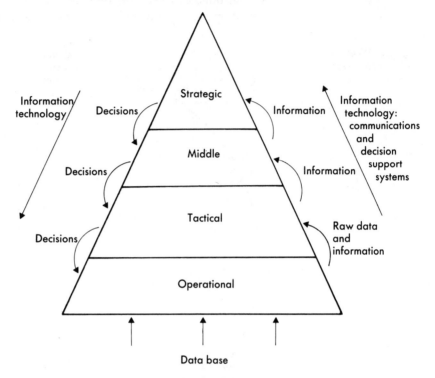

by the firm from its external environment, are transformed by the dataprocessing system into comprehensible, decision-specific information. A good management information system should be able to:

- Convert data from their base form into information relevant for decision-making purposes.

- Achieve that conversion within the activity cycle of the function to which the information will be directed.

- Adapt sufficiently to provide information for the unusual and unstructured decisions which managers (especially senior managers) have to make from time to time.

In addition, the management information system must also be amenable to independent verification and checking. In the terminology of the auditor, the points at which checks and controls can be made in an information system form the 'internal controls' of the organization. We have already discussed the concept of control in some detail in Chapter 8. An internal control system relies heavily upon the concept of feedback, where the actual performance of the information system is checked at various stages of its operation in order to ensure that discrepancies are eliminated and that a recognizable trail of activity is being maintained. Auditors recognize this as the maintenance of an 'audit trail' within the system.

We introduced, within the three criteria of an effective management information system outlined above, the concept of an 'activity cycle'.

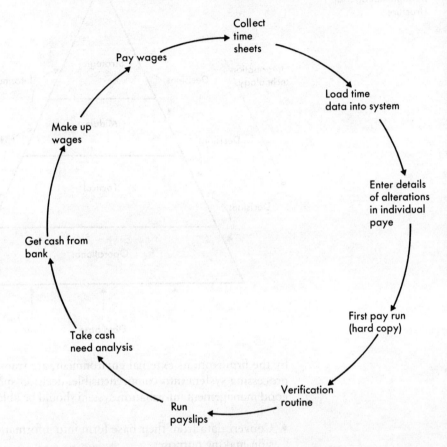

Fig 14.4 Weekly time cycle for cash-wages system

Many of the routine decisions and other activities of a firm occur in regular cycles. For example, wages are paid out weekly, salaries are paid out monthly, creditors are paid within a reasonable period of time and so forth. Each activity has its own time cycle and the management information system must be able to process the appropriate data and produce the necessary information within the time available. In Fig. 14.4 we show an example of a wages payment system in the form of a time cycle. The management information system of the firm must be able to turn this cycle within one week to be effective.

Effective computerization can greatly speed up the cycle time of the management information system as well as increase the system's scope in terms of the data which can be converted and the range of decisions that can be supported. Unfortunately, computerization of a management information system can easily lead to obscurity in the way data and information are handled, and make the problems of internal control much more difficult.

Management information systems and technology (MIST) is the study of how information technology can be used to enhance the creation and maintenance of organization-specific information systems. The study of MIST involves:

- An understanding of the current state-of-the-art of information technology.

- A knowledge of the possibilities available within the fields of computerized decision support systems (including artificial intelligence and expert systems).

- A profound knowledge and understanding of the behaviour of individuals within organizations, i.e. how they interrelate and communicate with one another.

> *Note:* There is much confusion about the meaning of the term 'information technology'. We take it to mean the implementation of the latest available computerized technology within the field of data handling, information processing and communication. The idea that modern computers can be effectively linked together (networked) into rapid information dissemination and communication systems is what distinguishes information technology from the computer science which preceded it.

Again, within the hierarchical structure outlined above (Fig. 14.3), we can view the management information system as a synthesis of the firm's structure and the various management functions within it. Computerization of such a system would produce a software structure as outlined in Fig. 14.5

Figure 14.5 nicely reinforces the fact that a computerized management information system is not so much a network of machines strategically placed in various offices, but rather a set of interdependent software suites. That is, a range of different computer programs performing different functions, but related to one another through their ability to access and interact with a common data base through the data-base management system (DBMS).

The lowest level of the diagram in Fig. 14.5 represents the operational software in the system, i.e. the suites of programs devoted to:

- The control and maintenance of the operational data base.

- The management of the firm's interaction with its data environment.

- The maintenance of the higher levels of the system.

At higher levels programs will be concerned with the interactive reporting from the system to managers requiring information for specific tactical and, at the highest levels, strategic decisions.

Within a matrix type organizational structure (see Chapter 2) the management information system must be able to support the decision-making needs of the groups and intergroup teams within the firm. In this type

Fig 14.5 Software hierarchy

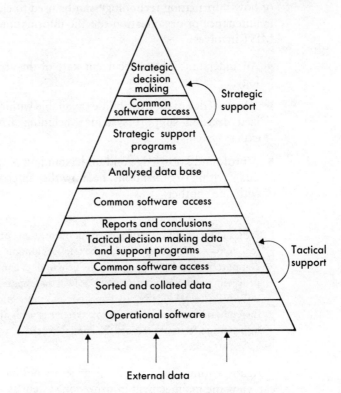

of structure we can envisage the data base as a 'protective' shell for the information system, absorbing data from the environment and forming a source of data for the various applications software which draw upon it (see Fig. 14.6).

The function of management accounting within the management information system

Throughout this book we have acknowledged as central, the idea that management accounting is concerned with the communication of information which is relevant to management's decision-making. As such, management accounting forms an integral part of the firm's management information system. As a result, the formal methods of data analysis, which we recognize as management accounting, are being subsumed in many firms into their management information systems. The result of this process is that the management accountant is now losing his or her identity and becoming part of the rather larger information management team of the firm. This is especially noticeable in those areas of management accounting which are concerned with the integrative aspects of the management:

Fig 14.6 The matrix
support system
Ⓕ Functional support
software
Ⓢ Strategic support
software

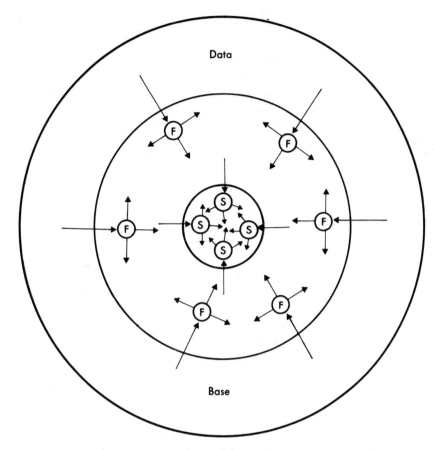

- The control of costs and the provision of exception (variance) reports.

- Planning and control through the budgeting systems of the firm.

However, as the effect of information technology spreads through the firm, specialist functions who make use of management-accounting information can now obtain that information through computerized communication and data management systems. Operations managers can now retrieve their specialized information needs from the firm's data base in a much more accessible form and much more rapidly. Furthermore, in some cases the new technology can give access to information which would have been too costly to prepare on a regular basis with a manual system.

In the next section of this chapter we will consider three important types of management decision-making which we have already considered in this book and examine how they could be serviced by a fully computerized management information system:

- Variance analysis and the control of costs.

- Linear programming and the production decision.

- Investment decision-making and strategic planning.

Information technology and corporate decision-making

We will examine the three areas of decision-making above in the following way: first, we will consider how the necessary information inputs for each decision type would have been provided under older types of computerized accounting systems. Second, we will consider how the older types of system have been improved by the advent of the new technology and, third, how these improved systems interact with the firm's data base.

Variance analysis and the control of costs

In many firms, variance analysis was a common by-product of large (mainframe) accounting programs; however, it was only a by-product and as such suffered accordingly. The computer-generated management report was usually a wad of computer printout several inches thick through which the hapless manager would have to search for relevant items amongst all of the other data produced by the system.

Given the high cost of managerial time, a more efficient information system would present only those items of information which the manager deemed relevant for his or her particular purpose. In older systems, where the cost of hardware and of associated processing times were much higher, the balance of technical effort was directed toward ensuring machine rather than user convenience. That balance has now changed as the cost of hardware (especially communication and peripheral equipment) has been reduced.

Another of the problems associated with older computerized accounting systems is that they were largely arranged around traditional data-processing functions (such as stock and payroll, for example) and so, to use their data files for other purposes was often both difficult and costly. As a result, the variances produced by the firm's costing system were often only a part of the overall, periodic output from its data-processing system. To allow for multiple use of data the tendency arose to keep separate files for specific programs. This in turn led to the same data being kept many times over in different forms.

The replication of data in many different files was very inefficient, not only in terms of the the storage space consumed but also in terms of making revisions of data throughout the system. Because storage space was at such a premium (largely because of its cost) data files were often kept on backing storage in the form of reels of magnetic tape which had to be loaded by hand each time the data were required. In order to surmount this problem a means of centralized data storage was needed which could be accessed by many different programs. This gave rise to the concept of a data base and the means of controlling it—the data-base management system. A data-base management system will allow data stored in a data base to be retrieved or updated on request.

In a fully integrated budgeting and control system, management will need to retrieve variances:

- At least within one activity cycle of the cost or revenue centre under control.

- In different and specific ways as different explanations for the variances materialize. In Chapter 9 we laid out a variance tree which showed the ranges of subsidiary variance which could be pulled out from the crude differences between actual and budgeted costs and revenues. Managers with responsibility for particular departments may wish to search particular branches of that variance tree looking for clues as to the reason for variances at higher levels within the tree.

Given the current state of the art, a modern variance analysis system should be able to:

- present calculations of all possible variances and report those variances which lie outside any preset range of acceptability,

and enable management to:

- investigate any subvariances belonging to a variance which lies outside the control limits and to suggest possible causes of that variance,

- examine any trend in variances of particular revenue or cost items and be able to advise management of the implications of that trend for their budgeting policy and

- conduct 'what if' type experiments in the examination of possible courses of corrective action.

This type of variance analysis system would have many of the attributes of an expert system in that it would be able to diagnose problems and give the sort of advice which a management accountant would normally give as to corrective action which should be taken. With this type of system the management accountant's role has moved away from the routine analysis and interpretation of data. In this new environment the management accountant's role will be to maintain and police the system, to provide expert diagnosis and advice in exceptional situations and to ensure that managers who are meant to access the system and act upon its recommendations are doing so.

Linear programming and production management

One application of variance analysis is in the control of production processes which would initially be planned using a tactical decision support program such as a linear programming package. The variance analysis would point to areas of the production budgets derived from the linear program which did not match reality. The initial figures for such a program would be obtained from widely different parts of the data base.

In early computerized production planning programs the user would, typically, have to prepare the data in a form appropriate for the technique to be employed. The user would then have to batch load the data (unless there was on-line access) into a special computer run of (say) a linear programming package. In a modern system most, if not all, of these processes can be achieved within the system itself.

In Fig. 14.7 we show the example of a linear programming problem included as one of the end of chapter exercises in Chapter 7.

Fig 14.7 Data sources for linear programming

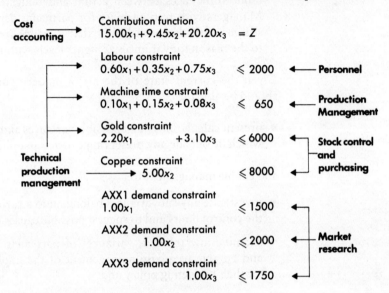

Cost accounting → Contribution function
$15.00x_1 + 9.45x_2 + 20.20x_3 = Z$

Labour constraint
$0.60x_1 + 0.35x_2 + 0.75x_3 \leqslant 2000$ ← Personnel

Machine time constraint
$0.10x_1 + 0.15x_2 + 0.08x_3 \leqslant 650$ ← Production Management

Gold constraint
$2.20x_1 \quad + 3.10x_3 \leqslant 6000$ ← Stock control and purchasing

Technical production management

Copper constraint
$5.00x_2 \leqslant 8000$

AXX1 demand constraint
$1.00x_1 \leqslant 1500$

AXX2 demand constraint
$1.00x_2 \leqslant 2000$ ← Market research

AXX3 demand constraint
$1.00x_3 \leqslant 1750$

An integrated production planning system would retrieve the necessary inputs for the Simplex algorithm from a number of sources. The estimates of unit contribution would be derived from the cost-accounting system with any necessary corrections to ensure that only the opportunity costs of the production decision were included. The production constraints would be derived as follows from:

- The levels of actual stocks of gold and copper mesh available from the updated inventory reports with revisions to accommodate expected additions to stock during the coming production period and deletions for any other commitments in the current period.

- The availability of labour hours can be accessed from the personnel data kept on the data base. The usages of particular types of labour can be derived from records of previous production runs, from work study and from union agreements.

- Market research reports for various products should allow the production planners to estimate the maximum demand for a particular product at a given price. This information could be retrieved and analysed from past sales records held on the data base.

- Orders which have been accepted for the production output during the coming period. This information can be fed into the algorithm as 'greater than' constraints upon production.

- The usages of materials and other input resources which can be obtained by analysis of the attributes of the particular product, from previous production budgets and from the product's technical specification—all of which should be held on the data base.

The retrieval of data from the data base and its manipulation and interpretation through a production planning algorithm (such as the Simplex) can form the backbone of that part of the firm's management information system concerned with production. The programs involved in production planning are referred to as 'tactical support programs' in opposition to the strategic support software which is necessary to service the long-term decision-making of management.

Investment appraisal and strategic planning

The implementation of computerization to support management decision-making has been largely concentrated at the operational and tactical levels of the firm. The reason for this is that decisions at this level are often perceived to be much more structured than decisions at the strategic level. As we have observed before in this book, the potential for automation and computerization has been largely ignored at the strategic level.

The principal applications of the old computer technology to investment appraisal and strategic planning were in the areas of project planning (using such techniques as 'critical path analysis' and 'programme evaluation and review techniques' or 'PERT'). Some work was done in the 1960s and 1970s in the area of technological forecasting and in the risk analysis of investment projects. However, none of these techniques has been widely adopted within British industry.

One problem with computerized support for strategic decision-making is that it invariably requires access to a much wider range of data than would be collected routinely by the firm and incorporated within its data base. For example, a major new investment in plant would require:

- Estimates of cash inflows and outflows over the life of the project.

- An estimate of the discount rate to be applied in assessing future cash flows.

- An estimate of the capital cost of the plant.

These requirements assume, of course, that management would be prepared to use discounting procedures as a means of structuring its investment decisions. However, whichever system of investment decision-making management prefers, it may be that the development of external data bases, such as British Telecom's Prestel service, will provide convenient 'on-line' access to much of the additional information that management needs.

The development of the 'silicon office'

Throughout this book we have suggested many different aspects of the management accountant's work. However, we have not said a lot about the way the management accountant should do that work. Old-fashioned textbooks in cost accounting are replete with the types of schedules and spreadsheets that the accountant can use to analyse data. However, the time is fast coming when schedules and working paper files will become a thing of the past. The use of microcomputers as office workstations has given rise to the concept of the 'silicon office'. Indeed, it is not beyond the bounds of possibility that many office activities can be conducted just as easily from home using a microcompter linked through a 'modem' to the central office computer system.

The main components of a silicon office (apart from the micro-computer) are:

- A method of communicating with a central, host computer which handles the firm's data base. For remote access this sort of communication can be achieved via the telephone system using a device (a 'modem') which converts the digital signals from the computer into frequency-modulated signals for transmission via the telephone network. Some long-distance, intercontinental computer communication can already be transmitted directly through any one of the many communications satellites in orbit above the Earth.

- A word-processing package. This book, for example, was written entirely on a microcomputer-based, word-processing package. One or two publishers now have the facilities for taking manuscripts in magnetic form, copy-editing them and composing the proofs without any paper being produced until the final proofs are sent to the author for checking. In the normal office environment; reports can be produced and corrected much more quickly through the editing facilities which are now available with word processors.

- A computerized filing system which manages the office's records such as its indexes, mailing lists, suppliers' and customers' names and addresses, etc.

- A 'spreadsheet' package which allows all of the work which the accountant would normally have prepared on handwritten schedules to be done on the microcomputer screen. These packages have simplified all of those processes where projections of figures were involved, often with numerous corrections to be made.

Note: If you, as an aspiring accountant, have not met a spreadsheet program make the opportunity to do so quickly. Once you have mastered the spreadsheet (and they are very easy) try any of the numerical questions at the end of the chapters in this book. Then look forward to the day when the professional bodies allow microcomputers and spreadsheet packages into the examinations.

The latest software can integrate these various packages together with the possibility of presenting information produced in graphical form. Finally, the professional office of the future will not be complete without a facility for users to create their own 'expert system' on any subject they like. Already there are packages which, given a user's knowledge on a particular subject, can create a knowledge base upon which the expert system can operate using the decision criteria supplied by the user.

For the management accountant of the future the outlook has never been better. The development of our understanding of the way that managers make decisions has given management accounting relevance. The advent of the modern information technology revolution has freed the management accountant from much of the drudgery associated with the preparation and dissemination of information.

Summary

In this chapter we have examined the role which management information systems and technology have to play in management accounting. Undoubtedly, modern technology can be used to improve the support which the management accountant can give to management decision-making. In one important sense, the recent advances in computer technology have brought the role of the management accountant into sharper focus. No longer is the management accountant required to spend inordinate amounts of time on the preparation of information—that, in the modern firm, can be computerized—rather he or she can spend more time on the design of information and the systems which transmit that information to its user.

Supplementary reading

DANIELS, A., and YEATES, D., *Practical Systems Design*, Pitman, 1984.

EDWARDS, C., *Developing Microcomputer-based Business Systems*, Prentice-Hall, 1982.

EISENBACH, S., and STOKES, A. V., Multi-user systems, *Personal Computer World*, Parts 1 and 2, 1981.

MASON, D., Information technology, *Management Accounting*, November 1983.

Questions

1 Discuss the role of information technology, in the following areas of management decision-making:
   (a) Product pricing.
   (b) Wage negotiating.
   (c) The financing decision.

You will find it helpful to reread the chapters concerned and make a careful note of the information requirements of each type of decision.

2   Using a spreadsheet package rework Martinez' problem in Chapter 13. What is the net present value of the project if (i) the sales price of alpha-nievene rises by 6 per cent per annum and (ii) materials costs rise by 10 per cent per annum.

3   Outline what is meant by the term 'management information system'. To what extent is the study of management information systems different from the study of management accounting?

15 Conclusion

In this book we have attempted to show the diversity of subject matter and perspectives contained within management accounting.

Management accounting, like many of the other areas within the social sciences, has an inner tension which is not yet fully resolved. At one level, the subject is concerned with the provision of information tailored for models which are derived from a formal analysis of diverse managerial decisions. At this level, management accounting can be said to be a 'prescriptive' discipline. The models which arise from such analysis match up to, at least, one view of what constitutes the best practice in, or the most 'rational' approach to, decision-making.

Our prescriptions of the most appropriate type of information for decision-making purposes presupposes that managers do make (or 'ought to make') decisions in accordance with our analytical formulations.

At another level we recognize that management accountants work in an environment where information also serves to modify and support the behaviour and relationships of individuals within the firm. We have devoted much space to the discussion of this 'behavioural' dimension of management accounting. There is, regrettably, a tendency in many first-level courses to ignore these issues because they can cloud the purity of a purely formal presentation (and examination) of the subject. This book has been a strong statement of our view that the purely formal approach to management accounting must be interpreted within the real behavioural and organizational dimensions of practical management. In our view, it is important to consider these wider dimensions of the discipline at an early stage.

In one important sense this book does not have a conclusion except in as far as we have now filled the word 'budget' agreed with our publisher! We have deliberately left many questions unresolved and a number of methods underdeveloped. This seems to us entirely appropriate for a text devoted to a first appreciation of the subject. There are many ways in which the subject of management accounting can be developed. Some of these are set out below.

The techniques of the subject

We have introduced a number of the basic techniques used by the management accountant although most can be developed far beyond the treatment given in this book. In the area of costing, for example, techniques such as process costing or variance analysis can be extended to include methods of accounting for scrap and wastage, interdepartmental transfers and so on. Professional examinations and practice will give you ample opportunity to develop your knowledge of these areas.

The subject-matter of management accounting

There are a number of issues which we have left unexplored. In the area of pricing, for example, we have not considered the problems of transfer pricing between divisions within the firm—not because the topic is unimportant (it is!) but because we believe the concept of opportunity cost needs time to mature and be examined before the problems of transfer pricing can be dealt with. Some topics we have excluded because they would distract us from what we believe to be a reasonably coherent and progressive treatment of the subject. One such topic is goal-programming which we believe to be an exciting method for applying non-optimizing logic to production problems.

Behavioural and organizational dimensions

This textbook attempts in many places to interpret the subject-matter of management accounting in a behavioural and organizational context. This is an area in which there is currently considerable research activity although little has penetrated to the initial treatments of management accounting offered by the majority of other texts. If you are interested in this aspect of the subject you might like to follow up the references given at the end of Chapters 2 and 3.

The technology of the disciplice

In this age of cheap, high-speed computers there is much to learn and be discovered about the way that the new technology can enhance the effectiveness of the management accountant. For example, exciting areas are now opening up in the fields of artificial intelligence and decision support systems which promise great things for management accountants in the future. In the Appendix to this book we outline the features of a software package which has been written to support this book. We urge you, if you have access to an appropriate microcomputer, to experiment with the programs in that package.

Finally, we hope that you have gained many useful insights and at least some satisfaction from studying this book. In fact we hope you have liked it so much that you will keep it as a permanent addition to your library and not try to sell it on the second-hand market.

Appendix

The computer software suite

There is a suite of software and a user guide which has been designed for use alongside this book. The programs cover the areas of:

- Statistical cost estimation.
- Break-even analysis and flexible budgeting.
- Linear programming.
- Stock control.
- Variance analysis.
- Investment analysis using discounting and non-discounting procedures.

These programs are capable of solving much larger and more complex problems than those we deal with in the book. The program disk also contains files of test data for a number of the problems dealt with in the book. You should also be able to apply the programs to many of the end of chapter exercises.

The programs are menu driven and have been tested using a wide range of test data. All of the programs permit data to be entered from the keyboard, saved on file and solved. Output can be either on a VDU or on a printer.

The programs are written in Microsoft BASIC and are available on the following machines:

- Sirius 256K.
- Apricot.
- IBM PC.
- Apple II with CPM card.

The programs are capable of operation on most machines which support CPM and Microsoft BASIC. We can configure the programs to run on such machines (apply to us for details).

Glossary ──────────────────────────────────

A.B.C. analysis   A technique for ranking stock or debtor balances in order to highlight the most significant amounts (by value).

Ability to pay   An estimate, based upon the increase in value added over an accounting period, of management's ability to pay a wage claim.

Activity   The level of production or creation of a service within a firm.

Activity variance   That part of the usage variance for a variable resource which can be attributed to an alteration in the overall level of output. The activity variance equals the difference between budgeted usage at actual output and budgeted usage at budgeted output times the budgeted price.

Annuity   The present value of a series of constant future receipts.

Annuity factor   The present value of a series of future receipts of £1 per period.

Barriers to entry   The transaction costs, set-up costs and/or legal constraints which act as a disincentive to firms attempting to enter a particular market. In perfectly competitive markets the barriers to entry are zero. The greater the degree of monopoly concentration in a market the higher the barrier to entry.

Beta (β)   A statistic which measures the sensitivity of a security to general market influences. A security whose returns move up and down exactly in line with the market (as measured by the returns on a broadly based stock market index) would have $\beta = 1$. A security which responds more rapidly to market-wide influences will have $\beta > 1$; conversely a security which is less influenced by market-wide factors than a broadly based stock market index has $\beta < 1$.

Bilateral monopsony   A market setting with one buyer and one seller.

Bureaucracy   (Literally: rule by offices.) A type of organizational structure analysed by the sociologist Max Weber. Bureaucratic organizations are characterized by functional 'offices' which have an existence over and above the individuals who are their temporary incumbents and by a rigid structure of authority and control.

Contingency theory   A theory of organizational behaviour which states that structure is dependent upon contingent environmental variables (broadly classified as economic and technological) and will adapt to meet the demands of those environmental variables. Contingency theory stands in opposition to the view that there is a single, ideal organizational structure suited to all firms at all times. (See *Requisite Variety* (*Law of*).)

Contribution   In decision analysis: projected sales revenue less the external opportunity cost of production.

In costing: actual sales revenue less the variable costs incurred in production.

Contribution margin	The contribution generated per unit of production.
Control	That process of reactive decision-making concerned with maintaining the performance of a system in accordance with some preset target or goal.
Cost centre	A location within a firm to which certain costs can be unambiguously allocated. Examples are the paint shop in a car-body plant or the marketing department of a firm. A cost centre need not, of necessity, be a revenue centre.
Cost-plus pricing	Pricing based upon the total cost of production (including allocated fixed overheads) plus a preset profit margin.
Degeneracy	The situation in linear programming where there are fewer variables in solution than there are binding constraints. In a two-product linear programme, degeneracy will occur if there are more than two constraints effectively limiting the production plan.
Deprival value	The loss which a firm would suffer if it were deprived of a particular asset. Deprival value is often referred to as 'current cost'.
Differentiation	(In organizational theory.) The process of creating diverse functions, specialisms and skills in order to cope with an uncertain economic and technological environment.
Dramaturgical	A sociological concept that individuals make choices on the basis of their preconceptions of how they should act in given situations. This stands in contrast to the idea that individuals rationally weigh up the costs and benefits of different alternatives before making their choices.
Dual price	(Also termed 'shadow price'.) The change in the objective function of a linear programme production plan brought about by a marginal change in the availability of a given scarce resource.
Economic order quantity	The amount of stock which should be reordered in order to minimize the total cost of holding stock within an accounting period.
Efficiency variance	That part of the quantity (usage) variance for a variable resource which cannot be attributed to alterations in the overall level of activity. The efficiency variance equals the difference between the actual usage and the budgeted usage at actual output, times the budgeted price.
Elasticity	A measure of the responsiveness of one economic variable (usually a product's price) to changes in another dependent variable (usually demand or income).
Expert system	A computer program which can make judgements on the basis of information given to it. The program will utilize a knowledge base of information and probabilities concerning the class of decisions about which judgements are to be made.
FIFO	(First in first out.) A historical cost, stock-valuation procedure which assumes (for valuation purposes only) that the first stock purchased or made is the first to be sold. The value of the stock on hand at the end of a given period will be based upon the most recent prices at which stock has been purchased (or made). The stock value taken to cost of goods sold in the profit and loss account will be based upon earlier prices.
Fixed cost	A cost which does not vary with production level (example: factory rent, rates, etc.). Costs are only fixed in the short term; in the very long term, no costs are fixed.

Flexible budget	A cost and revenue budget constructed under different output-level assumptions.
Gearing	The ratio of debt to equity (or total debt to total capital) in a firm's capital structure. Market gearing uses the total market values of debt and equity when calculating the ratio. Book or historical gearing uses the book values of debt and equity when calculating the ratio.
Income	The amount which an individual can consume during a period and still be as well off at the end of that period as at the beginning. For a business, the concept relates to the amount which can be distributed during a period leaving the capital value of the business unaltered. This raises problems of what is meant by leaving the capital base 'unaltered'—a topic which is outside the scope of this book.
Incrementalism	The view of human rationality which assumes that individuals seek solutions which are very close to the position which already exists. Once a satisfactory alternative is found the search process stops.
Incrementalist approach	(In budgeting.) Where budgets are created on the basis of changes to the current position. The incrementalist approach assumes that the current budgets represent a fair allocation of the organization's resources and that budgets created in subsequent periods should only represent modifications of the current position.
Information efficiency	The efficiency with which a market adjusts prices in accordance with new, economically significant information. Perfect efficiency is where market prices react instantaneously to new information and adjust to that price level which would have existed had the market known about the information all along.
Integration	The converse of differentiation. Within contingency theory, firms cope with uncertainty by differentiating their activities and hence attaining a greater degree of organizational variety. This poses problems for management which needs to synthesize (or integrate together) the resultant differences of interest which will arise as a result of the process of differentiation.
Internal rate of return	The discount rate which produces a zero net present value for a given project.
Job costing	A method of costing discrete processes which are deemed to have a start and an end within one accounting period.
LIFO	(Last in first out.) A historical cost stock-valuation method which assumes (for valuation purposes only) that the last stock purchased or made is the first to be used or sold. This method, in a period of rising prices, will tend to undervalue closing stocks for balance sheet purposes (relative to their current cost), while valuing stock for the cost of goods sold at the most recent price levels (cf. FIFO).
Linear programming	A technique for the solution of resource constraint problems such as those found in production planning and investment appraisal under capital rationing. The problem is specified in terms of a linear objective function and a series of linear constraints. When used for the solution of production problems, the technique provides the user with the output levels of each product required to maximize (or minimize) the value of the given objective function, the amount of resources which are unused

at optimal production and the values of the dual prices attaching to each constraint.

Marginal cost
The extra cost incurred through a marginal alteration in output level. Mathematically, marginal cost is the first differential of total cost with respect to output. At maximum profit, marginal cost equals marginal revenue (assuming differentiability of the cost and revenue functions to all degrees).

Marginal rate of time preference
(In economics.) An investor's marginal rate of substitution between current and future consumption. Alternatively, the marginal rate of time preference for an individual can be regarded as the minimum rate of return which will just induce him or her to commit a marginal amount of current wealth to investment.

Marginal revenue
The extra revenue derived from a marginal alteration in the level of output. Mathematically, marginal revenue is the first differential of total revenue with respect to output. At maximum profit, marginal revenue equals marginal cost (assuming differentiability of the cost and revenue functions to all degrees).

Money cash flows
Projections of cash flows which incorporate expectations of the effect of future price changes. In other words, future cash flows are projected in terms of the actual cash receivable at the future times. The term is also used in the context of past cash flows which have not been restated to current prices.

Money rate of return
Rates of return which incorporate a reward to the investor for the decline in the purchasing power of the capital invested.

Monopolistic competition
A market where a supplier creates some differentiation between his or her product and those of the competition. In this situation the supplier can only expect to make short-term monopoly profits.

Monopoly
A market consisting of a single seller and a number of buyers. In such a situation the monopolist represents the supply side of the industry.

Monopsony
A market setting of many suppliers and a single buyer.

Oligopoly
A market consisting of a few sellers and a number of buyers.

Opportunity cost
The cash change which follows necessarily and exclusively as a consequence of a decision to use a given resource.

Opportunity cost of capital
The rate of interest which a firm must pay as a consequence of its decision to use capital in investment. In most situations, the opportunity cost of capital will be the minimum rate of return (expressed as an interest rate) which the firm must offer to attract replacement funds in its current gearing ratio.

Overhead allocation
The practice of allocating overheads to different aspects of production on the basis of the usage of a particular resource (labour hours used, for example) or on the basis of production level.

Payback
The time period required to recoup the cash outlay on an investment project. Payback can be calculated using uncorrected cash flows or using discounted cash flows ('discounted payback').

Perfect competition
A market setting in which no single buyer or seller can, unilaterally, influence the market price of the commodity concerned. Perfect competition is an ideal market type and can only be approximated in practice. The assumptions of perfect competition are: there is a single, homogenous

product with many buyers and sellers, no barriers to entry to the market and zero information costs.

Present value
The current wealth value which is equivalent in an investor's view to a given stream of future cash flows. The investor will calculate present values by discounting the future cash flows at his or her marginal rate of time preference for cash.

Price variance
That part of the overall variance between a budgeted and actual cost or revenue figure which can be attributed to the change in price per unit purchased or sold. The price variance equals the change in price times the actual quantity.

Process costing
A technique for costing continuous processes based upon the notion of an equivalent unit. An equivalent unit represents the number of units of final production which would have been produced given the quantity of a particular resource tied up in work in progress.

Quantity variance
That part of the overall variance between a budgeted and actual cost or revenue figure which can be attributed to the change in quantity of a resource used or of a product sold. The quantity variance equals the change in quantity times the budgeted price.

Ratchet cost
A cost which increases (in some way) as output increases, but is fixed as output decreases. Example: labour costs, where additional labour is hired as output increases but which cannot be easily removed as output falls.

Real cash flows
Future cash flows projected under the assumption of current prices (i.e. in terms of pounds of current purchasing power). The term is also used to describe past cash flows which have been restated in current purchasing power terms.

Real rates of return
Rates of return which do not incorporate any expectation of future inflation and, therefore, do not incorporate any element of reward to the investor for loss of purchasing power. Real rates of return should only be used to evaluate real cash flows.

Realizable value
The sale value (after transactions cost) of an asset. Realizable can be calculated on a 'forced' sale basis or on an 'open' sale.

Replacement cost
The current buying price of an asset or resource.

Requisite Variety (Law of)
The proposition that organizations form specialist functions and activities to the degree required to cope with the uncertainty in their external environment.

Revenue centre
A location within a firm to which revenues, from the sale of products or services, can be attributed.

Satisficing
A model of individual decision-making behaviour proposed by H. A. Simon. Simon argued that individuals seek satisfactory as opposed to optimal solutions and do not search through all possible alternatives but settle for the first satisfactory solution available.

Semivariable cost
A cost pattern which contains both a fixed and a variable element.

Side payment
A payment made by management to a particular individual or group in order to purchase that individual or group's compliance with a particular organizational goal. The process of bargaining over side-payments is the principal mechanism whereby an organizational consensus is achieved (Cyert and March, *A Behavioural Theory of the Firm*).

Simplex	A technique used for the solution of linear-programming problems based upon the pivotal reduction of a matrix of linear equations.
Spreadsheet	The generic title given to a range of computer programs which simulate an accountant's spreadsheet (e.g. Supercalc, Visicalc, Perfect Calc, etc.). The spreadsheet offers the facilities of creating columnar schedules of data, of incorporating formulae and recalculating the whole spreadsheet if changes in data entry are made.
Sticky prices	A reaction model for oligopolistic pricing behaviour. A kinked demand curve is hypothesized, whereby one competitor's price decrease will induce induce others to follow suit. This reaction ensures that there is no long-term alteration in market shares and hence no increased revenue can be earned by the price cutter. Conversely, unilateral price increases are unlikely to be followed by equivalent increases by other competitors, and hence a decrease in volume is likely to result in a consequential loss in volume.
Strategic decisions	Decisions with long-term effects upon the firm. Technically, such long-term decisions are those where the time value of money has a significant influence on the outcome.
Tactical decisions	Decisions which have only short-term effects and which presuppose some prior long-run (strategic) decision and the concomitant commitment of fixed resources. Short-run decision analysis focuses on consequential cash changes only—the time value of money can usually be ignored.
Value added	The difference between the sales revenue earned in an accounting period and the cost of the goods and services bought in.
Variable cost	A cost which is linearly dependent upon the level of production. Few cost patterns are directly variable but exhibit some form of discontinuity (or break) or some alteration in their associated marginal cost because of yield or efficiency effects.
Variance analysis	A technique for separating the differences between budgeted and actual revenues and costs into their component parts. (See *Price, Quantity, Efficiency* and *Activity variances*.)
Wealth	The stock of consumption power possessed by an individual. In operational terms wealth is defined as the net present value of all actual and potential future cash flows which an individual can command.
Zero-base budgeting	The view that budgets should be created on an initial assumption of a zero allocation of resources to each activity. Each resource centre must then justify the absolute level of resources required to achieve its agreed targets.

Index

Index